TM

References for the Rest of Us!®

BESTSELLING BOOK SERIES

Do you find that traditional reference books are overloaded with technical details and advice you'll never use? Do you postpone important life decisions because you just don't want to deal with them? Then our *For Dummies*® business and general reference book series is for you.

For Dummies business and general reference books are written for those frustrated and hard-working souls who know they aren't dumb, but find that the myriad of personal and business issues and the accompanying horror stories make them feel helpless. *For Dummies* books use a lighthearted approach, a down-to-earth style, and even cartoons and humorous icons to dispel fears and build confidence. Lighthearted but not lightweight, these books are perfect survival guides to solve your everyday personal and business problems.

"More than a publishing phenomenon, 'Dummies' is a sign of the times."

— *The New York Times*

"…you won't go wrong buying them."

— *Walter Mossberg, Wall Street Journal, on For Dummies books*

"A world of detailed and authoritative information is packed into them…"

— *U.S. News and World Report*

Already, millions of satisfied readers agree. They have made For Dummies the #1 introductory level computer book series and a best-selling business book series. They have written asking for more. So, if you're looking for the best and easiest way to learn about business and other general reference topics, look to For Dummies to give you a helping hand.

Wiley Publishing, Inc.

5/09

Japanese
FOR
DUMMIES®

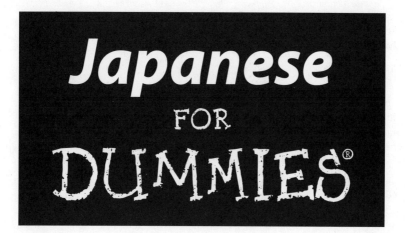

by Eriko Sato

WILEY

Wiley Publishing, Inc.

Japanese For Dummies®

Published by
Wiley Publishing, Inc.
111 River St.
Hoboken, NJ 07030
www.wiley.com

Copyright © 2002 by Wiley Publishing, Inc., Indianapolis, Indiana

Published simultaneously in Canada

For general information on our other products and services or to obtain technical support, please contact our Customer Care Department within the U.S. at 800-762-2974, outside the U.S. at 317-572-3993, or fax 317-572-4002.

Wiley also publishes its books in a variety of electronic formats. Some content that appears in print may not be available in electronic books.

Library of Congress Control Number: 2002100180

ISBN: 0-7645-5429-8

Printed in the United States of America

10 9 8 7

1B/RQ/QT/QU/IN

About the Author

Eriko Sato is a lecturer of Japanese language at the State University of New York at Stony Brook, where she received her PhD degree in linguistics. As soon as she started graduate work at Stony Brook in 1988, she decided to devote the rest of her career to Japanese-language education and research. She studied Japanese and English linguistics and foreign languages, including Chinese, French, and Korean, to prepare herself to be a teacher and researcher who understands students' linguistic backgrounds and difficulties. She has written many articles for linguistic and education journals, and she is currently writing three books on Japanese language: a textbook for young children, a textbook for college students, and a manual for Japanese/English translators. Many brilliant American educators have influenced Eriko. She believes that the learning process must be stimulating, challenging, and enjoyable for students.

Since moving to the United States, Eriko has developed an appreciation for the importance of helping Japanese Americans maintain the Japanese language and its cultural heritage. The Japanese language and its corresponding cultural heritage are the ways in which Japanese Americans can cherish their roots, their identities, and their strength. The language and culture are the ways to understand the contents of their parents' and grandparents' souls. Eriko founded a Japanese school in her community on Long Island, New York, with her friend, Megan Roth-Ueno, who shares the same philosophy on education and diversity. In their school, Japanese students, American students, and Japanese-American students, young and old, enjoy studying Japanese language and participating in cultural activities, creating a warm, family-oriented circle of friends.

About the Technical Reviewer

Tim Cook is the host and instructor of *Irasshai,* the Japanese language and culture distance-learning program from Georgia Public Broadcasting, which won a Southern Regional Emmy. Beamed by satellite around the United States, the program offers Japanese instruction to high school students who would otherwise not have such an opportunity.

Author's Acknowledgments

I want to thank all the people at Wiley Publishing, Inc., for including the Japanese language in their *For Dummies* series — the most unique, innovative, and trusted book series in publication history. It was my pleasure to be able to author *Japanese For Dummies.* My appreciation goes out to my friend, Jayne Matteo, and my literary agent, Grace Freedson, for bringing me this opportunity. My first impression of Wiley Publishing was very positive, thanks to an excellent acquisition editor, Roxane Cerda. My mission was to overcome the lack of parallelism between Japanese and European languages and to write a book that anyone can read at any time without having any difficulty. I couldn't have completed this important and challenging mission without the help of Kathleen Dobie, the project editor for this book. Kathleen's editorial leadership, passion, talent, and hard work made a huge difference. Thank you very much. I am also very grateful to Mike Baker, Tim Cook, and Marcia Johnson for editing this book so that it maintains the authentic spirit and the important philosophy of the *For Dummies* series. Their professional contributions were invaluable, and I can't thank them enough for their hard work. I'm also grateful to all the people on the CD production team, especially Constance Carlisle.

I am deeply indebted to Leslie Cloper, my dear friend and my greatest linguistic research partner for eight years. Leslie supported me and encouraged me from the beginning of this project to the end and contributed a great amount of her time, insight, and knowledge to this book. Her kindness will never be forgotten. I also want to thank my friend Susan Carter, the great artist who often travels to Japan for her art exhibitions, for sharing a number of her interesting interpretations of Japan with me. Susan and her husband Mike provided great insight on many topics in this book. I am also grateful to Mark Aronoff, Richard Larson, Sachiko Murata, and Eva Nagase at Stony Brook University and Shigeru Miyagawa at Massachusetts Institute of Technology for their warm encouragement. And I sincerely want to thank over 1,000 of my current and past students of Japanese at different schools and colleges for being the source of my never-ending energy. I remember each of you clearly.

Finally, I want to thank my family. My special thanks go out to my parents in Japan. They never stop thinking of me. Their support is especially appreciated while I'm working hard in front of the computer for 18 hours a day on the other side of the earth. Thank you for your weekly international phone calls and for reminding me to get more sleep. And my deepest thanks, of course, go to my husband, Yimei, and our daughter, Anna. They know how much enthusiasm and passion I have for Japanese-language education and how excited I was about working on this project. Thank you for understanding me, supporting me, and giving me a tremendous amount of help and happiness. We are a great team!

Publisher's Acknowledgments

We're proud of this book; please send us your comments through our Dummies online registration form located at www.dummies.com/register/.

Some of the people who helped bring this book to market include the following:

Acquisitions, Editorial, and Media Development

Project Editor: Kathleen A. Dobie

Acquisitions Editor: Roxane Cerda

Copy Editor: Mike Baker

Technical Reviewer: Tim Cook

Permissions Editor: Laura Moss

Media Development Specialist: Marisa E. Pearman

CD Producer: Her Voice Unlimited, LLC

Editorial Manager: Christine Meloy Beck

Media Development Manager: Laura VanWinkle

Editorial Assistant: Melissa Bennett

Production

Project Coordinator: Maridee Ennis

Layout and Graphics: Barry Offringa, Laurie Petrone, Jacque Schneider, Betty Schulte, Jeremey Unger, Erin Zeltner

Proofreaders: David Faust, John Greenough, Kyle Looper, Susan Moritz, Carl Pierce, Charles Spencer

Indexer: Sherry Massey

Illustrations: Elizabeth Kurtzman

Special Help
Marcia Johnson

Publishing and Editorial for Consumer Dummies

Diane Graves Steele, Vice President and Publisher, Consumer Dummies

Joyce Pepple, Acquisitions Director, Consumer Dummies

Kristin A. Cocks, Product Development Director, Consumer Dummies

Michael Spring, Vice President and Publisher, Travel

Brice Gosnell, Associate Publisher, Travel

Suzanne Jannetta, Editorial Director, Travel

Publishing for Technology Dummies

Andy Cummings, Vice President and Publisher, Dummies Technology/General User

Composition Services

Gerry Fahey, Vice President of Production Services

Debbie Stailey, Director of Composition Services

Contents at a Glance

Cartoons at a Glance

By Rich Tennant

page 65

page 7

page 317

page 335

page 197

Cartoon Information:
Fax: 978-546-7747
E-Mail: richtennant@the5thwave.com
World Wide Web: www.the5thwave.com

Table of Contents

Introduction

· ·

*W*e live on a wonderfully diverse planet and within amazingly diverse societies. Exchanging ideas, products, foods, and friendship across national and cultural boundaries is the key to making our lives richer and more meaningful and peaceful. Besides, traveling abroad is a lot cheaper than it used to be. It's always fun to grab your passport and set off on an adventure, but it can be even more fun if you can communicate with people in a different country in their own language.

If Japanese is the language you want to learn, for whatever reason, *Japanese For Dummies* can help. It's a great place to start: *Japanese For Dummies* provides instant results, plus some of the cultural background behind the language. I'm not saying that you'll be fluent overnight, but you will gain confidence, have fun, and continue to pick up more and more Japanese. Remember: A good start is essential for good progress and a good ending.

About This Book

Japanese For Dummies can help you whether you want to get familiar with Japanese because you're planning a trip to my island-nation homeland, or you deal with Japanese companies at work, or your new neighbor is Japanese and you want to be able to say *good morning!* (Try **ohayō gozaimasu** [oh-hah-yohh goh-zah-ee-mah-soo].) I give you the most important and most used Japanese words and phrases on subjects as diverse as shopping, money, food, and sports in self-contained chapters and sections.

You can read as much or as little as you want of this book and the chapters in it. You can decide what topic you're interested in, consult the index or the table of contents to find the proper section, and quickly discover everything you need to know about the subject. (Well, maybe not everything. I highly recommend Chapters 1 and 2, which contain the basics of Japanese pronunciation and grammar. These two chapters are always there for you to come back to if you get hung up on a pronunciation or grammar issue.)

Conventions Used in This Book

I use a few conventions in this book to help your reading go smoothly:

- ✔ Japanese terms are set in **boldface** to make them stand out.
- ✔ Pronunciations and meanings in parentheses follow the Japanese terms.
- ✔ Verb conjugations (lists that show you the basic forms of a verb) are given in tables in this order: the dictionary form, the negative form, the stem form, and the te-form. Pronunciations follow in the second column. The following is an example of the verb tables contained in this book using the verb **taberu** (tah-beh-roo; to eat):

Conjugation	*Pronunciation*
taberu	tah-beh-roo
tabenai	tah-beh-nah-ee
tabe	tah-beh
tabete	tah-beh-teh

Japanese verbs don't conjugate like English verbs. You can't find exact counterparts for English verb forms like infinitives, gerunds, and participles. In addition, you don't conjugate Japanese verbs in terms of the person and number. So, **taberu** can mean *I eat, you eat, he eats, she eats,* and *they eat.* This may take a little getting used to, but it should make your verb-learning life a little easier. With Japanese verbs, you use different forms in different contexts, but those forms usually follow pretty standard rules.

I explain everything you need to know about verbs in Chapter 2. Now, I didn't say that I explain everything *there is* to know about Japanese verbs — that would take a whole other book — but I explain the basics you need to feel comfortable and proficient.

To help you remember the most important new words and see the language in context, this book includes some special elements to reinforce the new Japanese terms you're studying:

- ✔ **Talkin' the Talk dialogues:** To see and hear actual Japanese conversations is the best way to learn Japanese. So I include many dialogues under the "Talkin' the Talk" heading. These exchanges show you the Japanese words, their pronunciations, and the English translations so that you can see how the language is actually used.

  The dialogues with an On the CD icon beside them appear, appropriately enough, on the CD that comes with this book.

✔ **Words to Know blackboards:** The words and phrases in the blackboard-like boxes are the ones I think are the most important words and phrases in the preceding section or sections.

When I include a verb on a Words to Know blackboard, I indicate the verb type with either [ru] for ru-verbs, [u] for u-verbs, or [irr] for irregular verbs so that you know how to conjugate the verb. (Chapter 2 has information on verb types and how to conjugate them.)

✔ **Fun & Games activities:** It's a good idea to check your grasp of important Japanese words and phrases after reading each chapter. The Fun & Game activities at the end of chapters provide a stimulating and fun review of some important words and phrases.

Different languages often express the same idea very differently, which sometimes is a result of the different cultures that underlie each language. English and Japanese are no exception: The two languages differ at times concerning what gets expressed and how it gets expressed. And Japanese has many words and phrases that you can't translate into English at all. In this book, I want you to know what is actually said (the content and intended meaning), rather than how it is said. So, instead of giving you a literal translation, I give you a non-literal, natural English translation. For example, the phrase **yoroshiku** (yoh-roh-shee-koo) can be literally translated as *appropriately,* but the phrase really means *pleased to meet you* if you say it when meeting someone new. This book gives the pleased-to-meet-you type translations — the non-literal translations — in the appropriate contexts. And one more thing: The way I translate Japanese phrases and sentences can be different depending on the context. For example, I may translate **yoroshiku** as *thanks for doing me a favor,* instead of *pleased to meet you,* if it's used right after asking a favor of someone.

Your exploration of the Japanese language will show you different ways of looking at the world of language because Japanese doesn't contain as many grammar-type things as European languages have. For example, Japanese doesn't have equivalents of English articles like *a* and *the.* And Japanese doesn't have a singular/plural distinction, such as *dog* and *dogs,* either.

Sometimes, Japanese has things that European languages don't have. For example, Japanese speech styles clearly indicate degrees of respect or familiarity within conversational contexts.

It's okay to be surprised at these differences, but make sure to enjoy them too. And the next time you see your friends or your relatives, proudly teach them an interesting fact like Japanese say *I'll be rude* when they leave their teacher's or boss's office. Isn't it weird? What they actually mean is *Goodbye.*

Foolish Assumptions

To write this special book, *Japanese For Dummies,* I had to come up with some assumptions. My foolish assumptions are:

- ✔ You don't know much Japanese, except maybe for a few words like **karate** and **sushi.**

- ✔ You're not planning on taking a language-proficiency test for Japanese next month. You're not planning on becoming a professional Japanese translator in the near future. You just want to be able to communicate basic information in Japanese and get to know the Japanese language.

- ✔ You don't have time to spend hours and hours memorizing vocabulary and grammar rules.

- ✔ You want to have fun in addition to learning Japanese.

If these assumptions apply to you, you're in business. Why don't you get started?

How This Book Is Organized

This book is divided into four parts and an appendix. Each part has a specific focus on one aspect of the Japanese language. Each part is further divided into several chapters that cover particular topics, such as using Japanese to dine at a restaurant, go shopping, or plan a vacation.

Part I: Getting Started

This part lets you get familiar with some Japanese words and then provides the basic information you need to read and understand the rest of the book. Part I presents all the possible Japanese sounds and shows you how the sounds are represented throughout the book. It also provides you with basic Japanese grammar rules so that you can easily understand the sentences that show up in each chapter — get used to looking for the verb at the end of a sentence.

Part II: Japanese in Action

This part gets you going. It provides Japanese words and phrases that you can start using in your daily life today. Here's where the real fun begins.

Part II explains greetings, provides words and phrases so that you can strike up conversations, and includes a ton of information on performing everyday activities at home and at the office in Japanese. Your everyday life is about to take on a Japanese flavor.

Part III: Japanese on the Go

This part lets you be even more active. Forget those daily routines and head for the hills, the beach, or some other fabulous destination. Part III provides all the info you need to manage your trip. It covers subjects like making a reservation, getting money from the bank, and dealing with emergencies all in Japanese.

Part IV: The Part of Tens

Part IV is the collection of simple phrases and facts that I want you to know and remember forever. It's like a mother's last reminder to a child about to take off for a long journey to an unknown place. In this book, the reminders include ten ways to learn Japanese quickly, ten things you should never do in front of Japanese folks, ten useful Japanese expressions, and ten phrases that make you sound like a native Japanese speaker.

Part V: Appendixes

This part includes helpful references that you may want to take a look at occasionally as you work on the rest of the chapters. It includes a giant verb table that shows you the conjugation patterns of all types of regular verbs and most of the irregular verbs. Appendix B is a very convenient mini-dictionary from both Japanese to English and English to Japanese. If you encounter an unfamiliar word, you can check it out here. The answers to the Fun & Games exercises at the end of the chapters are in Appendix C, and the last appendix provides a list of the tracks that appear on the audio CD. It's handy when you want to play a particular Talkin' the Talk dialogue from the book.

Icons Used in This Book

To help alert you to the type of information you come across, I placed some icons in the left-hand margins and next to some of the introductions to the Talkin' the Talk sections throughout the book. They can help you find certain types of information quickly. Here are the six icons to keep an eye out for:

This icon highlights tips that can make learning Japanese easier.

To ensure that you don't forget information important to the language, or just in the chapter, this icon serves as a reminder, like a string tied around your finger.

This icon can keep you from making embarrassing or really foolish mistakes.

If you're interested in information and advice about culture and travel, look for these icons. They draw your attention to interesting tidbits about Japan.

Languages are full of quirks that may trip you up if you're not prepared for them. This icon points to discussions of these weird grammar rules.

The audio CD that comes with this book gives you the opportunity to listen to real Japanese speakers so that you can get a better understanding of what Japanese sounds like. This icon marks the basic sounds and Talkin' the Talk dialogues you can find on the CD.

Where to Go from Here

Learning a language starts with simple tasks like listening and repeating, but the most important step is to use the words and phrases you learn. So, read the chapter that interests you, listen to the audio CD in your room or in your car, and then make sure to use your favorite Japanese phrases when you hang out with your friends or family. If you follow this plan, you'll be able to answer **Hai** (hah-ee; Yes!) confidently when people ask **Nihongo wa hanasemasu ka** (nee-hohn-goh wah hah-nah-seh-mah-soo kah; Can you speak Japanese?)

Part I
Getting Started

The 5th Wave   By Rich Tennant

"I don't know what you're so nervous about. Just use the phrase book and demand they upgrade us to a better room."

In this part . . .

Part I welcomes you to the Japanese language. Here,
I give you the basic facts on Japanese — how to pro-
duce Japanese sounds like a native speaker, how to put
Japanese words together appropriately, how to count in
Japanese, and how to communicate in Japanese with a
Japanese attitude. **Jā, hajimemashō** (jahh, hah-jee-meh-
mah-shohh; Let's start!).

Chapter 1

You Already Know a Little Japanese

Welcome to Japanese! This chapter lets you open your mouth and sound like a totally different person — a Japanese person! Isn't it exciting? In this chapter, I show you how to start saying familiar Japanese words like **sushi** with an authentic Japanese accent. Next time you go to a Japanese restaurant, you can amaze your server by pronouncing **sushi** properly. This chapter also provides you with some convenient Japanese phrases and interesting tips on Japanese body language.

Use your eyes, ears, mouth, and intuition a lot as you go over this chapter and apply what you see, hear, pronounce, and feel to your daily life. To practice the language, work with your family, your close friends, or even your pets until you get the chance to talk with a Japanese person. The more you apply a language in your daily life, the better you grasp its essence.

When you speak a foreign language, don't be afraid of making mistakes and be sure to keep smiling. If you speak even a little bit of their language, Japanese people will open their hearts to you right away and appreciate your effort. Simply making the effort to communicate in another person's language is one of the best ways to act as an ambassador and contribute to international friendship.

Learning to speak a foreign language perfectly should take a back seat to this cultural exchange. Foreign language education is the greatest way to explore a different culture and the related values and ways of living. Encountering another culture helps you know your own culture and values better. Opening your eyes to Japan is actually opening your eyes to yourself and to your roots.

Basic Japanese Sounds

Japanese sounds are very easy to hear and pronounce. Each syllable is simple, short, and usually pronounced very clearly. With a little practice, you'll get use to them quickly. This section gets you off on the right foot (or should I say the right sound) by looking at vowels, consonants, and a couple of combinations of each. All vowels and consonants are specified by **rōmaji** (rohh-mah-jee; Roman letters) in this book, so you see the familiar English alphabet. Japanese use their own system called **kana** (kah-nah) and about 2,000 Chinese characters in their daily life, but they also use **rōmaji** for the convenience of foreigners. In this book, you won't see any **kana** letters or Chinese characters, just **rōmaji.**

Vowel Sounds

The Japanese language only has five basic vowels — **a, e, i, o,** and **u** — all of which sound short and crispy — plus their longer counterparts, represented by **ā, ē, ī, ō,** and **ū** in this book.

The difference between short and long vowel sounds in Japanese is quite a bit different than in English. In Japanese, long vowels have the same sound as short vowels — you just draw out the sound for a moment longer. To an English-speaking ear, a long vowel sounds as if it's being stressed — as if it has an accent mark.

The difference between a long vowel and a short vowel can make all the difference in the meaning of a Japanese word. For example, **obasan** (oh-bah-sahn) with the short vowel **a** means *aunt,* but **obāsan** (oh-bahh-sahn) with the long vowel **ā** means *grandmother.* If you don't differentiate the vowel length properly, no one will understand who you're talking about when all of your relatives get together.

Not getting the vowels right is a very common mistake new Japanese speakers make and one that can cause a lot of confusion, so concentrate on getting the vowel sounds right as you go through this book.

Listen for the difference between short and long vowel sounds on the CD to get the idea about vowel length. Table 1-1 lists all the Japanese vowels. Listen to their pronunciation using the CD and imitate them a few times, pretending to be a parrot. Now you know what a day in a parrot's life is like. In this book, a straight bar (¯) over a vowel indicates that it's a long vowel.

Table 1-1		Japanese Vowel Sounds	
Letter	*Pronunciation*	*English Word with the Sound*	*Example*
a	ah	a<u>ha</u>	obasan (oh-bah-sahn; aunt)
ā	ahh		obāsan (oh-bahh-sahn; grandmother)
e	eh	b<u>e</u>d	Seto (seh-toh; a city in Japan)
ē	ehh		sēto (sehh-toh; pupil)
i	ee	f<u>ee</u>t	ojisan (oh-jee-sahn; uncle)
ī or ii	eee		ojīsan (oh-jeee-sahn; grandfather
o	oh	d<u>o</u>me	tori (toh-ree; bird)
ō	ohh		tōri (tohh-ree; street)
u	oo	f<u>oo</u>t	yuki (yoo-kee; snow)
ū	ooo		yūki (yooo-kee; courage)

Vowel combinations

In Japanese, any two vowels can be next to each other in a word, but you might hear them as one vowel sound. For example, the combination **ai** (ah-ee; love) sounds like one vowel sound, the English *i* (as in *eye*), but to Japanese, this is actually two vowels, not one. The Japanese word **koi** (koh-ee; carp) sounds like the English one-syllable word *coy,* but to Japanese, **koi** is a two-syllable word. Other common vowel combinations are in Table 1-2. To you, some of them may sound similar to each other, but Japanese speakers hear them differently. Try hearing and saying the difference.

Table 1-2	Vowel Combinations	
Japanese	*Pronunciation*	*Translation*
ai	ah-ee	love
mae	mah-eh	front
ao	ah-oh	blue

(continued)

Table 1-2 *(continued)*

Japanese	Pronunciation	Translation
au	ah-oo	meet
koi	koh-ee	carp
koe	koh-eh	voice
ue	oo-eh	up

Whispered vowels

The vowels **i** (ee) and **u** (oo) come out as a downright whisper whenever they fall between the consonant sounds **ch, h, k, p, s, sh, t,** or **ts** or whenever a word ends in this consonant-vowel combination. What do all those consonants have in common? They're what linguists call "voiceless," meaning that they don't make your vocal cords vibrate. Don't believe me? Put your hand over your vocal cords and say a voiceless consonant like the *k* sound. Then say a "voiced" consonant like the *g* sound. Feel the difference? Whispering **i** (ee) and **u** (oo) with these voiceless consonants almost makes it sound as though these vowels disappear. Listen to the examples from Tables 1-3 and 1-4 with and without the whispered vowels.

Table 1-3	Words with Whispered Vowels	
Japanese	*Pronunciation*	*Translation*
sukēto	skehh-to	skating
kusai	ksah-ee	stinky
ashita	ah-shtah	tomorrow
sō desu	sohh dehs	that's right

Table 1-4	Words without Whispered Vowels	
Japanese	*Pronunciation*	*Translation*
sugoi	soo-goh-ee	amazing; wow
kuni	koo-nee	country
kagu	kah-goo	furniture

Consonant Sounds

Good news. Most Japanese consonants are pronounced like they are in English. Check out the descriptions of the sounds you need to pay attention to in Table 1-5.

Table 1-5	Japanese Consonants Different from English	
Consonant	*Description of the Sound*	*Examples*
r	Almost like a Spanish **r**, where you tap your tongue on the roof of your mouth just once — almost like an English **d** or **l**, but not quite.	rakuda (rah-koo-dah; camel); tora (toh-rah; tiger); tori (toh-ree; bird)
f	A much softer sound than the English **f** — somewhere between an **f** and an **h** sound. Make it by bringing your lips close to each other and gently blowing air through them.	Fujisan (foo-jee-sahn; Mt. Fuji); tōfu (tohh-foo; bean curd); fūfu (fooo-foo; married couple)
ts	The combination of **t** and **s** is hard to pronounce at the beginning of a word, as in **tsunami,** although it's easy anywhere else. My advice is to say the word **cats** in your head and then say **tsunami.**	tsunami (tsoo-nah-mee; tidal wave); tsuki (tsoo-kee; the moon)
ry	The combination of **r** and **y** is difficult to pronounce when it occurs before the vowel **o.** If so, try saying **ri** (ree) and then **yo** (yoh). Repeat many times and gradually increase the speed until you can pronounce these two sounds simultaneously. Remember that the **r** sounds almost like a **d** in English	ryō (ryohh; dormitory); ryokan (ryoh-kahn; Japanese-style inn)

Like most other languages, Japanese has double consonants too. To say these double consonants — **pp, tt, kk,** and **ss** — you pronounce them as single consonants preceded by a brief pause. Check out the following examples and listen to the pronunciation on the CD.

> ✓ **kippu** (keep-poo; tickets)
>
> ✓ **kitte** (keet-teh; stamps)
>
> ✓ **kekkon** (kehk-kohn; marriage)
>
> ✓ **massugu** (mahs-soo-goo; straight)

Sounding Fluent

If you want to sound like a native Japanese speaker, you need to imitate the overall intonation, rhythm, and accent of native Japanese. These almost musical aspects of the language make a big difference, and they're not that difficult to achieve. In the following sections, I show you some tricks to make you sound like a Japanese.

Don't stress

English sentences sound like they're full of punches, one after another, because they contain English words that have stressed syllables followed by unstressed syllables. But Japanese sentences sound very flat because Japanese words and phrases don't have any stressed syllables. So unless you are very angry or excited, suppress your desire to stress syllables when you speak Japanese.

Get in rhythm

English sentences sound very smooth and connected, but Japanese sentences sound chopped up because each syllable is pronounced more clearly and separately in Japanese than in English. You can sound like a native speaker by pronouncing each syllable separately, not connecting them as you do in English.

Pitch perfectly

Although Japanese speakers don't punch their syllables, they may raise or lower their *pitch* on a specific syllable in certain words. A raised pitch may sound like a stress, but if you think in terms of music, the high notes aren't necessarily stressed more than the low notes. But pitch differences in Japanese are a lot more subtle than differences between musical notes. Sometimes this slight difference can change the meaning of a word. That, however, also depends on what part of Japan you're in. For example, in eastern Japan, the word **hashi** (hah-shee), said with high-to-low pitch means *chopsticks,* but with low-to-high pitch, it means *a bridge.* In western Japan, it's exactly the opposite: High-to-low pitch means *a bridge,* and low-to-high pitch means *chopsticks.* How can you tell what anyone means? For one thing, the eastern dialect is standard because that's where Tokyo, the capital of Japan, is located. In any event, the context usually makes it clear. If you're in a restaurant and you ask for **hashi,** you can safely assume that, no matter how you pitch this word, no one will bring you a bridge. Listen to this word said both ways on the CD and try to hear what I mean by pitch.

  ✔ **hashi** (hah-shee; chopsticks): The pitch goes from high to low.
  ✔ **hashi** (hah-shee; bridge): The pitch goes from low to high.

Okay, so they don't sound terribly different. Rather than getting all bothered about pitch, just know that it exists and try as best you can to mimic the pronunciations on the CD.

Another interesting fact about pitch: The Japanese raise their overall pitch range when they speak to their superiors. So, to a boss, client, customer or teacher, people speak as if they are chirping birds, and to their friends, assistants, and family members, they speak using their normal pitch range. This is most noticeable among women. Female workers raise their pitch greatly when they deal with business customers. They don't mean to scare their customers; they're just trying to be super polite. Women also raise their pitch when they speak to young children, just to indicate a friendly attitude toward the little ones. A Japanese woman's flattering high pitch in these contexts has a totally different tone of voice from the high pitch that she uses when she raises her pitch out of anger.

You Already Know a Little Japanese

Believe or not, you already know many Japanese words: Some are Japanese words that English borrowed and incorporated; others are English words used in Japan.

Japanese words in English

Do you love eating **sushi?** Do you practice **karate?** Do you hang out at **karaoke** bars? Even if you answered no to every question, you probably know what these words mean and that they come from Japanese, so you already know some Japanese.

One tip about pronunciation: Remember that there are no accented syllables in Japanese. So when you say **sushi,** don't stress the first syllable. I know the English-speaker in you wants to do it, but don't. Check out these words that traveled from Japan to become part of the English language:

- **hibachi** (hee-bah-chee): portable charcoal stove

- **jūdō** (jooo-dohh): Japanese martial art that redirects an attack back onto the attacker

- **karaoke** (kah-rah-oh-keh): form of entertainment that involves singing to prerecorded music

- **karate** (kah-rah-teh): Japanese form of self defense that relies on delivering quick, sharp blows with hands or feet

- **kimono** (kee-moh-noh): robe with wide sleeves and a sash; traditional Japanese clothing for women

- **origami** (oh-ree-gah-mee): the art of paper folding

- **sake** (sah-keh): Japanese rice wine

- **samurai** (sah-moo-rah-ee): professional warriors

- **sashimi** (sah-shee-mee): sliced raw fish

- **sukiyaki** (soo-kee-yah-kee): Japanese-style beef stew

- **sushi** (soo-shee): rice ball with sliced raw fish on top

- **tsunami** (tsoo-nah-mee): tidal wave

English words used in Japanese

A ton of English words have crossed the oceans to Japan, and the number is increasing quickly. You can use many English words in Japan, if you pronounce them with a heavy Japanese accent.

- **bāsudē kēki** (bahh-soo-dehh kehh-kee): birthday cake

- **jūsu** (jooo-soo): juice

- **kamera** (kah-meh-rah): camera

- **kōhī** (kohh-heee): coffee

- **nekutai** (neh-koo-tah-ee): necktie

- **pātī** (pahh-teee): party

- **rajio** (rah-jee-oh): radio

- **resutoran** (reh-soo-toh-rahn): restaurant

- **sutēki** (soo-tehh-kee): steak

- **sutoraiku** (soo-toh-rah-ee-koo): strike

Puzzling English words in Japan

Some English words changed their meanings after they were assimilated into the Japanese language. Don't be puzzled when you hear these words:

✔ Smart: **Sumāto** (soo-mahh-toh) does not mean *bright*. It means *skinny* or *thin* in Japan.

✔ Training pants: **Torēningu pantsu** (toh-rehh-neen-goo pahn-tsoo) are not for toddlers who are about to give up their diapers. They're gym pants, and adults also wear them.

✔ Mansion: **Manshon** (mahn-shohn) is not a huge, gorgeous house. It's just a small, neat-looking condominium in Japan.

How many English words can you find in the following dialogue?

Talkin' the Talk

Ken and Yōko are making plans for Michiko's birthday. They use a number of English-influenced words during their conversation.

Ken: **Michiko no tanjōbi wa pātī o shiyō.**
mee-chee-koh noh tahn-johh-bee wa pahh-teee oh shee-yohh.
For Michiko's birthday, let's throw a party.

Yōko: **Ōkē. Jā, watashi wa, bāsudē kēki o tsukuru ne.**
ohh-kehh. jahh, wah-tah-shee wah, bahh-soo-dehh kehh-kee oh tsoo-koo-roo neh.
Okay. Then I will make a birthday cake.

Ken: **Jā, boku wa kōhī to, jūsu o yōisuru.**
jahh, boh-koo wah kohh-heee toh, jooo-soo oh yohh-ee-soo-roo.
Then I will prepare coffee and juice.

Yōko: **Sorekara, kamera mo wasurenaide ne.**
soh-reh-kah-rah, kah-meh-rah moh wa-soo-reh-nah-ee-deh neh.
And don't forget to bring the camera.

Keeping English company names in Japan

If you walk down the street in Japan, looking at the signs of companies, restaurants, stores, hotels, and galleries, you may be amazed that many of the names are completely English or a combination of Japanese and English.

The Japanese also use English when naming products like cars, electronics, appliances, cosmetics, and even children's snacks! They think that things sound cool if their names are English or spelled with the English alphabet. Seeing English in Japan can certainly make you feel cool and comfortable!

- **Cars:** Corolla, Crown, Sprint, Civic
- **Companies:** Recruit, Sony, National, NEC, Sharp
- **Computers:** Valuestar
- **Galleries:** Gallery Ginza
- **Hotels:** Shinagawa Prince, Palace Tokyo
- **Restaurants:** Skylark, Oasis
- **Snacks:** Pocky, Milky, Chelsea
- **Stores:** Lawson, High Ace, Happy Mart

Basic Phrases

Start using the following short Japanese phrases at home. Make it a habit. You may need your family's cooperation with this, but if you get used to seizing the moment and saying the right phrase, you can seem like a Japanese even if you don't have black eyes. And the next time you associate with Japanese people, you can smoothly say these Japanese phrases:

- **Dōmo.** (dohh-moh): Thank you *or* Hi!

  Used for thanking, and also for brief greetings.

- **Ĭe.** (eee-eh): No *or* Don't mention it.

- **Sō, sō.** (sohh, sohh): You're right, you are right!

  Used when you agree with someone's statement. It's almost like what you mean when you say *yeah* in the middle of conversations just to let the other person know that you're listening and agreeing.

- **Dame.** (dah-meh): You are not allowed to do that *or* That's bad!

  Used when you want to stop someone doing something or when you want to say that something is bad or impermissible. You'd probably never say it to a superior or to someone older than you. You can say it to your children, your siblings, or your very close friends.

- **Zenzen.** (zehn-zehn): Not at all *or* It was nothing.

- **Ii desu ne.** (ee-ee deh-soo neh): That's a great idea!

- **Yatta.** (yaht-tah): Yahoo! I did it.

- **Gambatte.** (gahm-baht-teh): Go for it *or* Try your best!
- **Omedetŏ.** (oh-meh-deh-tohh): Congratulations!
- **Yŏkoso.** (yohh-koh-soh): Welcome!
- **Shinpai shinaide.** (sheen-pah-ee shee-nah-ee-deh): Don't worry!
- **Makasete.** (mah-kah-seh-teh): Count on me!
- **Sono tŏri.** (soh-noh tohh-ree): You're absolutely right!

Body Language

Gestures are very important for communication. Japanese probably use fewer gestures than Westerners. For example, they don't hug or kiss people in public. But they do have some unique gestures. If you know their meanings and functions, and if you can use them as you interact with Japanese people, you'll seem like part of the crowd. Try some of the following gestures yourself. And if you see native Japanese people in a Japanese grocery store, at the mall, at a party, or anywhere else, observe them carefully. You will definitely see some of these gestures used.

- **Banzai** (bahn-zah-ee): When a bunch of people gather to celebrate something, they often stand up at the same time, raise both arms over their heads simultaneously, and shout **banzai** (hurrah) together three times.

- **Bowing:** For Japanese, bowing is an absolutely important and necessary everyday communication tool. You bow to thank someone, to apologize, to greet, and even to say goodbye. By bowing, you express your politeness and respect for others. But you don't have to bow very deeply. In most cases, you can just tilt your head for a second or two. Save the deep bow, using the upper half of the body, for those times when you make a horrible mistake, receive overwhelming kindness, or associate with extremely formal people.

- **Nodding:** Whenever someone says something to you, nod immediately. Otherwise, the speaker will think that you're not paying attention or that you're upset.

- **Waving:** To have your waves understood, you must know that it's all in the wrist. If you greet your neighbor by moving your hand up and down from your wrist, like a toddler waving bye-bye, your American neighbor will understand that you mean to say *hi*. However, your Japanese neighbors will think that you're beckoning them to come to you. The Japanese use a sort of palm-down scooping motion to say *come here* — just a 180-degree turn from the palm-up scooping motion Americans use to say the same thing.

Fun & Games

Japanese has short and long vowels, and they make a difference in meaning. Think about how you say the following words in Japanese, and circle the correct word in the parentheses. The solution is in Appendix C.

1. grandmother (**obasan, obāsan**)

2. grandfather (**ojisan, ojīsan**)

3. Thank you. (**domo, dōmo**)

4. karaoke (**karaoke, karaōke**)

5. judo (**jūdō, judo**)

Chapter 2

The Nitty Gritty: Basic Japanese Grammar and Numbers

- -

In This Chapter

▶ Speaking with style

▶ Handing out sentences

▶ Questioning your English teacher

▶ Forming verbs

▶ Numbering your choices

- -

*1*f grammar rules are the branches of a tree, then words are the tree's beautiful leaves. Checking the branches before enjoying those leaves is the shortcut to your success in understanding the entire tree. This chapter shows you what the branches of the Japanese language tree look like.

Using Appropriate Speech Styles

Japanese use different speech styles depending on who they're talking to. For example, you ask a simple question like *Did you see it?* differently to different people. When speaking to your boss, use the *formal* style of speech and say **Goranninarimashita ka** (goh-rahn-nee-nah-ree-mah-shee-tah kah). When speaking to your colleague, use the *polite/neutral* style and say **Mimashita ka** (mee-mah-shee-tah kah). And with your kids, use the *plain/informal* style and say **Mita no** (mee-tah noh). Notice that the phrase becomes shorter and shorter as you go down in the relative hierarchy from your boss to your kids. Japanese use their mouth muscles more for their boss and less for their kids.

What if you use the plain/informal style with your boss? He or she will probably start looking for some official reason to kick you out of his or her group. What if you use a formal style to your own daughter? It will sound like you're just a commoner and your daughter got married to a royal prince. The tricky part is that the correct speech style depends on both social hierarchy,

in terms of position and age, and social grouping, such as insiders and out-
siders. The informal forms can sound rude, but they can also sound very
friendly; the formal forms can sound very polite, but they can also sound
awfully cold. What if your assistant is older than you are? What if your son is
your boss? In some cases, which style you should use can be very unclear.
Table 2-1 gives you some general guidelines.

Table 2-1	Speech Styles
Style	*Whom to Use It With*
Formal	your business customer, a person who is much older than you, your boss, your teacher
Polite/neutral	your classmate, your colleague, your neighbor, your acquaintance, your friend's parent
Plain/informal	your parent, your child, your spouse, your student, your assistant, your close friend

In this book, I use the speech style appropriate to the context, but don't
worry — I let you know whether I'm giving you formal, polite/neutral, or
plain/informal style.

My advice is to start from the polite/neutral style and gradually play with
formal and plain/informal styles.

Forming Sentences

It took me about twenty months to start forming a Japanese sentence after
I was born. Twenty months! I was very cute at that age, or so my mom says.
Today, you can start forming a Japanese sentence in just five minutes —
I promise. You're saving a lot of time!

Presenting the basic construction

The basic word order in English is subject-verb-object, but the order in
Japanese is subject-object-verb. Instead of saying *I watched TV,* you say *I TV*

watched. Instead of saying *I ate sushi,* say *I sushi ate.* Now you know the pattern. So repeat after me: Put the *verb at the end! Verb end! Verb end!* Go ahead and try it! *I sake drank, I karaoke did,* and *I money lost!* Good, you the basic word order in Japanese have.

Introducing particles

Subject-object-verb is the basic word order in Japanese, but object-subject-verb is also okay. As long as the verb is at the end of the sentence, Japanese grammar teachers are happy. For example, if Mary invited John, you can say either *Mary John invited* or *John Mary invited* in Japanese. Like I said, as long as the verb is at the end, the order of other phrases doesn't matter.

Although it sounds great, a smart person like you may be saying, "Wait a minute! How do you know who invited whom?" The secret is that Japanese use a little tag called a *particle* right after each noun phrase. The particle for the action performer is **ga** (gah), and the particle for the action receiver is **o** (oh). So, both of the following sentences mean *Mary invited John:*

- ✔ **Marī ga Jon o sasotta.** (mah-reee gah john oh sah-soht-tah)
- ✔ **Jon o Marī ga sasotta.** (john oh mah-reee gah sah-soht-tah)

Actually, **ga** is the subject-marking particle, and **o** is the direct object-marking particle. They can't be translated into English. Sorry, it's just Japanese.

Other Japanese particles include **kara** (kah-rah), **made** (mah-deh), **ni** (nee), **de** (deh), **to** (toh), and **ka** (kah). Luckily, they can be translated into English words like *from, until, to, with, by, at, in, on, and,* and *or.* But each particle is translated differently depending on the context. For example, the particle **de** corresponds to *in, by,* or *with* in English:

- ✔ **Bosuton de benkyōsuru.** (boh-soo-tohn deh behn-kyohh-soo-roo; I'll study in Boston.)
- ✔ **Takushī de iku.** (tah-koo-sheee deh ee-koo; I'll go by taxi.)
- ✔ **Fōku de taberu.** (fohh-koo deh tah-beh-roo; I eat with a fork.)

Translation is not always the best way to figure out a foreign language, so remember the particles in terms of their general functions, not their exact English translations. Table 2-2 presents Japanese particles and their various meanings. I provide translations where I can.

Table 2-2		Particles	
Particle	*Translation*	*General Function*	*Example*
ga (gah)	No English equivalent	Specifies the subject of the sentence.	Jon ga kita. (john gah kee-tah; John came.)
o (oh)	No English equivalent	Specifies the direct object of the sentence.	Marī ga Jon o sasotta. (mah-reee gah john oh sah-soht-tah; Mary invited John.)
kara (kah-rah)	from	Specifies the starting point of the action.	Ku-ji kara benkyōshita. (koo-jee kah-rah behn-kyohh-shee-tah; I studied from 9 o'clock.)
made (mah-deh)	until	Specifies the ending point of the action.	San-ji made benkyōshita. (sahn-jee mah-deh behn-kyohh-shee-tah; I studied until 3 o'clock.)
ni (nee)	to, on, at	Specifies the target of the action.	Nihon ni itta. (nee-hohn nee eet-tah; I went to Japan.) Tōkyō ni tsuita. (tohh-kyohh nee tsoo-ee-tah; I arrived at Tokyo.)
		Specifies the time of the event.	San-ji ni tsuita. (sahn-jee nee tsoo-ee-tah; I arrived at 3 o'clock.)
e (eh)	to, toward	Specifies the direction of the action.	Tōkyō e itta. (tohh-kyohh eh eet-tah; I went to/towards Tokyo.)
de (deh)	in, by, with, at	Specifies how the action takes place; indicates the location, the manner, or the background condition of the action.	Bosuton de benkyōshita. (boh-soo-tohn de behn-kyohh-shee-tah; I studied in Boston.) Takushī de itta. (tah-koo-sheee deh eet-tah; I went there by taxi.) Fōku de tabeta. (fohh-koo deh tah-beh-tah; I ate with a fork.)

Particle	Translation	General Function	Example
no (noh)	's	Creates a possessive phrase or a modifier phrase.	Marī no hon (mah-reee noh hohn; Mary's book) nihongo no hon (nee-hon-goh noh hohn; a Japanese language book)
to (toh)	and, with	Lists items.	Sushi to sashimi o tabeta. (soo-shee toh sah-shee-mee oh tah-beh-tah; I ate sushi and sashimi.)
		Specifies the co-agent of the action.	Jon ga Marī to utatta. (john gah mah-reee toh oo-taht-tah; John sang with Mary.)
ka (kah)	or	Lists choices.	Sushi ka sashimi o taberu. (soo-shee kah sah-shee-mee oh tah-beh-roo; I will eat sushi or sashimi.)

You can have a bunch of particles in a sentence:

- ✔ **Marī ga kuruma de Tōkyō e itta.** (mah-reee gah koo-roo-mah deh tohh-kyohh eh eet-tah; Mary went to Tokyo by car.)

- ✔ **Jon no otōsan kara bīru to osake to wain o moratta.** (john noh oh-tohh-sahn kah-rah beee-roo toh oh-sah-keh toh wah-een oh moh-raht-tah; I received beer, sake, and wine from John's dad.)

Japanese nouns need these particles; they don't need articles like *a* and *the* in English. Furthermore, there's no need to specify *singular* or *plural*. **Tamago** (tah-mah-goh) is either *an egg* or *eggs*.

Telling the topic

English doesn't have a topic phrase, but if you put a topic phrase at the beginning of whatever you say, you can sound a lot more like a native Japanese speaker. Japanese just love to mention topics at the beginning of their sentences.

At the very beginning of a statement, clarify what you're talking about — state the *topic* of the sentence. You need to provide the listener with a heads up: *What I will say from now is about* **topic,** *As for* **topic,** or *Speaking of* **topic.** Use the particle **wa** (wah) to mark the topic word.

Suppose you're talking about what you did *yesterday.* You start with the word for yesterday, **kinō** (kee-nohh), add **wa** after the word to alert the listener that *yesterday* is your topic, and then finish the sentence.

The following sentences differ in what the speaker is talking about. The statement can be about what happened *yesterday,* about what happened to *the teacher,* or about what happened to *John,* depending on what precedes **wa:**

- ✔ **Kinō wa sensē ga Jon o shikatta.** (kee-nohh wah sehn-sehh gah john oh shee-kaht-tah; As for yesterday, what happened is that the teacher scolded John.)

- ✔ **Sensē wa kinō Jon o shikatta.** (sehn-sehh wah kee-nohh john oh shee-kaht-tah; As for the teacher, what he did yesterday was to scold John.)

- ✔ **Jon wa sensē ga kinō shikatta.** (john wah sehn-sehh gah kee-nohh shee-kaht-tah; As for John, what happened to him was that the teacher scolded him yesterday.)

Any noun can be the topic. The subject noun can be the topic, and the object noun can be the topic too. When a noun is both the subject of the sentence and the topic of the sentence, you use only the topic particle **wa** — never **ga wa** — to mark the noun as both the subject and the topic. In the same way, when a noun is the direct object as well as the topic, mark it with just **wa** — never with both **o** and **wa.**

Asking Questions

If you can form a sentence, you can form a question very easily in Japanese. Unlike in English, you don't have to invert the subject and the verb when you ask a question in Japanese. And you don't use question marks either.

How you form a question depends on what you are expecting as an answer. Are you expecting *yes* or *no*? Or are you expecting a specific piece of information, like a name, place, date, or person? Each case is discussed in the following subsections.

Yes/no questions

To form a question that you expect a *yes* or *no* answer to, just add the question particle **ka** (kah) at the end of the statement sentence and use a rising intonation, just as you do in English. For example, **Jon wa kimasu** (john wah kee-mah-soo) means *John will come,* and **Jon wa kimasu ka** (john wah kee-mah-soo kah) means *Will John come?*

Content questions

To ask a question that expects specific information or content as an answer, use a question word in addition to the question particle **ka** at the end of the sentence. Just like in English, different question words must be used depending on what is being asked. Table 2-3 provides more information on question words.

Table 2-3	Typical Question Words	
Question Word	*Pronunciation*	*Translation*
dare	dah-ree	who
doko	doh-koh	where
donata	doh-nah-tah	who
dore	doh-reh	which one
dō	dohh	how
ikura	ee-koo-rah	how much
itsu	ee-tsoo	when
nani	nah-nee	what

Talkin' the Talk

Yōko is asking Ken who came to yesterday's party.

Yōko: **Kinō no pātī wa dare ga kimashita ka.**
kee-nohh noh pahh-teee wah dah-reh gah kee-mah-shee-tah ka.
Who came to yesterday's party?

Ken: **Jon to Marī ga kimashita.**
john toh mah-reee gah kee-mah-shee-tah.
John and Mary came.

Dropping Understood Words

You may have the impression that Japanese people are diligent and hard working — and that is certainly true in many areas — but when it comes to speaking, the Japanese use the minimum number of words necessary to convey their meaning. Minimalist speaking is the Japanese way.

One way to pare down sentences is to drop pronouns and words that are understood in the context, and Japanese drop both almost all the time. As a result, you often hear sentences without a subject, a direct object, a time phrase, or a location phrase. It's not uncommon to see a sentence that consists of just the verb or just the topic. For example, the words and phrases in the parentheses in the following sentences don't have to be spoken, and they usually aren't. It's better to say less.

- ✔ **(Anata wa kyō watashi no) uchi ni kimasu ka.** ([ah-nah-tah wah kyohh wah-tah-shee noh] oo-chee nee kee-mah-soo kah; Will you come to my house today?)
- ✔ **Hotto doggu wa (tabemasu ka).** (hoht-toh dohg-goo wah [tah-beh-mah-soo kah]; Will you eat a hot dog?)
- ✔ **(Watashi wa kinō tenisu o) shimashita.** ([wah-tah-shee wah kee-nohh teh-nee-soo oh] shee-mah-shee-tah; I played tennis yesterday.)

Using Pronouns

Pronouns are convenient shorthand for nouns that both English and Japanese make good use of. Check out the following instruction where I italicized all the pronouns:

> Mix *those* together like *this,* leave *it* right *there* for a while, and then give *it* to *him* with *that.*

Makes you realize how convenient pronouns are, doesn't it? And, take it from me, they become even more useful when your short-term memory worsens as you age and you start referring to everything as "that," "it," and "her."

Demonstrative pronouns

Demonstrative pronouns seems like much too big a phrase to talk about four little words: *this, that, these,* and *those.* Think about the donut shop. You point at all the goodies and say, "I want six of these, two of those, and that big one right there." You use demonstrative pronouns to point verbally. In Japanese, things are just a little more complicated than they are in English.

Suppose you're the speaker and your girlfriend is the listener, and just the two of you are sitting face to face at a cozy table in a fancy restaurant. How romantic! In this case, the half of the table on your side is your territory, and the other half on your girlfriend's side is her territory. Any other tables in the restaurant are outside of both your territories. With these boundaries drawn, you can use the following pronouns when referring to various foods throughout the restaurant.

- ✔ **kore** (koh-reh): Things in your territory
- ✔ **sore** (soh-reh): Things in her territory
- ✔ **are** (ah-reh): Things outside of both your territories

Do you get the idea? If you do, you can understand who is eating **tako** (tah-koh; octopus), who is eating **ika** (ee-kah; squid), and who is eating **ebi** (eh-bee; shrimp) at the Japanese restaurant in the following Talkin' the Talk section. Seafood can look similar when sliced, which may account for Michelle and Brandon's confusion.

Talkin' the Talk

Michelle and Brandon are sitting at a table in a fancy Japanese restaurant eating sashimi, which is sliced raw seafood.

Brandon: **Sore wa ika desu ka.**
soh-reh wah ee-kah deh-soo kah.
Is that squid?

Michelle: **Īe, kore wa tako desu. Sore wa ika desu ka.**
eee-eh, koh-ree wah tah-koh deh-soo.
soh-ree wah ee-kah deh-soo kah.
No, this one is octopus. Is that one squid?

Brandon: **Hai, kore wa ika desu.**
hah-ee, koh-reh wah ee-kah deh-soo.
Yes, this one is squid.

Michelle: **Jā, are wa nan desu ka.**
jahh, ah-reh wah nahn deh-soo kah.
Then, what is that one over there?

Brandon: **Are wa ebi desu.**
ah-reh wah eh-bee deh-soo.
That one over there is shrimp.

Personal pronouns

The first-person singular pronoun in Japanese is **watashi** (wah-tah-shee), and it corresponds to the English *I* and *me*. Japanese does have other personal pronouns, which you can check out in Table 2-4.

Table 2-4	Personal Pronouns	
Pronoun	*Pronunciation*	*Translation*
watashi	wah-tah-shee	I, me
watashitachi	wah-tah-shee-tah-chee	we, us
anata	ah-nah-tah	you (singular)
anatatachi	ah-nah-tah-tah-chee	you (plural)
kare	kah-reh	he, him
karera	kah-reh-rah	they, them (male and mixed genders)
kanojo	kah-noh-joh	she, her
kanojora	kah-noh-joh-rah	they, them (female)

The first-person singular pronoun is typically **watashi,** but you can say *I/me* more than one way. The formal version is **watakushi** (wah-tah-koo-shee). Men say **boku** (boh-koo) in informal and neutral contexts. In informal contexts, some men say **ore** (oh-reh), some older men say **washi** (wah-shee), and some young women say **atashi** (ah-tah-shee).

Don't ever use **ore, washi,** and **atashi** when talking with your teacher, boss, customer, or client. **Boku** is not that bad, but **watashi** is safer in formal situations.

The first-person pronouns are repeatedly used in conversations, but other pronouns aren't. In fact, the use of **anata** (ah-nah-tah; you, singular) is almost forbidden. The person who says **anata** sounds snobby, arrogant, or just foreign.

So, how can you ask a question like *Will you go there?* without using **anata?** One strategy is to drop the pronoun (see the "Dropping Understood Words" section earlier in this chapter). Just use the verb and the question particle: **Ikimasu ka** (ee-kee-mah-soo kah; Will [you] go [there]?). Another strategy to avoid **anata** is to repeatedly use the person's name. You can ask Yōko this question: **Yōko-san, Yōko-san wa ikimasu ka** (yohh-koh-sahn, yohh-koh-sahn wah ee-kee-mah-soo kah; *Literally:* Yoko, is Yoko going?), which actually means *Yoko, are you going there?*

Words to Know

are	ah-reh	that one (over there)
boku	boh-koo	I/me (for men)
kore	koh-reh	this one
sore	soh-reh	that one (near you)
watashi	wah-tah-shee	I/me

Working with Verbs

Good news! You don't need to conjugate verbs based on person, gender, or number in Japanese. You use the same form of a verb whether you're talking about yourself, your girlfriend, your boyfriend, or all your friends. For example, you use the verb **taberu** (tah-beh-roo) whether you want to say *I eat, you eat, he eats, she eats,* or *they eat.*

"That's great," you're thinking — no conjugation tables to memorize. Not so fast. I'm not saying that Japanese verbs don't conjugate at all — they do. In this section, I walk you through the various conjugations, showing you how to create present, past, negative, and polite verbs (and combinations of these as well). If you get confused, you can always check out the verb tables in Appendix A.

Japanese language places a lot of emphasis on verbs. Verbs not only express certain actions or states of being, they also indicate social status, respect, and humility. You can often tell if Japanese are talking to an esteemed guest, a colleague, a spouse, or even a dog, just by the verb they use. Throughout this book, I use examples of plain/informal verbs, polite/neutral verbs, and formal verbs. However, the most common verbs are in the plain/informal and polite/neutral categories.

It could be just a coincidence, but every negative form of Japanese verbs has the *n* sound somewhere in it, just as the negative forms in English and most European languages do.

Understanding basic verb forms

The variations on the verb **taberu,** or any other Japanese verb, are made from four basic verb forms. By adding things onto the end of these forms, replacing their ending sound with another sound, or in some cases using them the way they are, Japanese expresses tense and level of formality, as well as get the verb in the right condition to accept an auxiliary verb. The four forms are:

- ✔ **Dictionary form:** You see this verb form when you look up words in the dictionary. It's kind of like an infinitive in English, but without the *to*. It's also called the *informal* or *plain* form because you use it when speaking informally — to friends or family. It can, however, serve other functions.

- ✔ **Negative form:** The opposite of the dictionary form. If the dictionary form means *I do,* the negative form means *I don't.*

- ✔ **Stem form:** This is the shortest form of a verb, but it can't stand alone — it needs one of a variety of verb suffixes that indicate tense or some other condition. For example, you add **masu** (mah-soo) to this form to make affirmative polite verbs.

- ✔ **Te-form:** Called the te-form because it always ends in **te** (teh) or **de** (deh). This form is most commonly used in combination with other verbs or with other auxiliary verbs. By itself, it's understood as an informal request.

Throughout the book, when I introduce a new verb, I give you these four forms, in this order — dictionary, negative, stem, and te-forms — along with the pronunciation. The following is an example with **taberu** (tah-beh-roo; to eat):

Form	Pronuciation
taberu	tah-beh-roo
tabenai	tah-beh-nah-ee
tabe	tah-beh
tabete	tah-beh-teh

Doing the conjugation thing

As in English, Japanese has regular and irregular verbs. All regular verbs conjugate according to a predictable pattern, while irregular verbs deviate from the pattern to a greater or lesser extent. Luckily, most verbs are regular.

Conjugating verbs

Regular verbs come in two basic varieties depending on their endings in the dictionary form: *ru-verbs* and *u-verbs*. Before you can conjugate any regular verb, you have to determine which type you're dealing with. Unfortunately, a verb's ending only tells whether it's a ru-verb or a u-verb about 80 percent of the time. Although all ru-verbs end in **ru,** sometimes u-verbs do too. U-verbs add one more sound or one more syllable in the negative, stem, and te-forms, as can be seen with the verb **kaeru** (kah-eh-roo). **Kaeru** can be either a ru-verb (meaning *exchange*) or a u-verb (meaning *go home*). Here's how they conjugate:

Form	*ru-verb (to exchange)*	*u-verb (to go home)*
Dictionary	kaeru	kaeru
Negative	kaenai	kaeranai
Stem	kae	kaeri
Te	kaete	kaette

Table 2-5 lists the conjugations of some frequently used ru-, u-, and irregular verbs.

Table 2-5		Verb Forms			
	Meaning	*Dictionary Form*	*Negative Form*	*Stem Form*	*Te-form*
Ru-verbs					
	to eat	taberu	tabenai	tabe	tabete
	to watch	miru	minai	mi	mite
	to exist (people & animals)	iru	inai	i	ite
U-verbs					
	to speak	hanasu	hanasanai	hanashi	hanashite
	to write	kaku	kakanai	kaki	kaite
	to swim	oyogu	oyoganai	oyogi	oyoide
	to drink	nomu	nomanai	nomi	nonde
	to play	asobu	asobanai	asobi	asonde
	to die	shinu	shinanai	shini	shinde
	to buy	kau	kawanai	kai	katte
	to take	toru	toranai	tori	totte
	to wait	matsu	matanai	machi	matte

(continued)

Table 2-5 *(continued)*

	Meaning	Dictionary Form	Negative Form	Stem Form	Te-form
Irregular Verbs					
	to exist (inanimate things)	aru	nai	ari	atte
	to go	iku	ikanai	iki	itte
	to come	kuru	konai	ki	kite
	to exist, come, go (honorific)	irassharu	irassharanai	irasshai	irasshatte
	to do	suru	shinai	shi	shite

My recommendation is not to be overly concerned with conjugating verbs accurately. Pay more attention to how verbs are used in context throughout this book. When you get a grasp of functions and implications of each verb form in context, you can start working on remembering detailed rules for producing the correct form.

If you want to try conjugating, pay attention to the ending syllable and the type of the verb, and follow the pattern of one of the verbs in the above table. But which one? Pick the one with the same *ending syllable* and the same *verb type*. By the *ending syllable,* I mean the last *syllable,* not the last *sound.* That is, the last consonant and vowel combination. If there is no consonant right before the last vowel, the last vowel by itself is the ending syllable of the verb. All the verbs in the dictionary form in the preceding table end in one of these syllables: **ru, su, ku, gu, mu, bu, nu, u,** and **tsu,** and so does every other Japanese verb! By *verb type,* I mean the u-verb, ru-verb, or irregular verb distinction. Remember that you can't always tell a verb's type from its ending, so I let you know the verb's type whenever I give you a conjugation table or list a verb in a Words to Know section.

Deciding tense: Past or not past, that is the question

Japanese verbs have just two tenses: present and past. The dictionary form is present tense. Present tense refers to both present and future, which makes the verb **taberu** not just *I eat,* but also *I will eat.* Usually the context tells you which meaning the verb is expressing. As in English, the present tense often doesn't refer to this very moment, but to some habitual action, such as *I eat dinner every day at six.*

Forming the past tense

If you know a verb's te-form, expressing that verb in the past tense is easy. You simply change the final vowel. Because this is the te-form, you're always changing an **e** to an **a.** For example, **tabete** (tah-beh-teh; eat) becomes **tabeta** (tah-beh-tah; ate), and **nonde** (nohn-deh; drink) becomes **nonda** (nohn-dah; drank).

Creating negative past tense verbs

In order to say that you did not do something in the past, you need to be able to fashion verbs into their negative past forms. No problem. It's easy. Simply take the negative form, drop the final vowel, **i,** and add **-katta.** For example, **tabenai** (tah-beh-nah-ee; don't eat) becomes **tabenakatta** (tah-beh-nah-kaht-tah; didn't eat). Cool, huh?

Speaking politely

In Japanese, the verbs you choose to use say a lot about you. Although it's fine to use the plain/informal verb forms when you talk with close friends or family members, if you use them in a business situation or with strangers, the listener may think you're unsophisticated or even rude. The ability to judge the situation and know what level of formality is appropriate is an integral part of speaking Japanese.

Making polite/neutral verb forms is easy. You just have to remember four verb endings (one each for affirmative present, negative present, affirmative past, and negative past), and add one of them to the end of the verb in the stem form.

- ✔ For affirmative present verbs, add **-masu.**
- ✔ For negative present verbs, add **-masen.**
- ✔ For affirmative past verbs, add **-mashita.**
- ✔ For negative past verbs, add **-masendeshita.**

The following mini-table gives you some examples:

Verb	Stem	Affirmative Present	Negative Present	Affirmative Past	Negative Past
taberu (eat)	tabe	tabemasu	tabemasen	tabemashita	tabemasendeshita
miru (watch)	mi	mimasu	mimasen	mimashita	mimasendeshita
nomu (drink)	nomi	nomimasu	nomimasen	nomimashita	nomimasendeshita

Enhancing verbs with suffixes

Japanese has a rich inventory of verb suffixes that can add either concrete meaning or subtle implications to your language. Different suffixes require different verb forms: *plain/informal form* (dictionary form, negative form, past tense, or negative past tense), stem form, or te-form. You may think that I'm slipping a whole new form in on you, but *plain/informal form* is just the term I use to indicate that the verb form *isn't* the stem or te-form. Dictionary form, negative form, past tense, and negative past tense verbs all follow the same pattern, so I call them all the plain/informal form. Knowing verb suffixes can increase your communication power exponentially. Table 2-6 shows some of the most common suffixes.

Table 2-6	Common Verb Suffixes		
Meaning/ Function	*Suffix*	*Example*	*Translation*
Suffixes that follow Plain/Informal forms			
should	-bekidesu	taberu-bekidesu	I should eat.
probability	-deshō	taberu-deshō	I'll probably eat.
possibility	-kamoshiremasen	taberu-kamoshiremasen	I might eat.
person	-hito	taberu-hito	the person who eats
because	-kara	taberu-kara	because I eat
noun-maker	-koto	taberu-koto	the act of eating
things	-mono	taberu-mono	things to eat
time	-toki	taberu-toki	when I eat
intention	-tsumoridesu	taberu-tsumoridesu	I plan to eat.
Suffixes that follow Stem forms			
while	-nagara	tabe-nagara	while eating
purpose	-ni	tabe-ni	in order to eat

Meaning/ Function	Suffix	Example	Translation
difficulty	-nikui	tabe-nikui	It's hard to eat.
over-doing	-sugiru	tabe-sugiru	I over eat.
desire	-tai	tabe-tai	I want to eat.
Suffixes that follow Te-forms			
doing a favor	-ageru	tabete-ageru	I eat for you.
present perfect	-aru	tabete-aru	I have eaten.
present progressive	-iru	tabete-iru	I am eating.
requesting	-kudasai	tabete-kudasai	Please eat.
attempt	-miru	tabete-miru	I'll try to eat.
completion	-shimau	tabete-shimau	I finish eating.

Note: *In this table I use hyphens to show you the boundary between the verb and the verb suffix, but you pronounce the verbs as one word or phrase.*

Using the Verb Desu, to Be

Like the English verb *to be*, **desu** (deh-soo) expresses the identity or state of people and things. **Desu** is used in a construction, **X wa Y desu** (X wah Y deh-soo; X is Y). Instead of saying *X is Y*, Japanese say *X Y is*. The particle **wa** (wah) is the topic particle discussed in the "Telling the topic" section earlier in this chapter.

Desu follows either a noun or an adjective. For example, **Otōto wa gakusē desu** (oh-tohh-toh wah gah-koo-sehh deh-soo) means that *My little brother is a student.* **Watashi wa genki desu** (wah-tah-shee wah gehn-kee deh-soo) means that *I am fine.* Now you know why many Japanese sentences end in **desu.** And like the verb *to be*, **desu** can also express the location of people and things. For example, **Jon wa Bosuton desu** (john wah boh-soo-tohn deh-soo) means *John is in Boston.* Just be aware that the location of things and people also can be expressed by the verbs **aru** and **iru,** in addition to **desu.** To find out more about **aru** and **iru,** see Chapter 4.

Conjugation-wise, **desu** doesn't look like any other verb: You may wonder whether it's really a verb. This is because **desu** didn't start out as as stand-alone verb. It was the combination of the particle **de,** the verb **aru** (ah-roo; to exist), and the polite suffix -**masu.**

Table 2-7 shows you the patterns of **desu.** To help you see the point easily, I use the same noun **gakusē** (gah-koo-sehh; student) in each example. If you want to know how to use **desu** after an adjective, see the following "Describing Adjectives" section.

Table 2-7	Formal Form of Noun plus Desu	
Japanese	*Pronunciation*	*Translation*
gakusē desu	gah-koo-sehh deh-soo	is a student
gakusē ja arimasen	gah-koo-sehh jah ah-ree-mah-sehn	isn't a student
gakusē deshita	gah-koo-sehh deh-shee-tah	was a student
gakusē ja arimasendeshita	gah-koo-sehh jah ah-ree-mah-sehn-deh-shee-tah	wasn't a student

In an informal context, you can use the shorter version of **desu,** as Table 2-8 demonstrates.

Table 2-8	Informal Form of Noun plus Desu	
Japanese	*Pronunciation*	*Translation*
gakusē da	gah-koo-sehh dah	is a student
gakusē ja nai	gah-koo-sehh jah nah-ee	isn't a student
gakusē datta	gah-koo-sehh daht-tah	was a student
gakusē ja nakatta	gah-koo-sehh jah nah-kaht-tah	wasn't a student

Ja (jah), which you see in the negative forms in Tables 2-7 and 2-8, is the contraction of **dewa** (deh-wah). Most Japanese use **ja** in everyday conversation, but occasionally, they use **dewa.** Just be ready to hear either one of them.

Talkin' the Talk

Susan asks Ken some questions.

Susan: **Ano otoko no hito wa gakusē desu ka.**
ah-noh oh-toh-koh noh hee-toh wah gah-koo-sehh deh-soo ka.
Is that man a student?

Ken: **Īe, gakusē ja arimasen. Watashi no karate no sensē desu.**
eee-eh, gah-koo-sehh jah ah-ree-mah-sehn. wah-tah-shee noh kah-rah-teh noh sehn-sehh deh-soo.
No, he is not a student. He is my karate teacher.

Susan: **Ā, sō desu ka. Chotto kowasō desu ne.**
ahh, sohh deh-soo kah. choht-toh koh-wah-sohh deh-soo neh.
Oh, I see. He looks a little scary.

Words to Know

gakusē	gah-koo-sehh	student
kowasō	koh-wah-sohh	scarey-looking
sensē	sehn-sehh	teacher

Describing Adjectives

As in English, Japanese adjectives can be placed either before a noun as a noun modifier (a *good* book, for example) or at the end of a sentence (The book is *good.*).

Believe or not, all Japanese adjectives end in either **i** or **na** when they're placed before a noun. Adjectives that end in **i** are called *i-type adjectives,* and those that end in **na** are called *na-type adjectives*. Very simple. There's really no clear-cut distinction between the two groups in terms of meaning. For example, **taka-i** and **kōka-na** both mean *expensive,* but one is an i-type adjective and the other is a na-type adjective.

Look at some adjectives that modify the noun **hon** (hohn; book):

- ✔ **benri-na hon** (behn-ree-nah hohn; a convenient book)
- ✔ **kirĕ-na hon** (kee-rehh-nah hohn; a beautiful book)
- ✔ **kōka-na hon** (kohh-kah-nah hohn; an expensive book)
- ✔ **omoshiro-i hon** (oh-moh-shee-roh-ee hohn; an interesting book)
- ✔ **taka-i hon** (tah-kah-ee hohn; an expensive book)

Japanese adjectives consist of a *stem* (the part that remains the same) and an *inflection* part (the part that changes depending on the context). The endings **i** and **na** are inflection parts. I placed a little dash to show you the boundary between the *stem* and the *inflection* in this section, but you won't see it in other parts of this book.

English adjectives conjugate based on whether they're comparative or superlative, like *tall, taller,* and *tallest,* but Japanese adjectives don't. They conjugate based on different factors. For example, when they're placed at the end of a sentence, rather than before a noun, the **i** and **na** change or disappear, and an extra item like the verb **desu** (deh-soo; to be) shows up in various forms, all of which depend on the tense, whether it's affirmative or negative, and whether it's plain/informal or polite/neutral.

Look at the following sentences, all of which either include **taka-i** (tah-kah-ee; expensive), an i-type adjective, or **kōka-na** (kohh-kah-nah; expensive), a na-type adjective.

- ✔ **Are wa kōka ja arimasen.** (ah-reh wah kohh-kah jah ah-ree-mah-sehn; That is not expensive.)
- ✔ **Hanbāgā wa taka-ku arimasen.** (hahn-bahh-gahh wah tah-kah-koo ah-ree-mah-sehn; Hamburgers are not expensive.)
- ✔ **Kōka-na nekkuresu o kaimashita.** (kohh-kah nah nehk-koo-reh-soo oh kah-ee-mah-shee-tah; I bought an expensive necklace.)
- ✔ **Kore wa taka-katta.** (koh-reh wah tah-kah-kaht-tah; This was expensive.)
- ✔ **Taka-i hon o kaimashita.** (tah-kah-ee hohn oh kah-ee-mah-shee-tah; I bought an expensive book.)

All of the patterns for i-type and na-type adjectives are summarized in Table 2-9, along with some variations in parentheses.

Table 2-9	Adjective Patterns		
	Tense/Polarity	*I-type*	*Na-type*
Plain/Informal style			
	Present affirmative (is)	taka-i	kōka da
	Present negative (isn't)	taka-ku nai	kōka ja nai
	Past affirmative (was)	taka-katta	kōka datta
	Past negative (wasn't)	taka-ku nakatta	kōka ja nakatta
Polite/Neutral style			
	Present affirmative (is)	taka-i desu	kōka desu
	Present negative (isn't)	taka-ku arimasen (taka-ku nai desu)	kōka ja arimasen (kōka ja nai desu)
	Past affirmative (was)	taka-katta desu	kōka deshita
	Past negative (wasn't)	taka-ku arimasen deshita (taka-ku nakatta desu)	kōka ja arimasen deshita (kōka ja nakatta desu)

The irregular adjective most frequently used is **i-i** (ee-ee; good). Its stem part is **i**, and its inflection part is the second **i**. The stem part **i** becomes **yo** in all the forms except the present affirmative form, regardless of whether it's placed at the end of a sentence or right before a noun.

✔ **i-i hon desu** (ee-ee hohn deh-soo; is a good book)

✔ **i-i-desu** (ee-ee deh-soo; is good)

✔ **yo-katta desu** (yoh-kaht-tah deh-soo; was good)

✔ **yo-ku arimasendeshita** (yoh-koo ah-ree-mah-sehn-deh-shee-tah; wasn't good)

✔ **yo-ku arimasen** (yoh-koo ah-ree-mah-sen; isn't good)

In this book, when I list an adjective in the Words to Know section, I list na-type adjectives in the stem form without the **na** and i-type adjectives in the stem form plus the inflection **i**. It's just because **i** appears almost all the time, but **na** appears only when the adjective is followed by a noun.

Counting in Japanese

Numbers are definitely an indispensable part of life. When you cook, you count the number of eggs you put into your batter. When you're at a party, your wife counts the number of drinks you have. When you get paid, you count the number of bills in your hand. In this section, I show you numbers from 1 to 100,000 in Japanese. Think of it — you can increase your vocabulary by 100,000 words.

Numbers from 1 to 10

You can master the art of counting from one to ten right now. It'll be handy as you earn your belts at a **karate dōjō** (kah-rah-teh dohh-johh; karate training hall). At a **karate dōjō,** they never start from **rē** (rehh; zero). They always start from **ichi** (ee-chee; one) when they punch and kick. Many moms also count from **ichi** before they punish their kids. **Ichi** (ee-chee; one), **ni** (nee; two), **san** (sahn; three), **yon** (yohn; four), **go** (goh; five). *Now you have a time out!* Check out Table 2-10 to start counting in Japanese.

Table 2-10		Numbers from 1 to 10	
1	ichi (ee-chee)	6	roku (roh-koo)
2	ni (nee)	7	nana (nah-nah) *or* shichi (shee-chee)
3	san (sahn)	8	hachi (hah-chee)
4	yon (yohn) *or* shi (shee)	9	kyū (kyooo) *or* ku (koo)
5	go (goh)	10	jū (jooo)

The numbers that follow an *or* in Table 2-10 are usually only used for reciting numbers or doing arithmetic and not for actually counting things. You students of martial arts may be familiar with these numbers from counting while practicing kicks, punches, and so on. In martial-type language, syllables are often cut short, making counting practice sound like **ich, ni, san, shi, go, rok, shich, hach, ku, jū.** It also makes war movies hard to understand!

Numbers from 11 to 99

The Japanese number system is both somewhat cumbersome and very logical. The discussion about different words for four and nine in the "Lucky and unlucky numbers" sidebar in this chapter gives you an indication of the cumbersome part. But now for the logical part: To make any number from eleven to ninety-nine, you just combine the numbers from one to ten. For example, eleven is **jū-ichi** (jooo-ee-chee) — ten **(jū)** plus one **(ichi)**. How about twelve? Same thing: Twelve is **jū-ni** (jooo-nee). Twenty is two sets of ten, so you say "two-tens," **ni-jū** (nee-jooo). It may help you to think of twenty as two times ten. Twenty-one is **ni-jū-ichi** (nee-jooo-ee-chee).

Do you see the logic? You can use this pattern to count up to **kyū-jū-kyū** (kyooo-jooo-kyooo; ninety-nine, or nine tens plus nine).

Numbers from 100 to 9,999

If you want to go shopping in Japan, you need to master the numbers over one hundred because one hundred yen is just about one dollar, so you'll be dealing with hundreds and thousands of yen just to go grocery shopping.

To count over 100, keep using the pattern for numbers up to ninety-nine (see the previous section). One hundred is **hyaku** (hyah-koo). So, two hundred is **ni-hyaku** (nee-hyah-koo). One thousand is **sen** (sehn); therefore, two thousand is **ni-sen** (nee-sehn). I'm sure you can't wait to say 9,999. Yes. It's **kyū-sen kyū-hyaku kyū-jū kyū** (kyooo-sehn kyooo-hyah-koo kyooo-jooo kyooo).

Be aware of some irregular sound changes. When the words for one hundred, **hyaku,** and one thousand, **sen,** are preceded by the number three, **san,** they become **byaku** (byah-koo) and **zen** (zehn), respectively. So, three hundred is **san-byaku** and three thousand is **san-zen.** Other irregular sound changes are found in six hundred, **rop-pyaku** (rohp-pyah-koo), eight hundred, **hap-pyaku** (hahp-pyah-koo), and eight thousand **has-sen** (hahs-sehn). Table 2-11 lists some of the numbers from 100 to 9,000.

Lucky and unlucky numbers

Japanese think that 3, 5, and 7 are lucky numbers. One example of this is seen in the traditional ritual, **shichi-go-san** (shee-chee-goh-sahn; _Literally:_ seven-five-three). On November 15, many Japanese families cerebrate this gala day for three-year-old and five-year-old boys and three-year-old and seven-year-old girls by dressing their children in traditional clothes, such as kimono, and visiting Shinto shrines.

In contrast, Japanese think that 4 and 9 are unlucky numbers because the number four, when pronounced as **shi** (shee), sounds the same as the word _death,_ and the number nine, pronounced as **ku** (koo), sounds the same as the word _suffering._ So, Japanese table settings come with five plates, cups, knives, forks, and spoons — never in sets of four. The next time you give some cookies or candies to a Japanese, give him or her any number of them, except four or nine.

Table 2-11	Select Numbers from 100 to 9,000		
100	hyaku (hyah-koo)	1,000	sen (sehn)
200	ni-hyaku (nee-hyah-koo)	2,000	ni-sen (nee-sehn)
300	san-byaku (sahn-byah-koo)	3,000	san-zen (sahn-zehn)
400	yon-hyaku (yohn-hyah-koo)	4,000	yon-sen (yohn-sehn)
500	go-hyaku (goh-hyah-koo)	5,000	go-sen (goh-sehn)
600	rop-pyaku (rohp-pyah-koo)	6,000	roku-sen (roh-koo-sehn)
700	nana-hyaku (nah-nah-hyah-koo)	7,000	nana-sen (nah-nah-sehn)
800	hap-pyaku (hahp-pyah-koo)	8,000	has-sen (hahs-sehn)
900	kyū-hyaku (kyooo-hyah-koo)	9,000	kyū-sen (kyooo-sehn)

Numbers from 10,000 to 100,000

Unlike English, Japanese has a special digit name for ten thousand. It's **man** (mahn; ten thousand). For example, to mean fifty thousand (50,000), you may want to say **go-jū-sen** because your mathematical logic is **go-jū** (50) of **sen** (1,000), but Japanese don't say that. They say **go-man** (goh-mahn; 50,000) — a bit tricky for you. Ten thousand is **ichi-man** (ee-chee-mahn; 10,000), twenty thousand is **ni-man** (nee-mahn; 20,000), and thirty thousand is **san-man** (sahn-mahn; 30,000). Starting to get used to it? Check out Table 2-12 to compare digit names.

Table 2-12	English and Japanese Digit Names	
Number	*English*	*Japanese*
10	ten	jū
100	hundred	hyaku
1,000	thousand	sen
10,000	N/A	man
1,000,000	million	N/A
100,000,000	N/A	oku

Now, can you say 99,999? It's **kyū-man kyū-sen kyū-hyaku kyū-jū kyū.** Here's one more: One hundred thousand isn't 100 **sen** (thousand), but 10 **man: jū-man.** Now you can tell your mom or your friends that you can count up to one hundred thousand in Japanese. They'll think that you're a genius. But if you're not sure of your counting abilities just yet, look up the numbers over ten thousand in Table 2-13.

Table 2-13	Select Numbers from 10,000 to 100,000		
10,000	ichi-man (ee-chee-mahn)	60,000	roku-man (roh-koo-mahn)
20,000	ni-man (nee-mahn)	70,000	nana-man (nah-nah-mahn)
30,000	san-man (sahn-mahn)	80,000	hachi-man (hahr-chee-mahn)
40,000	yon-man (yohn-mahn)	90,000	kyū-man (kyooo-mahn)
50,000	go-man (goh-mahn)	100,000	jū-man (jooo-mahn)

Counting with Counters

If I say *I drank one sake,* you won't know whether I drank one *glass* of rice wine or one *bottle* of rice wine, although the state of my brain function would be dramatically different depending on which answer were correct. And if I eat two *dozen* eggs instead of two eggs every day, I won't live as long as I should. Words like *glasses, bottles,* and *dozens* express the amount or quantity unit. Other English unit words include *piece, sheet,* and *pair* (as in a *piece* of cake, a *sheet* of paper, and a *pair* of shoes).

Unless you're reciting numbers or doing arithmetic, you need to place a counter right after numbers. You need a *counter* to specify time and date, talk about your age, chat about your score on a test, and count days, cars, students, money, chairs, fish, and a ton of other things — even mosquitoes.

Hold onto your hat here — this is where numbers start getting bumpy. Depending on the shape, size, and type of the item, you use different counters. Here's how it works: If you count mechanical items such as cars, you need the counter **-dai** (dah-ee). Simply add the counter after the number of cars — **ichi-dai, ni-dai, san-dai,** and so on. If you count cylindrical items, you need a different counter, which is **-hon** (hohn). If you count animals, you need the counter **-hiki** (hee-kee).

The tricky part is that there can be more than one acceptable counter for an item. When you're at the fish market trying to buy five mackerel, you can use either **-hiki** or **-hon** as the counter. Some people prefer one over the other, often according to their age and the region where they live.

Table 2-14 lists some frequently used counters, including the ones I mentioned, along with their uses. Table 2-14 includes only *some* of many Japanese counters. Wow!

Table 2-14	Counters and Their Uses	
Counter	*Use*	*Examples*
-dai (dah-ee)	mechanical items	cars, typewriters, refrigerators
-hiki (hee-kee)	animals	mosquitoes, dogs, cats, frogs, fish
-hon (hohn)	cylindrical items	pens, pencils, bananas, sticks, umbrellas
-mai (mah-ee)	flat items	bed sheets, paper, stamps
-nin (neen)	people	students, children, women
-tsu (tsoo)	various inanimate items/ items that don't have a specific counter	furniture, apples, bags, traffic lights

Native Japanese numbers

The numbers predominantly used in daily life and in academic, business, and scientific fields in modern Japan are actually of Chinese origin. The numbers from **ichi** (ee-chee; one), **ni** (nee; two), and **san** (sahn; three), up to **jū-man** (jooo-mahn; 100,000) are all of Chinese origin. But Japanese also has native numbers from one to ten:

- **hito** (hee-toh; one)
- **futa** (foo-tah; two)
- **mi** (mee; three)
- **yo** (yoh; four)
- **itsu** (ee-tsoo; five)
- **mu** (moo; six)
- **nana** (nah-nah; seven)
- **ya** (yah; eight)
- **kokono** (koh-koh-noh; nine)
- **tō** (tohh; ten)

Most of the native Japanese numbers cannot be pronounced by themselves: They can be spoken only when they're combined with a native counter like **-tsu** (tsoo). Because **-tsu** is used for counting a variety of items and it can be used even when a specific counter is available, memorizing **hito-tsu** (hee-toh-tsoo; one), **futa-tsu** (foo-tah-tsoo; two), **mit-tsu** (meet-tsoo; three), and so on will serve you well. They'll become handy.

Take a look at the final counter in Table 2-14. Not every single thing in the universe has its own counter. For things that don't have a specific counter, you use the native Japanese counter **-tsu** with native Japanese numbers (see the nearby "Native Japanese numbers" sidebar). (Most numbers are actually of Chinese origin, as are a great many other Japanese words.)

Table 2-15 puts it all together for you, giving you the numbers from one to ten and showing you how to use various counters. Keep this table handy.

Table 2-15	Counting with Counters					
Number	*-dai* *Mechanical items*	*-hiki* *Animals*	*-hon* *Cylindrical items*	*-mai* *Flat items*	*-nin* *People*	*-tsu* *Various inanimate items*
1 ichi	ichi-dai	ip-piki	ip-pon	ichi-mai	hitori	hito-tsu
2 ni	ni-dai	ni-hiki	ni-hon	ni-mai	futari	futa-tsu
3 san	san-dai	san-biki	san-bon	san-mai	san-nin	mit-tsu
4 yon	yon-dai	yon-hiki	yon-hon	yon-mai	yo-nin	yot-tsu
5 go	go-dai	go-hiki	go-hon	go-mai	go-nin	itsu-tsu
6 roku	roku-dai	rop-piki	rop-pon	roku-mai	roku-nin	mut-tsu
7 nana	nana-dai	nana-hiki	nana-hon	nana-mai	nana-nin	nana-tsu
8 hachi	hachi-dai	hap-piki	hap-pon	hachi-mai	hachi-nin	yat-tsu
9 kyū	kyū-dai	kyū-hiki	kyū-hon	kyū-mai	kyū-nin	kokono-tsu
10 jū	jū-dai	jup-piki	jup-pon	jū-mai	jū-nin	tō

Using some counters causes sound changes in the numbers and in the counter itself. And the Japanese native word for number ten, **tō** (tohh; ten), cannot be followed by the counter **-tsu** for some historical reason. Don't be too concerned about these irregular changes. Even if you make a mistake here, you'll be understood perfectly by Japanese.

If you forget which counter to use, and you're counting no more than ten of something, the number phrases in the last column of Table 2-15 (the **-tsu** column) work for counting just about anything.

Fun & Games

Count to 15 by filling in the blanks with the correct numbers. Flip to Appendix C for the answers.

1. **ichi**
2. **ni**
3. _____
4. **yon**
5. **go**
6. _____
7. **nana**
8. _____
9. _____
10. **jū**
11. **jū-ichi**
12. **jū-ni**
13. **jū-san**
14. _____
15. **jū-go**

Chapter 3

Introductions and Greetings

Konnichiwa! (kohn-nee-chee-wa; Hi!) Communication starts by introducing yourself to new people, and you can strengthen relationships by using pleasant daily greetings. In this chapter, I show you how to display a friendly and positive attitude to those around you. And don't forget to smile when you greet someone — a smile needs no translation.

Making Introductions

Nothing is more exciting than getting to know new people at a **pātī** (pahh-teee; party), **kaigi** (kah-ee-gee; conference), **atarashī shokuba** (ah-tah-rah-sheee shoh-koo-bah; new job), or even on the **tōri** (tohh-ree; street). Tomorrow, you may meet someone who will be very important in your life! This section shows you how to make a good first impression.

Introducing yourself

The first word to say as you introduce yourself to someone for the first time is **hajimemashite** (hah-jee-meh-mah-shee-teh). This word literally means *beginning,* and it clarifies the fact that you're meeting that person for the very first time. After saying **hajimemashite,** say your name, and then say **yoroshiku** (yoh-roh-shee-koo). **Yoroshiku** is a set phrase that shows your modest attitude and asks the other party to be friendly and nice to you. No English translation exists for it.

Bowing

Bowing plays a very important role in Japanese communication. Phrases expressing gratitude, apologies, and greetings are almost always accompanied by a bow. Japanese also bow when meeting someone for the very first time. Occasionally, they shake hands, but most of the time, they just bow as they say **yoroshiku.** You don't need to bow very deeply in this context. Just slowly tilt your head and upper back slightly forward, and hold the position for two seconds. The deep, long bow is only needed when you make a horrible mistake, receive overwhelming kindness, or associate with people to whom you have to show a great deal of respect. Westerners are not expected to bow to be polite, but if they do, they'll certainly impress and please Japanese.

English speakers just say "Pleased to meet you" or "I'm very happy to meet you" when they meet someone. They don't beg people to like them as the Japanese do. But when speaking Japanese, do as the Japanese do and say **yoroshiku.**

The response to **yoroshiku** is usually **kochirakoso** (koh-chee-rah-koh-soh) **yoroshiku,** meaning *It's I who should say that.* So, if you beg someone to be friendly, they beg you right back. After all of that begging, you're friends!

Introducing your friends

Your friend can become your friend's friend if you introduce them to each other. When you want to introduce your friend to someone, say **kochira wa** (koh-chee-rah wah; as for this person), your friend's name, and the verb **desu** (deh-soo; is). If you want to say *This is John,* say **Kochira wa Jon-san desu** (koh-chee-rah wah john-sahn deh-soo). The short suffix **-san** (sahn) after the name **Jon** (john; John) is a respectful title. It adds a touch of politeness when you mention it with someone's name, and it's similar to *Mr.* or *Ms.* in English. I discuss respectful titles in detail in the "Addressing friends and strangers" section later in this chapter. As long as I'm talking about introductions, here's one more tip: Remember to introduce the person with the lower social status to the person with the higher social status.

Talkin' the Talk

Jun is introducing his friends, Lisa and Robert, to each other.

Jun: **Robāto-san, kochira wa Risa Jonson-san desu. Risa-san, kochira wa Robāto Rosu-san desu.**
roh-bahh-toh-sahn, koh-chee-rah wah ree-sah john-sohn-sahn deh-soo. ree-sah-sahn, koh-chee-rah wah roh-bahh-toh roh-soo-sahn deh-soo.
Robert, this is Lisa Johnson. Lisa, this is Robert Roth.

Lisa: **Hajimemashite. Risa Jonson desu. Yoroshiku.**
hah-jee-meh-mah-shee-teh. ree-sah john-sohn deh-soo. yoh-roh-shee-koo.
How do you do? I'm Lisa Johnson. I'm pleased to meet you.

Robert: **Hajimemashite. Robāto Rosu desu. Kochirakoso yoroshiku.**
hah-jee-meh-mah-shee-teh. roh-bahh-toh roh-soo deh-soo. koh-chee-rah-koh-soh yoh-roh-shee-koo.
How do you do? I'm Robert Roth. I'm pleased to meet you too.

Asking people their names

Usually, the more people you know, the happier you are. So, start asking people their **namae** (nah-mah-eh; names) and make **tomodachi** (toh-moh-dah-chee; friends). As in English, telling someone your name when speaking Japanese is more or less a cue for that person to tell you his or her name. If it doesn't turn out that way, you can just ask by saying **Shitsurē desu ga, o-namae wa** (shee-tsoo-rehh deh-soo gah, oh-nah-mah-eh wah; I may be rude, but what's your name?). Your own name is **namae,** but someone else's name is **o-namae.**

Being polite with o-

The polite prefix **o-** is used optionally to show respect to others and the things that belong to them. It's often translated in English as *honorable,* which is why a lot of Japanese characters in grade-B movies always say honorable this and honorable that. But *honorable* is a mouthful compared to **o-,** which attaches to words much more naturally. Sometimes, using **o-** is obligatory regardless of whether you're talking about yourself or about others. For example, the word for *money* is **kane** (kah-neh), but people almost always call it **okane** (oh-kah-neh), even if they're talking about their own money. Only bank robbers and drunks say **kane.** Likewise, *tea* and *souvenir* should be **ocha** (oh-chah) and **omiyage** (oh-mee-yah-geh), respectively, no matter what. But I need to let you know that some geographic differences with this concept exist, depending on the part of Japan you're in.

Greeting and Chatting

Aisatsu (ah-ee-sah-tsoo; greetings) are the most important communication tools. Start your day with a friendly and cheerful greeting to your family, friends, colleagues, teachers, and bosses. Chatting about the weather is a nice way to have a brief conversation. And don't forget to conclude your greeting with a smile.

After an introduction, chat a little so that you and your new acquaintance get to know each other better. You can talk about where you're from and perhaps make a connection on that basis. A small conversation can mark the beginning of a friendship. These sections give you essential phrases for these friendly contexts.

Addressing friends and strangers

In English, you address others by their first name ("Hi, Robert!"), by their nickname ("Hey, Bobby!"), by their position ("Excuse me, professor"), or by their family name and an appropriate title ("Hello, Mr. Right"), depending on your relationship and how close you are to that person. You don't want to sound too formal or distant, but you don't want to sound too friendly or presumptuous either.

In Japanese society, addressing people is something that you don't want to mess up. When you meet someone new at work and you know the person's occupational title (such as company president, professor, or division manager), use the title along with his or her family name — for example, **Sumisu-shachō** (soo-mee-soo-shah-chohh; President Smith). Following are some examples of occupational titles:

- ✔ **buchō** (boo-chohh; department manager)
- ✔ **gakuchō** (gah-koo-chohh; university president)
- ✔ **kōchō** (kohh-chohh; principal)

✔ **sensē** (sehn-sehh; teacher)

✔ **shachō** (shah-chohh; company president)

✔ **tenchō** (tehn-chohh; store manager)

If you don't know the person's occupational title, the safest way to address him or her is to use his or her family name plus the respectful title **-san** (sahn) — **Sumisu-san** (soo-mee-soo-sahn; Ms. Smith). The more polite version of **-san** is **-sama** (sah-mah), but it's too formal and business-like for most social situations. Other respectful titles include **-chan** (chahn) and **-kun** (koon), but they must be used very carefully. Check out Table 3-1 to see which titles are appropriate for your friends and acquaintances. The table contains examples of various ways you might address Robert and Susan Smith.

Table 3-1	Respectful Titles	
Title	*Function*	*Example*
-chan (chahn)	For children, used after a boy or girl's given name.	Sūzan-chan (sooo-zahn-chahn), Robāto-chan (roh-bahh-toh-chahn)
-kun (koon)	Used after a boy's given name.	Robāto-kun (roh-bahh-toh-koon)
	Also used after a subordinate's family name, regardless of gender.	Sumisu-kun (soo-mee-soo-koon)
-sama (sah-mah)	Used after a superior's or customer's name, regardless of gender. Also used when addressing letters (Dear. . .).	Sumisu-sama (soo-mee-soo-sah-mah), Sūzan-sama (sooo-zahn-sah-mah), Robāto Sumisu-sama (roh-bahh-toh soo-mee-soo-sah-mah)
-san (sahn)	Used with anyone if other titles are unavailable.	Sumisu-san (soo-mee-soo-sahn), Sūzan-san (sooo-zahn-sahn), Robāto Sumisu-san (roh-bahh-toh soo-mee-soo-sahn)

When introducing themselves, Japanese (as well as Chinese and Koreans) give their family name first and given name last. Most Japanese realize that Western names aren't in the same order, and they won't expect you to reverse the order of your own name to match the pattern of their names. Many Japanese also realize that Westerners tend to use their given names a lot, but you should use the family name for all but your closest friends and family.

If you use the Japanese word for *you* — **anata** (ah-nah-tah) — you'll sound boastful or rude. (Chapter 2 has a section on pronouns.) Japanese uses names or titles where English uses *you.* Instead of *you,* you can use interesting age- and gender-sensitive terms when addressing strangers in friendly contexts. For example, **ojisan** (oh-jee-sahn) literally means *uncle,* but you can use it to address any unfamiliar middle-aged man. The following list shows other general descriptions of strangers and the Japanese terms you can use to address them:

- **middle-aged man: ojisan** (oh-jee-sahn; *Literally:* uncle)
- **middle-aged woman: obasan** (oh-bah-sahn; *Literally:* aunt)
- **old man: ojīsan** (oh-jeee-sahn; *Literally:* grandfather)
- **old woman: obāsan** (oh-bahh-sahn; *Literally:* grandmother)
- **young boy: bōya** *or* **obocchan** (bohh-yah *or* oh-boht-chahn; *Literally:* son)
- **young girl: ojōsan** (oh-johh-sah; *Literally:* daughter)
- **young man: onīsan** (oh-neee-sahn; *Literally:* big brother)
- **young woman: onēsan** (oh-nehh-sahn; *Literally:* big sister)

Well-educated Japanese adults use a breaking-the-ice idiom, **otaku** (oh-tah-koo; *Literally:* your household), but it has a limitation — you can't simply say **otaku** as you might use *Hey, you!* to get someone's attention. You can only use **otaku** in a sentence, as in **Otaku wa dochira kara desu ka** (oh-tah-koo wah doh-chee-rah kah-rah deh-soo kah; Where are you from?). However, this once-safe word now has another meaning that you may want to avoid. Youngsters recently started using **otaku** as a label for someone who is obsessed with something. So, be careful when you use it.

Words to Know

Hajimemashite.	hah-jee-meh-mah-shee-teh	How do you do?
O-namae wa.	oh-nah-mah-eh wah	What's your name?
sensē	sehn-sehh	teacher/professor
shachō	shah-chohh	company president
Yoroshiku.	yoh-roh-shee-koo	Pleased to meet you.

Greeting all day long

In Japanese, as in every other language, what you say and do to greet people depends on the time of the day and the person you're greeting.

In the morning, as you greet family, friends, and colleagues, say **ohayō** (oh-hah-yohh) — the informal version of *good morning.* As you greet your boss or teacher, use the formal **ohayō gozaimasu** (oh-hah-yohh goh-zah-ee-mah-soo) and don't forget to bow as you say it.

In the afternoon, say **konnichiwa** (kohn-nee-chee-wah; good afternoon) to everyone, regardless of their position and status. When you can see the stars or the moon in the sky, say **konbanwa** (kohn-bahn-wah), regardless of who you greet. It means *good evening.*

And it's not very polite just to say *hi.* If you haven't seen someone in a while, ask him or her **O-genki desu ka** (oh-gehn-kee deh-soo kah; How are you?) as well.

When others ask you how you are, you can say **Hai, genki desu** (hah-ee, gehn-kee deh-soo; I'm fine), but if you want to sound a bit more sophisticated, say **Hai, okagesamade** (hah-ee oh-kah-geh-sah-mah-deh; Yes, I'm fine thanks to you and God.) or **Nantoka** (nahn-toh-kah; I'm barely managing things in my life *or* I'm barely coping). Those two expressions sound very modest and mature to Japanese, though they sound pretty negative to American ears. In America, you have to answer *Great!* when someone asks *How are you?*

English speakers make a habit of asking everyone, close friends and complete strangers alike, how they are, even if they know that the person is healthy and fine. Asking this question in Japanese is different. **O-genki desu ka** is a serious question about a person's mental and physical health. So, don't use it when greeting someone you saw yesterday. Say it when you mean it.

Talking about the weather

Japanese- and English-speaking people often talk about the **tenki** (tehn-kee; weather) right after they greet someone. The **tenki** seems to be a universally-neutral topic. On a nice clear day, try starting a conversation with **Ii tenki desu ne** (eee tehn-kee deh-soo neh; It's nice today, isn't it?). The following adjectives describe temperature and humidity:

- **atatakai** (ah-tah-tah-kah-ee; warm)
- **atsui** (ah-tsoo-ee; hot)
- **mushi-atsui** (moo-shee-ah-tsoo-ee; muggy)

- ✔ **samui** (sah-moo-ee; cold)
- ✔ **suzushii** (soo-zoo-sheee; cool)

You can use these adjectives by themselves in informal contexts. For example, when you're at home, you can scream **Atsui** (ah-tsoo-ee; Hot!) when it's very hot. If you want to mention to your mom that it's hot, hoping that she'll agree with you, you can add the particle **ne** (neh; isn't it?), as in **Atsui ne** (ah-tsoo-ee neh; It's hot, isn't it?). The sentence-ending particle **ne** is for confirmation. It invites your partner's agreement and makes your conversation flow more smoothly. If you feel hot, say it with **ne** because your conversation partner probably feels hot too, unless he or she is a cyborg.

In a polite/neutral or formal context, make sure to add **desu** (deh-soo; to be) to the adjective. Adjectives always sound polite if they end in **desu**. (See Chapter 2 for more about the verb **desu**.) For example, you can say **Atsui desu** (ah-tsoo-ee deh-soo; It's hot.) or **Atsui desu ne** (ah-tsoo-ee deh-soo neh; It's hot, isn't it?) to your teacher, colleague, and boss. You can also work these nouns into your weather-related conversations:

- ✔ **ame** (ah-meh; rain)
- ✔ **arashi** (ah-rah-shee; storm)
- ✔ **hare** (hah-reh; clear sky)
- ✔ **kumori** (koo-moh-ree; cloudy sky)
- ✔ **yuki** (yoo-kee; snow)

Paying attention and saying so

When someone says something to you or gives you some piece of information, you can't just stare at him or her. You must nod. You can also say **Ā, sō desu ka** (ahh, sohh deh-soo kah), which means *Oh, is that so? Oh, really?* or *Oh, I see.* Or you can just say **Ā** (ahh), as you nod, to convey the same message. By doing this, you acknowledge the information given by your conversational partner. If you don't do it, your partner may start to think that you're either upset or rude.

Obviously, you can't just nod when the conversation is taking place over the phone. You have to say **Ā, sō desu ka** or **Ā**; otherwise, your partner on the phone may wonder if you're still there.

Asking people where they're from

When you meet someone, a natural question is *Where are you from?* Pose this question by saying **Dochira kara desu ka** (doh-chee-rah kah-rah deh-soo kah).

Dochira is the polite form of **doko** (doh-koh; where). The particle **kara** means *from*. (See particles on the Cheat Sheet at the front of the book or in Chapter 2).

To answer the question **Dochira kara desu ka,** you just replace **dochira** with a place name and drop the question particle **ka,** as Ken and Susan do in the following Talkin' the Talk dialogue.

Talkin' the Talk

Ken Yamada has just introduced himself to Susan Brennan at their mutual friend's house. Ken asks Susan where she is from.

Ken: **Sūzan-san, Sūzan-san wa dochira kara desu ka.**
sooo-zahn-sahn, sooo-zahn-sahn wah doh-chee-rah kah-rah deh-soo kah.
Susan, where are you from?

Susan: **Watashi wa San Furanshisuko kara desu.**
wah-tah-shee wah sahn-foo-rahn-shee-soo-koh kah-rah deh-soo.
I'm from San Francisco.

Ken: **Ā, sō desu ka.**
ahh, sohh deh-soo kah.
Oh, really?

Susan: **Yamada-san wa.**
yah-mah-dah-sahn wah.
How about you, Mr. Yamada?

Ken: **Boku wa Tōkyō kara desu.**
boh-koo wah tohh-kyohh kah-rah deh-soo.
I am from Tokyo.

Susan: **Ā, sō desu ka.**
ahh, sohh deh-soo kah.
Oh, I see.

In the preceding Talkin' the Talk, Ken uses **boku** (boh-koo) when referring to himself instead of saying **watashi** (wah-tah-shee). Men and boys often substitute **boku** for **watashi,** which isn't very formal. But it isn't very informal either (see Chapter 2).

Talking about your language skills

Whenever you speak **Nihongo** (nee-hohn-goh; the Japanese language) to **Nihonjin** (nee-hohn-jeen; Japanese people), they'll say **Nihongo ga jōzu desu ne** (nee-hohn-goh gah johh-zoo deh-soo neh; Your Japanese is great!). Because Japan is a society where being bilingual is considered very special and admirable, Japanese are always impressed if you speak Japanese. They appreciate your effort to study and use their language. As a reply to a compliment on your Japanese skills, you can say **dōmo** (dohh-moh; thank you), or you can choose one of the following modest phrases. It's up to you.

- ✔ **Īe, heta desu.** (eee-eh, heh-tah deh-soo; No, I'm bad.)
- ✔ **Īe, madamada desu.** (eee-eh, mah-dah-mah-dah deh-soo; No, not yet, not yet.)
- ✔ **Īe, zenzen.** (eee-eh, zehn-zehn; No, not at all.)

If you reply modestly using one of the above expressions, the Japanese person will be further impressed by your ability and praise your Japanese again.

Talkin' the Talk

David has been studying Japanese for two years. He sits at the counter in a Japanese restaurant and chats with a Japanese waitress.

Waitress: **Nihongo ga jōzu desu ne.**
nee-hohn-goh gah johh-zoo deh-soo neh.
Your Japanese is excellent!

David: **Īe, madamada desu.**
eee-eh, mah-dah-mah-dah deh-soo.
No, not yet, not yet.

Waitress: **Hontōni jōzu yo. Nihonjin-mitai.**
hohn-tohh-nee johh-zoo yoh. nee-hohn-jeen-mee-tah-ee.
You're really good! You speak like a Japanese person.

David: **Oseji o iwanaide kudasai yo.**
oh-seh-jee oh ee-wah-nah-ee-deh koo-dah-sah-ee yoh.
Stop flattering me.

To pay someone a compliment in Japanese, you compare the person to some-one or something admirable. You state who or what a person is like using **mitai** (mee-tah-ee; just like), as in the following examples:

- ✔ **Haha wa tenshi mitai desu.** (hah-hah wah tehn-shee mee-tah-ee deh-soo; My mom is like an angel.)

- ✔ **Watashi no bōifurendo wa Tāzan mitai desu.** (wah-tah-shee noh bohh-ee-foo-rehn-doh wah tahh-zahn mee-tah-ee deh-soo; My boyfriend is like Tarzan!)

Saying Goodbye

When you leave a friend, say **jā, mata** (jahh mah-tah; see you again). You can also say **sayōnara** (sah-yohh-nah-rah; goodbye) if you're parting for a longer period of time, but don't use this option if you'll see the person later that same day. Otherwise, you can use either phrase or both of them together. When you interact with your boss or teacher, say **jā, mata** and **shitsurē shimasu** (shee-tsoo-rehh-shee-mah-soo). **Shitsurē shimasu** literally means *I'll be rude.* How do you get *goodbye* out of *I'll be rude?* It's as if you're saying *I'm being rude by leav-ing your presence.*

Don't ever say **sayōnara** to your family members when you leave home for school or work. It sounds like you'll never be back. And don't say **shitsurē shimasu** either. It's too formal. Instead, say **ittemairimasu** (eet-teh-mah-ee-ree-mah-soo; *Literally:* I'll go and come back) — a set phrase for this occasion.

Talkin' the Talk

Jessica runs into her professor in the morning.

Jessica: **Sensē, ohayō gozaimasu.**
sen-sehh, oh-hah-yohh goh-zah-ee-mah-soo.
Professor, good morning!

Professor: **Ā, Jeshika-san. Ohayō.**
ahh, jeh-shee-kah-sahn. oh-hah-yohh.
Oh, Jessica. Good morning.

Jessica: **Ii tenki desu ne.**
eee tehn-kee deh-soo neh.
It's a nice day, isn't it?

Professor:	**Ē, sō desu ne.** ehh, sohh deh-soo neh. Yes, it is.
Jessica:	**Jā, mata kurasu de. Shitsurē shimasu.** jahh, mah-tah koo-rah-soo deh. shee-tsoo-rehh shee-mah-soo. I'll see you again in class. Goodbye.
Professor:	**Hai. Jā, mata.** hah-ee. jahh, mah-tah. Yes. See you later.

Words to Know

Ii tenki desu ne.	eee tehn-kee deh-soo ne	It's a nice day, isn't it?
Jā, mata.	jahh mah-tah	See you again.
Konnichiwa.	kohn-nee-chee-wah	Good afternoon.
Konbanwa.	kohn-bahn-wah	Good evening.
O-genki desu ka.	oh-gehn-kee deh-soo kah	How are you?
Ohayō.	oh-hah-yohh	Good morning.
Sayōnara.	sah-yohh-nah-rah	Goodbye.

Expressing Gratitude and Regret

Phrases of gratitude and apology are the most important and essential phrases in any language. Suppose a stranger holds a door open for you when you're entering a building. What do you say? Suppose you accidentally step on someone's foot. How do you say *I'm sorry*? This section answers these questions.

Showing gratitude

You may know the word **arigatō** (ah-ree-gah-tohh; thanks), but did you know that you can use it only with family, friends, co-workers, subordinates, or strangers who look easy-going and younger than you? When talking to teachers, bosses, strangers who look older than you, and strangers who look as if they're not so easy-going, don't say **arigatō** to mean *thank you,* say one of the following:

> ✔ **Arigatō gozaimasu.** (ah-ree-gah-tohh-goh-zah-ee-mah-soo)
>
> ✔ **Dōmo arigatō gozaimasu.** (dohh-moh ah-ree-gah-tohh goh-zah-ee-mah-soo)
>
> ✔ **Dōmo.** (dohh-moh)

The easiest phrase of gratitude is **dōmo** — an adverb that literally means *indeed* or *very much* but can be understood as *thank you.* It's a short, convenient, and yet polite phrase of gratitude that can be used in any context. If you want to express a greater-than-normal degree of gratitude, you can use one of the longer, more fully-spelled-out phrases, like **Arigatō gozaimasu** or **Dōmo arigatō gozaimasu.**

Apologizing

To apologize for something you've done or for causing someone pain or inconvenience, say **Dōmo sumimasen** (dohh-moh soo-mee-mah-sehn; I'm very sorry.) or just **Sumimasen** in Japanese. **Dōmo** is an interesting adverb. Its function is to make you sound serious, and it can be used with either **Arigatō gozaimasu** (Thank you) or **Sumimasen** (I'm sorry.). If you just say **dōmo** by itself, it's interpreted as *thank you,* but not as *sorry.* So, watch out! In an informal context, **Gomennasai** (goh-mehn-nah-sah-ee; Sorry) is just fine.

To get someone's attention, say **Chotto sumimasen** (choht-toh soo-mee-mah-sehn; Excuse me a little) or just **Sumimasen.**

You may have noticed that **Sumimasen** means both *I'm sorry* and *Excuse me,* but the context and your facial expression will clarify which one you mean. Japanese even say **Sumimasen** in contexts where English speakers would say *Thank you,* as if to say *Excuse me for making you feel that you had to go to all that trouble.*

Talkin' the Talk

Paul bumps into a woman at the airport.

Woman: **Itai.**
ee-tah-ee.
Ouch!

Paul: **Ā, dōmo sumimasen. Daijōbu desu ka.**
                ahh, dohh-moh soo-mee-mah-sehn. dah-ee-johh-boo deh-soo kah.
                Oh, I'm sorry. Are you all right?

Woman: **Ē, daijōbu desu.**
                ehh, dah-ee-johh-boo deh-soo.
                Yes, I'm fine.

Paul picks up the little package on the floor right behind the woman.

Paul: **Kore wa otaku no desu ka.**
                koh-reh wah oh-tah-koo noh deh-soo kah.
                Is this yours?

Woman: **Hai, sō desu. Watashi no desu. Dōmo.**
                hah-ee, sohh deh-soo. wah-tah-shee noh deh-soo. dohh-moh.
                Yes, it is. It's mine. Thank you.

Words to Know

Arigatō	ah-ree-gah-tohh	Thanks
Chotto sumimasen.	choht-toh soo-mee-mah-sehn	Excuse me.
Daijōbu desu ka.	dah-ee-johh-boo deh-soo kah	Are you okay?
Dōmo	dohh-mo	Thank you
Dōmo sumimasen.	dohh-moh soo-mee-mah-sehn	I'm sorry.
Gomennasai	goh-mehn-nah-sah-ee	Sorry

Fun & Games

Match the situation with the appropriate expression. You can find the answers in Appendix C.

1. You accidentally break your neighbor's window.

2. You see your friend in the morning.

3. You meet someone for the very first time at a friend's house.

4. Your teacher gives you a present.

5. You want to ask for directions, and you see a gentleman who looks like he'd be willing to help you.

a. **Chotto sumimasen.**

b. **Dōmo arigatō gozaimasu.**

c. **Dōmo sumimasen.**

d. **Ohayō.**

e. **Hajimemashite.**

Part II
Japanese in Action

The 5th Wave — By Rich Tennant

In this part . . .

This part lets you put Japanese to work in your daily life. Chatting with friends, eating, drinking, shopping, working at the office, relaxing at home, and enjoying your free time — I cover it all so that you can do it in Japanese. **Gambatte** (gahm-baht-teh; Try your best!).

Chapter 4

Getting to Know You: Making Small Talk

· ·

In This Chapter

▶ Addressing where you live

▶ Conversing about your job

▶ Chatting about your family

▶ Understanding the verbs for exist/possess

▶ Exchanging telephone numbers

· ·

Do you remember the first time you met your spouse, significant other, or best friend? The first conversation was probably very trivial, like "Oops, sorry." But that person is still in your life, whether you like it or not, so small talk can be important. Isn't life fun?

Initiating Small Talk

Small talk can be the highlight of a long plane flight — maybe on your trip to Japan. When you get on the plane, the person seated next to you may start a brief conversation. What can you talk about? You can talk about where you're going. That's a nice start. Then you can talk about where you live and what you do for living. If you want, you can also talk about your family. And if you feel like meeting the person again, go ahead and exchange phone numbers.

Breaking the ice with "excuse me"

Usually, small talk starts with **sumimasen** (soo-mee-mah-sehn; excuse me). You use this phrase to break the ice. But afterwards, you usually need to ask a few questions to strike up conversation. Depending on the type of information you're looking for, you need to use different question words like **dare** (dah-reh; who), **nani** (nah-nee; what), and **nan-ji** (nahn-jee; what time). Chapter 2 summarizes the types of questions and provides a list of question words, but you can use these simple ice-breaking questions to make small talk:

✔ **Basutē wa doko desu ka.** (bah-soo-tehh wah doh-koh deh-soo kah; Where is the bus stop?)

✔ **Doko ni ikimasu ka.** (doh-koh nee ee-kee-mah-soo kah; Where are you going?)

✔ **Ima, nan-ji desu ka.** (ee-mah, nahn-jee deh-soo kah; What time is it now?)

✔ **Mein Sutorīto wa doko desu ka.** (meh-een soo-toh-reee-toh wah doh-koh deh-soo kah; Where is Main Street?)

Talkin' the Talk

Richard doesn't have a watch, and he wants to know what time it is. He asks a woman on the street.

Richard: **Sumimasen. Ima nan-ji desu ka.**
soo-mee-mah-sehn. ee-mah nahn-jee deh-soo kah.
Excuse me. What time is it?

Woman: **Yo-ji desu.**
yoh-jee deh-soo.
It is four o'clock.

Richard: **Ā, sō desu ka. Dōmo.**
ahh, sohh deh-soo-ka. dohh-mo.
Oh, really. Thank you.

Woman: **Īe.**
eee-eh.
Don't mention it.

Richard: **Anō.**
ah-nohh.
Ahh.

Woman: **Hai.**
hah-ee
Yes.

Richard:	**Basutē wa doko desu ka.**
	bah-soo-tehh wah doh-koh deh-soo kah.
	Do you know where the bus stop is?

Woman:	**Basutē wa asoko desu.**
	bah-soo-tehh wah ah-soh-koh deh-soo.
	The bus stop is right over there.

Richard:	**Ā, dōmo.**
	ahh, dohh-mo.
	Oh, thank you.

Woman:	**Īe.**
	eee-eh.
	No problem.

Talking about where you're going

When you strike up a conversation while traveling, talking about where you're from is usually followed by questions about where you're going. Asking someone where he or she is going is easy. Just replace the particle **kara** (kah-rah; from), in **Dochira kara desu ka** (doh-chee-rah kah-rah deh-soo kah; Where are you from?), with **made** (mah-deh; up to), and you get **Dochira made desu ka,** which means *Where are you heading to?*

Talkin' the Talk

Frank is waiting for his flight at an airport in Japan. He steps into a cafeteria in the airport and sits down. A Japanese woman sitting next to him starts a conversation.

Woman:	**Dochira made desu ka.**
	doh-chee-rah mah-deh deh-soo kah.
	Where are you going?

Frank:	**Sapporo made desu.**
	sahp-poh-roh mah-deh deh-soo.
	To Sapporo.

Woman:	**Hontōni. Watashi no uchi wa Sapporo desu yo.**
	hon-tohh-nee. wah-tah-shee noh oo-chee wah sahp-poh-roh deh-soo yoh.
	Really? My home is in Sapporo!

Frank: **Hontō desu ka. Gūzen desu ne.**
hon-tohh deh-soo kah. gooo-zehn deh-soo neh.
Is that true? What a coincidence!

Woman: **Ē, shinjirarenai.**
ehh, sheen-jee-rah-reh-nah-ee.
Yes, unbelievable!

Frank: **Ē, hontōni.**
ehh, hohn-tohh-nee.
Yes, really.

Talking about Your Job

What you do for a living tells others a lot about you. Talking about what you do can make your conversation even more exciting and interesting. To ask other people about their **shigoto** (shee-goh-toh; jobs), you say **O-shigoto wa nan desu ka** (oh-shee-goh-toh wah nahn deh-soo kah; What's your job?), or you can use the abbreviated version, **O-shigoto wa** (oh-shee-goh-toh wah; How about your job?). Following are some occupations you or your conversational partner may hold:

- **bengoshi** (behn-goh-shee; lawyer)
- **isha** (ee-shah; medical doctor)
- **jimuin** (jee-moo-een; secretary)
- **kangofu** (kahn-goh-foo; nurse)
- **kenkyūin** (kehn-kyooo-een; researcher)
- **kokku** (kohk-koo; chef)
- **konpyūtā puroguramā** (kohn-pyooo-tahh poo-roh-goo-rah-mahh; computer programmer)
- **kyōju** (kyohh-joo; professor)
- **kyōshi** (kyohh-shee; teacher)
- **uētā** (oo-ehh-tahh; waiter)
- **uētoresu** (oo-ehh-toh-reh-soo; waitress)

These terms express specific roles and functions. If you just want to say that you work for a **kaisha** (kah-ee-shah; company) or that you are an *office worker*, you can use the term **kaishain** (kah-ee-shah-een; company employee). In fact,

Japanese typically identify themselves as **kaishain** without specifying their specific job titles or roles in the **kaisha.**

Talkin' the Talk

Yumi meets Brian at their mutual friend's wedding reception, and she asks him what he does for living.

Yumi:	**Buraian-san, o-shigoto wa nan desu ka.** boo-rah-ee-ahn-sahn, oh-shee-goh-toh wah nahn deh-soo kah. Brian, what's your job?
Brian:	**Kameraman desu.** kah-meh-rah-mahn deh-soo. I'm a photographer.
Yumi:	**Mā, sugoi.** mahh, soo-goh-ee. Wow, great!
Brian:	**Yumi-san no o-shigoto wa.** yoo-mee-sahn noh oh-shee-goh-toh wah. How about your job?
Yumi:	**Konpyūtā puroguramā desu.** kohn-pyooo-tahh poo-roh-goo-rah-mahh deh-soo. Computer programmer.
Brian:	**Ā, sō desu ka. Taihen desu ka.** ahh, sohh deh-soo kah. tah-ee-hehn deh-soo kah. Oh really. Is it hard?
Yumi:	**Zenzen.** zehn-zehn. Not at all.

Talking about Your Family

Do you carry pictures of your **kazoku** (kah-zoh-koo; family), **gārufurendo** (gahh-roo-foo-rehn-doh; girlfriend), **bōifurendo** (bohh-ee-foo-rehn-doh;

boyfriend), or **mago** (mah-goh; grandchildren)? Oh yes, grandparents love to show their grandchildren's pictures to everyone. Just say **kawaĩ** (kah-wah-eee; cute) — no matter what.

Some of the words you can use to say nice things in Japanese are: **kakkoii** (kahk-koh eee; cool), **kawaii** (kah-wah-eee; cute), **kirē** (kee-rehh; pretty), and **subarashii** (soo-bah-rah-sheee; wonderful). These adjectives can be used by themselves in informal contexts, but in other situations, they should be followed by the verb **desu** (deh-soo; to be). So you can say **kawaii** at home, but you should say **kawaii desu** (kah-wah-eee deh-soo) at the office or school. Both phrases mean *Cute!*

Table 4-1 contains terms for family members. For each English term, there are two Japanese terms — a polite term and a plain term. Which version you use depends on the context. In this case, there are three contexts. When you refer to someone else's family, use the polite term. To talk about your own family members to nonfamily, use the plain term. When you talk to any one of your older family members other than your spouse, or when you talk about them in an informal way, you should use a polite term. For example, you can call out for your mother by saying **Okāsan! Doko** (oh-kahh-sahn doh-koh; Mom! Where are you?). Or you can ask your mom, **Okāsan, otōsan wa doko** (oh-kahh-sahn, oh-tohh-sahn wah doh-koh; Mom, where is Dad?). I know most of you don't have a Japanese mother, but you may have a Japanese host mother, or you can adopt a Japanese mother in your neighborhood.

Table 4-1	Family Terms	
English	*Polite Term*	*Plain Term*
family	gokazoku (goh-kah-zoh-koo)	kazoku (kah-zoh-koo)
siblings	gokyōdai (goh-kyohh-dah-ee)	kyōdai (kyohh-dah-ee)
parents	goryōshin (goh-ryohh-sheen)	ryōshin (ryohh-sheen)
father	otōsan (oh-tohh-sahn)	chichi (chee-chee)
mother	okāsan (oh-kahh-sahn)	haha (hah-hah)
older brother	onĩsan (oh-neee-sahn)	ani (ah-nee)
older sister	onēsan (oh-nehh-sahn)	ane (ah-neh)
younger brother	otōto-san (oh-tohh-toh-sahn)	otōto (oh-tohh-toh)
younger sister	imōto-san (ee-mohh-toh-sahn)	imōto (ee-mohh-toh)
husband	goshujin (goh-shoo-jeen)	shujin (shoo-jeen)
wife	okusan (oh-koo-sahn)	kanai (kah-nah-ee)

English	Polite Term	Plain Term
child	kodomo-san (koh-doh-moh-sahn)	kodomo (koh-doh-moh)
son	musuko-san (moo-soo-koh-sahn)	musuko (moo-soo-koh)
daughter	musume-san (moo-soo-meh-sahn)	musume (moo-soo-meh)
grandfather	ojīsan (oh-jeee-sahn)	sofu (soh-foo)
grandmother	obāsan (oh-bahh-sahn)	sobo (soh-boh)
uncle	ojisan (oh-jee-sahn)	oji (oh-jee)
aunt	obasan (oh-bah-sahn)	oba (oh-bah)

Talkin' the Talk

A high school student, Jason, visits the house of his classmate, Satoru, for the first time, and he talks with Satoru's mother, Etsuko. She's asking about Jason's family members.

Etsuko: **Go-kyōdai wa.**
goh-kyohh-dah-ee wah.
Do you have any siblings?

Jason: **Ane ga imasu.**
ah-neh gah ee-mah-soo.
I have an older sister.

Jason shows a picture of his family to Etsuko.

Jason: **Kore ga ane desu.**
koh-reh gah ah-neh deh-soo.
This one is my sister.

Etsuko: **Ā, onēsan desu ka. Kirē desu ne.**
ahh, oh-nehh-sahn deh-soo kah. kee-rehh deh-soo ne.
Oh, this is your older sister. She is pretty, isn't she?

Jason: **Īe, zenzen.**
eee-eh, zehn-zehn.
No, not at all.

Etsuko: **Onēsan no o-shigoto wa.**
oh-nehh-sahn noh oh-shee-goh-toh wah.
What is your sister's job?

Jason:	**Kangofu desu.**
	kahn-goh-foo deh-soo.
	She is a nurse.

Etsuko:	**Ā, ii desu ne.**
	ahh, eee deh-soo neh.
	Oh, that's great.

Japanese always **homeru** (hoh-meh-roo; praise) other's family members' houses, clothes, and even pets, but when they receive a compliment, they deny it no matter what. It's a part of Japanese **kenson** (kehn-sohn; modesty), but these responses sometimes puzzle non-Japanese who are used to saying or hearing *My mom is pretty* and *I love my house*. So, when you speak with Japanese, say nice things about them, but be ready to hear them reject your compliments.

Existing and Possessing: The Verbs Iru and Aru

To tell someone that you have or possess something, use the verbs **iru** (ee-roo) and **aru** (ah-roo). They both mean *to exist*. In Japanese, you use *to exist* to show possession — I know it sounds strange, but it's just one of those things. Another strange thing is that you choose the verb according to whether the item you possess is animate or inanimate:

- ✔ **Iru** shows possession of animate items — things that can move by themselves, such as people and animals.

- ✔ **Aru** is for inanimate items — things that don't move by themselves, such as books, money, plants, and houses.

So, *I have a boyfriend* is **Watashi wa bōifurendo ga iru** (wah-tah-shee wah bohh-ee-foo-rehn-doh gah ee-roo), which literally means *As for me, a boyfriend exists.* Similarly, *Alison has money* is **Arison wa okane ga aru** (ah-ree-sohn wah oh-kah-neh gah ah-roo), which literally means *As for Alison, money exists.* Getting used to the *exist* business?

Don't forget to put the particle **ga** at the end of the object or animal you're claiming exists — the particle tells your listener what the subject of your sentence is.

Now you can talk about what you have or you don't have, using the verbs **iru** and **aru.** When you're speaking in a polite/neutral context, use the polite form of the verbs, **imasu** (ee-mah-soo) and **arimasu** (ah-ree-mah-soo), respectively, which are both conjugated here. **Iru** is an ru-verb, but **aru** is slightly irregular, so pay close attention to the negative form.

Form	Pronunciation
iru	ee-roo
inai	ee-nah-ee
i	ee
ite	ee-teh

Form	Pronunciation
aru	ah-roo
nai	nah-ee
ari	ah-ree
atte	aht-teh

Look at the following examples and think about what you have and what you don't have:

- ✔ **Hima ga arimasen.** (hee-mah gah ah-ree-mah-sehn; I don't have free time.)

- ✔ **Petto ga imasu.** (peht-toh gah ee-mah-soo; I have a pet.)

- ✔ **Watashi wa kyōdai ga imasen.** (wah-tah-shee wah kyohh-dah-ee gah ee-mah-sehn; I don't have siblings.)

- ✔ **Chichi wa o-kane ga arimasu.** (chee-chee wah oh-kah-neh gah ah-ree-mah-soo; My father has money.)

- ✔ **Shukudai ga arimasu.** (shoo-koo-dah-ee gah ah-ree-mah-soo; I have homework.)

Talking about Your Regular Activities

To express that you do something regularly — run, play tennis, go to work, brush your teeth, and so on — use the verb that expresses the activity and the verb **iru** (ee-roo; to exist), in that order. You combine two verbs. Make

sure to conjugate the verb that expresses the action in the te-form.
(See Chapter 2 for the details on the te-form.) The verb **iru** can be left as
it is, or it can be in the polite form, **imasu** (ee-mah-soo). For example, you
can combine the verbs **hashiru** (hah-shee-roo; to run) and **iru** to get **hashitte
iru** (hah-sheet-teh ee-roo) or **hashitte imasu** (hah-sheet-teh ee-mah-soo).
Both phrases mean that someone runs regularly. It's sort of like saying,
"I run and exist every day." Just be careful: **hashitte iru** also has an on-going
action interpretation that translates to *I'm in the middle of running*. Which
interpretation the phrase takes on, regular activity or on-going action,
depends on the context. If you say **mainichi** (mah-ee-nee-chee; every day)
before saying **hashitte imasu,** it obviously means a regular activity, like
I run every day. If you say **ima** (ee-mah; now) instead, the sentence means
I'm in the middle of running now. The following sentences all express regular
actions:

- ✔ **Ken wa mainichi piza o tabete imasu.** (kehn wah mah-ee-nee-chee
  pee-zah oh tah-beh-teh ee-mah-soo; Ken eats pizza every day.)

- ✔ **Otōto wa kyonen kara daigaku ni itte imasu.** (oh-tohh-toh wah kyoh-
  nehn kah-rah dah-ee-gah-koo nee eet-teh ee-mah-soo; My younger brother
  has been going to the college since last year.)

- ✔ **Otōsan wa itsumo nete iru yo.** (oh-tohh-sahn wah ee-tsoo-moh neh-teh
  ee-roo yoh; My dad is always sleeping!)

- ✔ **Shujin wa maishū tenisu o shite imasu.** (shoo-jeen wah mah-ee-shooo
  teh-nee-soo oh shee-teh ee-mah-soo; My husband plays tennis every
  week.)

Words to Know

kirē	kee-rehh	pretty
okāsan	oh-kahh-sahn	mother
onīsan	oh-neee-sahn	older brother
onēsan	oh-nehh-sahn	older sister
otōsan	oh-tohh-sahn	father
suteki	soo-teh-kee	gorgeous

Giving Out Your Contact Information

After having a good time chatting with a stranger on a train or airplane, or at a party or conference, you may want to contact him or her again. These days, the easiest way to keep in touch with someone is to get his or her **denshi mēru adoresu** (dehn-shee mehh-roo ah-doh-reh-soo; e-mail address), but if you want to take the orthodox approach, you can ask for his or her **denwa bangō** (dehn-wah bahn-gohh; phone number). Which one do you like to get — **denshi mēru adoresu** or **denwa bangō?** Do you like to know someone's **jūsho** (jooo-shoh; address) and **fakkusu bangō** (fahk-koo-soo bahn-gohh; fax number) too? If you sense that the person may become an important part of your professional or social life, make sure to collect all the information accurately. It's also a good idea to exchange **mēshi** (mehh-shee; business cards). These phrases are useful when exchanging contact information:

- ✔ **Denshi mēru de renraku shimasu.** (dehn-shee mehh-roo deh rehn-rah-koo shee-mah-soo; I'll contact you via e-mail.)

- ✔ **Denwa bangō wa nan desu ka.** (dehn-wah bahn-gohh wah nahn deh-soo kah; What's your telephone number?)

- ✔ **Denwa o shite kudasai.** (dehn-wah oh shee-teh koo-dah-sah-ee; Please call me.)

- ✔ **Jūsho o oshiete kudasai.** (jooo-shoh oh oh-shee-eh-teh koo-dah-sah-ee; Please let me know your address.)

- ✔ **Kore wa watashi no mēshi desu.** (koh-reh wah wah-tah-shee noh mehh-shee deh-soo; This is my business card.)

- ✔ **Yokattara, renraku kudasai.** (yoh-kaht-tah-rah, rehn-rah-koo koo-dah-sah-ee; Get in touch, if you like.)

Conjugate the verb **sumu** (soo-moo; to live/reside). It's a u-verb. If you want to say that you live somewhere, use the te-form of **sumu** and add the verb **iru** (ee-roo; to exist) right after it. For example, **Tōkyō ni sunde iru** (tohh-kyohh nee soon-deh ee-roo) and its polite version, **Tōkyō ni sunde imasu** (tohh-kyohh nee soon-deh ee-mah-soo), both mean *I live in Tokyo.*

Form	Pronunciation
sumu	soo-moo
sumanai	soo-mah-nah-ee
sumi	soo-mee
sunde	soon-deh

Talkin' the Talk

Mr. Suzuki meets Mr. White at a conference in Seattle, and he thinks that Mr. White may make a great partner on his research project.

Mr. Suzuki:	**Kore wa watashi no mēshi desu. Dōzo.** koh-reh wah wah-tah-shee noh mehh-shee deh-soo. dohh-zoh. This is my business card. Here you are.
Mr. White:	**Ā, dōmo.** ahh, dohh-moh. Oh, thank you.
Mr. Suzuki:	**Kore ga denwa-bangō desu.** koh-reh gah den-wah-bahn-gohh deh-soo. This is my telephone number.
Mr. White:	**Dōmo.** dohh-moh. Thank you.
Mr. Suzuki:	**Yokattara, renraku kudasai.** yoh-kaht-tah-rah, rehn-rah-koo koo-dah-sah-ee. Get in touch, if you like.
Mr. White:	**Hai, kanarazu shimasu.** hah-ee, kah-nah-rah-zoo shee-mah-soo. Yes, I certainly will.

Fun & Games

• •

Match these family members with the words that identify them. Check out
Appendix C for the answers.

1. 2. 3. 4.

a. okāsan   b. onēsan   c. obāsan   d. otōsan

• •

Chapter 5

Eating and Drinking: Itadakimasu!

*F*or some reason, **tabemono** (tah-beh-moh-noh; food) always seems to make people happy. Friendships grow faster when people chat in front of delicious **tabemono.** Trying authentic Japanese cuisine is something that you can do in any large city today. The guiding principles of **nihon ryōri** (nee-hohn ryohh-ree; Japanese cuisine) are delicate tastes, artistic presentations, fresh ingredients, an appreciation of nature, and the great hospitality of the person who cooks. This chapter gives you useful phrases and tips to enjoy your meals in Japan and your Japanese meals anywhere else.

Making the Most of Meals

How many times a day do you have a **shokuji** (shoh-koo-jee; meal)? If you're lucky, you can **taberu** (tah-beh-roo; eat) three times a day. If you're too busy, you may eat just once or twice. If you're obsessed with food, you may eat all the time.

I'm sorry to have to tell you this, but Japanese doesn't have one convenient adjective like *hungry.* To express *hungry,* you have to say **onaka ga suita** (oh-nah-kah gah soo-ee-tah), or with the polite suffix, **onaka ga sukimashita** (oh-nah-kah gah soo-kee-mah-shee-tah). **Onaka** means belly or stomach, and **suita** and **sukimashita** mean *became empty.* You're saying that your *stomach became empty.* It's a bit inconvenient, but say **onaka ga suita** to your mom when you feel hungry. If you're lucky, she'll feed you. The following are typical **shokuji** and **oyatsu** (oh-yah-tsoo; snacks):

✔ **asagohan** *or* **chōshoku** (ah-sah-goh-hahn *or* chohh-shoh-koo; breakfast)

✔ **hirugohan** *or* **chūshoku** (hee-roo-goh-hahn *or* chooo-shoh-koo; lunch)

✔ **bangohan** *or* **yūshoku** (bahn-goh-hahn *or* yooo-shoh-koo; supper)

✔ **yashoku** (yah-shoh-koo; midnight snack)

If you noticed **shoku** in several of the words related to eating, it's no accident. This word stem often (although not always) means *eat*.

My favorite **yashoku** is **rāmen** (rahh-mehn) noodles. If you think you know what **rāmen** are from the instant ramen available in your grocery store, you have only a slight hint of the real thing. Japanese **rāmenya** (rahh-mehn-yah; ramen shops) pride themselves on their secret ramen recipes, as immortalized in the movie *Tampopo*. Oh, I love **rāmen** noodles for my **yashoku.**

Check out Chapter 2 to see how to conjugate the verb **taberu** (tah-beh-roo; to eat), but read on to see how to conjugate the verb **nomu** (noh-moo; to drink). It's a u-verb.

Form	Pronunciation
nomu	noh-moo
nomanai	noh-mah-nah-ee
nomi	noh-mee
nonde	nohn-deh

Eating breakfast in two cultures

Even for the gastronomically adventurous, breakfast is not a meal that many people want to experiment with. Too bad. A Japanese **asagohan** (ah-sah-goh-hahn; breakfast) can be downright exquisite, if you have the eyes (and palate) to see it that way.

Enjoying breakfast Japanese style

Before stepping into a Japanese-style **shokudō** (shoh-koo-dohh; dining room) for breakfast, check out what they serve.

✔ **gohan** (goh-hahn; cooked rice)

✔ **hōrensō no ohitashi** (hohh-rehn-sohh noh oh-hee-tah-shee; boiled spinach seasoned with soy sauce)

✔ **misoshiru** (mee-soh-shee-roo; soybean-paste soup)

✔ **nama tamago** (nah-mah tah-mah-goh; raw eggs)

✔ **nori** (noh-ree; seaweed)

✔ **onsen tamago** (ohn-sehn tah-mah-goh; hot-spring boiled egg/ soft-boiled egg)

- ✔ **tsukemono** (tsoo-keh-moh-noh; pickled vegetables)
- ✔ **yakizakana** (yah-kee-zah-kah-nah; grilled/broiled fish)

Another common breakfast dish is **nattō** (naht-tohh; fermented soybeans). Don't worry, these fermented soybeans aren't alcoholic. A rough analogy: **Nattō** is fermented as yogurt is cultured. If sticky, strong-smelling soybeans are a little more than you can bear, well, it's admittedly an acquired taste. More than a few Japanese themselves never acquire it, even though soybeans are about the most nutritionally perfect food on the planet. The high-quality protein and digestive enzymes help prevent blood clots in the brain. Maybe some Japanese mustard can help you acquire the taste.

Eggs are a breakfast food that Japan shares with many countries, but the Japanese preparation is a little different. If you're afraid to try the traditional Japanese raw egg, you can choose the **onsen tamago,** an interesting soft-boiled egg. **Onsen tamago** is made by simmering an egg in a hot spring for about 40 minutes. The water temperature must be between 149° F (65° C) and 154° F (68° C), which is much lower than the boiling point for water — 212° F (100° C). The result of this process is that the egg yolk is settled, but the texture of the egg white is still soft and pudding-like.

Do you want to experiment by cooking an egg in your bathtub instead of a hot spring? If you succeed, it will be the *bathtub egg!* I hope it's not soapy. Actually, you don't need a hot spring or a bathtub. As long as you consistently keep the water between the specified temperatures for 40 minutes, you can make **onsen tamago** in a pot on your kitchen stove.

Digging into a Western-style breakfast

Breakfast is the first meal of the day. How you eat and what you eat for breakfast can affect the rest of your day. I can sympathize with people who eat the same thing for breakfast everyday. In 20 years, I haven't missed out on **kōhī** (kohh-heee; coffee) with my breakfast. And I haven't skipped my morning **bēguru** (behh-goo-roo; bagel) and **kurīmu chīzu** (koo-reee-moo cheee-zoo; cream cheese) in the last ten years. You may think I'm boring, but my breakfast has to be just right for me. What are your favorite breakfast foods? Or let me put this way: What are you addicted to?

- ✔ **batā** (bah-tahh; butter)
- ✔ **bēkon** (behh-kohn; bacon)
- ✔ **hamu** (hah-moo; ham)
- ✔ **jamu** (jah-moo; jam)
- ✔ **kurowassan** (koo-roh-wahs-sahn; croissant)
- ✔ **kōcha** (kohh-chah; black tea)
- ✔ **medamayaki** (meh-dah-mah-yah-kee; fried egg)

✔ **miruku** (mee-roo-koo; milk)

✔ **orenji jūsu** (oh-rehn-jee jooo-soo; orange juice)

✔ **sukuranburu eggu** (soo-koo-rahn-boo-roo ehg-goo; scrambled eggs)

✔ **sōsēji** (sohh-sehh-jee; sausage)

✔ **tōsuto** (tohh-soo-toh; toast)

Words to Know

chōshoku	chohh-shoh-koo	breakfast
kōhī	kohh-heee	coffee
shokudō	shoh-koo-dohh	dining room/restaurant
tamago	tah-mah-goh	eggs

Munching your lunch

In Japan, noodles are always popular lunchtime meals. The thick, white noodles that you may have seen in soups are **udon** (oo-dohn), and buckwheat noodles are **soba** (soh-bah). And, don't forget **rāmen** (rahh-mehn) noodles, which Japanese adopted from China. Rice dishes in big bowls are also very popular for lunch. These meals are called **donburi** (dohn-boo-ree; big bowl). They're a bowl of rice with different toppings. If you have cooked chicken and egg over the rice, it's called **oyako donburi** (oh-yah-koh dohn-boo-ree). **Oyako** literally means *parent-child;* it describes the chicken and the egg.

What do you usually eat for lunch?

✔ **chīzu** (cheee-zoo; cheese)

✔ **hanbāgā** (hahn-bahh-gahh; hamburger)

✔ **piza** (pee-zah; pizza)

✔ **sandoicchi** (sahn-doh-eet-chee; sandwich)

✔ **sarada** (sah-rah-dah; salad)

✔ **supagettī** (soo-pah-geht-teee; spaghetti)

✔ **sūpu** (sooo-poo; soup)

I usually use these tasty items to give my **sandoicchi** a little kick:

- ✔ **kechappu** (keh-chahp-poo; ketchup)
- ✔ **masutādo** (mah-soo-tahh-doh; mustard)
- ✔ **mayonēzu** (mah-yoh-nehh-zoo; mayonnaise)
- ✔ **pikurusu** (pee-koo-roo-soo; pickle)

Dining Out

You can find American-style fast food restaurants all over the world — even in Japan. In this section, I not only give you fast-food words, but I also give you the words you need to have a more elegant meal in a restaurant.

Ordering fast food

Whether you're ordering **piza** (pee-zah; pizza) with friends or grabbing a **sandoicchi** (sahn-doh-eet-chee; sandwich) for lunch, you probably spend a fair amount of money enriching fast-food chains. This section tells you how to **chūmon suru** (chooo-mohn soo-roo; order) a **hanbāgā** (hahn-bahh-gahh; hamburger) and **furaido poteto** (foo-rah-ee-doh poh-teh-toh; fries) in Japan — or at least in Japanese. Check out some other major fast-food dishes:

- ✔ **chikin bāgā** (chee-keen bahh-gahh; chicken patty)
- ✔ **chīzu bāgā** (cheee-zoo bahh-gahh; cheeseburger)
- ✔ **furaido chikin** (foo-rah-ee-doh chee-keen; fried chicken)
- ✔ **hotto doggu** (hoht-toh dohg-goo; hot dog)
- ✔ **miruku shēku** (mee-roo-koo shehh-koo; milkshakes)

Now that you have a handle on the menu, practice conjugating the verb **chūmon suru** (chooo-mohn soo-roo; to order). It's actually a combination of the noun **chūmon** (order) and the verb **suru** (to do), so just conjugate the **suru** part. Yes, it's an irregular verb.

Form	*Pronunciation*
chūmon suru	chooo-mohn soo-roo
chūmon shinai	chooo-mohn shee-nah-ee
chūmon shi	chooo-mohn shee
chūmon shite	chooo-mohn shee-teh

You may have to answer a few questions when you order at a fast-food joint. **Omochi kaeri desu ka** (oh-moh-chee kah-eh-ree deh-soo kah) means *Will you bring it home?* or *To go?* **Kochira de omeshiagari desu ka** (koh-chee-rah deh oh-meh-shee-ah-gah-ree deh-soo kah) means *Will you eat here?* or *For here?* If you hear one of these questions, just answer with **hai** (hah-ee; yes) or **īe** (eee-eh; no).

Liking with adjectives

When you talk about your preferences in English, you use verbs such as *to like, to love,* and *to hate*. It may seem strange to you, but in Japanese, you use adjectives to express your likes and dislikes. For example, **suki** (soo-kee; to like) is an adjective. If you want to say that you like pizza, you say **Watashi wa piza ga suki desu** (wah-tah-shee wah pee-zah gah soo-kee deh-soo; I like pizza.) The translation becomes misleading here, so watch out. The item you like, *pizza* in this case, is marked by the subject-marking particle **ga**. You can't use the direct object-marking particle **o** because you use **o** only with a verb. So don't be misled by English translations.

Express what you like with an adjective and the particle **ga** in Japanese. You can use either **ga suki** or its polite counterpart, **ga suki desu**. If you know **suki**, you also have to know **kirai** (kee-rah-ee; to hate). And, if you like or hate something *a lot,* add **dai-** (dah-ee), which means *big,* before **suki** or **kirai**, as in **daisuki** (dah-ee-soo-kee; to like it a lot), and **daikirai** (dah-ee-kee-rah-ee; to hate it a lot). Now you have four adjectives that you can use to express your likes and dislikes! Get used to these words by looking at the following examples:

- ✔ **Benkyō ga kirai desu.** (behn-kyohh gah kee-rah-ee deh-soo; I hate studying.)
- ✔ **Sensē ga suki desu.** (sehn-sehh gah soo-kee deh-soo; I like the teacher.)
- ✔ **Watashi wa sakana ga daisuki desu.** (wah-tah-shee wah sah-kah-nah gah dah-ee-soo-kee deh-soo; I love fish a lot!)
- ✔ **Otōto wa yasai ga daikirai desu.** (oh-tohh-toh wah yah-sah-ee gah dah-ee-kee-rah-ee deh-soo; My little brother hates vegetables a lot.)

Talkin' the Talk

Tanya and Yukiko are about to order a pizza for a party. They're wondering what toppings they should ask for.

Tanya: **Toppingu wa.**
           tohp-peen-goo wah.
           How about toppings?

Yukiko: **Watashi wa masshurūmu ga suki. Tānya wa.**
wah-tah-shee wah mahs-shoo-rooo-moo gah soo-kee.
tahh-nyah wah.
I like mushrooms. How about you Tanya?

Tanya: **Watashi wa peparoni ga suki. Demo, masshurūmu
wa kirai.**
wah-tah-shee wah peh-par-roh-nee gah soo-kee.
deh-moh, mahs-shoo-rooo-moo wah kee-rah-ee.
I like pepperoni, but I don't like mushrooms.

Yukiko: **Ā, sō. Jā, onion wa.**
ahh, sohh. jahh, oh-nee-ohn wah.
All right. Then how about onions?

Tanya: **Onion wa daisuki.**
oh-nee-ohn wah dah-ee-soo-kee.
I love onions.

Yukiko starts placing an order for their pizza.

Yukiko: **Sumimasen. Rāji piza onegaishimasu.**
soo-mee-mah-sehn. rahh-jee pee-zah oh-neh-gah-ee-
shee-mah-soo.
Excuse me. A large pizza please.

Server: **Toppingu wa.**
tohp-peen-goo wah.
What toppings?

Yukiko: **Peparoni to masshurūmu.**
peh-pah-roh-nee toh mahs-shoo-rooo-moo.
Pepperoni and mushrooms.

Tanya: **Chigau, chigau. Peparoni to onion.**
chee-gah-oo, chee-gah-oo. peh-pah-roh-nee toh
oh-nee-ohn.
No, no. Pepperoni and onions.

Yukiko: **Ā, gomennasai. Peparoni to onion.**
ahh, goh-mehn-nah-sah-ee. peh-pah-roh-nee toh oh-
nee-ohn.
Oh, I'm sorry. Pepperoni and onions please.

In the preceding Talkin' the Talk, **onion** (onions) and **masshurūmu** (mushrooms) are marked by the particle **wa**, not by the particle **ga**. Tanya says
Onion wa daisuki (I love onions), for example. Why? This is because **onion**

happens to be the topic of the sentence, as well as the item being liked. Yes, **wa** is the topic-marking particle. (To find out more about particles, see Chapter 2.) So, a more literal translation of this sentence is *As for onions, I love them*. Why doesn't Tanya say **Onion ga wa daisuki** ? It's strange, but the particles **ga** and **wa** can't occur next to each other: **ga** must be deleted if **wa** is next to it. That's why there's no **ga** after **onion.**

Making time for dinner

Japanese are gourmets. They often line up in front of the most popular restaurants, and they don't mind waiting for an hour or more. But if you don't want to wait in line, make a **yoyaku** (yoh-yah-koo; reservation) over the phone.

Japanese say *to make a reservation* by saying *to do a reservation,* which is **yoyaku o suru** (yoh-yah-koo oh soo-roo). Remember that **suru** (soo-roo; to do) is an irregular verb. Conjugate **yoyaku o suru.** Because **yoyaku** is a noun, all you have to worry about is the **suru** part.

Form	*Pronunciation*
yoyaku o suru	yoh-yah-koo oh soo-roo
yoyaku o shinai	yoh-yah-koo oh shee-nah-ee
yoyaku o shi	yoh-yah-koo oh shee
yoyaku o shite	yoh-yah-koo oh shee-teh

First, let the restaurant's host or hostess know when you want to arrive. The basics of how to tell time in Japanese, including the concepts of *a.m., p.m.,* and *o'clock,* are all explained in Chapter 7. In Table 5-1, I just provide the time ranges that you will most likely need to make a reservation for dinner.

Table 5-1	A Time Table	
Time	*Japanese*	*Pronunciation*
6:00	roku-ji	roh-koo-jee
6:15	roku-ji jūgo-fun	roh-koo-jee jooo-goh-foon
6:30	roku-ji han	roh-koo-jee hahn
6:45	roku-ji yonjūgo-fun	roh-koo-jee yohn-jooo-goh-foon
7:00	shichi-ji	shee-chee-jee
8:00	hachi-ji	hah-chee-jee
9:00	ku-ji	koo-jee

When you talk about an approximate time, add **goro** (goh-roh) after the time phrase. **Roku-ji goro** (roh-koo-jee goh-roh) means *about 6:00,* and **roku-ji han goro** (roh-koo-jee hahn goh-roh) means *about 6:30.*

After you establish a reservation time, let the restaurant know how many people are in your party. Japanese even use a counter to count people. Counters are short suffixes that directly follow numbers. Which counter you use depends on the item you're counting. So, you can't just say **go** (goh; five) when you have five people in your party. You have to say **go-nin** (goh-neen). Right, **-nin** (neen) is the counter for people. But watch out for the irregular **hitori** (hee-toh-ree; one) and **futari** (foo-tah-ree; two). (To find out more about counters, see Chapter 2.) Check out Table 5-2 to start counting people.

Table 5-2	Expressing the Number of People	
Number of People	*Japanese*	*Pronunciation*
1	hitori	hee-toh-ree
2	futari	foo-tah-ree
3	san-nin	sahn-neen
4	yo-nin	yoh-neen
5	go-nin	goh-neen
6	roku-nin	roh-koo-neen
7	nana-nin	nah-nah-neen
8	hachi-nin	hah-chee-neen
9	kyū-nin	kyooo-neen
10	jū-nin	jooo-neen

Talkin' the Talk

Makoto Tanaka is trying to make a reservation at Fuguichi, a blowfish restaurant, over the phone.

Hostess: **Maido arigatō gozaimasu. Fuguichi de gozaimasu.**
mah-ee-doh ah-ree-gah-tohh goh-zah-ee-mah-soo.
foo-goo-ee-chee deh goh-zah-ee-mah-soo.
Thank you for your patronage. This is Fuguichi. How can I help you?

Makoto:	**Anō, konban, yoyaku o shitai-n-desu ga.**
	ah-nohh, kohn-bahn, yoh-yah-koo oh shee-tah-een-deh-soo gah.
	I would like to make a reservation for tonight.

Hostess:	**Hai, arigatō gozaimasu. Nan-ji goro.**
	hah-ee, ah-ree-gah-tohh goh-zah-ee-mah-soo. nahn-jee goh-roh.
	Yes, thank you. About what time?

Makoto:	**Shichi-ji desu.**
	shee-chee-jee deh-soo.
	Seven o'clock, please.

Hostess:	**Hai. Nan-nin-sama.**
	hah-ee. nahn-neen-sah-mah.
	Certainly. How many people?

Makoto:	**Go-nin desu.**
	goh-neen deh-soo.
	Five people.

Hostess:	**Hai, kashikomarimashita. O-namae wa.**
	hah-ee, kah-shee-koh-mah-ree-mah-shee-tah. oh-nah-mah-eh wa.
	Certainly. Your name?

Makoto:	**Fuji Bōeki no Tanaka desu.**
	foo-jee bohh-eh-kee noh tah-nah-kah deh-soo.
	I'm Tanaka from Fuji Trade Company.

Hostess:	**Fuji Bōeki no Tanaka-sama de gozaimasu ne.**
	foo-jee bohh-eh-kee noh tah-nah-kah-sah-mah deh goh-zah-ee-mah-soo neh.
	Mr. Tanaka from Fuji Trade Company. Is that correct?

Makoto:	**Hai.**
	hah-ee.
	Yes.

Hostess:	**Dewa, shichi-ji ni.**
	deh-wah, shee-chee-jee nee.
	Then, at seven o'clock, we'll be expecting you.

Makoto:	**Hai. Yoroshiku.**
	hah-ee. yoh-roh-shee-koo.
	Yes. Thank you.

Eating blowfish carefully

For a long time, Japanese have admired **fugu** (foo-goo; blowfish) as *the* most delicious fish. There's only one problem: It's poisonous; or rather, the ovaries and liver are especially poisonous. If the person preparing it accidentally slices into either of those two places, you could die from it. There have been some actual deaths caused by improper preparation of **fugu** by unlicensed chefs in Japan.

Only trained and licensed chefs are legally permitted to cut, clean, and serve **fugu**. They remove the dangerous parts and wash the remaining portion of the fish very carefully, using a tremendous amount of water.

Fugu is one of the most expensive delicacies in Japan and costs about $200 for a single fish. Japanese are truly gourmets. They seek out exquisite tastes, while risking their lives and paying a fortune in the process.

In Japanese, you often form a statement using **-n-desu** (n-deh-soo) in conversation, as Makoto does in the previous Talkin' the Talk. The effect of **-n-desu** is to encourage your partner to respond to your statements. Saying **Yoyaku o shitai-n-desu** (yoh-yah-koo oh shee-tah-een-deh-soo: I'd like to make a reservation.) sounds much more inviting and friendly than saying **Yoyaku o shitai desu.** It shows your willingness to listen to your partner's comments and opinions. Therefore, use **-n-desu** in informal conversation, but not in written form or public speech. When a verb is followed by **-n-desu,** it must be in the informal/plain form. Ending your statement with the particle **ga** (gah; but), as in **Yoyaku oshitai-n-desu ga,** makes it very clear that you're waiting for the other person to reply.

Japanese say **yoroshiku** (yoh-roh-shee-koo) after asking a favor of someone or after making a request, such as a reservation at a restaurant as seen in the previous Talkin' the Talk section. In this context, it means *Please take good care of it for me.* You don't say anything like that in English, so just think of it as *thank you.* **Yoroshiku** is one of those phrases that you have to use your intuition and cultural understanding, rather than translations, to understand. But if you can use it appropriately, you'll really sound like a native Japanese speaker!

Ordering in a restaurant

How do you order in a restaurant? Do you carefully go over the **menyū** (meh-nyooo; menu), or do you look to see what other people are eating? Do you ask the **uētā** (oo-ehh-tahh; waiter) or **uētoresu** (oo-ehh-toh-reh-soo; waitress) for some direction as to what's good? I like the second and the third options. Do you routinely order a **zensai** (zehn-sah-ee; appetizer), an **o-nomimono** (oh-noh-mee-moh-noh; beverage), and a **dezāto** (deh-zahh-toh; dessert) in addition to your entrée? If you order all of them, I'm sure that you're usually satisfied, but I'm also sure that your bill is large. In this section, I provide you with phrases and concepts that you need to place an order in a restaurant.

Whether you go to a four-star restaurant or the corner pub, your waiter or waitress will ask you questions like:

- ✔ **Gochūmon wa.** (goh-chooo-mohn wah; Your order?)
- ✔ **Nani ni nasaimasu ka.** (nah-nee nee nah-sah-ee-mah-soo kah; What will you have?)
- ✔ **O-nomimono wa.** (oh-noh-mee-moh-noh wah; Anything to drink?)

And here are a few phrases that you can use while talking to the wait staff:

- ✔ **Rāmen o mittsu onegaishimasu.** (rahh-mehn oh meet-tsoo oh-neh-gah-ee-shee-mah-soo; Can we have ramen noodles for three please?)
- ✔ **Sushi to sashimi to misoshiru o onegaishimasu.** (soo-shee toh sah-shee-mee toh mee-soh-shee-roo oh oh-neh-gah-ee-shee-mah-soo; Can I have sushi, sashimi, and miso soup please?)
- ✔ **Wain wa arimasu ka.** (wah-een wah ah-ree-mah-soo kah; Do you have wine?)
- ✔ **Watashi wa sutēki o kudasai.** (wah-tah-shee wah soo-tehh-kee oh koo-dah-sah-ee; Can I have steak please?)
- ✔ **Watashi wa razānya o onegaishimasu.** (wah-tah-shee wah rah-zahh-nyah oh oh-neh-gah-ee-shee-mah-soo; Can I have lasagna please?)

To list several dishes, use **to** (toh) between each dish to link them. (Think of **to** as a verbal comma or the word *and*.) To specify the quantity of each item that you want to order, use the counter that applies to food items, **-tsu** — **hito-tsu** (hee-toh-tsoo; one), **futa-tsu** (foo-tah-tsoo; two), **mit-tsu** (meet-tsoo; three), and so forth. (See Chapter 2 for a more in-depth explanation of counters.)

If you really don't know what to order, ask **Osusumehin wa?** (oh-soo-soo-meh-hin wah; What do you recommend?).

Are you wondering what to do if you can't read the Japanese menu at a restaurant? Don't worry. Most restaurants in Japan have colored pictures on the menus or life-sized wax models of the food in their windows. The easiest way to order food is to follow this simple formula: Say **watashi wa** (wah-tah-shee wah; as for me), point to the picture of the dish on the menu, say **kore o** (koh-reh oh; this one), and say **onegaishimasu** (oh-neh-gah-ee-shee-mah-soo; I'd like to ask you) or **kudasai** (koo-dah-sah-ee; please give me) at the end.

Do you see any of your favorites on this dinner menu?

- ✔ **bifuteki** (bee-foo-teh-kee; beef steak)
- ✔ **bīfu shichū** (beee-foo shee-chooo; beef stew)

- **masshu poteto** (mas-shoo poh-teh-toh; mashed potato)
- **mīto rōfu** (meee-toh rohh-foo; meatloaf)
- **pan** (pahn; bread)
- **sake** (sah-keh; salmon)
- **sarada** (sah-rah-dah; salad)
- **sūpu** (sooo-poo; soup)

Which of the following Japanese dishes would you like to try?

- **gyūdon** (gyooo-dohn; a bowl of rice topped with cooked beef and vegetables)
- **oyako donburi** (oh-yah-koh dohn-boo-ree; a bowl of rice topped with cooked chicken and eggs)
- **tempura** (tehm-poo-rah; deep-fried vegetables or seafood)
- **unagi** (oo-nah-gee; eel)

Talkin' the Talk

 Matt and Yumiko are going to place an order at a restaurant inside the Tokyo station.

Matt:	**Sumimasen. Menyū o onegaishimasu.** soo-mee-mah-sehn. meh-nyooo oh oh-neh-gah-ee-shee-mah-soo. Excuse me. Menu, please.
Server:	**Dōzo.** dohh-zoh. Here you are.
Matt:	**Dōmo.** dohh-moh. Thank you.
Server:	**Nani ni nasaimasu ka.** nah-nee nee nah-sah-ee-mah-soo kah. What would you like to have?
Matt:	**Boku wa tempura to sashimi.** boh-koo wah tehm-poo-rah toh sah-shee-mee. I'll have tempura and sashimi.
Server:	**Hai, tempura to sashimi.** hah-ee, tehm-poo-rah toh sah-shee-mee. Yes, tempura and sashimi.

Yumiko:	**Watashi wa supagettī o onegaishimasu.** wah-tah-shee wah soo-pah-geht-teee oh oh-neh-gah-ee-shee-mah-soo. I'll have spaghetti.
Server:	**Sumimasen. Supagettī wa gozaimasen.** soo-mee-mah-sehn. soo-pah-geht-teee wah goh-zah-ee-mah-sehn. I'm sorry. We don't have spaghetti.
Yumiko:	**Jā, chikin tēshoku o onegaishimasu.** jahh, chee-keen tehh-shoh-koo oh oh-neh-gah-ee- shee-mah-soo. In that case, I'll have the chicken dinner.
Server:	**Hai, kashikomarimashita.** hah-ee, kah-shee-koh-mah-ree-mah-shee-tah. Yes, certainly.

If you want to have a complete meal that comes with rice, soup, and a salad, order a **tēshoku** (tehh-shoh-koo; set meal), like **sashimi tēshoku** and **tempura tēshoku.**

Setting your table

If there's anything missing on your table, ask the waiter or waitress for it. If you're eating at home, get it yourself, or if you have children, ask them to do it for you. Does Table 5-3 have what you need for your table?

Table 5-3	Dining Utensils	
Japanese	*Pronunciation*	*Translation*
fōku	fohh-koo	fork
gurasu	goo-rah-soo	glass
kappu	kahp-poo	cup
naifu	nah-ee-foo	knife
napukin	nah-poo-keen	napkin
o-sara	oh-sah-rah	plate
supūn	soo-pooon	spoon

If you're having Japanese food, you may need some of these:

- **hashi** (hah-shee; chopsticks)
- **o-chawan** (oh-chah-wahn; rice bowl)
- **o-wan** (oh-wahn; Japanese lacquered soup bowl)

Chatting with the waiter or waitress

Ask questions of your **uētā** (oo-ehh-tahh; waiter) or **uētoresu** (oo-ehh-toh-reh-soo; waitress). Or, just chat with them about the food they served.

- **Chotto henna aji desu.** (choh-toh hehn-nah ah-jee-deh-soo; It tastes sort of strange.)
- **Kore wa nan desu ka.** (koh-reh wah nahn deh-soo kah; What is this?)
- **Kore wa yakete imasu ka.** (koh-reh wah yah-keh-teh ee-mah-soo kah; Is it well done?)
- **Oishii desu ne.** (oh-ee-sheee deh-soo neh; Isn't this delicious?)
- **Omizu o kudasai.** (oh-mee-zoo oh koo-dah-sah-ee; Water, please.)
- **Toire wa doko desu ka.** (toh-ee-ree wah doh-koh deh-soo kah; Where is the bathroom?)
- **Totemo oishikatta desu.** (toh-teh-moh oh-ee-shee-kaht-tah deh-soo; That was very delicious!)
- **Watashi wa ebi ga taberaremasen.** (wah-tah-shee wah eh-bee gah tah-beh-rah-reh-mah-sehn; I can't eat shrimp.)

Paying for your meal

When and how you pay for your meal can vary by restaurant. You may have to pay up front, or you may be able to pay after eating. You may be able to use your credit card, but some places only accept cash. It's best to clarify these details before eating. When you eat with your friends, do you **warikan ni suru** (wah-ree-kahn nee soo-roo; go Dutch), or does one person **ogoru** (oh-goh-roo; treat) everyone? How about when you eat with your boss? He or she probably pays, but it never hurts to say **O-kanjō o onegaishimasu** (oh-kahn-johh oh oh-neh-gah-ee-shee-mah-soo; Check please), especially if you know that your boss won't let you pay. The following phrases are handy when you pay for your meal:

- **Betsubetsu ni onegaishimasu.** (beh-tsoo-beh-tsoo nee oh-neh-gah-ee-shee-mah-soo; Please give us separate checks.)
- **Isshoni onegaishimasu.** (ees-shoh-nee oh-neh-gah-ee-shee-mah-soo); Please give us one check.)

    ✔ **O-kanjō o onegaishimasu.** (oh-kahn-johh oh oh-neh-gah-ee-shee-mah-soo; Check please.)

    ✔ **Ryōshūsho o onegaishimasu.** (ryohh-shooo-shoh oh oh-neh-gah-ee-shee-mah-soo; Receipt please.)

You don't have to tip at any restaurant in Japan, but you still get very good service about 99 percent of the time. For very expensive meals, the tip is automatically included in your bill as a **sābisuryō** (sahh-bee-soo-ryohh; service fee). Most restaurants accept **kurejitto kādo** (koo-reh-jeet-toh kahh-doh; credit cards), but many of them still only accept **genkin** (gehn-keen; cash). If you're not sure about a particular restaurant's policy, simply ask before you're seated.

Words to Know

chūmon	chooo-mohn	order
o-kanjō	oh-kan-johh	check, bill
o-mizu	oh-mee-zoo	water
yoyaku	yoh-yah-koo	reservation

Going Grocery Shopping

Restaurants are great, but if you want to save time or money, go shopping for food. If you go to a **sūpāmāketto** (sooo-pahh-mahh-keht-toh; supermarket), you can get most of the items you need in one trip. You can buy **niku** (nee-koo; meat), **yasai** (yah-sah-ee; vegetables), **kudamono** (koo-dah-moh-noh; fruit), **sakana** (sah-kah-nah; fish), and other foods like:

    ✔ **aisukurīmu** (ah-ee-soo-koo-reee-moo; ice cream)

    ✔ **gyūnyū** (gyooo-nyooo; milk)

    ✔ **jūsu** (jooo-soo; juice)

    ✔ **o-kome** (oh-koh-meh; uncooked rice)

    ✔ **pan** (pahn; bread)

    ✔ **tamago** (tah-mah-goh; eggs)

Buying ready-made dishes

When you feel a little hungry, try some of the following Japanese snacks on the way home from work, school, or a weekend outing.

✔ **dorayaki** (doh-rah-yah-kee): Round, Japanese-style pancake with red-bean paste inside

✔ **okonomiyaki** (oh-koh-noh-mee-yah-kee): Japanese-style pancake with vegetables and seafood or meat

✔ **taiyaki** (tah-ee-yah-kee): Japanese-style pancake with red-bean paste inside, just like **dorayaki**, but shaped like **tai** (tah-ee; red snapper)

✔ **takoyaki** (tah-koh-yah-kee): Japanese-style, bite-sized, ball-shaped pancake with a little piece of octopus in it

You can get any of these quick and tasty snacks at supermarket food courts, department stores, or railroad stations. You can eat them on the run or take them home to enjoy later.

Going to a butcher

Many people are **niku** (nee-koo; meat) eaters. **Niku, niku, niku** — that's all they want to eat. How about your family? Which **niku** do they like? You can find these items at a **nikuya-san** (nee-koo-yah-sahn; meat store):

✔ **butaniku** (boo-tah-nee-koo; pork)

✔ **gyūniku** (gyooo-nee-koo; beef)

✔ **maton** (mah-tohn; mutton)

✔ **shichimenchō** (shee-chee-mehn-chohh; turkey)

✔ **toriniku** (toh-ree-nee-koo; chicken)

Processed, cured, and cooked meats are very convenient. If you need to whip up a quick dinner, you may want to buy one of these:

✔ **hamu** (hah-moo; ham)

✔ **kōn bīfu** (kohhn beee-foo; corned beef)

✔ **rōsuto bīfu** (rohh-soo-toh beee-foo; roast beef)

✔ **sōsēji** (sohh-sehh-jee; sausage)

Buying vegetables and fruit

You can buy **yasai** (yah-seh-ee; vegetables) and **kudamono** (koo-dah-moh-noh; fruit) in supermarkets, but if you go to a farm stand or a **yaoya-san** (yah-oh-yah-sahn; vegetable and fruit store/green market), you can get the freshest produce. Include some of the following items on your **shoppingu risuto** (shohp-peen-goo ree-soo-toh; shopping list) — they're good for you.

- **banana** (bah-nah-nah; bananas)
- **jagaimo** (jah-gah-ee-moh; potatoes)
- **mikan** (mee-kahn; oranges)
- **ninjin** (neen-jeen; carrots)
- **pīman** (peee-mahn; green peppers)
- **remon** (reh-mohn; lemons)
- **retasu** (reh-tah-soo; lettuce)
- **ringo** (reen-goh; apples)
- **tamanegi** (tah-mah-neh-gee; onions)
- **tomato** (toh-mah-toh; tomatoes)
- **ichigo** (ee-chee-goh; strawberries)

Buying fresh fish

Japanese are big fish-eaters. My parents eat fish every morning and night. They either don't know that meat exists, or they're just health conscious — I'm not sure which. If you're also a fish lover, the fish market is the place for you. Remember the names of your favorite fish when you make the trip:

- **maguro** (mah-goo-roh; tuna)
- **masu** (mah-soo; trout)
- **nishin** (nee-sheen; herring)
- **sake** (sah-keh; salmon)
- **tai** (tah-ee; red snapper)
- **tara** (tah-rah; cod)

Basements of department stores

Don't ever skip the basements of department stores while you're in Japan. The entire basement floor is a beautiful, mouth-watering, food market. The atmosphere is lively and friendly. All sorts of take-home dishes, condiments, desserts, and even individually wrapped sushi pieces are waiting for you. You can certainly try the free food samples. It's a great opportunity for you to enjoy a large sampling of foods and to practice your Japanese with the friendly sales people.

If you go to Japan, try buying fresh fish at the Tsukiji (tsoo-kee-jee) Market. Tsukiji is the largest and most famous fish market in Tokyo, and it's always crowded with professional fresh-fish buyers and sellers. Major sushi restaurants in Tokyo buy fish directly from Tsukiji. There's no room in the market for formality, and everyone is friendly.

Talkin' the Talk

Shōko is buying shrimp at the fish market.

Shōko: **Sono ebi wa atarashii.**
soh-noh eh-bee wah ah-tah-rah-sheee.
Are those shrimp fresh?

Fishmonger: **Mochiron. Mada ikiteru yo.**
moh-chee-rohn. mah-dah ee-kee-teh-roo-yo.
Of course. They are still alive!

Shōko: **Jā 300 guramu.**
jahh sahn-byah-koo goo-rah-moo.
Then give me 300 grams of those.

Fishmonger: **Maido. Hoka wa.**
mah-ee-doh. hoh-kah wah.
Thanks. Anything else?

Shōko: **Saba o go-hon.**
sah-bah oh goh-hohn.
Give me five mackerels.

Fishmonger: **Hai yo. Zenbu de 2,300-en.**
hah-ee yoh. zehn-boo deh nee-sehn-sahn-byah-koo-ehn.
Okay. All together, 2,300 yen.

Shōko: **Hai, 3,000-en.**
hah-ee, sahn-zehn-ehn.
Okay, here you are, 3,000 yen.

Fishmonger: **Jā, 700-en no otsuri.**
jahh, nah-nah-hyah-koo-ehn noh oh-tsoo-ree.
Then, here's your change, 700 yen.

Shōko: **Arigatō.**
ah-ree-gah-tohh.
Thanks.

Words to Know

gyūnyū	gyooo-nyooo	milk
kudamono	koo-dah-moh-noh	fruit
mochiron	moh-chee-rohn	of course
niku	nee-koo	meat
sakana	sah-kah-nah	fish
tamago	tah-mah-goh	eggs
yasai	yah-sah-ee	vegetables

Being Invited to a Party

Because Japanese houses are typically small and Japanese are so modest about them, they only invite their closest friends over for a party. If you're one of them, consider yourself honored.

For a friendly and easy home party, Japanese often serve dishes that they cook right at the table using a portable stove or electric hot plate. Instead of being stuck in the kitchen and missing the fun, the hosts can cook, eat, and chat with their friends at the same time. Enjoy fun and delicious dishes with your Japanese friends, and deepen your friendships at the same time. Many restaurants in Japan specialize in tabletop cooking and dining experiences too. Here are a few dishes that you can order at a restaurant or cook up with your friends:

- ✔ **shabushabu** (shah-boo-shah-boo): Beef and vegetables cooked in a pot of boiling broth
- ✔ **sukiyaki** (soo-kee-yah-kee): Beef and vegetables cooked in **warishita** (wah-ree-shee-tah; mixture of soy sauce, sugar, and liquor)
- ✔ **yosenabe** (yoh-seh-nah-beh): Japanese casserole of vegetables, fish, or meat
- ✔ **yakiniku** (yah-kee-nee-koo): Korean-style barbecue

Fondue, Japanese style

Japanese often serve a sort of fondue called **shabushabu** (shah-boo-shah-boo) — a big pot of kelp broth placed on a portable stove on the dining table. You pick up a thin slice of beef with chopsticks, immerse it in the boiling broth, and swish it around for several seconds. You eat it right away with the dip of your choice (such as sesame-paste dip or soy sauce and lime dip). Other ingredients include Chinese cabbage, garland chrysanthemum leaves, mushrooms,

soybean curds, and gelatin noodles. Some people add thick white noodles called **udon** (oo-dohn), leeks, and other ingredients.

Japanese beef is very expensive, but it's also very tender and delicious. To produce this quality beef, farmers feed the cows beer and massage them with big brushes. So the next time meet a well-groomed cow with beer on its breath, you'll know that it has recently been to Japan.

Using Proper Table Manners

When you're invited for dinner, you always have to be polite. But what qualifies as polite depends on the culture and customs of your hosts. Japanese drink soup directly from an **o-wan** (oh-wahn; Japanese lacquered soup bowl) without using a spoon. And that's polite. Japanese slurp **ramen** noodles in soup. That's polite too.

When you start eating, always say **itadakimasu** (ee-tah-dah-kee-mah-soo). It's a very humble word for *receive,* but in this context, there's really no good translation. Just remember that it's a set phrase used to express humble gratitude to those who made the meal that you are about to receive possible. Even young kids say it in Japan. If they forget, their moms scold them. So, never forget **itadakimasu,** even if you're not with your mother in Japan. And when you're done with your meal, say **gochisōsama** (goh-chee-sohh-sah-mah). This is another word of gratitude for which there's no English equivalent, but you never want to leave the table without saying it.

You can also use some of these phrases at the table:

- ✔ **Oishii desu.** (oh-ee-sheee deh-soo; Delicious!)
- ✔ **Okawari onegaishimasu.** (oh-kah-wah-ree oh-neh-gah-ee-shee-mah-soo; May I have another serving?)
- ✔ **O-mizu o onegaishimasu.** (oh-mee-zoo oh oh-neh-gah-ee-shee-mah-soo; May I have some water?)

Rice and the Japanese diet

Rice is a very essential ingredient for Japanese meals. The average Japanese person eats rice twice a day. Like Eskimo languages that have many words to describe different types of snow, the Japanese language has many words associated with rice. Cooked rice is **gohan** (goh-hahn), and uncooked rice is **okome** (oh-koh-meh). There are also a variety of rice dishes and products in Japan:

- **mochi** (moh-chee; rice cakes)

- **ojiya** (oh-jee-yah; rice porridge with bits of vegetables, meat, or fish)

- **okayu** (oh-kah-yoo; rice porridge)

- **okowa** (oh-koh-wah; steamed sweet rice)

- **sekihan** (seh-kee-hahn; steamed sweet rice with red beans)

- **senbē** (sehn-behh; rice crackers)

- **shiratama** (shee-rah-tah-mah; rice-flour dumplings)

TIP

If you're the host or the hostess, offer food to your guest by saying **wa ikaga** (wah ee-kah-gah; How about. . . ?). For example, you can offer mashed potato to your guest by saying **Masshupoteto wa ikaga desu ka** (mahs-shoo poh-teh-toh wah ee-kah-gah deh-soo kah; How about mashed potato?). But remember, Japanese guests tend to be shy. They often say **Ie** (eee-eh; No thank you.) to be polite even when they're hoping for more. If you offer again, saying **enryo shinaide** (ehn-ryoh shee-nah-ee-deh; Don't be shy.), your guests will probably accept.

Talkin' the Talk

Yumiko invited Richard and a few other friends to her house for dinner.

Yumiko: **Tabemashō.**
tah-beh-mah-shohh.
Let's eat!

Everyone: **Itadakimasu.**
ee-tah-dah-kee-mah-soo.
I'll start eating!

Richard: **Oishii desu ne.**
oh-ee-sheee deh-soo neh.
It's delicious, isn't it?

Yumiko: **Ā, yokatta. Enryo shinaide ne.**
ahh, yoh-kaht-tah. ehn-ryoh shee-nah-ee-deh neh.
Oh, good. Don't hesitate. Have more.

Richard: **Ā, dōmo.**
ahh, dohh-moh.
Oh, thank you.

Yumiko: **Gohan no okawari wa.**
goh-hahn noh oh-kah-wah-ree wah.
How about another bowl of rice?

Richard: **Jā, onegaishimasu.**
jahh, oh-neh-gah-ee-shee-mah-soo.
Yes, please.

Yumiko: **Hai.**
hah-ee.
Okay.

Words to Know

Enryo shinaide.	ehn-ryoh shee-nah-ee-deh	Don't be shy.
Gochisōsama.	goh-chee-sohh-sah-mah	Thank you for the great meal.
Itadakimasu.	ee-tah-dah-kee-mah-soo	I'll start eating.
Oishii desu.	oh-ee-sheee deh-soo	It's delicious.
okawari	oh-kah-wah-ree	another serving

Fun & Games

Identify the various fruits and vegetables in this market stall. Take a look at Appendix C for the answers.

A. _____

B. _____

C. _____

D. _____

E. _____

F. _____

G. _____

H. _____

Chapter 6

Shopping Around

1 love shopping. When I feel great, I shop. When I feel depressed, I shop. And when I get a raise — you guessed it — I shop. If you love shopping as much as I do, grab a **kurejitto kādo** (koo-reh-jeet-toh kahh-doh; credit card) or some **genkin** (gehn-keen; cash), and start **kaimono** (kah-ee-moh-noh; shopping). This chapter helps you to get a handle on prices, evaluate products, and make purchases in Japanese.

You may or may not have a lot of **o-kane** (oh-kah-neh; money). Either way, buy the things that you really like or you really need. Don't **dakyōsuru** (dah-kyohh-soo-roo; compromise) in terms of value or quality. Look for the **shōhin** (shohh-heen; merchandise) of your dreams! If you buy something you're not crazy about, you probably won't use it. It will sit in your closet, garage, or attic, collecting dust and taking up space — like the fabulous treadmill I bought a few years back. When you do find yourself with a bunch of items you no longer use, don't throw them away. Donate the goods to less fortunate people — they'll be used rather than wasted, and you can help someone. That's what goes through my mind every time I donate a five-ton bag of **yōfuku** (yohh-foo-koo; clothes)!

Asking for a Particular Item

If you have a particular item in mind, step into a store and say **wa arimasu ka** (wah ah-ree-mah-soo kah; do you have. . .?). In January five years ago, I was desperately looking for an American flag. Everywhere I went, even in a supermarket, I asked, **Amerika no hata wa arimasu ka** (ah-meh-ree-kah noh hah-tah wah ah-ree-mah-soo kah; Do you have an American flag?). No luck — I had to wait until July when flags were all over the place. If you really want something, don't give up and continue to **sagasu** (sah-gah-soo; look for) what you want. Conjugate the verb **sagasu** (sah-gah-soo; to look for). It's a u-verb.

Form	Pronunciation
sagasu	sah-gah-soo
sagasanai	sah-gah-sah-nah-ee
sagashi	sah-gah-shee
sagashite	sah-gah-shee-teh

If you go to Japan, visit the fun and friendly souvenir shops in **Kyōto** (kyohh-toh), **Nara** (nah-rah), and **Asakusa** (ah-sah-koo-sah). **Kankōkyaku** (kahn-kohh-kyah-koo; tourists) from all over the **sekai** (seh-kah-ee; world) flock to these cities, and the souvenir stores sell things like those listed in Table 6-1.

Table 6-1	Japanese Souvenirs	
Japanese	*Pronunciation*	*Translation*
geta	geh-tah	type of wooden clogs
hashi	hah-shee	chopsticks
kabin	kah-been	vase
kasa	kah-sah	umbrella
kimono	kee-moh-noh	kimono
kushi	koo-shee	comb
ningyō	neen-gyohh	doll
o-cha	oh-chah	green tea
origami	oh-ree-gah-mee	origami/square, colored paper for the art of paper folding
osara	oh-sah-rah	plate
senbē	sehn-behh	rice cracker
sensu	sehn-soo	fan
yunomi	yoo-noh-mee	teacup

Furoshiki (foo-roh-shee-kee; wrapping cloths) may be a nice choice for your souvenir from Japan. They're big square cloths that Japanese use to tie things up and carry them in. They have beautiful patterns and colors and smooth textures. You could use one as a tablecloth or as a cover for your computer. Be creative!

Souvenir shopping in Asakusa

If you want to buy inexpensive Japanese arts and crafts for souvenirs in the **Tōkyō** (tohh-kyohh; Tokyo) area, go to **Asakusa** (ah-sah-koo-sah). It's a neighborhood in Tokyo. When you exit the subway station, you'll see a huge red lantern, about ten feet long, hanging on the gate called **Kaminarimon** (kah-mee-nah-ree-mohn; Lightening Gate). After you pass through the gate, you'll be at the beginning of **Nakamise-dōri** (nah-kah-mee-seh-dohh-ree; Nakamise Street).

It's a long, wide, roofed, pedestrian-only street, and it's always packed with **kankōkyaku** (kahn-kohh-kyah-koo; tourists). Hundreds of small gift shops tightly line both sides of this street. The atmosphere is lively and conveys the spirit of old, friendly Tokyo. You can buy Japanese confectioneries, dolls, green teas, kimonos, teacups, and much, much more.

Express your request using a verb in the te-form (see Chapter 2) and **kudasai** (koo-dah-sah-ee).

> ✔ **Sore o misete kudasai.** (soh-reh oh mee-seh-teh koo-dah-sah-ee; Please show me that.)

> ✔ **Tabete kudasai.** (tah-beh-teh koo-dah-sah-ee; Please eat.)

In the following Talkin' the Talk, Joan wants to **kau** (kah-oo; buy) a Japanese souvenir. Before you read the dialogue, conjugate the verb **kau** (to buy). It's a u-verb. Watch out for the **w** sound that appears in the negative form.

Form	Pronunciation
kau	kah-oo
kawanai	kah-wah-nah-ee
kai	kah-ee
katte	kaht-teh

Talkin' the Talk

Joan wants to buy a Japanese souvenir and steps into a souvenir store in Asakusa.

Joan: **Sumimasen. Furoshiki wa arimasu ka.**
soo-mee-mah-sehn. foo-roh-shee-kee
wah ah-ree-mah-soo kah.
Excuse me. Do you have furoshiki?

Clerk: **Furoshiki wa arimasen.**
            foo-roh-shee-kee wah ah-ree-mah-sehn.
            Furoshiki? We don't have it.

Joan: **Ā, sō desu ka.**
            ahh, sohh deh-soo kah.
            Oh, I see.

Joan sees a nice teacup in the window.

Joan: **Sumimasen. Chotto kore o misete kudasai.**
            soo-mee-mah-sehn. choht-toh koh-reh oh
            mee-seh-teh koo-dah-sah-ee.
            Excuse me. Could you show me this please?

Clerk: **Kore desu ka.**
            koh-reh deh-soo kah.
            This one?

Joan: **Hai.**
            hah-ee.
            Yes.

Clerk: **Dōzo.**
            dohh-zo.
            Here you are.

If you see a nice item in a store window, ask the clerk to show it to you. How do you specify the item that you want to see? You can point at it with your index finger and say **kore** (koh-reh; this one). **Kore** works most of the time. But what if a **yunomi** (yoo-noh-mee; teacup) and a **kyūsu** (kyooo-soo; teapot) are right next to each other, and your index finger doesn't have a laser pointer attached to it? If you say **kore,** the clerk will say **dore** (doh-reh; which one?), and you'll have to say **kore** again, and the clerk will have to say **dore** again. To end this frustrating and repetitious conversation, say **kono yunomi** (koh-noh yoo-noh-mee; this teacup) or **kono kyūsu** (koh-noh kyooo-soo; this teapot). Yes, you can add a common noun, such as **yunomi** or **kyūsu,** to the Japanese word for *this,* but you must change **kore** to **kono.**

Similarly, **sore** (soh-reh; that one near you) and **are** (ah-reh; that one over there) become **sono** (soh-noh) and **ano** (ah-noh), respectively, when followed by a common noun. (If you want to know more about **sore** and **are,** see Chapter 2.) Even the question word **dore** (doh-reh; which one) must become **dono** when followed by a common noun. Wow, too many forms? If you think about it, the change is very systematic: The ending **re** becomes **no.** Check out Table 6-2 and the following examples to straighten everything out.

Table 6-2	This, That, and Which
Term Used Independently	*Term Followed by a Common Noun*
kore (koh-reh; this one)	kono (koh-noh; this . . .)
sore (soh-reh: that one near you)	sono (soh-noh: that . . . near you)
are (ah-reh; that one over there)	ano (ah-noh; that . . . over there)
dore (doh-reh; which one)	dono (doh-noh; which . . .)

> ✔ **Ano biru wa nan desu ka.** (ah-noh bee-roo wah nahn deh-soo kah; What is that building?)
>
> ✔ **Are wa kafeteria desu.** (ah-reh wah kah-feh-teh-ree-ah deh-soo; That one is a cafeteria.)
>
> ✔ **Sono nekkuresu wa takai desu ka.** (soh-noh nehk-koo-reh-soo wah tah-kah-ee deh-soo kah; Is that necklace expensive?)

Comparing Merchandise

Finding a good deal is impossible without carefully comparing the **shōhin** (shohh-heen; merchandise). When you shop, look at the **hinshitsu** (heen-shee-tsoo; quality) and the **kinō** (kee-nohh; functions) of the **sēhin** (sehh-heen; product) closely and compare several similar items you're interested in. Ask yourself which one is better and which one is the best. Making comparisons, grammar-wise, is much easier in Japanese than in English. Unlike in English, you don't have to conjugate adjectives, adding *-er* or *-est* to show different degrees: **Takai** (tah-kah-ee) remains **takai,** whether you want to say expensive, more expensive, or most expensive. The following sections show you how to make different comparisons.

Saying cheaper, more expensive, better, or worse

When you say *Videotapes are cheaper than DVDs, Old furniture is better than new furniture,* and *My car is more expensive than your car,* you're comparing two items. In Japanese, there's no need to add *-er* or *more* to make a comparison. You just need the Japanese equivalent of *than,* which is the particle **yori** (yoh-ree). Place **yori** right after the second item in the comparison. Using the first example in this paragraph, *than DVDs* has to be *DVDs than* in Japanese. It's a mirror-image situation. Take a look at a few examples to see this concept in action:

- **Bideo tēpu wa DVD yori yasui desu.** (bee-deh-oh tehh-poo wah deee-beee-deee yoh-ree yah-soo-ee deh-soo; Videotapes are cheaper than DVDs.)

- **Furui kagu wa atarashii kagu yori ii desu.** (foo-roo-ee kah-goo wah ah-tah-rah-sheee kah-goo yoh-ree eee deh-soo; Old furniture is better than new furniture.)

- **Watashi no kuruma wa anata no kuruma yori takai desu.** (wah-tah-shee noh koo-roo-mah wah ah-nah-tah noh koo-roo-mah yoh-ree tah-kah-ee deh-soo; My car is more expensive than your car.)

Comparing two items

Life is full of out-of-two comparison questions, like *Which one is better, this one or that one?*; *Who do you like better, Mary or me?*; and *Which is more important, money or reputation?*

Which one in Japanese is **dochira** (doh-chee-rah). Just keep in mind that **dochira** is used only when the question is about two items. (To find out how to ask a question about three or more items, see the section entitled "Comparing three or more items" later in this chapter.) Here are the steps for constructing an out-of-two comparison question.

1. List the two items being compared at the beginning of the sentence.

2. Add the particle **to** (toh; and) after each item, just to make it look like a list.

3. Insert the question word **dochira,** followed by the subject-marking particle **ga** (gah).

   You can't use the topic particle **wa** (wah) after **dochira.** Acutally, you can't use **wa** after any question word. So, your choice is limited to **ga** in this case.

4. Add the adjective with the question particle **ka** (kah).

Did you get lost? I hope not. If you did, these examples will probably help clear things up:

- **Kore to, are to, dochira ga ii desu ka.** (koh-reh toh, ah-reh toh, doh-chee-rah gah eee deh-soo kah; Which one is better, this one or that one?)

- **Marī to, watashi to, dochira ga suki desu ka.** (mah-reee toh, wah-tah-shee toh, doh-chee-rah gah soo-kee deh-soo kah; Which one do you like better, Mary or me?)

✔ **O-kane to, mēsē to, dochira ga daiji desu ka.** (oh-kah-neh toh, mehh-sehh toh, doh-chee-rah gah dah-ee-jee deh-soo kah; Which one is more important, money or reputation?)

There are a few different ways to answer these comparison questions, but here's the simplest one. Just say the item of your choice with the verb **desu** (deh-soo; to be). For example, if someone asks you **Piza to, sushi to, dochira ga suki desu ka** (pee-zah toh, soo-shee toh, doh-chee-rah gah soo-kee deh-soo kah; Which one do you like better, pizza or sushi?), you can answer with **Piza desu** (pee-zah deh-soo; Pizza!) or **Sushi desu** (soo-shee deh-soo; Sushi!), depending on which one you like better. Which one do you like better?

Pointing out the best one

When shopping, you want to find the best merchandise you can buy while staying within your budget. If you like big cars, look for the *biggest* car your money can buy. If you like luxury cars, look for the *most luxurious* car you can afford. If you don't have a preference, look for the *cheapest* car. In Japanese, there's no need to add *-est* or *most* to adjectives to express *the best* or *the most*. Just use the adverb **ichiban** (ee-chee-bahn; the most/the best), which literally means *number one*. Simply place **ichiban** right before the adjective Look at the following examples and see how easy it is to form *-est* and *most* sentences in Japanese.

✔ **Kono kuruma wa ichiban ōkii desu.** (koh-noh koo-roo-mah wah ee-chee-bahn ohh-keee deh-soo; This car is the biggest.)

✔ **Kono kuruma wa ichiban kōkyū desu.** (koh-noh koo-roo-mah wah ee-chee-bahn kohh-kyooo deh-soo; This car is most luxurious.)

✔ **Tomu wa ichiban yasashii desu.** (toh-moo wah ee-chee-bahn yah-sah-sheee deh-soo; Tom is the kindest.)

If you want to specify the domain in which an item is *the most* or *the best,* such as "in the class," "in the U.S.," or "in the world," insert a noun that specifies the domain, along with the particle **de** (deh), right before **ichiban.**

✔ **Kono kuruma wa Amerika de ichiban ōkī desu.** (koh-noh koo-roo-mah wah ah-meh-ree-kah deh ee-chee-bahn ohh-keee deh-soo; This car is the biggest in America.)

✔ **Kono kuruma wa sekai de ichiban kōkyū desu.** (koh-noh koo-roo-mah wah seh-kah-ee deh ee-chee-bahn kohh-kyooo deh-soo; This car is the most luxurious in the world.)

✔ **Tomu wa kurasu de ichiban yasashii desu.** (toh-moo wah koo-rah-soo deh ee-chee-bahn yah-sah-sheee deh-soo; Tom is the kindest in the class.)

Comparing three or more items

To ask which item is the best among three or more items that you list one by one, use the question words **dare** (dah-reh), **doko** (doh-koh), and **dore** (doh-reh). Use **dare** for people, use **doko** for places, and use **dore** for other items including foods, cars, animals, plants, games, and academic subjects. All three words mean *which one*. You can't use **dochira** (doh-chee-rah) to mean *which one* in this context because you use **dochira** only for asking a question about two items. (See the "Comparing two items" section earlier in this chapter.)

To ask a question comparing three or more items, list the items with the particle **to** (toh) after each item. Ask the question using the question words **dare, doko,** or **dore.** Again, **ichiban** (ee-chee-bahn; the best/the most) is the key. Take a look:

✔ **Besu to, Marī to, Ken to, Jon to, dare ga ichiban yasashii desu ka.** (beh-soo toh, mah-reee toh, kehn toh, john toh, dah-reh gah ee-chee-bahn yah-sah-sheee deh-soo kah; Among Beth, Mary, Ken, and John, who is the kindest?)

✔ **Bosuton to, Tōkyō to, Shikago to, doko ga ichiban samui desu ka.** (boh-soo-tohn toh, tohh-kyohh toh, shee-kah-goh toh, doh-koh gah ee-chee-bahn sah-moo-ee deh-soo kah; Among Boston, Tokyo, and Chicago, which one is the coldest?)

✔ **Hanbāgā to, hotto doggu to, piza to, dore ga ichiban suki desu ka.** (hahn-bahh-gahh toh, hoht-toh dohg-goo toh, pee-zah toh, doh-reh gah ee-chee-bahn soo-kee deh-soo kah; Among hamburgers, hot dogs, and pizza, which one do you like the best?)

Sometimes you want to specify the category of the items among which the comparison is made, like *out of foods, out of the students in the class,* or *among the cities in the country.* If so, specify the category at the beginning of the question and place two particles, **de** (deh) and **wa** (wah), right after it. And one thing you need to remember is that **nani** (nah-nee; what) must be used instead of **dore** (doh-reh; which one). So, if you're specifying a category rather than giving a list, use **dare** (dah-reh; who) for people, **doko** (doh-koh; where) for locations, and **nani** (nah-nee; what) for other items. It's a bit cumbersome to switch **dore** and **nani,** isn't it? You deserve a table to help you sort things out, so check out Table 6-3.

Table 6-3	Saying *which one* in Japanese		
Category	Out of two items	Out of three or more items	Out of a category of items
people	dochira	dare	dare
locations	dochira	doko	doko
other items	dochira	dore	nani

Look at some "which one" questions concerning a category of items:

- **Kurasu no gakusē de wa dare ga ichiban yasashii desu ka.** (koo-rah-soo noh gah-koo-sehh deh wah dah-reh gah ee-chee-bahn yah-sah-sheee deh-soo kah; Among the students in the class, who is the kindest?)

- **Nihon no machi de wa doko ga ichiban kirē desu ka.** (nee-hohn noh mah-chee deh wah doh-koh gah ee-chee-bahn kee-rehh deh-soo kah; Out of Japanese cities, which one is most beautiful?)

- **Tabemono de wa nani ga ichiban suki desu ka.** (tah-beh-moh-noh deh wah nah-nee gah ee-chee-bahn soo-kee deh-soo kah; Among foods, which one do you like the best?)

The simplest way to answer these questions is to use **desu** (deh-soo; to be). If someone asks you **Amerika de wa doko ga ichiban samui desu ka** (ah-meh-ree-kah deh wah doh-koh gah ee-chee-bahn sah-moo-ee deh-soo kah; Which place is the coldest in America?), you can answer by saying **Arasuka desu** (ah-rah-soo-kah deh-soo; Alaska!).

Talkin' the Talk

Tamiko is buying a refrigerator at an appliance store. The salesperson showed her one, but Tamiko didn't like it very much. Now the salesperson is about to show her another model.

Salesperson: **Jā, kore wa. Kore-wa 150,000-en desu yo.**
jahh, koh-reh wah. koh-reh wah jooo-goh-mahn-ehn deh-soo yoh.
Then, how about this? This one is 150,000 yen.

Tamiko: **Demo, sore wa kore yori takai desu yo.**
deh-moh, soh-reh wa koh-reh yoh-ree tah-kah-ee deh-soo yoh.
But that one is more expensive than this one.

Salesperson: **Demo, shōene taipu desu yo.**
deh-moh, shohh-eh-neh tah-ee-poo deh-soo yoh.
But it's an energy-efficient model.

The salesperson notices that Tamiko is unimpressed with his explanation.

Salesperson: **Jā, kore wa. Kore-wa 120,000-en desu yo.**
jahh, koh-reh wah. koh-reh wah jooo-nee-mahn-ehn deh-soo yoh.
Well, how about this? This one is 120,000 yen.

The most convenient way to say *how about* is to simply say **wa** — the particle that designates the topic — with a rising intonation. It's the short form of **wa dō desu ka** (wah dohh deh-soo kah; how is). In the preceding Talkin' the Talk section, the salesperson introduces different refrigerators one by one, just by pointing at them while saying **kore wa** — another handy use for the topic marker **wa**.

Words to Know

Kore wa.	koh-reh wah	How about this?
rēzōko	rehh-zohh-koh	refrigerator
takai	tah-kah-ee	expensive
yasui	yah-soo-ee	cheap

Shopping for Clothes

Where do you buy your **yōfuku** (yohh-foo-koo; clothes)? Do you look for quality items that you can wear for ten years or more? Or, do you buy cheap items that you just wear for one season? Both approaches to shopping for clothes have their good points. When you buy **yōfuku**, make sure to choose the right **saizu** (sah-ee-zoo; size) and **iro** (ee-roh; color). What are you looking for? Check out Table 6-4 for a list of clothes and accessories.

Table 6-4	Articles of Clothing and Accessories	
Item	*Pronunciation*	*Translation*
jaketto	jah-keht-toh	jacket
kōto	kohh-toh	coat
kutsu	koo-tsoo	shoes
kutsushita	koo-tsoo-shee-tah	socks
sētā	sehh-tahh	sweater
shatsu	shah-tsoo	shirt
shitagi	shee-tah-gee	underwear
suetto shatsu	soo-eht-toh shah-tsoo	sweatshirt
sukāto	soo-kahh-toh	skirt
zubon	zoo-bohn	pants/slacks

Asking about color

When you buy **yōfuku** (yohh-foo-koo; clothes), check out all the **iro** (ee-roh; colors) and pick the one that looks best on you. Do you like **hade na iro** (hah-deh nah ee-roh; vivid colors) or **jimi na iro** (jee-mee nah ee-roh; conservative colors)? I like **kīro** (keee-roh; yellow) the best because the sweet old lady who used to live next door to me said that yellow is a **shiawase no iro** (shee-ah-wah-seh noh ee-roh; happy color). What's your favorite **iro?**

- **aka** (ah-kah; red)
- **ao** (ah-oh; blue)
- **chairo** (chah-ee-roh; brown)
- **kīro** (keee-roh; yellow)
- **kuro** (koo-roh; black)
- **midori** (mee-doh-ree; green)
- **murasaki** (moo-rah-sah-kee; purple)
- **orenji** (oh-rehn-jee; orange)
- **pinku** (peen-koo; pink)
- **shiro** (shee-roh; white)

The particle **ga** (gah; but), as it's used in the following Talkin' the Talk, connects two contrasting or conflicting sentences. Simply add the particle **ga** (gah; but) at the end of the first sentence as in the following examples.

- **Jaketto wa arimasu ga, rongu kōto wa arimasen.** (jah-keht-toh wa ah-ree-mah-soo gah, rohn-goo kohh-toh wah ah-ree-mah-sehn; We have jackets, but we don't have long coats.)

- **Watashi wa Amerikajin desu ga, Nihongo o hanashimasu.** (wah-tah-shee wah ah-meh-ree-kah-jeen deh-soo gah, nee-hohn-goh oh hah-nah-shee-mah-soo; I'm American, but I speak Japanese.)

Talkin' the Talk

Kanako wants to buy a leather skirt, so she visits a small boutique in her neighborhood.

Kanako: **Sumimasen. Kawa no sukāto wa arimasu ka.**
soo-mee-mah-sehn. kah-wah noh soo-kahh-toh wah ah-ree-mah-soo kah.
Excuse me. Do you have leather skirts?

Clerk: **Kawa no jaketto wa arimasu ga, kawa no sukāto wa arimasen.**
kah-wah noh jah-keht-toh wah ah-ree-mah-soo gah, kah-wah noh soo-kahh-toh wah ah-ree-mah-sehn.
We have leather jackets, but we don't have any leather skirts.

Kanako: **Ā, sō desu ka. Kawa no jaketto wa nani iro desu ka.**
ahh, sohh deh-soo kah. kah-wah noh jah-keht-toh wah nah-nee ee-roh deh-soo kah.
Oh, okay. What color are the leather jackets?

Clerk: **Kuro desu.**
koo-roh deh-soo.
Black.

Kanako: **Chigau iro wa.**
chee-gah-oo ee-roh wah.
Do you have a different color?

Clerk: **Arimasen.**
ah-ree-mah-sehn.
No, we don't.

Using "chotto" for a variety of reasons

Chotto (choht-toh) is one of those wonderful words that every language has, a word with far more uses than a dictionary can suggest. The English translation is usually *a little,* but you hear it in situations where no literal translation works. You can use **chotto** to make your request, complaint, or refusal sound understated, which makes you appear sensitive and modest — a good thing to Japanese. Check out the many uses of **chotto:**

- ✔ **Asking a favor:** To ask a favor of someone, start with **chotto,** as in **Chotto oshiete kudasai** (choht-toh oh-shee-eh-teh koo-dah-sah-ee). This phrase translates literally as *Please teach me a little,* but in more natural English, it means something like *I'd like to ask you something if I could.*

- ✔ **Asking for permission:** When you need to get permission to do something, start with **chotto.** You can think of the phrase **Chotto kite mite mo ii desu ka** (choht-toh kee-teh-mee-teh moh eee deh-sooo kah; *Literally:* Can I try it on a little?) as having a meaning close to *Can I try it on for a minute?* In this context, **chotto** makes it sound as if you'll be done as soon as possible.

  Ask for permission by using the verb in the te-form (see Chapter 2) with the phrase **mo ii desu ka** (moh eee deh-soo kah). For example, **Tabete mo ii desu ka** (tah-beh-teh moh eee deh-soo kah) means *Is it okay to eat?*

- ✔ **Complaining: Chotto chīsai desu** (choht-toh cheee-sah-ee deh-soo; It's a little small) sounds gracious when everyone knows that you really mean *It's too small.*

- ✔ **Objecting: Chotto yamete kudasai** (choht-toh yah-meh-teh koo-dah-sah-ee; Please stop that a little) sounds mild, but it works — even when you mean *Please stop that completely.*

In many contexts, you can just say **chotto** without completing the sentence. Here are a few examples: You want to call your assistant to your desk. You notice a stranger sitting on your coat. Your houseguest asks you whether he can smoke. In these cases, saying **chotto** brings the assistant to your desk, gets the stranger off your coat, and tells your guest that you hate the smell of cigarettes. All that with one little word! Of course, you need to use your facial expressions and your intonation appropriately in each context.

Checking the size

If you're in a store staring at a piece of clothing, wondering if it's your **saizu** (sah-ee-zoo; size), don't let a lack of words inhibit you from trying it on. Ask the clerk **Chotto kite mite mo ii desu ka** (choht-toh kee-teh mee-teh moh eee deh-soo kah; Can I try it on a little?). If the clerk says okay, go to the **shichakushitsu** (shee-chah-koo-shee-tsoo; fitting room) and try it on to see whether it's a **chōdo ii** (chohh-doh eee; exact fit). If not, you can use one of the following phrases:

- ✔ **Chotto chīsai desu.** (choht-toh cheee-sah-ee deh-soo; A little small.)
- ✔ **Chotto ōkii kana.** (choht-toh ohh-keee kah-nah; Is it a little big for me?)
- ✔ **Nagai desu.** (nah-gah-ee deh-soo; It's long.)
- ✔ **Sukoshi mijikai desu.** (soo-koh-shee mee-jee-kah-ee deh-soo; A little short.)

The verb **kiru** (kee-roo; to wear) is a ru-verb.

Form	Pronunciaiton
kiru	kee-roo
kinai	kee-nah-ee
ki	kee
kite	kee-teh

When you want to try doing something, use the verb in the te-form and add **miru.** For example, **tabete miru** (tah-beh-teh mee-roo) means *to try eating.* **Kite miru** (kee-teh mee-roo) means *to try wearing,* or *to try on.*

Trying on clothing is important, but shopping for a **T-shatsu** (teee-shah-tsoo; T-shirt) is pretty easy. You can often avoid going to the **shichakushitsu** if you know your size.

- ✔ **S** (eh-soo; small)
- ✔ **M** (eh-moo; medium)
- ✔ **L** (eh-roo; large)
- ✔ **XL** (ehk-koo-soo eh-roo; extra large)

Buying a dress is more complicated than shopping for a T-shirt. What's your dress size? Size 8, 12, or 16? Use the counter **-gō** (gohh) when sizing up your choices. (For more info on using Japanese counters, check out Chapter 2; the Cheat Sheet has a list of numbers.)

Women's dress sizes in Japan are one size less than they are in America. Here are the rough equivalents for women's dress sizes:

American	6	8	10	12	14	16
Japanese	5	7	9	11	13	15

Men's suit and coat sizes are expressed in letters in Japan. Compare American sizes and Japanese sizes:

American	34	36	38	40	42	44	46
Japanese	S		M		L		LL

In Japan, length is specified using the metric system. If your waist is **30 inchi** (sahn-jooo-een chee; 30 inches), it's **76.2 senchi** (nah-nah-jooo-roh-koo tehn nee sehn-chee; 76.2 centimeters). To find your size in centimeters, just multiply your size in inches by 2.54 (1 inch = 2.54 centimeters). Carry a little **dentaku** (dehn-tah-koo; calculator) with you if you shop in Japan.

Talkin' the Talk

Lori has found a nice-looking jacket in a store, but she doesn't like the color. She's about to ask the clerk if they have the same jacket in a different color.

Lori: **Chigau iro wa arimasu ka.**
chee-gah-oo ee-roh wah ah-ree-mah-soo kah.
Do you have a different color?

Clerk: **Jā, kono aka wa.**
jahh, koh-noh ah-kah wah.
Well, how about this red one?

Lori: **Sore wa kirē ne. Chotto kite mite mo ii desu ka.**
soh-reh wah kee-rehh neh. choht-toh kee-teh mee-teh moh eee deh-soo kah.
That's beautiful. Can I try it on?

Clerk: **Dōzo.**
dohh-zo.
Go ahead.

Lori tries it on.

Lori: **Chotto chīsai desu. Ōkii saizu wa arimasu ka.**
choht-toh cheee-sah-ee deh-soo. ohh-keee sah-ee-zoo wah ah-ree-mah-soo kah.
It's a little small. Do you have a bigger size?

Clerk: **Jā, kore wa. Kore wa L desu yo.**
jahh, koh-reh wah. koh-reh wah eh-roo deh-soo yoh.
Then, how about this? This one is L (large).

Lori tries it on.

Lori: **Ā, kore wa chōdo ii. Kore o kudasai.**
ahh, koh-reh wah chohh-doh eee. koh-reh oh koo-dah-sah-ee.
Wow, this one fits just right. I'll take this one please.

Clerk: **Hai.**
hah-ee.
Okay.

Words to Know

chīsai	cheee-sah-ee	small
chōdo ii	chohh-doh eee	exact fit
kiru [ru]	kee-roo	to wear
mijikai	mee-jee-kah-ee	short
nagai	nah-gah-ee	long
ōkii	ohh-keee	big
saizu	sah-ee-zoo	size
shichakushitsu	shee-chah-koo-shee-tsoo	fitting room

Going to a Department Store

Depāto (deh-pahh-toh; department stores) are very convenient. Their **nedan** (neh-dahn; prices) are a little high, but they offer a variety of quality items and **burandohin** (boo-rahn-doh-heen; designer-brand items). They also offer good **sābisu** (sahh-bee-soo; service), I suppose. Which departments interest you in a **depāto**?

- **fujinfuku** (foo-jeen-foo-koo; women's clothes)
- **gakki** (gahk-kee; musical instruments)

- ✔ **hōseki** (hohh-seh-kee; jewelry)

- ✔ **kaban** (kah-bahn; luggage)

- ✔ **kagu** (kah-goo; furniture)

- ✔ **keshōhin** (keh-shohh-heen; cosmetics)

- ✔ **kodomofuku** (koh-doh-moh-foo-koo; children's clothes)

- ✔ **kutsu** (koo-tsoo; shoes)

- ✔ **shinshifuku** (sheen-shee-foo-koo; men's clothes)

- ✔ **shoseki** (shoh-seh-kee; books)

- ✔ **supōtsu yōhin** (soo-pohh-tsoo yohh-heen; sporting goods)

Which floor do you want to go to? To answer this question, use the counter **-kai.** (For more info on Japanese counters, see Chapter 2). Now, you can go from the first floor to the tenth floor: **ik-kai** (eek-kah-ee; first floor), **ni-kai** (nee-kah-ee; second floor), **san-kai** (sahn-kah-ee; third floor), **yon-kai** (yohn-kah-ee; fourth floor), **go-kai** (goh-kah-ee; fifth floor), **rok-kai** (rohk-kah-ee; sixth floor), **nana-kai** (nah-nah-kah-ee; seventh floor), **hachi-kai** (hah-chee-kah-ee; eighth floor), **kyū-kai** (kyooo-kah-ee; ninth floor), **juk-kai** (jook-kah-ee; tenth floor).

Store clerks speak very politely. One of the polite phrases that they often use is **de gozaimasu** (deh goh-zah-ee-mah-soo). It's a polite version of the verb **desu** (deh-soo; to be). So instead of saying **Hōseki wa nana-kai desu** (hohh-seh-kee wah nah-nah-kah-ee deh-soo; Jewelry is on the seventh floor.), they say **Hōseki wa nana-kai de gozaimasu** (hohh-seh-kee wah nah-nah-kah-ee deh goh-zah-ee-mah-soo). **De gozaimasu** shows up in the following Talkin' the Talk section.

Talkin' the Talk

Brian enters a department store in Tokyo.

Clerk: **Irasshaimase.**
ee-rahs-shah-ee-mah-seh.
Welcome!

Brian: **Anō, hōseki wa nan-kai desu ka.**
ah-nohh, hohh-seh-kee wah nahn-kah-ee
deh-soo kah.
Which floor is jewelry on?

Clerk:	**Hōseki wa nana-kai de gozaimasu.** hohh-seh-kee wah nah-nah-kah-ee deh goh-zah-ee-mah-soo. Jewelry is on the seventh floor.
Brian:	**Ā, sō desu ka.** ahh, sohh deh-soo kah. Oh, okay.
Clerk:	**Achira no erebētā o go-riyō kudasai.** ah-chee-rah noh eh-reh-behh-tahh oh goh-ree-yohh koo-dah-sah-ee. Please use the elevator over there.
Brian:	**Ā, dōmo.** ahh, dohh-moh. Oh, thank you.

Words to Know

burandohin	boo-rahn-doh-heen	designer-brand item
depāto	deh-pahh-toh	department store
erebētā	eh-reh-behh-tahh	elevator
irasshaimase	ee-rahs-shah-ee-mah-seh	welcome
sābisu	sahh-bee-soo	service

Identifying Prices and Negotiating

Kaimono (kah-ee-moh-noh; shopping) can be exciting. Visiting different **mise** (mee-seh; stores), checking out all the **mono** (moh-noh; things), comparing **nedan** (neh-dahn; prices), and asking for a **nebiki** (neh-bee-kee; discount) is my idea of a great afternoon. Every family needs at least one **kaimono jōzu** (kah-ee-moh-noh johh-zoo; shopping expert).

Department stores in Japan

When you enter a prestigious **depāto** (deh-pahh-toh; department store) in Japan, female clerks, in their handsome **sēfuku** (sehh-foo-koo; uniforms) and **bōshi** (bohh-shee; hats), greet you by saying **irasshaimase** (ee-rahs-shah-ee-mah-seh; welcome), especially in the morning. They also assist you in the **erebētā** (eh-reh-behh-tahh; elevator) by holding the door and pressing the floor button for you.

Another interesting part of Japanese department stores is that they have high-class restaurant complexes featuring different ethnic cuisines on their top floors and amusement parks on their roofs. Some of them even have a small museum, gallery, or auditorium. And don't forget the **chika** (chee-kah; basement) — a floor with a variety of foods for sale that appeals to **gurume** (goo-roo-meh; gourmets) .

Are you good at asking for **nebiki** (neh-bee-kee; discounts)? You can't just expect a discount — you have to be firm about asking for it. If you're not good at asking for a **nebiki,** ask your mom — she probably knows a few tricks.

In Japan, bargaining is not a common practice except in a few places, like **Akihabara** (ah-kee-hah-bah-rah), the famous Electric Town.

Here are a few phrases for talking about **nedan:**

- ✔ **Chotto takai desu.** (choht-toh tah-kah-ee deh-soo; It's a little expensive.)
- ✔ **Ikura desu ka.** (ee-koo-rah deh-soo kah; How much is it?)
- ✔ **Mō chotto yasuku shite kudasai.** (mohh choht-toh yah-soo-koo shee-teh koo-dah-sah-ee; Make it a bit cheaper please.)
- ✔ **Māmā yasui desu ne.** (mahh mahh yah-soo-ee deh-soo neh; It's relatively cheap.)

Talkin' the Talk

Hiroya is buying a camera in Akihabara, the famous Electric Town in Japan.

Hiroya: **Kono kamera wa ikura.**
koh-noh kah-meh-rah wah ee-koo-rah.
How much is this camera?

Salesman: **40,000-en.**
yohn-mahn-ehn.
40,000 yen.

Hiroya frowns a bit.

Salesman: **Tonari wa 50,000-en da yo.**
toh-nah-ree wah goh-mahn-ehn dah yoh.
In the next store, it's 50,000 yen.

Hiroya: **Tonari mo 40,000-en datta yo.**
toh-nah-ree moh yohn-mahn-ehn daht-tah yoh.
It was 40,000 yen in the next store too.

Salesman: **Jā, 39,000-en.**
jahh, sahn-mahn-kyooo-sehn-ehn.
Then, 39,000 yen.

Hiroya: **30,000-en.**
sahn-mahn-ehn.
How about 30,000 yen?

Salesman: **Zettai dame.**
zeht-tah-ee dah-meh.
Absolutely impossible.

Hiroya: **Jā, 35,000-en.**
jahh, sahn-mahn-goh-sehn-ehn.
Then, 35,000 yen.

Salesman: **Dame, dame, dame, dame. 39,000-en.**
dah-meh, dah-meh, dah-meh, dah-meh.
sahn-mahn kyooo-sehn-ehn.
No, no, no, no. 39,000 yen.

Hiroya: **Mō chotto yasuku shite kudasai yo.**
mohh choht-toh yah-soo-koo shee-teh
koh-doh-sah-ee yoh.
Make it a bit cheaper.

Electric Town: Akihabara

Akihabara (ah-kee-hah-bah-rah) is the world-famous **Denkigai** (dehn-kee-gah-ee; Electric Town) in Tokyo. As soon as you step out of the Akihabara railway station, you'll see a number of tall buildings with shiny **neon** (neh-ohn; neon) and big **kanban** (kahn-bahn; signs) that say computer, refrigerator, TV, radio, watch, or camera in Japanese and English. You can find some **menzēten** (mehn-zeh-tehn; duty-free stores) here. Bring your passport if you plan to shop in **menzēten**, because the merchandise is tax-free only if you're taking it to a foreign country after purchase.

A few sales representatives stand in front of each **mise** (mee-seh; store), and try to hustle **kyaku** (kyah-koo; customers) inside. They don't look very friendly, but they'll talk with you if you show an interest in any of their products. You can certainly negotiate for a better price in Akihabara, but you won't get a dramatic discount.

Words to Know

dame	dah-meh	no way
Ikura desu ka?	ee-koo-rah deh-soo kah	How much?
takai	tah-kah-ee	expensive
yasui	yah-soo-ee	cheap

Paying for Your Purchase

What do you have in your **saifu** (sah-ee-foo; wallet)? If you're going shopping, you'll need a **kurejitto kādo** (koo-reh-jeet-toh kahh-doh; credit card) or some **o-satsu** (oh-sah-tsoo; bills) and a few **kōka** (kohh-kah; coins). When you harau (hah-rah-oo; pay), don't forget your **o-tsuri** (oh-tsoo-ree; change).

Conjugate the verb **harau** (hah-rah-oo; to pay). It's a u-verb. Watch out for the **w** sound that shows up in the negative form.

Form	*Pronunciation*
harau	hah-rah-oo
harawanai	hah-rah-wah-nah-ee
harai	hah-rah-ee
haratte	har-raht-teh

Talkin the Talk

Michiko is paying a cashier for a pair of sneakers and a racket in a sporting-goods store.

Michiko: **Kore to kore o kudasai.**
koh-reh toh koh-reh o koo-dah-sah-ee.
I want this and this please.

Clerk: **Hai. Shōhizē o irete, 3,225-en de gozaimasu.**
hah-ee. shohh-hee-zehh oh ee-reh-teh, sahn-zehn-nee-hyah-koo-nee-jooo-goh-ehn deh goh-zah-ee-mah-soo.
Sure. Including the sales tax — 3,225 yen.

Michiko: **Yasui desu ne. Zenbu de desu ka.**
yah-soo-ee deh-soo neh. zehn-boo deh deh-soo kah.
That's cheap. Is that all together?

Clerk: **Hai. Kyō wa subete 50 pāsento biki desu.**
hah-ee. kyohh wah soo-beh-teh goh-joop-pahh-sehn-toh bee-kee deh-soo.
Sure. Everything is 50 percent off today.

Michiko: **Mā, ureshii. Jā, 4,000-en kara onegai shimasu.**
mahh, oo-reh-sheee. jahh, yohn-sehn-en kah-rah oh-neh-gah-ee shee-mah-soo.
Wow, that makes me happy. Then, please take it out of 4,000 yen.

Clerk: **Hai. Dewa, 775-en no o-kaeshi de gozaimasu. Ryōshūsho wa kochira de gozaimasu. Dōmo arigatō gozaimashita.**
hah-ee. deh-wah, nah-nah-hyah-koo-nah-nah-jooo-goh-ehn noh oh-kah-eh-shee deh goh-zah-ee-mah-soo. ryohh-shooo-shoh wah koh-chee-rah deh goh-zah-ee-mah-soo. dohh-moh ah-ree-gah-tohh goh-zah-ee-mah-shee-tah.
Sure. Your change is 775 yen. Here's the receipt. Thank you very much.

Words to Know

50 pāsento biki	goh-joop-pahh-sehn-toh bee-kee	50 percent off
o-kaeshi	oh-kah-eh-shee	return
o-tsuri	oh-tsoo-ree	change
ryōshūsho	ryohh-shooo-shoh	receipt
shōhizē	shohh-hee-zehh	sales tax
subete	soo-beh-teh	everything
zenbu de	zehn-boo deh	all together

Fun & Games

Match the following illustrations with the words for the Japanese items. The solution is in Appendix C.

1.   origami

2.    kimono

3.   yunomi

4.    geta

Chapter 7

Exploring the Town

· ·

· ·

Don't just sit around and do nothing when you visit new **machi** (mah-chee; towns). Check out a few **shō** (shohh; shows) or **ibento** (ee-behn-toh; events). You may even find **waribiki chiketto** (wah-ree-bee-kee chee-keht-toh; discount tickets). If you don't know your way around, ask for **ikikata** (ee-kee-kah-tah; directions), look at a **chizu** (chee-zoo; map), and take the most convenient form of **kōtsūkikan** (kohh-tsooo-kee-kahn; transportation). But first, check out what forms of transportation are available. What day is it **kyō** (kyohh; today)? What time is it **ima** (ee-mah; now)? Are the trains running? How about the subway?

Knowing the Time and Day

What day is it today? Is it **kinyōbi** (keen-yohh-bee; Friday), when you get to leave **shigoto** (shee-goh-toh; work) at **3-ji** (sahn-jee; 3:00)? Is it **suiyōbi** (soo-ee-yohh-bee; Wednesday), when you're going to an **ēga** (ehh-gah; movie) at **gogo 7-ji** (goh-goh shee-chee-jee; 7:00 p.m) with a friend, or **kayōbi** (kah-yohh-bee; Tuesday), when your favorite **terebi bangumi** (teh-reh-bee bahn-goo-mee; TV program) starts at **9-ji** (koo-jee; 9:00)? Are you looking forward to the **konsāto** (kohn-sahh-toh; concert) on **doyōbi** (doh-yohh-bee; Saturday)? When do you need to leave the house to get there on time? **Gozen 11-ji** (goh-zehn jooo-ee-chee-jee; 11:00 a.m.)? **Gogo 1-ji** (goh-goh ee-chee-jee; 1:00 p.m.)?

Talking about the days of the week

Time flies. **Isshūkan** (ees-shooo-kahn; one week) is over before you know it. And the **shūmatsu** (shooo-mah-tsoo; weekend) is too short! It's always **getsuyōbi** (geh-tsoo-yohh-bee; Monday) again!

Both American and Japanese weeks only have seven days. An American week starts on **nichiyōbi** (nee-chee-yohh-bee; Sunday) and ends on **doyōbi** (doh-yohh-bee; Saturday), but a Japanese week starts on **getsuyōbi** (geh-tsoo-yohh-bee; Monday) and ends on **nichiyōbi** (nee-chee-yohh-bee; Sunday). Japanese work first and rest later. Table 7-1 lists the days of the week, starting with Monday, in true Japanese fashion.

Table 7-1	Days of the Week	
Day	*Japanese*	*Pronunciation*
Monday	getsuyōbi	geh-tsoo-yohh-bee
Tuesday	kayōbi	kah-yohh-bee
Wednesday	suiyōbi	soo-ee-yohh-bee
Thursday	mokuyōbi	moh-koo-yohh-bee
Friday	kinyōbi	keen-yohh-bee
Saturday	doyōbi	doh-yohh-bee
Sunday	nichiyōbi	nee-chee-yohh-bee

What's your weekly routine like? What are your plans for this week? Are you going to have a busy day today? **Kyō wa nanyōbi desu ka** (kyohh wah nahn-yohh-bee deh-soo kah; What day is it today?).

- ✔ **Kyō wa doyōbi desu.** (kyohh wah doh-yohh-bee deh-soo; Today is Saturday.)

- ✔ **Getsuyōbi kara kinyōbi made hatarakimasu.** (geh-tsoo-yohh-bee kah-rah keen-yohh-bee mah-deh hah-tah-rah-kee-mah-soo; I work from Monday to Friday.)

- ✔ **Konsāto wa doyōbi desu.** (kohn-sahh-toh wa doh-yohh-bee deh-soo; The concert is on Saturday.)

⤴ **Nichiyōbi wa yukkuri shimasu.** (nee-chee-yohh-bee wah yook-koo-ree shee-mah-soo; I relax on Sundays.)

Telling time

Look at your **tokē** (toh-kehh; watch) and find out the current **jikoku** (jee-koh-koo; time). You can express time in Japanese by using the counters **-ji** (jee; o'clock) and **-fun** (foon; minutes), as shown in Table 7-2. **-Fun** sometimes changes to **-pun** (poon), so watch out.

Table 7-2	Time
On the Hour	*On the Minute*
1-ji (ee-chee-jee; 1 o'clock)	1-pun (eep-poon; 1 minute)
2-ji (nee-jee; 2 o'clock)	2-fun (nee-foon; 2 minutes)
3-ji (sahn-jee; 3 o'clock)	3-pun (sahn-poon; 3 minutes)
4-ji (yoh-jee; 4 o'clock)	4-fun (yohn-foon; 4 minutes)
5-ji (goh-jee; 5 o'clock)	5-fun (goh-foon; 5 minutes)
6-ji (roh-koo-jee; 6 o'clock)	6-pun (rohp-poon; 6 minutes)
7-ji (shee-chee-jee; 7 o'clock)	7-fun (nah-nah-foon; 7 minutes)
8-ji (hah-chee-jee; 8 o'clock)	8-pun (hahp-poon; 8 minutes)
9-ji (koo-jee; 9 o'clock)	9-fun (kyooo-foon; 9 minutes)
10-ji (jooo-jee; 10 o'clock)	10-pun (joop-poon; 10 minutes)
11-ji (jooo-ee-chee-jee; 11 o'clock)	11-pun (jooo-eep-poon; 11 minutes)
12-ji (jooo-nee-jee; 12 o'clock)	12-fun (jooo-nee-foon; 12 minutes)

If you want to specify **gozen** (goh-zehn; a.m.) or **gogo** (goh-goh; p.m.), put the appropriate word in front of the number. Here are a few examples:

⤴ **gozen 2-ji** (goh-zehn nee-jee; 2:00 a.m.)

⤴ **gozen 9-ji 30-pun** (goh-zehn koo-jee sahn-joop-poon; 9:30 a.m.)

⤴ **gogo 3-san-ji 17-fun** (goh-goh sahn-jee jooo-nah-nah-foon; 3:17 p.m.)

You can use the convenient phrase **han** (hahn; half) for *half an hour* or *30 minutes*. **Mae** (mah-eh; before) and **sugi** (soo-gee; after) are also convenient for telling time. Sorry, but there's no simple phrase for *a quarter* or *15 minutes* in Japanese. **Ima nan-ji desu ka** (ee-mah nahn-jee deh-soo kah; What time is it now?).

- ✔ **1-ji han** (ee-chee-jee hahn; 1:30)

- ✔ **2-ji 5-fun mae** (nee-jee goh-foon mah-eh; 5 minutes before 2:00)

- ✔ **3-ji 5-fun sugi** (sahn-jee goh-foon soo-gee; 5 minutes after 3:00)

Japanese train schedules usually follow the 24-hour system. For example, **1-ji** (ee-chee-jee) only means *1:00 a.m.*, and **13-ji** (jooo-sahn-jee) only means *1:00 p.m.* This system eliminates a.m./p.m. ambiguity, and you don't need to say **gozen** or **gogo**.

To ask questions like *at what time, from what time, and until what time,* you need a particle like **ni** (nee; at), **kara** (kah-rah; from), or **made** (mah-deh; until). Make sure to place it after, not before, the time phrase. Grammatically speaking, Japanese is often the mirror image of English, and this is one of those times. *At five o'clock* is *five o'clock at* in Japanese, *from seven o'clock* is *seven o'clock from* in Japanese, and *until nine o'clock* is *nine o'clock until* in Japanese.

- ✔ **Nan-ji kara desu ka. — Ni-ji kara desu.** (nahn-jee kah-rah deh-soo kah. — nee-jee kah-rah deh-soo; From what time is it? — From two o'clock.)

- ✔ **Nan-ji made desu ka. — San-ji made desu.** (nahn-jee mah-deh deh-soo kah.— sahn-jee mah-deh deh-soo; Until what time is it? — Until three o'clock.)

- ✔ **Konsāto wa nan-ji ni hajimarimasu ka. — San-ji ni hajimarimasu.** (kohn-sahh-toh wah nahn-jee nee hah-jee-mah-ree-mah-soo kah. — sahn-jee nee hah-jee-mah-ree-mah-soo; What time does the concert start? — It starts at three o'clock.)

- ✔ **Ēga wa 11-ji kara 12-ji made desu.** (ehh-gah wah jooo-ee-chee-jee kah-rah jooo-nee-jee mah-deh deh-soo; The movie is from 11:00 to 12:00.)

If you don't need to know or express the exact time, you can vaguely specify the time of day using the following terms:

- ✔ **asa** (ah-sah; morning)

- ✔ **hiru** (hee-roo; noon)

- ✔ **ban** (bahn; evening)

- ✔ **mayonaka** (mah-yoh-nah-kah; midnight)

Words to Know

-fun	foon	minute
gogo	goh-goh	p.m.
gozen	goh-zehn	a.m.
han	hahn	half an hour
-ji	jee	o'clock
jikoku	jee-koh-koo	time
mae	mah-eh	before
nan-ji	nahn-jee	what time
sugi	soo-gee	past, after

Telling time relative to now

When dealing with time, the concepts of *before* and *after,* or *previous* and *following,* are very useful. Words like *next year* and *last week* are essential for grasping the time concept. Check out the expressions in Table 7-3 and start talking about time in relative terms.

Table 7-3	Relative Time Expressions	
Previous	*Current*	*Future*
sakki (sahk-kee; a little while ago)	ima (ee-mah; now)	chotto ato (choht-toh ah-toh; a little bit later)
kinō (kee-nohh; yesterday)	kyō (kyohh; today)	ashita (ah-shee-tah; tomorrow)
senshū (sehn-shooo; last week)	konshū (kohn-shooo; this week)	raishū (rah-ee-shooo; next week)

(continued)

Table 7-3 (continued)

Previous	Current	Future
sengetsu (sehn-geh-tsoo; last month)	kongetsu (kohn-geh-tsoo; this month)	raigetsu (rah-ee-geh-tsoo; next month)
kyonen (kyoh-nehn; last year)	kotoshi (koh-toh-shee; this year)	rainen (rah-ee-nehn; next year)

Exploring Fun Places

I bet that your **machi** (mah-chee; town) is full of great opportunities for fun. (If not, maybe you should consider moving to my **machi.**) Read the **shinbun** (sheen-boon; newspaper), pick up a few **zasshi** (zahs-shee; magazines), or surf the **Intānetto** (een-tahh-neht-toh; Internet) to find out what's going on. Come on — get up off the couch, grab your friends, and go have some fun.

Pick your favorite type of entertainment. Do you want to **odoru** (oh-doh-roo; dance), **utau** (oo-tah-oo; sing), **gēmu o suru** (gehh-moo oh soo-roo; play games), or **o-sake o nomu** (oh-sah-keh oh noh-moo; drink)? No need to limit yourself here. You can do all four at the same time! You could also visit a **bijutsukan** (bee-joo-tsoo-kahn; art museum) or catch a **shō** (shohh; show). I hear that *Cats* is still playing.

Visiting museums and galleries

If your daily life is filled with continuous hassles and headaches, your **kokoro** (koh-koh-roh; heart) deserves to be cleansed, nourished, and rejuvenated at a **bijutsukan** (bee-joo-tsoo-kahn; art museum). I especially love museum **baiten** (bah-ee-tehn; shops), where I can buy replicas of a great **gējutsuhin** (gehh-joo-tsoo-heen; work of art) to take home. The **hagaki** (hah-gah-kee; postcards) and **posutā** (poh-soo-tahh; posters) are great too.

Art **garō** (gah-rohh; galleries) are also cool. Sometimes, you can meet the featured **ātisuto** (ahh-tee-soo-toh; artist). If you want to know more about our planet, the **chikyū** (chee-kyooo; earth), go to **hakubutsukan** (hah-koo-boo-tsoo-kahn; museums). And if you're in a studious mood, check out a few **toshokan** (toh-shoh-kahn; libraries) and strengthen your intellectual side.

Here are some questions that you may want to ask in a museum or galary:

✔ **Baiten wa nan-ji kara nan-ji made desu ka.** (bah-ee-tehn wah nahn-jee kah-rah nahn-jee mah-deh deh-soo kah; From what time to what time is the shop open?)

- **Hakubutsukan wa nan-ji ni akimasu ka.** (hah-koo-boo-tsoo-kahn wah nahn-jee nee ah-kee-mah-soo kah; What time does the museum open?)

- **Nan-ji ni shimarimasu ka.** (nahn-jee nee shee-mah-ree-mah-soo kah; What time does it close?)

- **Nichiyōbi wa oyasumi desu ka.** (nee-chee-yohh-bee wah oh-yah-soo-mee deh-soo kah; Is it closed on Sundays?)

- **Postuā wa arimasu ka.** (poh-soo-tahh wah ah-ree-mah-soo kah; Do you have posters?)

Conjugate the verbs **aku** (ah-koo; to open) and **shimaru** (shee-mah-roo; to close). Both are u-verbs.

Form	Pronunciation
aku	ah-koo
akanai	ah-kah-nah-ee
aki	ah-kee
aite	ah-ee-teh

Form	Pronunciation
shimaru	shee-mah-roo
shimaranai	shee-mah-rah-nah-ee
shimari	shee-mah-ree
shimatte	shee-maht-teh

Talkin' the Talk

Carol arrives at a museum in the late afternoon.

Carol: **Sumimasen. Koko wa nan-ji ni shimarimasu ka.**
soo-mee-mah-sehn. koh-koh wah nahn-jee nee shee-mah-ree-mah-soo kah.
Excuse me. What time do you close?

Clerk: **Roku-ji desu.**
roh-koo-jee deh-soo.
Six o'clock.

Carol: **Ā, sō desu ka. Baiten wa nan-ji ni shimarimasu ka.**
ahh, sohh deh-soo kah. bah-ee-tehn wah nahn-jee nee shee-mah-ree-mah-soo kah.
Oh, really. What time does the museum store close?

Clerk:	**Go-ji desu.**
	goh-jee deh-soo.
	Five o'clock.

Carol:	**Ashita wa oyasumi desu ka.**
	ah-shee-tah wah oh-yah-soo-mee deh-soo kah.
	Are you closed tomorrow?

Clerk:	**Īe, ashita wa yatte imasu.**
	eee-eh, ah-shee-tah wah yaht-teh ee-mah-soo.
	No, we're open tomorrow.

Words to Know

aku [u]	ah-koo	to open
baiten	bah-ee-tehn	store/shop
bijutsukan	bee-joo-tsoo-kahn	art museum
garō	gah-rohh	gallery
hakubutsukan	hah-koo-boo-tsoo-kahn	museum
shimaru [u]	shee-mah-roo	to close
toshokan	toh-shoh-kahn	library

Exploring theaters

Visiting **gekijō** (geh-kee-johh; theaters) lets you really feel the passion of the performers. And just about everyone enjoys going to an **ēgakan** (ehh-gah-kahn; movie theater) to watch a newly-released **ēga** (ehh-gah; movie).

Before you attend an **o-shibai** (oh-shee-bah-ee; play) or catch an **ēga**, you have to buy a **chiketto** (chee-keht-toh; ticket). These phrases cover your Japanese ticket-buying needs:

- ✔ **Ichiman-en no seki o ni-mai onegaishimasu.** (ee-chee-mahn-ehn noh seh-kee oh nee-mah-ee oh-neh-gah-ee-shee-mah-soo; Two for the 10,000-yen seats, please.)

✔ **Otona futari onegaishimasu.** (oh-toh-nah foo-tah-ree oh-neh-gah-ee-shee-mah-soo; Two adults, please.)

✔ **Otona futari to kodomo hitori onegaishimasu.** (oh-toh-nah foo-tah-ree toh koh-doh-moh hee-toh-ree oh-neh-gah-ee-shee-mah-soo; Two adults and one child, please.)

✔ **Shinia hitori onegaishimasu.** (shee-nee-ah hee-toh-ree oh-neh-gah-ee-shee-mah-soo; One senior citizen, please).

Use the counter **-mai** (mah-ee) for counting tickets because tickets are usually flat. (See Chapter 2 for a discussion on counters.)

Talkin' the Talk

Doug is buying tickets at the theater box office at Tokyo's Kabukiza Theater.

Doug: **Sumimasen. Konban no o-shibai wa nan-ji kara desu ka.**
soo-mee-mah-sehn. kohn-bahn noh oh-shee-bah-ee wah nahn-jee kah-rah deh-soo kah.
Excuse me. What time does today's play start?

Clerk: **Yo-ji han kara ku-ji made desu.**
yoh-jee hahn kah-rah koo-jee mah-deh deh-soo.
It's from 4:30 to 9:00.

Doug: **Ā, sō desu ka. Mada ii seki wa arimasu ka.**
ahh, sohh deh-soo kah. mah-dah eee seh-kee wah ah-ree-mah-soo kah.
Oh, okay. Do you still have good seats?

Clerk: **10,500-en no seki wa mada arimasu.**
ee-chee-mahn-goh-hyah-koo-ehn noh seh-kee wah mah-dah ah-ree-mah-soo.
We still have some seats for 10,500 yen.

Doug: **Jā, 10,500-en no seki o ni-mai onegaishimasu.**
jahh, ee-chee-mahn-goh-hyah-koo-ehn noh seh-kee oh nee-mah-ee oh-neh-gah-ee-shee-mah-soo.
Then, give me two tickets for the 10,500-yen seats, please.

Clerk: **Hai.**
hah-ee.
Sure.

Kabuki

Kabuki (kah-boo-kee), which began in the seventeenth century, is the most popular type of traditional theater in Japan. All the action takes place on a dynamic, revolving stage.

The actors wear heavy makeup and colorful, spectacular costumes. Did you know that male actors play the roles of women in **Kabuki**? The male actors are more feminine than real women!

Watch how they move their necks and fingers and how they walk and sit down. It's amazing.

The Kabukiza Theater in Tokyo is world famous. The theater has large restaurants where you can grab a quick dinner during intermission. They also rent earphones that provide English commentary and explanations on the play's plot, music, and actors.

Words to Know

chiketto	chee-keht-toh	ticket
ēga	ehh-gah	movie
ēgakan	ehh-gah-kahn	movie theater
gekijō	geh-kee-johh	theater
konban	kohn-bahn	tonight
o-shibai	oh-shee-bah-ee	theatrical play
otona	oh-toh-nah	adult
seki	seh-kee	seat

Going to bars and clubs

O-sake (oh-sah-keh) means both *Japanese rice wine* and *alcoholic beverages* in general. If you like **bīru** (beee-roo; beer), try some Japanese-brand beers like **Asahi** (ah-sah-hee), **Kirin** (kee-reen), or **Sapporo** (sahp-poh-roh). These beers are sold in many countries throughout the world, including the United States and Canada. Now, take a walk over to the bar and order your favorite **o-sake**:

- **atsukan** (ah-tsoo-kahn; hot Japanese rice wine)

- **bīru** (beee-roo; beer)

- **burandē** (boo-rahn-dehh; brandy)

- **chūhai** (chooo-hah-ee; **shōchū** and tonic)

- **hiya** (hee-yah; cold sake)

- **jin** (jeen; gin)

- **kakuteru** (kah-koo-teh-roo; cocktail)

- **mizuwari** (mee-zoo-wah-ree; whiskey and water)

- **onzarokku** (ohn-zah-rohk-koo; whiskey on the rocks)

- **ramushu** (rah-moo-shoo; rum)

- **shōchū** (shohh-chooo; a Japanese liquor)

- **sutorēto** (soo-toh-rehh-toh; whiskey straight)

- **uisukī** (oo-ee-soo-keee; whiskey)

- **wokka** (wohk-kah; vodka)

- **wain** (wah-een; wine)

Where do you **nomu** (noh-moo; drink)? If you have a drink at home, it's usually a lot cheaper than going to a bar. But sometimes, it's fun to go to these places to have a drink in an exciting or fancy atmosphere:

- **bā** (bahh; bar)

- **izakaya** (ee-zah-kah-yah; casual Japanese-style bar)

- **naitokurabu** (nah-ee-toh-koo-rah-boo; nightclub)

Talkin' the Talk

Makoto Tanaka goes into an **izakaya** (ee-zah-kah-yah) — a casual bar with home-style food — after work.

Cook:	**Irasshai. O-hitori.** ee-rahs-shah-ee. o-hee-toh-ree. Welcome! Just yourself?
Makoto:	**Sō.** sohh. Right.

Cook: **Jā, koko dōzo.**
jahh, koh-koh dohh-zoh.
Then, please sit here. What will you drink?

Makoto: **Bīru.**
beee-roo.
Beer.

Cook: **Hai yo.**
hah-ee yoh.
Okay.

Makoto looks at the menu on the wall, wondering what to order.

Makoto: **Kyō wa nani ga oishii.**
kyohh wah nah-nee gah oh-ee-sheee.
What's good today?

Cook: **Kyō wa aji ga oishii yo.**
kyohh wah ah-jee gah oh-ee-sheee yoh.
The horse mackerel is delicious today.

Makoto: **Jā, sore.**
jahh, soh-reh.
Then, I'll have that.

Cook: **Hai yo.**
hah-ee yoh.
Sure.

Words to Know

bā	bahh	bar
bīru	beee-roo	beer
izakaya	ee-zah-kah-yah	casual Japanese-style bar
naitokurabu	nah-ee-toh-koo-rah-boo	nightclub
o-sake	oh-sah-keh	rice wine or alcohlic beverage in general

CULTURAL WISDOM

Bars and clubs in Japan

Japanese **otoko no hito** (oh-toh-koh noh hee-toh; men) love **o-sake** (oh-sah-keh; alcoholic beverages). Drinking is almost obligatory for a Japanese **bijinesuman** (bee-jee-neh-soo-mahn; businessman). Part of a businessman's **shigoto** (shee-goh-toh; job) involves entertaining his **o-kyaku-san** (oh-kyah-koo-sahn; clients) in **bā** (bahh; bars) and **naitokurabu** (nah-ee-toh-koo-rah-boo; nightclubs). It's still very rare to see Japanese businesswomen taking their clients to these places, but we may be seeing more and more of them in the future.

Both Japanese men and women drink with their **tomodachi** (toh-moh-dah-chee; friends) and **dōryō** (dohh-ryohh; colleagues) in **izakaya** (ee-zah-kah-yah; casual Japanese-style bars). It's something like the Japanese equivalent of a British pub. In **izakaya,** you don't hear wordy, honorific phrases very much. Waiters and waitresses treat you like you're a member of their family. Sitting at the counter is definitely fun. You can watch the chefs cook, and you can chat with them. Trust me — enjoy several appetizers. You can always share dishes with your friends at the table. Eat some of these foods at **izakaya:**

- **hiyayakko** (hee-yah-yahk-koh; chilled tofu with sauce and spices)
- **kaki furai** (kah-kee foo-rah-ee; deep-fried oyster)
- **nikujaga** (nee-koo-jah-gah; beef and potatoes)
- **oden** (oh-dehn; Tokyo-style stew)
- **sunomono** (soo-noh-moh-noh; vinegared food)
- **yakizakana** (yah-kee-zah-kah-nah; grilled fish)

During the day, Japanese workers appear very quiet, serious, formal, and diligent. But when they drink with their **tomodachi** and **dōryō** after **shigoto** (shee-goh-toh; work), they can really have a good time.

Singing like a star at a karaoke bar

Karaoke (kah-rah-oh-keh) is an abbreviation of **karappo ōkesutora** (kah-rahp-poh ohh-keh-soo-toh-rah), which means *empty orchestra*. So, you can think of it as an orchestra in search of a singer.

Karaoke started in Japan about 20 years ago as a form of after-work entertainment for Japanese business people. Karaoke was viewed as a great way of releasing the daily **sutoresu** (soo-toh-reh-soo; stress) related to **shigoto** (shee-goh-toh; work). Today, karaoke is popular among everyone — men and women, young and old. It's an artistic, intelligent, accessible, and healthy **shumi** (shoo-mee; hobby). And karaoke bars have spread all over the world.

If you go to Japan, visit a karaoke **bā** (bahh; bar) at least once and sing while you drink. Check the index of **kyoku** (kyoh-koo; musical pieces) and ask for the song that you want to **utau** (oo-tah-oo; sing). When it's your **ban** (bahn; turn), sing into the **maiku** (mah-ee-koo; microphone) as you watch the **kashi** (kah-shee; lyrics) scroll across the **gamen** (gah-mehn; monitor). Sing like a **sutā** (soo-tahh; star), even if you're **onchi** (ohn-chee; tone-deaf).

The other **o-kyaku-san** (oh-kyah-koo-sahn; customers) in the bar become an instant audience. They'll probably give you a warm reception no matter how bad you sing. Remember, it is a bar after all, and people do tend to drink at bars.

If you really want to practice singing while you're in Japan, you can go to a **karaoke bokkusu** (kah-rah-oh-keh bohk-koo-soo; karaoke box) — an insulated, individual room with a karaoke set where you can practice. In a **karaoke bokkusu,** you can sing as often as you want, without waiting for your turn and without spending too much money on **o-sake** (oh-sah-keh; alcoholic beverages).

Conjugate the verb **utau** (oo-tah-oo; to sing). It's a u-verb.

Form	Pronunciation
utau	oo-tah-oo
utawanai	oo-tah-wah-nah-ee
utai	oo-tah-ee
utatte	oo-taht-teh

Words to Know

karaoke	kah-rah-oh-keh	karaoke
kashi	kah-shee	lyrics
kyoku	kyoh-koo	musical piece
onchi	ohn-chee	tone-deaf person
utau [u]	oo-tah-oo	to sing

Giving and Receiving Invitations

It's always fun to hang out with friends. **Sasou** (sah-soh-oo; invite) your friends for a night out on the town. You can go to bars or theaters **isshoni** (ees-shoh-nee; together). But you don't always have to go out to be with your friends and have a good time. You can throw a **hōmu pātī** (hohh-moo pahh-teee; home party) or simply invite some people over to watch a movie. This section lets you get more socially active with Japanese. Who do you want to **sasou?** Your girlfriend? Your classmate? Your colleague? To start with, why don't you conjugate the verb **sasou** (sah-soh-oo; to invite)? It's a u-verb.

Form	Pronunciation
sasou	sah-soh-oo
sasowanai	sah-soh-wah-nah-ee
sasoi	sah-soh-ee
sasotte	sah-soht-teh

Making a suggestion with "why don't we"

If you want to go somewhere with your friend, make a suggestion by saying *Why don't we go there? How about going there?* or *Would you like to go there?* The easiest, most natural, and least pushy way of making a suggestion in Japanese is to ask a question that ends in **-masen ka** (mah-sehn kah). **-Masen ka** is the polite negative ending **-masen** plus the question particle **ka**. Why negative? In English, you say things like *Why don't we go to the bar tonight?* That's negative too, so fair is fair. Make sure the verb before **-masen ka** is in the stem form, as in **Ikimasen ka** (ee-kee-mah-sehn kah; Why don't we go there?). The **iki** part is the stem form of the verb **iku** (ee-koo; to go). If you want to do something, use other verbs like **suru** (soo-roo; to do), **utau** (oo-tah-oo; to sing), and **taberu** (tah-beh-roo; to eat).

- ✔ **Ēgakan ni ikimasen ka.** (ehh-gah-kahn nee ee-kee-mah-sehn kah; Why don't we go to a movie theater tonight?)

- ✔ **Itsuka isshoni tenisu o shimasen ka.** (ee-tsoo-kah ees-shoh-nee teh-nee-soo oh shee-mah-sehn kah; Why don't we play tennis together someday?)

- ✔ **Kondo isshoni utaimasen ka.** (kohn-doh ees-shoh-nee oo-tah-ee-mah-sehn kah; How about singing together next time?)

- ✔ **Kondo isshoni robusutā o tabemasen ka.** (kohn-doh ees-shoh-nee roh-boo-soo-tahh oh tah-beh-mah-sehn kah; How about eating lobster together next time?)

Saying "let's go" and "shall we go"

In English, you can enthusiastically invite your friends to an activity by saying *Let's go there* or *Let's do it*. How do you say *let's* in Japanese? It's easy: Get a verb in the stem form, and add the ending **-mashō** (mah-shohh), as in **ikimashō** (ee-kee-mah-shohh; let's go), **shimashō** (shee-mah-shohh; let's do it), **utaimashō** (oo-tah-ee-mah-shohh; let's sing), and **tabemashō** (tah-beh-mah-shohh; let's eat).

- ✔ **Isshoni utaimashō.** (ees-shoh-nee oo-tah-ee-mah-shohh; Let's sing together.)

- ✔ **Konban isshoni nomimashō.** (kohn-bahn ees-sho-nee noh-mee-mah-shohh; Let's drink together tonight.)

- ✔ **Kondo isshoni ēga o mimashō.** (kohn-doh ees-shoh-nee ehh-gah oh mee-mah-shohh; Let's see a movie together next time.)

If you make a question using **-mashō,** it means *Shall we?*

- ✔ **Chesu o shimashō ka.** (cheh-soo oh shee-mah-shohh kah; Shall we play chess?)

- ✔ **Kantorī Gāden ni ikimashō ka.** (kahn-toh-reee gahh-dehn nee ee-kee-mah-shohh kah; Shall we go to Country Garden?)

-Mashō ka also means *Shall I?* So, it's useful when you want to say something like *Shall I bring something?* and *Shall I help you?* Usually context clarifies whether **-mashō ka** means *Shall we?* or *Shall I?*

- ✔ **Nanika motteikimashō ka.** (nah-nee-kah moht-teh-ee-kee-mah-shohh kah; Shall I bring something?)

- ✔ **Tetsudaimashō ka.** (teh-tsoo-dah-ee-mah-shohh kah; Shall I help you?)

Talkin' the Talk

Allison asks her colleague, Liz, whether she wants to go to a beer hall together after work.

Allison:	**Konban hima desu ka.**
	kohn-bahn hee-mah deh-soo kah.
	Are you free tonight?

Liz:	**Ē.**
	ehh.
	Yes.

Allison:	**Biyahōru ni ikimasen ka.**
	bee-yah-hohh-roo nee ee-kee-mah-sehn kah.
	How about going to a beer hall?

Liz:	**Ē, ii desu yo. Ikimashō.**
	ehh, eee deh-soo yoh. ee-kee-mah-shohh.
	Sure. Let's go there.
Allison:	**Jā, roku-ji ni Kantorī Gāden de.**
	jahh, roh-koo-jee nee kahn-toh-reee gahh-dehn deh.
	Then, at six o'clock, at Country Garden.
Liz:	**Hai. Jēson mo sasoimashō ka.**
	hah-ee. jehh-sohn moh sah-soh-ee-mah-shohh kah.
	Sure. Shall we invite Jason too?
Allison:	**Ē, sasoimashō.**
	ehh, sah-soh-ee-mah-shohh.
	Sure, let's invite him.

Inviting your friends to your house

Clean up your house and buy some drinks and chips. Then, you're ready to have some friends over! Use the verb **kuru** (koo-roo; to come) when you call. But before you invite anyone, practice conjugating the verb **kuru** (koo-roo; to come) so that they can **kuru** to your house. It's an irregular verb.

Form	Pronunciation
kuru	koo-roo
konai	koh-nah-ee
ki	kee
kite	kee-teh

Now, you're ready to invite your friends over:

- **Uchi ni kimasen ka.** (oo-chee nee kee-mah-sehn kah; Would you like to come to my house?)

- **Ashita watashi no apāto ni kimasen ka.** (ah-shee-tah wah-tah-shee noh ah-pahh-toh nee kee-mah-sehn kah; Would you like to come to my apartment tomorrow?)

If you're the one who gets invited, it's a good idea to ask your friend what you can **motteiku** (moht-teh-ee-koo; bring). Japanese hosts and hostesses tend to tell their guests not to bring anything, but it's better if guests bring something anyway.

Talkin' the Talk

Helen invites George to her house.

Helen: **Kondo no nichiyōbi, uchi ni kimasen ka.**
kohn-doh noh nee-chee-yohh-bee, oo-chee nee kee-mah-sehn kah.
Would you like to come to my house this Sunday?

George: **Ā, dōmo.**
ahh, dohh-moh.
Oh, thank you.

Helen: **Isshoni bābekyū o shimashō.**
ees-shoh-nee bahh-beh-kyooo oh shee-mah-shohh.
Let's have barbecue together.

George: **Ā, ii desu ne.**
ahh, eee deh-soo neh.
That sounds great.

Helen: **Supearibu wa suki desu ka.**
soo-peh-ah-ree-boo wah soo-kee deh-soo kah.
Do you like spareribs?

George: **Hai, suki desu.**
hah-ee, soo-kee deh-soo.
Yes, I like them.

Helen: **Jā, supearibu o tabemashō.**
jahh, soo-peh-ah-ree-boo oh tah-beh-mah-shohh.
Then, let's have spareribs.

George: **Ā, dōmo. Nanika motteikimashō ka.**
ahh, dohh-moh. nah-nee-kah moht-teh-ee-kee-mah-shohh kah.
Shall I bring something?

Helen: **Īe, irimasen.**
eee-eh, ee-ree-mah-sehn.
No, you don't need to.

Words to Know

biya hōru	bee-yah hohh-roo	beer hall
bābekyū	bahh-beh-kyooo	barbecue
isshoni	ees-shoh-nee	together
konban	kohn-bahn	tonight
kuru [irr]	koo-roo	to come
nanika	nah-nee-kah	something
sasou [u]	sah-soh-oo	to invite
uchi	oo-chee	house

Fun & Games

In the puzzle below, try to find these words in Japanese:

gallery, art museum, movie theater, library, museum, izakaya bar, theater

The solution is in Appendix C.

ā	w	u	r	y	z	i	d	f	b	f	ō
g	e	k	i	j	ō	z	p	d	i	h	t
a	b	t	h	ī	e	a	a	k	j	p	r
r	h	o	k	o	s	k	z	k	u	r	h
ō	i	s	ī	ō	t	a	ā	h	t	k	e
ū	o	h	b	w	ā	y	ē	f	s	h	ō
k	ā	o	k	m	t	a	z	ē	u	t	u
h	a	k	u	b	u	t	s	u	k	a	n
ē	y	a	n	j	t	z	ā	u	a	u	ī
n	f	n	e	ē	g	a	k	a	n	o	ō

Chapter 8

Enjoying Yourself: Recreation

. . . .

In This Chapter

▶ Expressing *to do* with **suru**

▶ Finding a hobby

▶ Getting back to nature in all seasons

▶ Playing sports

▶ Harnessing artistic talent

▶ Making beautiful music

▶ Playing Japanese pinball and other games

. . . .

No matter how much you love your **shigoto** (shee-goh-toh; job), your life can't be entirely healthy if it only consists of work. Make it a goal to set some time aside for **rikuriēshon** (ree-koo-ree-ehh-shohn; recreation). Expanding your interests will make you an even more interesting and attractive person. What? Your favorite form of **rikuriēshon** is studying Japanese? I like that!

Using the Verb Suru (To Do)

The verb **suru** (soo-roo; to do) is the most frequently used verb in Japanese. You can use **suru** when you want to talk about doing many different types of activities, including most of the recreational activities discussed in this chapter.

To start with, conjugate the verb **suru** (soo-roo; to do). It's an irregular verb.

Form	Pronunciation
suru	soo-roo
shinai	shee-nah-ee
shi	shee
shite	shee-teh

You can use **suru** to express many activities, from sports to working to sight-seeing. Table 8-1 shows some of the many deeds you can do with **suru.**

Table 8-1	Suru Activities	
Japanese	*Pronunciation*	*Translation*
benkyō o suru	behn-kyohh oh soo-roo	to study
denwa o suru	dehn-wah oh soo-roo	to telephone someone
kaimono o suru	kah-ee-moh-noh oh soo-roo	to do the shopping
kankō o suru	kahn-kohh oh soo-roo	to go sightseeing
karate o suru	kah-rah-teh oh soo-roo	to do karate
ryōri o suru	ryohh-ree oh soo-roo	to cook
sentaku o suru	sehn-tah-koo oh soo-roo	to do laundry
shigoto o suru	shee-goh-toh oh soo-roo	to work
shukudai o suru	shoo-koo-dah-ee oh soo-roo	to do homework
sōji o suru	sohh-jee oh soo-roo	to clean
tenisu o suru	teh-nee-soo oh soo-roo	to play tennis
toranpu o suru	toh-rahn-poo oh soo-roo	to play cards
yamanobori o suru	yah-mah-noh-boh-ree o soo-roo	to mountain climb
zangyō o suru	zahn-gyohh oh soo-roo	to work overtime

Japanese have created many verbs by adding the verb **suru** to a foreign word.

- ✔ **chekku suru** (chehk-koo soo-roo; to check)
- ✔ **kyanseru suru** (kyahn-seh-roo soo-roo; to cancel)
- ✔ **rirakkusu suru** (ree-rahk-koo-soo soo-roo; to relax)

You form lots of Japanese verbs by putting a noun in front of **suru** and conjugating just **suru.**

Talking about Your Hobbies

If you get to know a Japanese person socially, he or she may ask you, **Shumi wa** (shoo-mee wah; What's your hobby?). Having at least one **shumi** (shoo-mee;

hobby) that you can proudly talk about is nice. Is your **shumi** athletic, artistic, or academic in nature? Or is it just amusing? Do you **suru** (soo-roo; do) any of the following activities?

- ✔ **dokusho** (doh-koo-shoh; reading)
- ✔ **engē** (ehn-gehh; gardening)
- ✔ **ikebana** (ee-keh-bah-nah; flower arranging)
- ✔ **kitte no korekushon** (keet-teh noh koh-reh-koo-shohn; stamp collecting)
- ✔ **ryōri** (ryohh-ree; cooking)
- ✔ **tsuri** (tsoo-ree; fishing)

My friend's **shumi** is **dokusho**. He **yomu** (yoh-moo; reads) **hon** (hohn; books), **zasshi** (zahs-shee; magazines), and anything else that he can get his hands on. He reads everything — the nutritional information on cereal boxes, the lists of chemicals in his wife's cosmetic goods, and even entire software manuals. Why don't you conjugate the verb **yomu** (yoh-moo; to read)? It's a u-verb.

Form	Pronunciation
yomu	yoh-moo
yomanai	yoh-mah-nah-ee
yomi	yoh-mee
yonde	yohn-deh

Talkin' the Talk

Tatsuya has just gotten to know Joanna at an informal party at a mutual friend's house.

Tatsuya: **Joana-san. Shumi wa nan desu ka.**
joh-ah-nah-sahn. shoo-mee wah nahn deh-soo kah.
Joanna, what's your hobby?

Joanna: **Shumi wa dokusho desu.**
shoo-mee wah doh-koo-shoh deh-soo.
My hobby is reading.

Tatsuya: **Hē. Sugoi desu ne.**
hehh. soo-goh-ee deh-soo neh.
Wow, that's great.

Joanna:	**Sō desu ka. Tatsuya-san no shumi wa.**
	sohh deh-soo kah. tah-tsoo-yah-sahn noh shoo-mee wah.
	Really? How about yours Tatsuya?
Tatsuya:	**Boku no shumi wa taberu koto desu.**
	boh-koo noh shoo-mee wah tah-beh-roo koh-toh deh-soo.
	My hobby is eating!

If you want to place a verb in a sentence where you usually find nouns, make the verb noun-like by adding the noun **koto** (kohh-toh) after the verb, as Tatsuya does in the last line of the preceding conversation. **Koto** doesn't have any specific meaning by itself, and it makes sense only if it follows another word. For example, **taberu koto** means the *act of eating*.

Words to Know

dokusho	doh-koo-sho	reading
engē	ehn-gehh	gardening
shumi	shoo-mee	hobby
suru [irr]	soo-roo	to do
tsuri	tsoo-ree	fishing
yomu [u]	yoh-moo	to read

Exploring Nature

If you're tired of working in front of your **konpyūtā** (kohn-pyooo-tahh; computer), take a trip to the **yama** (yah-mah; mountains) or the **umi** (oo-mee; sea). Your eyes need a change of pace, and the beautiful **kumo** (koo-moh; clouds), the tall **ki** (kee; trees), and a **yotto** (yoht-toh; sailboat) or two on the **suihēsen** (soo-ee-hehh-sehn; horizon) can provide a nice break.

Admiring and discovering the landscape

While enjoying healthy and athletic **rikuriēshon** (ree-koo-ree-ehh-shohn; recreation) in **shizen** (shee-zehn; nature), you may want to use a few of the words in Table 8-2.

Table 8-2	Nature Nouns	
Japanese	*Pronunciation*	*Translation*
bīchi	beee-chee	beach
kaigan	kah-ee-gahn	shoreline
kawa	kah-wah	river
kazan	kah-zahn	volcano
mizuumi	mee-zoo-oo-mee	lake
sabaku	sah-bah-koo	desert
sanmyaku	sahn-myah-koo	mountain range
sunahama	soo-nah-hah-mah	sandy beach
taki	tah-kee	waterfall
umi	oo-mee	sea/ocean
yama	yah-mah	mountain

Beyond admiring the scenery, you may want to get out into nature and go **haikingu** (hah-ee-keen-goo; hiking) or **kyanpu** (kyahn-poo; camping) or **saikuringu** (sah-ee-koo-reen-goo; cycling) or **suiē** (soo-ee-ehh; swimming).

Words to Know

rikuriēshon	ree-koo-ree-ehh-shohn	recreation
suiē	soo-ee-ehh	swimming
shizen	shee-zehn	nature
umi	oo-mee	sea/oean
yama	yah-mah	mountain

Changing with the seasons

Does your part of the world have **shiki** (shee-kee; four seasons)? Or does it only have some combination of **haru** (hah-roo; spring), **natsu** (nah-tsoo; summer), **aki** (ah-kee; fall), and **fuyu** (foo-yoo; winter)? Does it cost a lot to heat and cool your house? What kind of trees and flowers can you plant in your area? When you want to explore nature, the season is the most important factor to take into account.

Like most of North America, Japan has **shiki: haru, natsu, aki,** and **fuyu.** To take advantage of the best Japan has to offer, follow this seasonal mini-tour of things to do on the Japanese islands. If it's **haru,** don't miss **hanami** (hah-nah-mee; flower viewing). In **natsu,** go to the **inaka** (ee-nah-kah; countryside) for **Bon** (bohn; the Buddhist festival of the dead) and experience **Bon matsuri** (bohn mah-tsoo-ree; Bon festivals) and **Bon odori** (bohn oh-doh-ree; Bon dancing). **Odoru** (oh-doh-roo; dance) with the crowd! In **aki,** drive around in the **yama** (yah-mah; mountains) and enjoy the **kōyō** (kohh-yohh; colored leaves). If it's **fuyu,** go to the **yuki matsuri** (yoo-kee mah-tsoo-ree; snow festival) in **Hokkaidō** (hohk-kah-ee-dohh; Hokkaido) and see the huge and magnificent snow sculptures.

To make a suggestion, you take the stem form of a verb and add a verb suffix — **-masen ka** (mah-sehn kah; why don't we), as in **odorimasen ka** (oh-doh-ree-mah-sehn kah; Why don't we dance?), or **-mashō** (mah-shohh; let's), as in **odorimashō** (oh-doh-ree-mah-shohh; Let's dance!). Examples of these two endings are in the following Talkin' the Talk section and in Chapter 7.

Talkin' the Talk

The cherry trees have just started to bloom. Yoshiko works for a small company in Tokyo and asks the president of the company to hold a flower-viewing party at a local park for all company employees.

Yoshiko: **Shachō, sakura ga sakimashita yo.**
              shah-chohh, sah-koo-rah gah sah-kee-mah-shee-tah yoh.
              President, the cherry trees have started to bloom.

President: **Ā, sō.**
              ahh, sohh.
              Really?

Yoshiko: **Minna de Ueno Kōen de hanami o shimasen ka.**
meen-nah deh oo-eh-noh kohh-ehn deh han-nah-
mee oh shee-mah-sehn kah.
Why don't we go flower viewing with everyone at
Ueno Park!

President: **Ii desu yo. Jā, kinyōbi no shigoto wa san-ji ni
owarimashō.**
eee deh-soo yoh. jahh, keen-yohh-bee
noh shee-goh-toh wah sahn-jee nee
oh-wah-ree-mah-shohh.
All right then, let's close at 3:00 on Friday.

Yoshiko: **Jā, watashi wa sunakku to o-sake o yōi shimasu.**
jahh, wah-tah-shee wah soo-nahk-koo toh oh-sah-keh
oh yohh-ee shee-mah-soo.
Then I'll bring snacks and sake.

President: **Ā, arigatō.**
ahh, ah-ree-gah-tohh.
Oh, thanks.

Yoshiko: **Sorekara, basho o totteokimasu kara, watashi wa
shigoto o ichi-ji ni owatte mo ii desu ka.**
soh-reh-kah-rah, bah-shoh oh toht-teh-
oh-kee-mah-soo kah-rah, wah-tah-shee wah
shee-goh-toh oh ee-chee-jee nee oh-waht-teh
moh eee deh-soo kah.
And I'll save a spot at the park, so is it okay for me to
be dismissed at 1:00?

President: **Mmmmm.**
mmmmm.
Well. . . .

CULTURAL WISDOM

Welcoming spring

Japanese celebrate the arrival of **haru** (hah-roo; spring) by having an informal party under the **sakura no ki** (sah-koo-rah noh kee; cherry trees) when the trees are in bloom. They spread out a blanket, eat food, drink **o-sake** (oh-sah-keh; Japanese rice wine or any alcoholic beverage), play music, sing, dance, and get drunk. Parks with cherry trees become very crowded in the spring, and groups compete for places to party. As in the Japanese proverb **hana yori dango** (hah-nah yoh-ree dahn-go; dumplings rather than flowers), many people enjoy eating and drinking more than appreciating the beautiful flowers above their heads!

Remember that you can ask for permission by using a verb in the te-form and adding **mo ii desu ka** to it. For example, **tabete mo ii desu ka** (tah-beh-teh moh eee deh-soo kah) means *Is it okay to eat?* In the above Talkin' and Talk section, Yoshiko asks **Ichi-ji ni shigoto o owatte mo ii desu ka.** She's asking for permission to leave the office early.

Words to Know

haru	hah-roo	spring
natsu	nah-tsoo	summer
aki	ah-kee	fall
fuyu	foo-yoo	winter

Living the Sporting Life

Do you participate in or watch **supōtsu** (soo-pohh-tsoo; sports)? Whether you **suru** (soo-roo; play) or **miru** (mee-roo; watch), sports probably take up some of your time.

Conjugate the verb **miru** (mee-roo; to watch), which is a ru-verb.

Form	Pronunciation
miru	mee-roo
minai	mee-nah-ee
mi	mee
mite	mee-teh

Yakyū (yah-kyooo; baseball) and **sakkā** (sahk-kahh; soccer) are the most popular sports in Japan, but people also enjoy other sports, such as

- **barēbōru** (bah-rehh-bohh-roo; volleyball)
- **basukettobōru** (bah-soo-keht-toh-bohh-roo; basketball)
- **futtobōru** (foot-toh-bohh-roo; football)

- **gorufu** (goh-roo-foo; golf)
- **sukēto** (soo-kehh-toh; skating)
- **sukī** (soo-keee; skiing)
- **sāfin** (sahh-feen; surfing)
- **tenisu** (teh-nee-soo; tennis)

Also, check out traditional Japanese sports. **Sumō** (soo-mohh; sumo wrestling) is the national sport in Japan. The object of **sumō** is to push your opponent out of a ring or to force any part of his body, other than the soles of his feet, to touch the ground. Believe it or not, many strong **sumō** wrestlers are from America! If you're interested in becoming a **sumō** wrestler in Japan, start overeating and gain at least 300 pounds! The heavier, the better.

You may want to look into these other traditional Japanese sports:

- **karate** (kah-rah-teh; a Japanese system of self-defense, using quick, sharp blows from the hands and feet)
- **kendō** (kehn-dohh; Japanese fencing)
- **kyūdō** (kyooo-dohh; archery)

Talkin' the Talk

The following dialogue is a telephone conversation between Pete and Dan. Pete is asking Dan to play tennis with him.

Pete: **Ashita isshoni tenisu o shimasen ka.**
ah-shee-tah ees-shoh-nee teh-nee-soo oh
shee-mah-sehn kah.
Why don't we play tennis together tomorrow.

Dan: **Doko de.**
doh-koh deh.
Where?

Pete: **Daigaku no tenisu kōto de.**
dah-ee-gah-koo noh teh-nee-soo kohh-toh deh.
At the university tennis courts.

Dan: **Ā, ii desu ne.**
ahh, eee deh-soo neh.
Oh, that's great.

Pete:	**Raketto wa arimasu ka.**
	rah-keht-toh wah ah-ree-mah-soo kah.
	Do you have a racket?

Dan:	**Raketto wa arimasu. Demo, bōru wa arimasen.**
	rah-keht-toh wah ah-ree-mah-soo. deh-moh,
	bohh-roo wah ah-ree-mah-sehn.
	I have a racket. But I don't have tennis balls.

Pete:	**Daijōbu. Bōru wa arimasu.**
	dah-ee-johh-boo. bohh-roo wah ah-ree-mah-soo.
	That's fine. I have tennis balls.

Words to Know

bōru	bohh-roo	ball
daijōbu	dah-ee-johh-boo	that's fine/no problem
raketto	rah-keht-toh	racket
tenisu	teh-nee-soo	tennis
tenisu kōto	teh-nee-soo kohh-toh	tennis court

CULTURAL WISDOM

Baseball in Japan

Japanese have loved **yakyū** (yah-kyooo; baseball) ever since American Abner Doubleday introduced the sport in the late 1800s. Instead of the American League and the National League, Japan has the **se rīgu** (seh reee-goo; Central League) and **pa rīgu** (pah reee-goo; Pacific League). As in the States, teams compete for the pennant, and then the two league-championship teams compete in the **Nihon shirīzu** (nee-hohn shee-reee-zoo; Japan series).

Many American professional baseball players compete in Japan. In summer, Japanese also excitedly follow the **kōkō yakyū** (kohh-kohh yah-kyooo; high school baseball) series on TV.

Saying "I Can"

To say that you *can do* something rather than that you *do* something, add a suffix (**-eru** or **-rareru**) to the verb. Sorry, there's no convenient word like *can* in Japanese. You need to do a little surgery on the verb to securely attach the suffix. Don't worry — verbs don't bleed. The amount of verb surgery necessary and the suffix you add both depend on the class of the verb.

If the verb is a u-verb, remove the **u** at the end of the verb in the dictionary form, and add **-eru.** For example, **aruku** (ah-roo-koo; to walk) is a u-verb. Removing the final **u** and adding **-eru** gives you **arukeru** (ah-roo-keh-roo). **Aruku** means *I walk,* but **arukeru** means *I can walk.* Your surgery was a great success! You can walk! Congratulations!

If the verb is a ru-verb, remove the **ru** at the end of the verb in the dictionary form, and add **-rareru.** For example, the verb **okiru** (oh-kee-roo; to sit up) is a ru-verb. Removing the **ru** and adding **-rareru** gives you **okirareru** (oh-kee-rah-reh-roo). **Okirareru** means *I can sit up.* Just remember these two surgical procedures to make any action possible and express what you can do.

The only necessary sound adjustment in this whole process is to change **ts** to **t** before adding **-eru.** So, the "can" form of the verb **motsu** (moh-tsoo; to hold) is **moteru** (moh-teh-roo; can hold), not **motseru** (moh-tseh-roo). It doesn't mean that **motsu** is an irregular verb. It's a regular verb. It's just that **tse** (tseh) is not an authentic Japanese sound, so it gets simplified to **te** (teh). That's a reasonable and minor sound adjustment, right? And I should tell you what happens to two of the major irregular verbs, **suru** (soo-roo; to do) and **kuru** (koo-roo; to come), in the "can" situation. The "can" form of the verb **suru** is **dekiru** (deh-kee-roo; can do), and the "can" form of the verb **kuru** is **korareru** (koh-rah-reh-roo; can come).

When you use these "can" forms in a sentence, replace the direct object particle **o** (oh) with the particle **ga** (gah). I know — it's not a subject, but you have to mark it with the particle **ga** anyway. Strange, isn't it? So, **sushi o tsukuru** (soo-shee oh tsoo-koo-roo) means *you make sushi,* but **sushi ga tsukureru** (soo-shee gah tsoo-koo-reh-roo) means *you can make sushi.* Now, tell me what you can do, what your friends can do, and what your family members can do.

- ✔ **Adamu wa karate ga dekimasu.** (ah-dah-moo wah kah-rah-teh gah deh-kee-mah-soo; Adam can do karate.)

- ✔ **Chichi wa Nihongo ga hanasemasen.** (chee-chee wah nee-hohn-goh gah han-nah-seh-mah-sehn; My father can't speak Japanese.)

- ✔ **Kurisu wa hashi ga tsukaemasu.** (koo-ree-soo wah hah-shee gah tsoo-kah-eh-mah-soo; Chris can use chopsticks.)

- ✔ **Watashi wa Nihongo ga hanasemasu.** (wah-tah-shee wah nee-hohn-goh gah hah-nah-seh-mah-soo; I can speak Japanese.)

Using Your Artistic Talent

Don't be afraid of expressing your **kimochi** (kee-moh-chee; feelings) and **kangae** (kahn-gah-eh; ideas) artistically. Use your **sōzōryoku** (sohh-zohh-ryoh-koo; creativity). No need to follow strict rules or **jōshiki** (johh-shee-kee; common sense) in art. Be brave. You can even use the same techniques that you used as a **kodomo** (koh-doh-moh; child). Just look at Pablo Picasso and Jackson Pollock. They didn't let **jōshiki** stifle their artistic **sōzōryoku.**

Which of the following art forms interests you?

- **chōkoku** (chohh-koh-koo; sculpting/engraving)
- **kaiga** (kah-ee-gah; painting/drawing)
- **kirutingu** (kee-roo-teen-goo; quilting)
- **tōgē** (tohh-gehh; pottery)

If you go to Japan, visit **karuchā sentā** (kah-roo-chahh sehn-tahh; cultural centers or cultural schools). You can observe classes in traditional Japanese arts like

- **ikebana** (ee-keh-bah-nah; flower arranging)
- **ryōri** (ryohh-ree; cooking)
- **sadō** (sah-dohh; tea ceremony)
- **shodō** (shoh-dohh; calligraphy)

Did someone say **ryōri** isn't an art? Sure, it is. **Ryōri** is an art that pleases both the eye and the palate.

Talkin' the Talk

Yoshiko's mother is recommending that she take cooking lessons.

Mother: **Yoshiko. O-ryōri kyōshitsu ni ikanai.**
yoh-shee-koh. oh-ryohh-ree kyohh-shee-tsoo nee ee-kah-nah-ee.
Yoshiko. Why don't you go to cooking classes?

Yoshiko: **Hitsuyō nai yo.**
hee-tsoo-yohh nah-ee yoh.
It's not necessary.

Mother:	**Demo yudetamago shika tsukurenai deshō.**
	deh-moh yoo-deh-tah-mah-goh shee-kah
	tsoo-koo-reh-nah-ee deh-shohh.
	But you can only make boiled eggs!
Yoshiko:	**Medamayaki mo tsukureru yo.**
	meh-dah-mah-yah-kee moh tsoo-koo-reh-roo yoh.
	I can make fried eggs, too.

To say *only* in Japanese, you add the particle **shika** (shee-kah) to the end of the noun and make the verb negative, as Yoshiko's mother does in the preceding Talkin' the Talk section. Also, if **shika** follows the subject particle **ga** or the object particle **o,** you drop the particle and just use **shika.** Particles other than **ga** and **o** stay, as the following examples show.

- ✔ **Fugu wa resutoran de shika tabemasen.** (foo-goo wah reh-soo-toh-rahn deh shee-kah tah-beh-mah-sehn; I eat blowfish only at a restaurant.)

- ✔ **Nihongo shika hanashimasen.** (nee-hohn-goh shee-kah hah-nah-shee-mah-sehn; I only speak Japanese.)

- ✔ **Tanaka-san shika kimasendeshita.** (tah-nah-kah-sahn shee-kah kee-mah-sehn-deh-shee-tah; Only Mr. Tanaka came.)

Words to Know

chōkoku	chohh-koh-koo	sculpting/engraving
ikebana	ee-keh-bah-nah	flower arranging
kaiga	kah-ee-gah	painting/drawing
ryōri	ryohh-ree	cooking

Playing Musical Instruments

Like many children, Japanese kids take **piano** (pee-ah-noh; piano) and **baiorin** (bah-ee-oh-reen; violin) **ressun** (rehs-soon; lessons) because their moms want them to. But when they become teenagers, they play the **erekigitā** (eh-reh-kee gee-tahh; electric guitar) in **rokku bando** (rohk-koo bahn-doh; rock bands).

Do you play a **gakki** (gahk-kee; musical instrument)? If you don't, try the **piano, baiorin,** or one of these **gakki.** It's never too late.

- **doramu** (doh-rah-moo; drums)
- **furūto** (foo-rooo-toh; flute)
- **gitā** (gee-tahh; guitar)
- **sakusofon** (sah-koo-soh-fohn; saxophone)
- **toranpetto** (toh-rahn-peht-toh; trumpet)

You'll look fabulous if you can play any of the above instruments like a pro, but that won't be possible if you don't **renshū suru** (rehn-shooo soo-roo; practice). If you don't **renshū suru,** you won't perfect your conjugation skills either. So, **renshū suru** conjugating the verb **renshū suru.** Actually, you just have to conjugate the irregular verb **suru** (to do), which I go over in the very first section in this chapter.

If you've seen old Japanese films or visited a traditional Japanese town, you've probably heard one of these Japanese **gakki:**

- **fue** (foo-eh; Japanese flute or pipe)
- **koto** (koh-toh; long Japanese zither with 13 strings)
- **shamisen** (shah-mee-sehn; three-stringed Japanese banjo)
- **taiko** (tah-ee-koh; Japanese drums)

For different types of musical instruments, you use different verbs to mean *to play.* For wind instruments, use the verb **fuku** (foo-koo). For a stringed instrument or a keyboard, use the verb **hiku** (hee-koo). Other instruments need specific verbs.

- **baiorin o hiku** (bah-ee-oh-reen oh hee-koo; to play the violin)
- **doramu o tataku** (doh-rah-moo oh tah-tah-koo; to play the drums)
- **furūto o fuku** (foo-rooo-toh oh foo-koo; to play the flute)
- **orugan o hiku** (oh-roo-gahn oh hee-koo; to play the organ)
- **piano o hiku** (pee-ah-noh oh hee-koo; to play the piano)
- **toranpetto o fuku** (toh-rahn-peht-toh oh foo-koo; to play the trumpet)

Express a **mērē** (mehh-rehh; command) or give an order by using a verb in its stem form plus **-nasai.** For example, **tabenasai** (tah-beh-nah-sah-ee) means *Eat!* It's an order. Now you're the boss. Order your child to do the following:

✔ **Baiorin o renshū shinasai.** (bah-ee-oh-reen oh rehn-shooo shee-nah-sah-ee; Practice violin!)

✔ **Benkyō shinasai.** (behn-kyohh shee-nah-sah-ee; Study!)

✔ **Kikinasai.** (kee-kee-nah-sah-ee; Listen!)

✔ **Sōji o shinasai.** (sohh-jee oh shee-nah-sah-ee; Clean!)

Don't use this type of speech with your spouse if you want to stay happily married.

Talkin' the Talk

Midori is seven years old. She's watching TV in the living room, and her mother asks her to practice her violin.

Mother: **Baiorin o renshū shinasai.**
bah-ee-oh-reen oh rehn-shooo shee-nah-sah-ee.
Practice your violin.

Midori: **Atode.**
ah-toh-deh.
Later.

Mother: **Dame. Sakini renshū shinasai.**
dah-meh. sah-kee-nee rehn-shooo shee-nah-sah-ee.
Not good. Practice first.

Midori: **Dōshite.**
dohh-shee-teh.
Why?

Mother: **Raishū wa happyōkai yo.**
rah-ee-shooo wah hahp-pyohh-kah-ee yoh.
Your recital is next week.

Midori: **Daijōbu.**
dah-ee-johh-boo.
I'll be all right.

Mother: **Daijōbu ja arimasen. Renshū shinasai.**
dah-ee-johh-boo jah ah-ree-mah-sehn. rehn-shooo shee-nah-sah-ee.
You won't be all right. Practice!

Words to Know

baiorin	bah-ee-oh-reen	violin
furūto	foo-rooo-toh	flute
happyōkai	hahp-pyohh-kah-ee	recital
piano	pee-ah-noh	piano
renshū suru [irr]	rehn-shooo soo-roo	to practice

Playing Games

You can always play a game when you have some free time. These games aren't artistic, academic, or athletic, but they can make you forget about the real world for a while:

- **chesu** (cheh-soo; chess)
- **famikon** (fah-mee-kohn; computer games)
- **go** (goh; go, a kind of Japanese chess)
- **mājan** (mahh-jahn; mahjongg, a kind of Chinese chess)
- **pachinko** (pah-cheen-koh; a Japanese pinball game)
- **toranpu** (toh-rahn-poo; cards)

When you want to say *to play a game,* use the verb **suru** (soo-roo; to do), as in **chesu o suru** (cheh-soo oh soo-roo; to play chess), and just conjugate **suru.**

Fun & Games

Identify the seasons. Answers are in Appendix C.

A. _____ C. _____

B. _____ D. _____

Chapter 9

Talking on the Telephone

Denwa (dehn-wah; telephones) are an indispensable part of daily life. **Denshi mēru** (dehn-shee mehh-roo; e-mail) is also great, but it can't replace the sense of connection that you get from hearing your friend or family's **koe** (koh-eh; voice). This chapter gives you the essential phrases that you need to have **denwa no kaiwa** (dehn-wah noh kah-ee-wah; telephone conversations) in Japanese.

Using a Telephone

Think about it. **Denwa** (dehn-wah; telephones) are everywhere. How many **denwa** do you have at home? How many **denwa** are there in your office? Do you carry a **kētai-denwa** (kehh-tah-ee-dehn-wah; cellular phone)? How about **kōshū-denwa** (kohh-shooo-dehn-wah; public phones)? Count them all. You really are surrounded by **denwa.**

Before you get ready to make a call in Japanese, get used to the Japanese words and terms related to telephone equipment, systems, and accessories:

✓ **denwa o kakeru** (dehn-wah oh kah-keh-roo; to make a phone call)

✓ **denwa o morau** (dehn-wah oh moh-rah-oo; to receive a phone call)

✓ **denwa-bangō** (dehn-wah-bahn-gohh; telephone number)

✓ **denwachō** (dehn-wah-chohh; telephone book)

✓ **kētai-denwa** (kehh-tah-ee-dehn-wah; cellular phone)

✓ **kōshū-denwa** (kohh-shooo-dehn-wah; public phone)

✓ **terefon-kādo** (teh-reh-fohn-kahh-doh; telephone card)

Telephone cards

These days, most people use cellular phones in Japan, but **kōshū-denwa** (kohh-shooo-dehn-wah; public phones) are still available. If you go to Japan and you need to use **kōshū-denwa** (kohh-shooo-dehn-wah; public phones) a lot, buy a **terefon-kādo** (teh-reh-fohn-kahh-doh; telephone card). **Terefon-kādo** are much more convenient than using **koin** (koh-een; coins). The cards are nicer looking too — they have beautiful pictures on them. You can even create cards with your name on them to give out to your friends as little gifts.

You can buy a **terefon-kādo** from a **jidō-han-baiki** (jee-dohh-hahn-bah-ee-kee; vending machine). The machines usually are located near public phones and in airports and train stations. You also can buy a card at a variety of stores.

To make a call with a **terefon-kādo,** just insert it into the **denwa** (dehn-wah; telephone) and start dialing the **denwa-bangō** (dehn-wah-bahn-gohh; telephone number). There's no need to call the **denwa-gaisha** (dehn-wah-gah-ee-sha; telephone company) or input any codes or PIN numbers. Right after you insert your **terefon-kādo,** your card's balance appears on a monitor, and you can watch your money disappear as you talk.

Conjugate the verb **kakeru** (kah-keh-roo). You can use it in the phrase **denwa o kakeru** (dehn-wah oh kah-keh-roo; to make a phone call). It's a ru-verb.

Form	Pronunciation
kakeru	kah-keh-roo
kakenai	kah-keh-nah-ee
kake	kah-keh
kakete	kah-keh-teh

Making a Phone Call

Moshimoshi (moh-shee-moh-shee) in Japanese is a kind of a line-testing phrase like *Hello, are you there?* or *Can you hear me?* Before you start talking, say **moshimoshi**. If the other party on the phone doesn't speak at all, say **moshimoshi** again. If you still don't hear anything, repeat it more loudly — **MOSHIMOSHI!!! MO SHI MO SHI!!!!!** If you still don't hear anything, hang up!

Calling your friends

It's late at night. Do you need to call your **tomodachi** (toh-moh-dah-chee; friend) to **hanasu** (hah-nah-soo; talk) about the **shukudai** (shoo-koo-dah-ee; homework) you haven't done yet? Maybe you're thinking about inviting your **tomodachi** to the big **pātī** (pahh-teee; party). Or, maybe you want to call your **tomodachi** just to **oshaberi o suru** (oh-sha-beh-ree oh soo-roo; chat). Regardless of your situation, this section contains the info to get you started off on the right foot.

When you call your friend's home and someone other than your friend picks up, her **okāsan** (oh-kahh-sahn; mom) for example, say your name before asking her to get your friend. So, if your name were Suzuki, you would say **Suzuki desu ga** (soo-zoo-kee deh-soo gah; This is Mr./Ms. Suzuki speaking) and then **Ken-san o onegaishimasu** (kehn-sahn oh oh-neh-gah-ee-shee-mah-soo; May I talk to Ken please?). If you don't tell her your name, she'll say **Dochira-sama desu ka** (doh-chee-rah-sah-mah deh-soo kah; Who is calling please?).

To make an informal suggestion to your close friend, just use the negative verb form with a rising question intonation, as in **konai** (koh-nah-ee; Wouldn't you like to come here?), as Andy does in the following Talkin' the Talk dialogue. It's short and easy and very handy when you want to invite a friend to join you someplace, as in *Hello. It's me. I'm at the bar now. **Konai?***

Talkin' the Talk

Andy Fraser is having a good time with his friend at a club in Shinjuku, Tokyo. Andy is calling Shin Yoshikawa, another friend of his, to see whether he can join them.

Shin's mom: **Yoshikawa de gozaimasu.**
yoh-shee-kah-wah deh goh-zah-ee-mah-soo.
This is the Yoshikawa residence.

Andy: **Furēzā desu ga, Shin-san o onegaishimasu.**
foo-rehh-zahh deh-soo gah, sheen-sahn oh
oh-neh-gah-ee-shee-mah-soo.
This is Mr. Fraser speaking. May I speak to Shin please?

Shin's mom: **Hai, chotto matte kudasai ne.**
hah-ee, choht-toh maht-teh koo-dah-sah-ee neh.
Yes, hold on please.

Shin: **Moshimoshi.**
moh-shee-moh-shee.
Hello.

Andy:	**Shin.**
	sheen.
	Shin?

Shin:	**Ā, Andī. Ima doko.**
	ahh, ahn-deee. ee-mah doh-koh.
	Oh, Andy. Where are you?

Andy:	**Ima Shinjuku. Shin mo konai.**
	ee-mah sheen-joo-koo. sheen moh koh-nah-ee.
	I'm in Shinjuku. How about coming out?

Words to Know

_____-san o onegaishimasu.	-sahn oh oh-neh-gah-ee-shee-mah-soo	May I talk to Mr./Ms. _____ please?
Chotto matte kudasai.	choht-toh maht-teh koo-dah-sah-ee	Hold on please.
Dochira-sama desu ka.	doh-chee-rah-sah-mah deh-soo kah	Who's calling?

Calling hotels and stores

When you call commercial institutions, such as **hoteru** (hoh-teh-roo; hotels), **mise** (mee-seh; stores), and **resutoran** (reh-soo-toh-rahn; restaurants), the employees introduce their business first, right after they pick up the phone, by saying **de gozaimasu** (deh goh-zah-ee-mah-soo). It's the super-polite version of the verb **desu** (deh-soo; to be). Of course, with Japanese sentence construction, you'll hear the name of the business before **de gozaimasu.** For example, **Hoteru Sanraizu de gozaimasu** (hoh-teh-roo sahn-rah-ee-zoo deh goh-zah-ee-ma-soo) means *This is Hotel Sunrise.*

After an employee answers the phone, tell him or her who you want to speak to or who you're looking for:

- **Adamu Jonson-san o onegaishimasu.** (ah-dah-moo john-sohn-sahn oh oh-neh-gah-ee-shee-mah-soo; May I speak to Mr. Adam Johnson please?)

- **Naisen 403-ban ni tsunaide kudasai.** (nah-ee-sehn yohn-hyah-koo-sahn-bahn nee tsoo-nah-ee-deh koo-dah-sah-ee; Please connect me to extension 403.)

✔ **Ēgyōbu no kata o onegaishimasu.** (ehh-gyohh-boo noh kah-tah oh oh-neh-gah-ee-shee-mah-soo; I'd like to speak someone in the sales department.)

When you call a commercial institution, they may put you on hold for several minutes. I'm sure you don't like it, but while you're waiting, check out the phrases for *waiting.*

✔ **Mō 30-pun matte iru-n-desu ga.** (mohh sahn-joop-poon maht-teh ee-roon-deh-soo gah; I've been waiting for 30 minutes.)

✔ **O-matase shimashita.** (oh-mah-tah-seh shee-mah-shee-tah; Sorry to have kept you waiting.)

✔ **Shōshō o-machi kudasai.** (shohh shohh oh-mah-chee koo-dah-sah-ee; Could you wait a little please?)

Asking for what you want

Why do you make a phone call? Because you *want* to talk to someone, right? Why do you *want* to talk to someone? Maybe you *want* to tell him or her what you *want.* But how do you say *to want* in Japanese? Well, I have two confessions to make. First, although Japanese do *want* things, there's no Japanese verb that means *to want.* But fear not, Japanese has an adjective that means *to want.* Now you're probably wondering, "What's the Japanese adjective that means *to want?*" Here's my second confession. Japanese use different adjectives to express *to want* depending on whether they want to perform an action or they want some item. (I could make a couple more confessions about expressing a desire, but I don't have the space to go into them here — and you don't need to know about them to carry on a simple conversation. Welcome to Japanese!)

Wanting to do something

What do you *want* to do now? Do you *want* to **kau** (kah-oo; buy) a big house with a tennis court and a swimming pool without worrying about property taxes? Do you *want* to **taberu** (tah-beh-roo; eat) as much as you want without worrying about your health or your weight? Or do you *want* to **iku** (ee-koo; go) to Japan (with this book in your hand, of course) without worrying about how much the trip will cost? Saying these phrases, *to want to buy, to want to eat,* and *to want to go,* in Japanese is easy. Simply add the suffix **-tai** (tah-ee) to the end of the stem form of a verb, as in **kaitai** (kah-ee-tah-ee; to want to buy), **tabetai** (tah-beh-tah-ee; to want to eat), and **ikitai** (ee-kee-tah-ee; to want to go). Use these **tai** phrases just like you use regular i-type adjectives (Chapter 2 has more on these adjectives). Check out these examples:

✔ **Watashi wa yasumitai desu.** (wah-tah-shee wah yah-soo-mee-tah-ee deh-soo; I want to rest.)

- **Watashi wa atarashii kuruma o kaitai desu.** (wah-tah-shee wah ah-tah-rah-sheee koo-roo-mah oh kah-ee-tah-ee deh-soo; I want to buy a new car.)

- **Kyō wa sutēki o tabetai desu.** (kyohh wah soo-tehh-kee oh tah-beh-tah-ee deh-soo; I want to eat a steak today.)

- **Hawai ni ikitai desu.** (hah-wah-ee nee ee-kee-tah-ee deh-soo; I want to go to Hawaii.)

- **Nani o shitai desu ka.** (nah-nee oh shee-tah-ee deh-soo kah; What do you want to do?)

- **Uchi ni kaeritai desu.** (oo-chee nee kah-eh-ree-tah-ee deh-soo; I want to return home.)

When you tell someone what you want, you should end your statement with **-n-desu ga** (n-deh-soo gah). It injects a nice, friendly, and cooperative attitude into your statement. The function of **-n-desu** is to show your willingness to hear the other person's response to what you're saying. (See Chapter 5 for more on **-n-desu**.) The last **ga** is actually the sentence-ending particle that means *but*. So, you're literally saying *I want to do such and such, but*. What you actually mean is something like *I want to do such and such, but is it okay with you?*

Suppose you call a hotel to make a **yoyaku** (yoh-yah-koo; reservation). If you say **yoyaku o shitai desu** (yoh-yah-koo oh shee-tah-ee deh-soo), it just means *I want to make a reservation*. But, phrasing your statement this way sounds too blunt in Japanese, and you almost sound like you're making a protest or stating a demand. By contrast, if you say **yoyaku o shitai-n-desu ga** (yoh-yah-koo oh shee-tah-een-deh-soo gah), it means something like *I'd like to make a reservation, but could you help me with it?* Now, your statement sounds soft, and you're kindly inviting the hotel clerk's reply. I recommend that you use **-n-desu ga** whenever you call a store, restaurant, or hotel to tell them what you want. Check out these examples that contain a more realistic translation of two statements that use **-n-desu ga**:

- **Yoyaku o kakunin shitai-n-desu ga.** (yoh-yah-koo oh kah-koo-neen shee-tah-een-deh-soo gah; I'd like to confirm the reservation, but is it okay with you?)

- **Ēgyō jikan o shiritai-n-desu ga.** (ehh-gyohh jee-kahn oh shee-ree-tah-een-deh-soo gah; I'd like to know your business hours, but could you help me with this?)

Talkin' the Talk

Roberta Brown has just arrived at the Narita airport in Japan. She's trying to confirm her reservation at Hotel Yamato over the phone.

Clerk: **Hoteru Yamato de gozaimasu.**
             hoh-teh-roo yah-mah-toh deh goh-zah-ee-mah-soo.
             This is Hotel Yamato.

Roberta: **Yoyaku o kakunin shitai-n-desu ga.**
             yoh-yah-koo oh kah-koo-neen shee-tah-een-
             deh-soo gah.
             I'd like to confirm my reservation.

Clerk: **Hai, kashikomarimashita. O-namae wa.**
             hah-ee, kah-shee-koh-mah-ree-mah-shee-tah.
             oh-nah-mah-eh wah.
             Certainly. What's your name, ma'am?

Roberta: **Robāta Buraun desu.**
             roh-bahh-tah boo-rah-oon deh-soo.
             Roberta Brown.

Clerk: **Robāta Buraun sama de gozaimasu ne.**
             roh-bahh-tah boo-rah-oon sah-mah deh
             goh-zah-ee-mah-soo neh.
             Ms. Roberta Brown, is that correct?

Roberta: **Hai.**
             hah-ee.
             Yes.

Clerk: **Shōshō o-machi kudasai.**
             shohh-shohh oh-mah-chee koo-dah-sah-ee.
             Could you hold on please?

Roberta: **Hai.**
             hah-ee.
             Yes.

Clerk: **Moshimoshi. O-matase itashimashita. Buraun-sama
             de yoyaku wa gozaimasen ga.**
             moh-shee-moh-shee. oh-mah-tah-seh ee-tah-shee-
             mah-shee-tah. boo-rah-oon-sah-mah deh yoh-yah-
             koo wah goh-zah-ee-mah-sehn gah.
             Hello. Sorry to keep you waiting. I can't find your
             reservation though.

Roberta: **Ē.**
             ehh.
             What?

Wanting something

In *The Wizard of Oz,* the scarecrow *wants* a **chie** (chee-eh; brain), the tin man *wants* a **kokoro** (koh-koh-roh; heart), and the lion *wants* **yūki** (yooo-kee; courage). All right, back to reality. What do you *want* the most — **o-kane** (oh-kah-neh; money), **jikan** (jee-kahn; time), or **tomodachi** (toh-moh-dah-chee; friends)? Sometimes it's hard to have all of three at once.

To say that you *want* something, use the adjective (not the verb) **hoshii** (hoh-sheee; want) or its polite/neutral counterpart **hoshii desu** (hoh-sheee deh-soo). Place it at the end of the sentence and place the subject particle **ga** (gah) after the item that you want, as in **Watashi wa o-kane ga hoshii desu** (wah-tah-shee wah oh-kah-neh gah hoh-sheee deh-soo; I want money). The item that you want isn't the subject, but you need to use **ga** here. Now, I can ask you, **Nani ga hoshii desu ka** (nah-nee gah hoh-sheee deh-soo kah; What do you want?):

- ✔ **Watashi wa o-kane ga hoshii desu.** (wah-tah-shee wah oh-kah-neh gah hoh-sheee deh-soo; I want money.)

- ✔ **Jikan ga ichiban hoshii desu.** (jee-kahn gah ee-chee-bahn hoh-sheee deh-soo; I want time the most.)

- ✔ **Kuruma ga hoshii desu.** (koo-roo-mah gah hoh-sheee deh-soo; I want a car.)

Calling your client

If you're a businessperson, you probably call your **shigoto no o-kyaku-san** (shee-goh-toh noh oh-kyah-koo-sahn; business clients) constantly. And you probably know the important role telephone conversations play in maintaining good relationships. You don't want to sound pushy or arrogant. But you don't want to sound unsophisticated or unintelligent, either.

When you call your **shigoto no o-kyaku-san,** remember that you're representing your **kaisha** (kah-ee-shah; company) or **mise** (mee-seh; store). That's the Japanese way to make a business call. Don't forget to mention the name of your **kaisha** or **mise** first, before mentioning your own name. Instead of saying *This is Mr. White,* for example, say *This is ABC Technology's Mr. White.*

Greet your **o-kyaku-san** (oh-kyah-koo-sahn; client) and her **hisho** (hee-shoh; secretary) with **O-sewa ni natte orimasu** (oh-seh-wah nee naht-teh oh-ree-mah-soo; Thank you for doing business with us.). It's one of the essential set phrases in Japanese business.

And, when you ask for your call to be transferred to a specific person, don't forget to specify his title and department. This little tip is important, especially when more than one person in the company has the same last name.

Talkin' the Talk

Patrick White at ABC Technology has just prepared an estimate for his client, Mr. Tanaka, at the Yamato Kinzoku Company. Patrick is calling Mr. Tanaka to tell him about the estimate.

Secretary: **Yamato Kinzoku de gozaimasu.**
yah-mah-toh keen-zoh-koo deh goh-zah-ee-mah-soo.
This is Yamato Kinzoku Company.

Patrick: **Anō, ABC Tekunorojī no Howaito desu. Itsumo o-sewa ni natte orimasu.**
ah-nohh, ehh-beee-sheee teh-koo-noh-roh-jeee noh hoh-wah-ee-toh deh-soo. ee-tsoo-moh oh-seh-wah nee naht-te oh-ree-mah-soo.
This is Mr. White from ABC Technology. Thank you for doing business with us.

Secretary: **Kochira koso o-sewa ni natte orimasu.**
koh-chee-rah koh-soh oh-seh-wah nee naht-teh oh-ree-mah-soo.
Thank you, too.

Patrick: **Anō, ēgyō-bu no Tanaka buchō-sama wa irasshaimasu ka.**
ah-nohh, ehh-gyohh-boo noh tah-nah-kah boo-chohh-sah-mah wah ee-rahs-shah-ee-mah-soo ka.
Ahh, is Mr. Tanaka, the head of the sales department, available?

Secretary: **Hai, shōshō o-machi kudasai.**
hah-ee, shohh-shohh oh-mah-chee koo-dah-sah-ee.
Yes. Could you hold on please?

Patrick: **Hai.**
hah-ee.
Sure.

Tanaka: **Moshimoshi, Tanaka desu.**
moh-shee-moh-shee, tah-nah-kah deh-soo.
Hello, this is Mr. Tanaka speaking.

Patrick: **Ā, Tanaka-buchō. Howaito desu. Itsumo o-sewa ni natte orimasu.**
ahh, tah-nah-kah-boo-chohh. hoh-wah-ee-toh deh-soo. ee-tsoo-moh oh-seh-wah nee naht-teh oh-ree-mah-soo.
Oh, Division Chief Tanaka. This is Mr. White. I appreciate your doing business with us all this time.

Tanaka: **Īe, Īe. Kochira koso.**
eee-eh, eee-eh. koh-chee-rah koh-soh.
No, No. It is we who should say that.

Patrick: **Anō, mitsumorisho ga dekimashita.**
ah-nohh, mee-tsoo-moh-ree-shoh gah deh-kee-mah-shee-tah gah.
Well, the estimate is ready.

Words to Know

hisho	hee-shoh	secretary
kaisha	kah-ee-shah	company
mise	mee-seh	store
o-kyaku-san	oh-kyah-koo-sahn	customer/client
O-sewa ni natte orimasu.	oh-seh-wah nee naht-teh oh-ree-mah-soo	Thank you for doing business with us.

Leaving a Message

Talking to someone voice-to-voice can be very difficult nowadays. We often communicate by leaving **dengon** (dehn-gohn; messages) for each other while our **isogashii sēkatsu** (ee-soh-gah-sheee sehh-kah-tsoo; busy lives) keep going. You may leave a message on a **rusuban-denwa** (roo-soo-bahn-dehn-wah; answering machine), or you may leave a message with **dareka** (dah-reh-kah; someone).

Recording a message

When I get home, a few **dengon** are usually waiting for me on my **rusuban-denwa** (roo-soo-bahn-dehn-wah; answering machine). But most of the time when I try to return the calls, I end up leaving a **dengon** of my own! What do you do with a **dengon**? You **nokosu** (noh-koh-soo; leave) it. So, conjugate the verb **nokosu**. Remember, it means *to leave* in the sense of leaving a message, but not *to leave* in the sense of going away or departing. It's a u-verb.

Form	*Pronunciation*
nokosu	noh-koh-soo
nokosanai	noh-koh-sah-nah-ee
nokoshi	noh-koh-shee
nokoshite	noh-koh-shee-teh

A message between friends, Alex and Yukiko, may sound like this:

> **Moshimoshi. Yukiko-san. Arekkusu desu. Ashita isshoni ēga o mimasen ka. Yokattara o-denwa o kudasai. 03-3355-5532 desu. Dōmo.**
>
> moh-shee-moh-shee. yoo-kee-koh-sahn. ah-rehk-koo-soo deh-soo. ah-shee-tah ees-shoh-nee ehh-gah oh mee-mah-sehn kah. yoh-kaht-tah-rah oh-dehn-wah oh koo-dah-sah-ee. zeh-roh-sahn sahn-sahn-goh-goh goh-goh-sahn-nee deh-soo. dohh-moh.
>
> Hello Yukiko. This is Alex. Would you like to see a movie with me tomorrow? Please call me at 03-3355-5532 if it's okay with you. Thanks.

When you leave a message on an answering machine, clarify which person will call the other back:

- ✔ **Kaettara denwa o kudasai.** (kah-eht-tah-rah dehn-wah oh koo-dah-sah-ee; When you get back, please give me a call.)

- ✔ **Mata denwa o shimasu.** (mah-tah dehn-wah oh shee-mah-soo; I'll call you again.)

- ✔ **Yokattara o-denwa o kudasai.** (yoh-kaht-tah-rah oh-dehn-wah oh koo-dah-sah-ee; If you don't mind, could you give me a call?)

Leaving a message with a person

When you leave a message with a person, be clear about what you want. If you're leaving a message for a business contact, use polite phrases, such as the following:

- ✔ **Denwa ga atta koto o o-tsutae kudasai.** (dehn-wah gah aht-tah koh-toh oh oh-tsoo-tah-eh koo-dah-sah-ee; Please tell him/her that I called.)

- ✔ **Mata kochira kara o-denwa o itashimasu.** (mah-tah koh-chee-rah kah-rah oh-dehn-wah oh ee-tah-shee-mah-soo; I will call him/her again.)

- ✔ **O-denwa o itadakitai-n-desu ga.** (oh-dehn-wah oh ee-tah-dah-kee-tah-een-deh-soo gah; Would you kindly ask him/her to please call me back?)

- ✔ **Sukoshi okureru to tsutaete kudasai.** (soo-koh-shee oh-koo-reh-roo toh tsoo-tah-eh-teh koo-dah-sah-ee; Please tell him/her that I'll be a little late.)

The particle **to**, as in **"to tsutaete kudasai"** from the following Talkin' the Talk section, is a quotation particle. Place it right after your message to indicate what your message is. Use it with verbs like **iu** (ee-oo; to say), **kaku** (kah-koo; to write), and **tsutaeru** (tsoo-tah-eh-roo; to report/tell), as in the following examples:

- ✔ **10,000-en karita to kakimashita.** (ee-chee-mahn-ehn kah-ree-tah toh kah-kee-mah-shee-tah; I wrote that I borrowed 10,000 yen.)

- ✔ **Tanaka-san wa kuru to īmashita.** (tah-nah-kah-sahn wah koo-roo toh eee-mah-shee-tah; Mr. Tanaka said that he will come.)

- ✔ **Mata kimasu to tsutaete kudasai.** (mah-tah kee-mah-soo toh tsoo-tah-eh-teh koo-dah-sah-ee; Could you tell him/her that I'll come again?)

Go- (goh) is another polite prefix, just like **o-** (oh), which I discuss in Chapter 3. You can add **go-** to the beginning of a noun to refer respectfully to other people's items. Whether you should use **go-** or **o-** depends on the noun, and you just have to memorize which prefix goes with which nouns. Check out some examples:

- ✔ **go-dengon** (goh-dehn-gohn; message)

- ✔ **go-shōtai** (goh-shohh-tah-ee; invitation)

- ✔ **o-denwa** (oh-dehn-wah; telephone)

- ✔ **o-mizu** (oh-mee-zoo; water)

- ✔ **o-sake** (oh-sah-keh; rice wine *or* alcoholic beverage in general)

Talkin' the Talk

Mr. Isobe of A&A Company wants to visit his client, Ms. Takahashi, at Yamakawa Denki Company tomorrow morning. He's calling her company, but she's unavailable, so Mr. Isobe leaves a message with her secretary.

Secretary: **Yamakawa Denki de gozaimasu.**
yah-mah-kah-wa dehn-kee deh goh-zah-ee-mah-soo.
This is Yamakawa Denki Company.

Mr. Isobe: **A&A no Isobe desu ga, Takahashi-sama wa irasshaimasu ka.**
ehh-ahn-doh-ehh noh ee-soh-beh deh-soo gah, tah-kah-hah-shee-sah-mah wah ee-rahs-shah-ee-mah-soo kah.
This is Mr. Isobe from A&A. Is Ms. Takahashi available?

Secretary: **Ainiku gaishutsuchū desu. Nanika go-dengon wa.**
ah-ee-nee-koo gah-ee-shoo-tsoo-chooo deh-soo.
nah-nee-kah goh-dehn-gohn wah.
Unfortunately, she is not here. May I take a message?

Mr. Isobe: **Jā, ashita mata denwa o shimasu to tsutaete kudasai.**
jahh, ah-shee-tah mah-tah dehn-wah oh shee-mah-soo
toh tsoo-tah-eh-teh koo-dah-sah-ee.
Yes, could you tell her that I'll call her again tomorrow?

Secretary: **Hai, kashikomarimashita.**
hah-ee, kah-shee-koh-mah-ree-mah-shee-tah.
Certainly.

Mr. Isobe: **Jā, yoroshiku onegai shimasu.**
jahh, yoh-roh-shee-koo oh-neh-gah-ee shee-mah-soo.
Thank you for doing me a favor.

Fun & Games

Match each of the Japanese phrases to the correct English phrase. Turn to Appendix C for the answers.

1. Hold on please.

2. Shall I take a message?

3. Hello.

4. I'll call him again.

5. Sorry to have kept you waiting.

a. **Moshimoshi.**

b. **Go-dengon wa.**

c. **Mata o-denwa shimasu.**

d. **O-matase shimashita.**

e. **Shōshō o-machi kudasai.**

Chapter 10

At the Office and Around the House

• •

In This Chapter

▶ Managing yourself at the office

▶ Landing your dream job

▶ Hanging out at home

▶ Furnishing your pad

• •

*I*f you're a workaholic and you spend a lot of time in your **jimusho** (jee-moo-shoh; office), you should make your surroundings as homey and comfortable as possible. If you're more of a homebody and you spend a lot of time in your **ie** (ee-eh; house) or **apāto** (ah-pahh-toh; apartment), try decorating it using your own personal sense of style. But remember to make it cozy!

In major Japanese cities, most offices, houses, and apartments are very **semai** (seh-mah-ee; small). But most people get used to the small rooms and tiny pieces of furniture in a week or so. If you visit Japan, you may even find the cramped quarters convenient — you can reach everything in your room by simply stretching your arms a bit. According to Mr. Darwin, only those who are able to adapt to their environment survive. That's the spirit I like. I'm happy anywhere!

Managing Your Office Environment

If you're a **sēshain** (sehh-shah-een; full-time employee), you probably spend about one-third of your time at the office. Why not make your **shokuba** (shoh-koo-bah; work place) as **igokochi ii** (ee-goh-koh-chee eee; comfortable) as possible? Make it a point to **nakayoku suru** (nah-kah-yoh-koo soo-roo; get along) with your **dōryō** (dohh-ryohh; colleagues). And do an **ii shigoto** (eee shee-goh-toh; good job) so that you can be proud of yourself (and you can keep the boss off of your back).

Supplying your office

While you're sitting in your **isu** (ee-soo; chair) at your **tsukue** (tsoo-koo-eh; desk), take a look around. What do you have on your desktop? What don't you have?

- **denwa** (dehn-wah; telephone)
- **fakushimiri** (fah-koo-shee-mee-ree; fax machine)
- **konpyūtā** (kohn-pyooo-tahh; computer)
- **kopīki** (koh-peee-kee; copier)
- **purintā** (poo-reen-tahh; printer)

Check inside your **hikidashi** (hee-kee-dah-shee; drawers) to see what office supplies you have.

- **bōrupen** (bohh-roo-pehn; ballpoint pen)
- **enpitsu** (ehn-pee-tsoo; pencil)
- **hochikisu** (hoh-chee-kee-soo; stapler)
- **keshigomu** (keh-shee-goh-moo; eraser)
- **nōto** (nohh-toh; notebook)
- **nori** (noh-ree; glue)
- **shāpen** (shahh-pehn; mechanical pencil)
- **serotēpu** (seh-roh-tehh-poo; tape)

If you can't find a pen, an eraser, or a paper clip, ask a colleague. He or she probably has one that you can use. Use the verb **aru** (ah-roo; to exist) to ask *Do you have?* It's strange to use the verb *to exist* in this case, isn't it? (To see more examples of this strange use of the verb **aru,** see Chapter 4.) Add the polite suffix **-masu** (mah-soo), to the stem form of **aru,** as in **arimasu** (ah-ree-mah-soo), and make the phrase into a question by adding the question particle **ka** (kah), as in **arimasu ka** (ah-ree-mah-soo kah). But, if you just ask someone **arimasu ka,** he or she won't understand what you want. Mention the item you're asking about at the very beginning of the sentence. And place the topic particle **wa** (wah) right after the item that you're inquiring about. Now you can start bothering your colleagues:

- **Hochikisu wa arimasu ka.** (hoh-chee-kee-soo wah ah-ree-mah-soo kah; Do you have a stapler?)
- **Keshigomu wa arimasu ka.** (keh-shee-goh-moo wah ah-ree-mah-soo kah; Do you have an eraser?)

Talkin' the Talk

Patrick is working at the office. He checked in his drawer, but he couldn't find a pen. He's about to borrow one from a colleague.

Patrick: **Sumimasen. Pen wa arimasu ka.**
soo-mee-mah-sehn. pehn wah ah-ree-mah-soo kah.
Excuse me. Do you have a pen?

Colleague: **Hai, arimasu yo. Dōzo.**
hah-ee, ah-ree-mah-soo yoh. dohh-zoh.
Yes, I do. Here you are.

Patrick: **Dōmo.**
dohh-moh.
Thank you.

Words to Know

bōrupen	bohh-roo pehn	ballpoint pen
enpitsu	ehn-pee-tsoo	pencil
hochikisu	hoh-chee-kee-soo	stapler
jimusho	jee-moo-shoh	office
jōshi	johh-shee	boss
tsukue	tsoo-koo-eh	desk

Searching for a great job

When you **sagasu** (sah-gah-soo; look for) a **shigoto** (shee-goh-toh; job), you need to get ready for the **mensetsu** (mehn-seh-tsoo; interview). Be prepared to talk about your **shokureki** (shoh-koo-reh-kee; work history) and your career goals. Before you accept a job, check out all the **jōken** (johh-kehn; conditions) and benefits that go along with the position. I hope you're not so desperate that you have to take the job no matter what.

Conjugate the verb **sagasu** (sah-gah-soo; to look for) and go **sagasu** a good **shigoto! Sagasu** is a u-verb.

Form	Pronunciation
sagasu	sah-gah-soo
sagasanai	sah-gah-sah-nah-ee
sagashi	sah-gah-shee
sagashite	sah-gah-shee-teh

Some of the issues you probably want to address are:

- **kenkō hoken** (kehn-kohh hoh-kehn; health insurance)

- **kyūjitsu shukkin** (kyooo-jee-tsoo shook-keen; working on a holiday)

- **kyūryō** (kyooo-ryohh; salary)

- **shotokuzē** (shoh-toh-koo-zehh; income tax)

- **yūkyūkyūka** (yooo-kyooo-kyooo-kah; paid vacation)

- **zangyō** (zahn-gyohh; overtime)

- **zangyō teate** (zahn-gyohh teh-ah-teh; overtime pay)

Talkin' the Talk

Takeshi Sakai is desperately looking for a job. He's in the middle of his 19th job interview this month!

Interviewer: **Kyūryō wa amari takaku arimasen ga.**
kyooo-ryohh wah ah-mah-ree tah-kah-koo ah-ree-mah-sehn ga.
Your salary won't be great, though.

Takeshi: **Ii desu.**
eee deh-soo.
That's okay.

Interviewer: **Kenkō hoken mo arimasen yo.**
kehn-kohh hoh-kehn moh ah-ree-mah-sehn yo.
And you won't get health insurance either.

Takeshi: **Sore wa chotto komarimasu. Kodomo ga san-nin imasu kara.**
soh-reh wah choht-toh koh-mah-ree-mah-soo.
koh-doh-moh gah sahn-neen ee-mah-soo kah-rah.
That's a problem because I have three children.

Interviewer: **Ā, sō desu ka. Sore wa komarimasu ne.**
                 ahh, sohh deh-soo kah. soh-reh wah
                 koh-mah-ree-mah-soo neh.
                 Oh, really. That will be a problem.

In Japanese, you don't say *because I have three children;* you say *I have three children because,* as Takeshi does in the previous dialogue. You use the particle **kara** (kah-rah; because) as the final particle in the phrase.

Here are a few more examples:

- ✔ **Mensetsu o ukemasu kara, sūtsu o kaimasu.** (mehn-seh-tsoo oh oo-keh-mah-soo kah-rah, sooo-tsoo oh kah-ee-mah-soo; Because I'm going to have an interview, I'll buy a suit.)

- ✔ **Takai desu kara, kaimasen.** (tah-kah-ee deh-soo kah-rah, kah-ee-mah-sehn; Because it is expensive, I won't buy it.)

Words to Know

kenkō hoken	kehn-kohh hoh-kehn	health insurance
komaru	koh-mah-roo	to be in trouble
kyūryō	kyooo-ryohh	salary
sagasu [u]	sah-gah-soo	to look for
shigoto	shee-goh-toh	job

Clarifying your duties

When you're searching for a new job, it's always a good idea to clarify the duties, responsibilities, and obligations associated with the position. Even after you start working in a new place, you'll have to constantly figure out what you have to do each day. This section shows you how to figure out your duties in Japanese. Go ahead and start **hataraku** (hah-tah-rah-koo; working)!

Addressing your boss appropriately

Japan is very modern, but a shadow of feudalism still falls on the **shokuba** (shoh-koo-bah; workplace). **Buka** (boo-kah; subordinates) never address their **jōshi** (johh-shee; superiors) by their first names. If you work in Japan, address your **jōshi** using their titles and last names. So, if your **jōshi** is the **shachō** (shah-chohh; company president) and his last name is Smith, call him **Sumisu-shachō.** Address your **buka** by their last names, plus **-san** or **-kun.** In a business context, both **-san** (sahn) and **-kun** (koon) can be used for women and men. So, if Mr. Smith is your assistant, call him **Sumisu-san** (soo-mee-soo-sahn) or **Sumisu-kun** (soo-mee-soo-koon).

Some titles Japanese companies use are:

- **buchō** (boo-chohh; department chief)
- **fukushachō** (foo-koo-shah-chohh; company vice-president)
- **kachō** (kah-chohh; section chief)
- **kakarichō** (kah-kah-ree-chohh; subsection chief)
- **shachō** (shah-chohh; company president)

Conjugate the verb **hataraku** (hah-tah-rah-koo; to work). It's a u-verb.

Form	*Pronunciation*
hataraku	hah-tah-rah-koo
hatarakanai	hah-tah-rah-kah-nah-ee
hataraki	hah-tah-rah-kee
hataraite	hah-tah-rah-ee-teh

Now, it's time to find out about your duties and responsibilities. For starters, you can use these phrases:

- **Watashi no shigoto wa nan desu ka.** (wah-tah-shee noh shee-goh-toh wah nahn deh-soo kah; What is my job?)

- **Doyōbi mo hatarakanakute wa ikemasen ka.** (doh-yohh-bee mo hah-tah-rah-kah-nah-koo-teh wah ee-keh-mah-sehn kah; Do I have to work on Saturdays too?)

- **Sōji wa watashi no shigoto desu ka.** (sohh-jee wah wah-tah-shee noh shee-goh-toh deh-soo kah; Is cleaning my job?)

When you discuss an obligation and you need to use the phrase *I have to* or *I must,* use the verb in the negative form (see the Cheat Sheet or Chapter 2 for more on verb forms) and change it a bit: Drop the final **i** (ee) from the negative form and add **-kute wa ikemasen** (koo-teh wah ee-keh-mah-sehn) or **-kutewa ikenai** (koo-teh wah ee-keh-nah-ee). For example, the negative form of **taberu** (tah-beh-roo) is **tabenai** (tah-beh-nah-ee). By dropping the **i** from **tabenai** and adding -**kute wa ikemasen,** you get **tabenakute wa ikemasen** (tah-beh-nah-koo-teh wah ee-keh-mah-sehn), which means *I have to eat.* It's long, I admit that, but it's the easiest way to express *have to* or *must* in Japanese. Take a look at these examples:

- ✔ **Ii shigoto o sagasanakute wa ikemasen.** (eee shee-goh-toh oh sah-gah-sah-nah-koo-teh wah ee-keh-mah-sehn; I have to look for a good job.)

- ✔ **Kyō wa zangyō o shinakute wa ikenai-n-desu.** (kyohh wa zahn-gyohh oh shee-nah-koo-teh wah ee-keh-nah-een-deh-soo; I have to work over-time today.)

- ✔ **Mō kaeranakute wa ikemasen ka.** (mohh kah-eh-rah-nah-koo-teh wah ee-keh-mah-sehn kah; Do you have to go home already?)

You can express a ton of activities using the verb **suru** (soo-roo; to do), including many job-related actions. (See Chapter 8 for a detailed discussion of uses for **suru.**) Here are a few **suru** phrases that may come up in your workplace:

- ✔ **chekku suru** (chehk-koo-soo-roo; to check)

- ✔ **fakkusu suru** (fahk-koo-soo soo-roo; to fax)

- ✔ **kopī suru** (koh-peee soo-roo; to make copies)

- ✔ **sōji suru** (sohh-jee soo-roo; to clean)

Talkin' the Talk

Two colleagues, Mr. Ogawa and Mr. Mihara, are making plans for after work.

Ogawa: **Kyō kaeri ni isshoni nomimasen ka.**
kyohh kah-eh-ree nee ees-shoh-nee noh-mee-mah-sehn ka.
Why don't we have a drink together on the way home today?

Mihara: **Īe, kyō wa zangyō o shinakute wa ikenai-n-desu.**
eee-eh, kyohh wah zahn-gyohh oh shee-nah-koo-teh wah ee-keh-nah-een-deh-soo.
No. I have to work overtime today.

Ogawa: **Ano mitsumorisho desu ka.**
ah-noh mee-tsoo-moh-ree-shoh deh-soo kah.
On that estimate?

Mihara :	**Hai.**
	hah-ee.
	Yes.
Ogawa:	**Jā, tetsudaimasu.**
	jahh, teh-tsoo-dah-ee-mah-soo.
	Then I'll help you.
Mihara:	**Sō desu ka. Arigatō gozaimasu.**
	sohh deh-soo kah. ah-ree-gah-tohh
	goh-zah-ee-mah-soo.
	Really? Thank you.

Living the Good Life at Home

After moving to a new **machi** (mah-chee; town), the first thing that you need to do is to find a **sumu tokoro** (soo-moo toh-koh-roh; place to live). Finding a nice **apāto** (ah-pahh-toh; apartment) can solve all your problems. Pick out some trendy **kagu** (kah-goo; furniture). Greet your new **otonari-san** (oh-toh-nah-ree-sahn; next-door neighbor) and introduce yourself. Don't forget to invite your **tomodachi** (toh-moh-dah-chee; friends) over to your new **uchi** (oo-chee; home)! But you may want to wait until the boxes and crumpled-up newspapers aren't piled to the ceiling.

Finding an apartment

If you're a student, you may live in a **ryō** (ryohh; dormitory), an **apāto** (ah-pahh-toh; apartment), or even a **manshon** (mahn-shohn; condominium). Down the road, you may eventually want to buy your own **ie** (ee-eh; house).

Although it looks and sounds like *mansion*, **manshon** (mahn-shohn) does not mean a huge, luxurious house. It means an apartment in a relatively new multistory building. You can either rent or purchase a **manshon.**

If you need help **mitsukeru** (mee-tsoo-keh-roo; finding) a nice apartment, condo, or house, you can always talk to a **fudōsanya-san** (foo-dohh-sahn-yah-sahn; real estate agent). I hope you find a great place. Conjugate the verb **mitsukeru** (mee-tsoo-keh-roo; to find) for good luck. It's a ru-verb.

Form	*Pronunciation*
mitsukeru	mee-tsoo-keh-roo
mitsukenai	mee-tsoo-keh-nah-ee
mitsuke	mee-tsoo-keh
mitsukete	mee-tsoo-keh-teh

Talkin' the Talk

Jenny is looking for an apartment in a convenient, downtown location, possibly near the railway station. She decides to visit a real estate agent.

Agent: **Yachin wa ikura gurai.**
yah-cheen wa ee-koo-rah goo-rah-ee.
What is your price range for the rent?

Jenny: **Nanahyaku-doru ika desu.**
nah-nah-hyah-koo-doh-roo ee-kah deh-soo.
Seven hundred dollars or less.

Agent: **Jā, kore wa. Kore wa shinshitsu futa-tsu desu yo.**
jahh, koh-reh wah. koh-reh wah sheen-shee-tsoo
foo-tah-tsoo deh-soo yoh.
Okay. How about this? This one has two bedrooms.

Jenny : **Eki no chikaku desu ka.**
eh-kee noh chee-kah-koo deh-soo kah.
Is it near the train station?

Agent: **Eki made kuruma de 25-fun.**
eh-kee mah-deh koo-roo-mah deh
nee-jooo-goh-foon.
It's 25 minutes from the station by car.

Jenny: **Dame desu. Watashi wa kuruma ga nai-n-desu.**
dah-meh deh-soo. wah-tah-shee wah koo-roo-mah
gah nah-een-deh-soo.
No way. I don't have a car.

Agent: **Jā, kuruma o katte kudasai yo.**
jahh, koo-roo-mah oh kaht-teh koo-dah-sah-ee yoh.
Well, buy a car please.

Words to Know

ijō	ee-johh	or more
ika	ee-kah	or less
apāto	ah-pahh-toh	apartment
fudōsanya-san	foo-dohh-sahn-yah-sahn	real estate agent
ie	ee-eh	house
mitsukeru [ru]	mee-tsoo-keh-roo	to find
yachin	yah-cheen	rent

Naming that room

Think about your **apāto** (ah-pahh-toh; apartment) or **ie** (ee-eh; house). How many **heya** (heh-yah; rooms) does it have?

- ✔ **daidokoro** (dah-ee-doh-koh-roh; kitchen)
- ✔ **genkan** (gehn-kahn; foyer)
- ✔ **ima** (ee-mah; living room)
- ✔ **shinshitsu** (sheen-shee-tsoo; bedroom)
- ✔ **shokudō** (shoh-koo-dohh; dining room)

And look around the house. Do you have any of these?

- ✔ **hē** (hehh; fence)
- ✔ **maeniwa** (mah-eh-nee-wah; front yard)
- ✔ **shako** (shah-koh; garage)
- ✔ **uraniwa** (oo-rah-nee-wah; backyard)

Most Japanese apartments and houses have at least one **washitsu** (wah-shee-tsoo; Japanese-style room) with a **tatami** (tah-tah-mee; straw mat) floor. Most Japanese houses also have separate **o-furoba** (oh-foo-roh-bah; bathrooms) where you bathe and **toire** (toh-ee-reh; toilet rooms), although newer houses have Western-style bathrooms with both a toilet and bathtub.

Getting furniture

After you find a new apartment, you need to figure out where to put all of your **kagu** (kah-goo; furniture). If you're moving to a smaller place, you may have to give up some of your stuff. If you're moving to a larger place, you may have to go out and buy additional furniture. I think the shopping option sounds like the better choice. What **kagu** do you have, and what don't you have?

- **beddo** (behd-doh; bed)
- **honbako** (hohn-bah-koh; bookcase)
- **isu** (ee-soo; chair)
- **kyōdai** (kyohh-dah-ee; dresser)
- **sofā** (soh-fahh; couch)
- **tēburu** (tehh-boo-roo; table)
- **terebidai** (teh-reh-bee-dah-ee; TV stand)

Denki sēhin (dehn-kee sehh-heen; electric appliances) really make life **benri** (behn-ree; convenient). We have the scientists who discovered **denki** (dehn-kee; electricity) to thank for these wonderful gadgets. Don't forget to pay the **denkidai** (dehn-kee-dah-ee; electricity bill), or you'll have to reheat that tuna casserole over an open flame in the backyard.

- **denshi renji** (dehn-shee rehn-jee; microwave)
- **kansōki** (kahn-sohh-kee; dryer)
- **konro** (kohn-roh; stove)
- **kūrā** (kooo-rahh; air conditioner)
- **ōbun** (ohh-boon; oven)
- **rēzōko** (rehh-zohh-koh; refrigerator)
- **sara-araiki** (sah-rah-ah-rah-ee-kee; dishwasher)
- **sentakuki** (sehn-tah-koo-kee; washing machine)
- **sutereo** (soo-teh-reh-oh; stereo)
- **sutōbu** (soo-tohh-boo; space heater)
- **terebi** (teh-reh-bee; television)

Talkin' the Talk

Marge has had a backache for three weeks, and she's complaining about it to Sachiko.

Marge: **Mō san-shūkan koshi ga itai-n-desu.**
mohh sahn-shooo-kahn koh-shee gah ee-tah-een-deh-soo.
I've been having back pain for three weeks now.

Sachiko: **Beddo ga warui kamoshirenai yo.**
behd-doh gah wah-roo-ee kah-moh-shee-reh-nah-ee yoh.
Your bed may be bad.

Marge: **Ē, sō kamoshirenai.**
ehh, sohh kah-moh-shee-reh-nah-ee.
Yes, that may be.

Sachiko: **Futon ni nenai.**
foo-tohn nee neh-nah-ee.
Why don't you sleep on a futon?

Marge: **Sore nani.**
soh-reh nah-nee.
What's that?

Sachiko: **Nihon no mattoresu yo.**
nee-hohn noh maht-toh-reh-soo yoh.
It's a Japanese mattress.

CULTURAL WISDOM

Futon

Futons recently have become a trendy piece of furniture in the West. Like most cultural imports, however, the real thing is quite a bit different. For starters Japanese **futon** isn't pronounced *foo-tahn*, as you may be accustomed to, but *foo-tohn*, with an "o" sound in the second syllable.

A Western futon is just the mattress you sleep on — the comforter or blankets you use to keep warm are separate items. In Japan, however, both the matress and covering make up a **futon**.

At night, you lay out your **futon** on the floor, and in the morning, you fold it up and put in a closet. The same room can serve as a bedroom at night and as a living room during the day — quite convenient in a country where space is at a premium. If sleeping on the floor seems a little uncomfortable, rest assured that a Japanese **futon** is actually quite comfortable, and it gives you a good night's rest. On top of that, sleeping on a **futon** is good for your back as well.

If you aren't so sure about something, but you think *maybe* or *possibly,* say it with the verb suffix **kamoshiremasen** or with the informal version, **kamoshirenai.** For example, **taberu kamoshiremasen** (tah-beh-roo kah-moh-shee-reh-mah-sehn) and **taberu kamoshirenai** (tah-beh-roo kah-moh-shee-reh-nah-ee) both mean *he may eat.* Add the verb suffix to the plain/informal verb form.

Conjugate the verb **neru** (neh-roo; to sleep). It's a ru-verb.

Form	Pronunciation
neru	neh-roo
nenai	neh-nah-ee
ne	neh
nete	neh-teh

Words to Know

beddo	behd-doh	bed
denki sēhin	dehn-kee sehh-heen	electric appliances
futon	foo-tohn	futon (Japanese mattress and bedding)
heya	heh-yah	room
kagu	kah-goo	furniture
neru[ru]	neh-roo	to sleep

Keeping your apartment safe

You don't want to have a **kaji** (kah-jee; fire) while you're sleeping or a **dorobō** (doh-roh-bohh; thief) break into your home when you're on vacation. Go over the following checklist when you go out and when you go to bed:

 ✔ **danbō o kiru** (dahn-bohh oh kee-roo; to shut off the heat)

 ✔ **dengen o kiru** (dehn-gehn oh kee-roo; to shut off the power supply)

- **doa no kagi o kakeru** (doh-ah noh kah-gee oh kah-keh-roo; to lock the door)
- **denki o kesu** (dehn-kee oh keh-soo; to turn off the light)
- **gasu no motosen o shimeru** (gah-soo noh moh-toh-sehn oh shee-meh-roo; to close the main gas valve)
- **mado o shimeru** (mah-doh oh shee-meh-roo; to close the window)
- **tōsutā no konsento o nuku** (tohh-soo-tahh noh kohn-sehn-toh oh noo-koo; to unplug the toaster)

Keeping your home clean

Keeping your home **kirē** (kee-rehh; clean) can make life a lot more comfortable. A clean apartment can also keep your **ōya-san** (ohh-yah-sahn; landlord *or* landlady) happy. You may use these phrases as you do your weekly, or yearly, **sōji** (sohh-jee; cleaning):

- **heya o katazukeru** (heh-yah oh kah-tah-zoo-keh-roo; to tidy up the room)
- **mado o fuku** (mah-doh oh foo-koo; to clean the windows)
- **sōjiki o kakeru** (sohh-jee-kee oh kah-keh-roo; to vacuum)
- **yuka o fuku** (yoo-kah oh foo-koo; to mop the floor)

Mitai, which Michiko uses in the next Talkin' the Talk section, is similar to *like* or *as* in English. You use it to compare a person or thing to someone or something else. If you want to brag about your daughter's intelligence (which would be a very rude thing to do in Japan), you might say, "My daughter is like Einstein." The following examples give you more of a taste for this concept.

- **Richādo wa Nihonjin mitai desu.** (ree-chahh-doh wah nee-hohn-jeen mee-tah-ee deh-soo; Richard is like a Japanese.)
- **Watashi no sensē wa tenshi mitai desu.** (wah-tah-shee noh sehn-sehh wah tehn-shee mee-tah-ee deh-soo; My teacher is just like an angel.)

Talkin' the Talk

David is talking with his friend, Michiko, about Janet's house.

David: **Michiko wa Janetto no uchi ni itta.**
mee-chee-koh wah jah-neht-toh noh oo-chee nee eet-tah.
Michiko, have you been to Janet's house?

Michiko: **Īe, mada.**
             eee-eh, mah-dah.
             Not yet.

David: **Sugoku kirē. Soreni, jūtan ga shiroi.**
             soo-goh-koo kee-rehh. soh-reh-nee, jooo-tahn gah
             shee-roh-ee.
             It's immaculate. And she has a white carpet.

Michiko: **Hē.**
             hehh.
             Really?

David: **Uchi no naka wa kutsu wa genkin.**
             oo-chee noh nah-kah wah koo-tsoo wah gehn-keen.
             No shoes allowed in the house.

Michiko: **Nihonjin mitai.**
             nee-hohn-jeen mee-tah-ee.
             She's like a Japanese.

When you enter Japanese homes, make sure you **nugu** (noo-goo; take off) your **kutsu** (koo-tsoo; shoes). Before you visit, repair the **ana** (ahn-nah; holes) in your **kutsushita** (koo-tsoo-shee-tah; socks) if you don't want to be embarrassed. Usually, you'll be asked to wear **surippa** (soo-reep-pah; slippers) right after you enter the house. You can wear slippers anywhere inside the house except in **tatami** (tah-tah-mee; straw mat) floored rooms. You have to take off your slippers before entering **tatami** rooms.

Words to Know

jūtan	jooo-tahn	carpet/rug
kirē	kee-rehh	clean/beautiful/tidy
sōji	sohh-jee	cleaning

Fun & Games

• •

Name each of these pictured rooms and items in the house in Japanese. Check Appendix C for the answers.

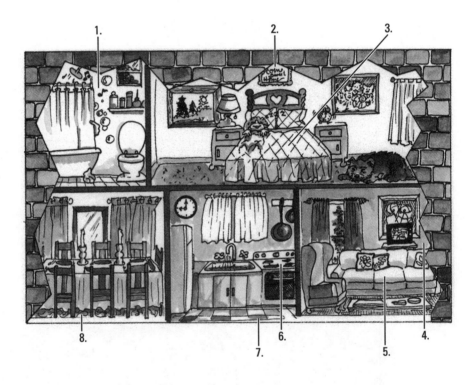

1. _____   5. _____

2. _____   6. _____

3. _____   7. _____

4. _____   8. _____

• •

Part III
Japanese on the Go

The 5th Wave   By Rich Tennant

Now c'mon Darryl. Japanese grammatical order is subject-object-verb. Not smile-point-shrug.

In this part . . .

1n Part III, you can escape that nine-to-five life and travel the globe. Are you ready to plan a trip, reserve a hotel, find transportation, ask directions, go through customs, exchange currency, and handle emergencies? Are you ready to do it all in Japanese? This part gets you ready for the fun, and the logistical, aspects of travel. **Yoi tabi o** (yoh-ee tah-bee oh; Have a nice trip!).

Chapter 11

Money, Money, Money

• •

In This Chapter

▶ Visiting the bank

▶ Withdrawing money from the ATM

▶ Paying with cold, hard cash

▶ Burning up the plastic

• •

Kane wa tenka no mawari mono (kah-neh wah tehn-kah noh mah-wah-ree-moh-noh; Money goes around the world.). This Japanese proverb means that the **o-kane** (oh-kah-neh; money) you spend today will come back to you in the future. You buy other people's products, but they also buy yours. Use your **o-kane** to make yourself, your family, and your friends happy.

In this chapter, I give you important words and phrases for handling **o-kane.** The information explains how to acquire and spend **o-kane** in Japanese.

Getting Money

You have to work if you want to make **o-kane** (oh-kah-neh; money), unless your parents or grandparents are extremely rich. But I'm not concerned about where your income comes from in this section. What I'm concerned about is how you access your money. You can get your money from an ATM machine, a foreign-currency exchange counter, or a bank. I know you have some under your mattress too. Oh, not under your mattress? Then, where is it? You can tell me.

Exchanging money

If you're in Japan, the **en** (ehn; yen) is the only acceptable **tsūka** (tsooo-kah; currency). Don't say *yen;* say **en.** Drop that *y* sound. You can **ryōgae suru** (ryohh-gah-eh soo-roo; exchange) your money for **en** at the **kūkō** (kooo-kohh; airport) or at major **ginkō** (geen-kohh; banks). Check out Table 11-1 and find the **gaika** (gah-ee-kah; foreign currency) that you have in your pocket.

Table 11-1	Currencies	
Currency	*Pronunciation*	*Translation*
Amerika doru	ah-meh-ree-kah doh-roo	U.S. dollar
Chūgoku gen	chooo-goh-koo gehn	Chinese yuan
Igirisu pondo	ee-gee-ree-soo pohn-doh	British pound
Kanada doru	kah-nah-dah doh-roo	Canadian dollar
Mekishiko peso	meh-kee-shee-koh peh-soh	Mexican peso
Ōsutoraria doru	ohh-soo-toh-rah-ree-ah doh-roo	Australian dollar
yūro	yooo-roh	European Union euro

Ask for the current **kawase rēto** (kah-wah-seh rehh-toh; exchange rate) and **ryōgae suru** (ryohh-gah-eh soo-roo; exchange) your currency for **en.** The following phrases may be helpful:

✔ **Gaika no ryōgae wa dekimasu ka.** (gah-ee-kah noh ryohh-gah-eh wah deh-kee-mah-soo kah; Can you exchange foreign currency?)

✔ **Ima ichi-doru nan-en desu ka.** (ee-mah ee-chee-doh-roo nahn-ehn deh-soo kah; How many yen for a dollar now?)

✔ **Kyō no kawase rēto o oshiete kudasai.** (kyohh noh kah-wah-seh rehh-toh oh oh-shee-eh-teh koo-dah-sah-ee; Please let me know today's exchange rate.)

✔ **Amerika doru o en ni ryōgae shi-tai-n-desu ga.** (ah-meh-ree-kah doh-roo oh ehn nee ryohh-gah-eh shee-tah-een-deh-soo gah; I'd like to exchange some American dollars for yen, is that okay?)

✔ **500-doru o en ni ryōgae shite kudasai.** (goh-hyah-koo-doh-roo oh ehn nee ryohh-gah-eh shee-teh koo-dah-sah-ee; Please exchange 500 dollars for yen.)

Some of the responses you may get when you exchange currency are:

✔ **Kai wa ichi-doru 123-en, uri wa ichi-doru 130 en desu.** (kah-ee wa ee-chee-doh-roo hyah-koo-nee-jooo-sahn-ehn, oo-ree wah ee-chee-doh-roo hyah-koo-sahn-jooo-ehn deh-soo; For exchanging dollars for yen, you get 123 yen for a dollar, and for exchanging yen for dollars, 130 yen equals a dollar.)

✔ **Tesūryō wa fukumarete imasu.** (teh-sooo-ryohh wah foo-koo-mah-reh-teh ee-mah-soo; The fee is already included.)

✔ **Kyō no kawase rēto wa kinō to onaji desu.** (kyohh noh kah-wah-seh rehh-toh wah kee-nohh toh oh-nah-jee deh-soo; Today's exchange rate is the same as yesterday's.)

Talkin' the Talk

Natalie has just arrived at Narita Airport in Tokyo, and she's about to exchange her U.S. dollars for Japanese yen at the exchange counter.

Natalie: **Sumimasen. Amerika doru kara en no ryōgae wa dekimasu ka.**
soo-mee-mah-sehn. ah-meh-ree-kah doh-roo kah-rah ehn noh ryohh-gah-eh wah deh-kee-mah-soo kah.
Excuse me. Can I change American dollars for yen?

Clerk: **Hai.**
hah-ee.
Sure.

Natalie: **Kyō no kawase rēto wa ikura desu ka.**
kyohh noh kah-wah-seh rehh-toh wah ee-koo-rah deh-soo kah.
What is today's exchange rate?

Clerk: **Ichi-doru 115-en desu.**
ee-chee-doh-roo hyah-koo-jooo-goh-ehn deh-soo.
One hundred and fifteen yen for one dollar.

Natalie: **Jā, 700-doru onegaishimasu.**
jahh, nah-nah-hyah-koo-doh-roo oh-neh-gah-ee-shee-mah-soo.
Then, I'd like to exchange 700 dollars please.

Clerk: **Pasupōto wa gozaimasu ka.**
pah-soo-pohh-toh wah goh-zah-ee-mah-soo kah.
Do you have your passport?

Natalie: **Hai. Dōzo.**
hah-ee. dohh-zoh.
Yes. Here you are.

Words to Know

en	ehn	Japanese yen
doru	doh-roo	American dollar
gaika	gah-ee-kah	foreign currency
kawase rēto	kah-wah-seh rehh-toh	exchange rate
ryōgae suru	ryohh-gah-eh soo-roo	to exchange
tesūryō	teh-sooo-ryohh	fee

Opening a bank account

Bank is **ginkō** (geen-kohh) in Japanese. It sounds like the popular dietary supplement, *ginko biloba,* which is supposed to increase your brainpower, but it has nothing to do with that. I know a lot of people who don't use their brains at all when they withdraw money from the **ginkō.**

You can open a **kōza** (kohh-za; account) at a **ginkō.** Your money will be safe, and you can earn **risoku** (ree-soh-koo; interest). It's very convenient, too. If you run out of **o-kane** (oh-kah-neh; money), you can always ask your mother to **densō suru** (dehn-sohh soo-roo; wire) some money to your **kōza.** What type of **kōza** are you interested in?

Account	*Pronunciation*	*Translation*
futsū yokin kōza	foo-tsoo yoh-keen kohh-zah	savings account
tēki yokin kōza	tehh-kee yoh-keen kohh-zah	fixed-deposit account/CD
tōza yokin kōza	tohh-zah yoh-keen kohh-zah	checking account

When you enter a **ginkō** in Japan, you'll hear **irasshaimase** (ee-rahs-shah-ee-mah-sehh; welcome) right away. The bank tellers dress in **sēfuku** (sehh-foo-koo; uniforms), and they treat you like **kami-sama** (kah-mee-sah-mah; God). After you enter the **ginkō,** pick up a ticket and wait until your number is called. The banks have comfy couches, current magazines, and TVs that make your wait almost enjoyable. When your number is called, go to the designated

madoguchi (mah-doh-goo-chee; window). Japanese banks have low windows so that customers can sit down while they perform their transactions.

Personal checks are not common in Japan. Most companies and institutions have **tōza yokin kōza** (tohh-zah yoh-keen kohh-zah; checking accounts), but individuals usually don't.

To open a **kōza** at a **ginkō,** you need **mibun shōmēsho** (mee-boon shohh-mehh-shoh; identification), as well as some money for your initial deposit. Are you ready to **hiraku** (hee-rah-koo; open) a **kōza?** Before you **hiraku** a **kōza,** practice conjugating the verb **hiraku** (hee-rah-koo; to open). It's a u-verb. Notice the **k** in all the forms except in the te-form.

Form	*Pronunciation*
hiraku	hee-rah-koo
hirakanai	hee-rah-kah-nah-ee
hiraki	hee-rah-kee
hiraite	hee-rah-ee-teh

Now, go to the bank and say that you want to **hiraku** an account. How do you say it? The best way is to say it with **tai-n-desu ga.** This ending makes your demand sound soft and friendly, and invites the clerk's reply. The verb before **tai-n-desu ga** must be in the stem form. For more about **tai,** see Chapter 9. And check out Chapter 5 for information on **-n-desu** and **ga.**

When you open a bank account, the bank clerk will ask you to fill out a **yōshi** (yohh-shee; form) and present your identification. Bank clerks speak to customers using super-polite words and phrases. To make their request very polite, they may use a verb in the stem form and place it between **o** (oh) and **kudasai** (koo-dah-sah-ee), as in **o-kaki kudasai** (oh-kah-kee koo-dah-sah-ee; please write it) and **o-mise kudasai** (oh-mee-seh koo-dah-sah-ee; please show it to me). In addition, many words that bank tellers use start with **go** or **o. Go** and **o** are polite prefixes. (See Chapters 3 and 9 for more about polite prefixes.) Be ready for the following super-polite demands from people at the bank:

- **Go-jūsho to o-denwa-bangō o onegaishimasu.** (goh-jooo-shoh toh oh-dehn-wah-bahn-gohh oh oh-neh-gah-ee-shee-mah-soo; Your address and your telephone number please.)

- **Mibun shōmēsho o o-mise kudasai.** (mee-boon shohh-mehh-shoh oh oh-mee-seh koo-dah-sah-ee; Please show me your identification.)

- **O-namae o o-kaki kudasai.** (oh-nah-mah-eh oh oh-kah-kee koo-dah-sah-ee; Please write your name.)

Talkin' the Talk

 Margaret is opening a bank account.

Teller: **Irasshaimase.**
ee-rahs-shah-ee-mah-seh.
Welcome.

Margaret: **Anō, futsū yokin kōza o hiraki-tai-n-desu ga.**
ah-nohh, foo-tsooo yoh-keen kohh-zah oh
hee-rah-kee-tah-een-deh-soo gah.
Hi, I'd like to open a savings account.

Teller: **Arigatō gozaimasu. Dewa, kono yōshi ni o-namae
to, go-jūsho to, o-denwa bangō o o-kaki kudasai.**
ah-ree-gah-tohh goh-zah-ee-mah-soo. deh-wah,
koh-noh yohh-shee nee oh-nah-mah-eh toh, goh-
jooo-shoh toh, oh-dehn-wah bahn-gohh oh oh-
kah-kee koo-dah-sah-ee.
Thank you very much. Please write your name,
address, and telephone number on this form.

Margaret: **Kore de ii desu ka.**
koh-reh deh eee deh-soo kah.
Is this okay?

Teller: **Hai. Mibun shōmēsho wa.**
hah-ee. mee-boon shohh-mehh-shoh wah.
Yes. And may I see your identification?

Margaret: **Hai. Dōzo.**
hah-ee. dohh-zoh.
Sure. Here it is.

Teller: **Dōmo.**
dohh-moh.
Thank you.

The teller checks Margaret's identification.

Teller: **Kyasshu kādo wa.**
kyahs-shoo kahh-doh wah.
How about an ATM card?

Margaret: **Kyasshu kādo wa irimasen.**
kyahs-shoo kahh-doh wah ee-ree-mah-sehn.
I don't need an ATM card.

In the above dialogue, the bank teller says **dewa** (deh-wah) right before asking Margaret to fill out the form. **Dewa** is just the non-abbreviated, very polite form of **jā** (jahh). Bank clerks and other service people use it instead of **jā**. Neither word has a concrete meaning — they're just interjections that mean something like *okay, then, now,* and *the next step is.*

Words to Know

futsū yokin kōza	foo-tsooo yoh-keen kohh-zah	savings account
hiraku [u]	hee-rah-koo	to open
kōza	kohh-zah	account
mibun shōmēsho	mee-boon shohh-mehh-shoh	personal identification
risoku	ree-soh-koo	interest
shomē	shoh-mehh	signature
tōza yokin kōza	tohh-zah yoh-keen kohh-zah	checking account
yōshi	yohh-shee	form

Making withdrawals and deposits

You can use the **jidō hikiotoshi** (jee-dohh hee-kee-oh-toh-shee; automatic payment) service offered by banks to pay your monthly bills. If you sometimes forget to pay your bills, **jidō hikiotoshi** is wonderful.

If you have too much **genkin** (gehn-keen; cash) in your **saifu** (sah-ee-foo; wallet), go to a **ginkō** (geen-kohh; bank) and make a **yokin** (yoh-keen; deposit). Don't make a mistake when you fill in your **kōza bangō** (kohh-zah bahn-gohh; account number) to make a deposit, or you may make some stranger extremely happy.

And when you run out of **genkin,** go to your **ginkō** or a **kyasshu mashīn** (kyahs-shoo mah-sheeen; ATM) and **hikidasu** (hee-kee-dah-soo; withdraw) more.

Words to Know

genkin	gehn-keen	cash
hikidasu [u]	hee-kee-dah-soo	to withdraw
kōza bangō	kohh-zah bahn-gohh	account number
yokin	yoh-keen	deposit

Using an ATM

ATMs are all over Japan, all over the United States, and all over Europe — it won't be long before they're all over the world. They make getting cash easy: All you need is your **kyasshu kādo** (kyahs-shoo kahh-doh; ATM card). You can make a **hikiotoshi** (hee-kee-oh-toh-shee; withdrawal), **yokin** (yoh-keen; deposit), **furikomi** (foo-ree-koh-mee; transfer), or **zandaka shōkai** (zahn-dah-kah shohh-kah-ee; balance inquiry). When you withdraw money from an ATM, you may hear instructions like the following:

✔ **Kādo o o-ire kudasai.** (kahh-doh oh oh-ee-reh koo-dah-sah-ee; Insert your card please.)

✔ **Anshō bangō o dōzo.** (ahn-shohh bahn-gohh oh dohh-zoh; Enter your PIN.)

✔ **Shibaraku o-machi kudasai.** (shee-bah-rah-koo oh-mah-chee koo-dah-sah-ee; Please wait.)

✔ **Kingaku o dōzo.** (keen-gah-koo oh dohh-zoh; Enter the amount please.)

✔ **Kakunin shite kudasai.** (kah-koo-neen shee-teh koo-dah-sah-ee; Confirm the amount.)

✔ **Genkin o o-uketori kudasai.** (gehn-keen oh oh-oo-keh-toh-ree koo-dah-sah-ee; Take the cash.)

✔ **Kādo o o-tori kudasai.** (kahh-doh oh oh-toh-ree koo-dah-sah-ee; Remove your card.)

✔ **Arigatō gozaimashita.** (ah-ree-gah-tohh goh-zah-ee-mah-shee-tah; Thank you very much.)

These instructions may appear in Japanese script on the screens of ATMs in Japan.

Conjugate the important verb **toru** (toh-roo; to take). It's a regular u-verb. Notice that the **r** appears in all the forms except the te-form. Just swallow the **r** in the te-form. How did it taste? Not bad, right?

Form	*Pronunciation*
toru	toh-roo
toranal	toh-rah-nah-ee
tori	toh-ree
totte	toht-teh

Spending Money

If you can pay your own bills, you're a big boy or girl. If you can pay your kids' or spouse's bills, you're a great man or woman. If you can pay your parents' bills, you're an extraordinary individual. Congratulations! Spending money shouldn't always be a pain; it should be a rewarding experience as well. There's no point in saving all your cash until you can no longer use it. Taking money to the grave is a big mistake.

Do you only believe in spending **genkin** (gehn-keen; cash), or are you a **kurejitto kādo** (koo-reh-jeet-toh kahh-doh; credit card) worshipper? If you're like a lot of people, you probably fall somewhere in between. **Genkin** and **kurejitto kādo** are convenient for making everyday payments. Take advantage of them. And if you're not allergic to computers, you can enjoy online forms of payment too.

Using cash

Genkin (gehn-keen; cash) is convenient for buying things like a cup of coffee, a magazine, or a snack from the vending machine. Most countries' currency includes both **shihē** (shee-hehh; bills) and **kōka** (kohh-kah; coins). When you refer to a **shihē** or **kōka,** place the numerical value before the word for bill or coin. For example, you can call a *five-dollar bill* and a *five-cent coin* **go-doru shihē** (goh-doh-roo shee-hehh) and **go-sento kōka** (goh-sehn-toh kohh-kah), respectively. Very simple. You may also hear **go-doru-satsu** (goh-doh-roo-sah-tsoo; five-dollar bill) and **go-sento koin** (goh-sehn-toh koh-een; five-cent coin) — **shihē** and **satsu** both mean *bill* or *note,* and **kōka** and **koin** both mean *coin.* Now, list all the **shihē** and **kōka** that you use:

- ✔ **100-doru-satsu** (hyah-koo-doh-roo-sah-tsoo; 100-dollar bill)
- ✔ **50-doru-satsu** (goh-jooo-doh-roo-sah-tsoo; 50-dollar bill)
- ✔ **20-doru-satsu** (nee-jooo-doh-roo-sah-tsoo; 20-dollar bill)
- ✔ **10-doru-satsu** (jooo-doh-roo-sah-tsoo; 10-dollar bill)
- ✔ **5-doru-satsu** (goh-doh-roo-sah-tsoo; 5-dollar bill)
- ✔ **1-doru-satsu** (ee-chee-doh-roo-sah-tsoo; 1-dollar bill)
- ✔ **25-sento koin** (nee-jooo-goh-sehn-toh koh-een; 25-cent coin)
- ✔ **10-sento koin** (joos-sehn-toh koh-een; 10-cent coin)
- ✔ **5-sento koin** (goh-sehn-toh koh-een; 5-cent coin)
- ✔ **kuŏtă** (koo-ohh-tahh; quarter)
- ✔ **daimu** (dah-ee-moo; dime)
- ✔ **nikkeru** (neek-keh-roo; nickle)
- ✔ **penĭ** (peh-neee; penny)

To count coins and bills, use the counter **-mai,** as in **ichi-mai** (eeh-chee-mah-ee), **ni-mai** (nee-mah-ee), **san-mai** (sahn-mah-ee), and so on. See Chapter 2 for more about **-mai** and other counters. Now, you're ready to count, spend, and save your **genkin.** If you don't have any **genkin,** you can always **kariru** (kah-ree-roo; borrow) some. Conjugate the verb **kariru** (to borrow). It's a ru-verb.

Form	*Pronunciation*
kariru	kah-ree-roo
karinai	kah-ree-nah-ee
kari	kah-ree
karite	kah-ree-teh

Here are a few phrases that you can use to get started talking about **genkin:**

- ✔ **Chichi kara gohyaku-doru karimashita.** (chee-chee kah-rah goh-hyah-koo-doh-roo kah-ree-mah-shee-tah; I borrowed five hundred dollars from my father.)
- ✔ **Go-doru kashite kudasai.** (goh-doh-roo kah-shee-teh koo-dah-sah-ee; Please loan me five dollars.)
- ✔ **Ichi-doru-satsu jū-mai arimasu ka.** (ee-chee-doh-roo-sah-tsoo jooo-mah-ee ah-ree-mah-soo kah; Do you have ten one-dollar bills?)
- ✔ **Ichi-doru-satsu wa san-mai shika arimasen.** (ee-chee-doh-roo-sah-tsoo wah sahn-mah-ee shee-kah ah-ree-mah-sehn; As for one-dollar bills, I have only three of them.)
- ✔ **Nijū-doru-satsu shika arimasen.** (nee-jooo-doh-roo-sah-tsoo shee-kah ah-ree-mah-sehn; I have only twenty-dollar bills.)

CULTURAL WISDOM

Dealing with Japanese currency

Can you identify Japanese **shihē** (shee-hehh; bills) and **kōka** (kohh-kah; coins)? The largest Japanese **shihē** is an **10,000-en-satsu** (ee-chee-mahn-ehn-sah-tsoo; 10,000-yen bill), and the highest Japanese coin is a **500-en-dama** (goh-hyah-koo-ehn-dah-mah; 500-yen coin). You'll like Japanese **50-en-dama** (goh-jooo-ehn-dah-mah; 50-yen coins) and **5-en-dama** (goh-ehn-dah-mah; 5-yen coins): They have a hole in the middle.

- ✔ **10,000-en-satsu** (ee-chee-mahn-ehn-sah-tsoo; 10,000-yen bill)

- ✔ **5,000-en-satsu** (goh-sehn-ehn-sah-tsoo; 5,000-yen bill)

- ✔ **2,000-en-satsu** (nee-sehn-ehn-sah-tsoo; 2,000-yen bill)

- ✔ **1,000-en-satsu** (sehn-ehn-sah-tsoo; 1,000-yen bill)

- ✔ **500-en-dama** (goh-hyah-koo-ehn-dah-mah; 500-yen coin)

- ✔ **100-en-dama** (hyah-koo-ehn-dah-mah; 100-yen coin)

- ✔ **50-en-dama** (goh-jooo-ehn-dah-mah; 50-yen coin)

- ✔ **10-en-dama** (jooo-ehn-dah-mah; 10-yen coin)

- ✔ **5-en-dama** (goh-ehn-dah-mah; 5-yen coin)

- ✔ **1-en-dama** (ee-chee-ehn-dah-mah; 1-yen coin)

Did you notice that the Japanese currency system doesn't use *quarters?* The only popular Japanese fractions are *half* and *one-tenth*. *Quarter* just isn't used.

GRAMMATICALLY SPEAKING

To say *only,* place the particle **shika** (shee-kah) at the end of the noun and make the verb negative, as in the last two sentences in the preceding bulleted list. See Chapter 8 for additional info on **shika.**

Talkin' the Talk

Addie wants to buy a candy bar from the vending machine, but she only has a ten-dollar bill. She asks Erik if he has change for her ten.

Addie: **Ichi-doru-satsu jū-mai aru.**
ee-chee-doh-roo-sah-tsoo jooo-mah-ee ah-roo.
Do you have ten one-dollar bills?

Erik: **Nana-mai shika nai.**
nah-nah-mah-ee shee-kah nah-ee.
I only have seven.

Addie: **Jā, go-doru-satsu wa aru.**
         jahh, goh-doh-roo-sah-tsoo wah ah-roo.
         Then, do you have any five-dollar bills?

Erik: **Un. Ichi-mai aru yo.**
         oon. ee-chee-mah-ee ah-roo yoh.
         Yes. I have one of them.

Addie: **Jā, ichi-doru-satsu go-mai to go-doru-satsu ichi-mai
         chōdai.**
         jahh, ee-chee-doh-roo-sah-tsoo goh-mah-ee toh goh-
         doh-roo-sah-tsoo ee-chee-mah-ee chohh-dah-ee.
         Then, give me five one-dollar bills and one five-dollar
         bill.

Erik: **Dōshite.**
         dohh-shee-teh.
         Why?

Addie: **Daijōbu. Jū-doru-satsu ichi-mai ageru yo.**
         dah-ee-johh-boo. jooo-doh-roo-sah-tsoo ee-chee-
         mah-ee ah-geh-roo yoh.
         Don't worry. I'll give you a ten-dollar bill.

Erik: **Ā, jā, ii yo.**
         ahh, jahh, eee yoh.
         Oh. Then it's okay.

Words to Know

500-en-dama	*goh-hyah-koo-ehn-dah-mah*	*500 yen coin*
kariru [ru]	*kah-ree-roo*	*to borrow*
kōka	*kohh-kah*	*coins*
shihē	*shee-hehh*	*bills*

Paying with plastic

A **kurejitto kādo** (koo-reh-jeet-toh kahh-doh; credit card) is almost a must-have in our modern lives. You need a credit card for **rentakā o suru** (rehn-tah-kahh oh soo-roo; renting a car) and **hoteru o yoyaku suru** (hoh-teh-roo oh yoh-yah-koo soo-roo; reserving a hotel room). In Japan, credit cards are accepted in many stores, hotels, and restaurants, but they're not as widely accepted as they are in the United States. Use these questions to determine if a store accepts credit cards:

- ✔ **Kurejitto kādo wa tsukaemasu ka.** (koo-reh-jeet-toh kahh-doh wa tsoo-kah-eh-mah-soo kah; Can I use a credit card?)

- ✔ **Biza ka Masutā kādo wa tsukaemasu ka.** (bee-zah kah mah-soo-tahh kahh-doh wah tsoo-kah-eh-mah-soo kah; Can I use Visa or MasterCard?)

The particle **ka** (kah) that you see between **Biza** and **Masutā** in the above sentence means _or._ You can use it for listing two or more choices. Place it after each noun except the last one. A few more examples may be helpful:

- ✔ **Amerikan Ekisupuresu ka Disukabā wa tsukaemasu.** (ah-meh-ree-kahn eh-kee-soo-poo-reh-soo kah dee-soo-kah-bahh wa tsoo-kah-eh-mah-soo; If it's American Express or Discover, you can use it.)

- ✔ **Kūkō ka ginkō de ryōgae o shimasu.** (kooo-kohh kah geen-kohh deh ryohh-gah-eh oh shee-mah-soo; I'll exchange money at the airport or at the bank.)

- ✔ **Genkin ka, kogitte ka, debitto kādo de haraimasu.** (gehn-keen kah, koh-geet-teh kah, deh-beet-toh kahh-doh deh hah-rah-ee-mah-soo; I'll pay by cash, check, or debit card.)

Perhaps you like to use your **debitto kādo** (deh-beet-toh kahh-doh; debit card) to pay for everyday expenses. **Debitto kādo** have one advantage over **kurejitto kādo** (koo-reh-jeet-toh kahh-doh; credit cards). When the money is deducted from your bank account, you can't spend more than you have.

Tsukaimasu (tsoo-kah-ee-mah-soo) means _I use it,_ but **tsukaemasu** (tsoo-kah-eh-mah-soo), as seen in some bullet items above, means _I can use it._ For more info on how to form "can do" verbs like **tsukaemasu,** see Chapter 8.

Conjugate the verb **tsukau** (tsoo-kah-oo; to use). It's a u-verb.

Form	*Pronunciation*
tsukau	tsoo-kah-oo
tsukawanai	tsoo-kah-wah-nah-ee
tsukai	tsoo-kah-ee
tsukatte	tsoo-kaht-teh

Talkin' the Talk

Yoshiko is about to buy a dress in a department store.

Yoshiko: **Kurejitto kādo wa tsukaemasu ka.**
koo-reh-jeet-toh kahh-doh wa tsoo-kah-eh-mah-soo kah.
Can I use a credit card?

Clerk: **Hai. Biza ka Masutā kādo wa tsukaemasu yo.**
hah-ee. bee-zah kah mah-soo-tahh kahh-doh wa tsoo-kah-eh-mah-soo yoh.
Sure. If it's Visa or MasterCard, you can use it.

Yoshiko: **Jā, Masutā kādo de onegaishimasu.**
jahh, mah-soo-tahh kahh-doh deh oh-neh-gah-ee-shee-mah-soo.
Then, I'll charge it on my MasterCard.

Clerk: **Koko ni go-shomē o onegaishimasu.**
koh-koh nee goh-shoh-mehh oh oh-neh-gah-ee-shee-mah-soo.
Please sign here.

Words to Know

debitto kādo	deh-beet-toh kahh-doh	debit card
kurejitto kādo	koo-reh-jeet-toh kahh-doh	credit card
Kurejitto kādo wa tsukaemasu ka.	koo-reh-jeet-toh kahh-doh wa tsoo-kah-eh-mah-soo kah	Can I use a credit card?
tsukau [u]	tsoo-kah-oo	to use

Fun & Games

Fill in the boxes in this crazy crossword puzzle with the correct Japanese words. Answers are in Appendix C.

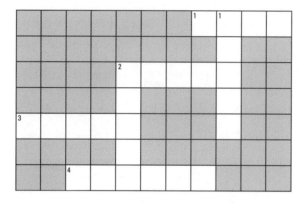

Across

   1. dollar

   2. foreign currency

   3. deposit

   4. to exchange currency

Down

   1. money

   2. bank

Chapter 12

Asking Directions

. . . .

In This Chapter

▶ Asking and answering "where" questions

▶ Providing directions like a pro

▶ Asking and answering "how do I get to" questions

▶ Using landmarks in your directions

. . . .

Don't hesitate to ask for directions in a new town. Everyone has to ask for directions sometimes, and it can be fun. If you can ask for directions in Japanese, you're ready to go anywhere in Japan. Japanese will enjoy talking to you and offering their help.

This chapter gives you the words and phrases necessary for giving and receiving directions. Where are you going? Is your destination **tōi** (tohh-ee; far) or **chikai** (chee-kah-ee; near)? Do you need to take a **chikatetsu** (chee-kah-teh-tsoo; subway), or are you going to **aruku** (ah-roo-koo; walk)?

Asking "Where" Questions

Suppose you want to go to **shiyakusho** (shee-yah-koo-shoh; city hall). You know it's near the **chikatetsu no eki** (chee-kah-teh-tsoo noh eh-kee; subway station), but you can't see it. What do you do? Check the **jūsho** (jooo-shoh; address)? Look at a **chizu** (chee-zoo; map)? Walk around a bit more? If none of these methods works, ask a kind-looking stranger. If no one looks nice, ask someone who looks mean. People are usually nicer than they look.

Where in Japanese is **doko** (doh-koh). But you can't just say **doko.** You'll sound like you have a very bad concussion and don't know where you are. Mention what you're looking for first. Here are a few places you may be looking for:

✔ **Amerika taishikan** (ah-meh-ree-kah tah-ee-shee-kahn; American embassy)

✔ **ēgakan** (ehh-gah-kahn; movie theater)

- **gakkō** (gahk-kohh; school)

- **gasorin sutando** (gah-soh-reen soo-tahn-doh; gas station)

- **ginkō** (geen-kohh; bank)

- **hakubutsukan** (hah-koo-boo-tsoo-kahn; museum)

- **shiyakusho** (shee-yah-koo-shoh; city hall)

- **shoppingu sentā** (shohp-peen-goo sehn-tahh; shopping mall)

- **toshokan** (toh-shoh-kahn; library)

- **yūbinkyoku** (yooo-been-kyoh-koo; post office)

Put the topic particle **wa** after the place you're looking for. Then, add **doko desu ka** (doh-koh deh-soo kah; where is) or **doko ni arimasu ka** (doh-koh nee ah-ree-mah-soo kah; where is it located). You can use either one, but **doko desu ka** is shorter, and probably easier for you to say, though you may hear either one of them.

- **Byōin wa doko desu ka.** (byohh-een wah doh-koh deh-soo kah; Where is the hospital?)

- **Ginkō wa doko ni arimasu ka.** (geen-kohh wah doh-koh nee ah-ree-mah-soo kah; Where is the bank located?)

Words to Know

chikai	chee-kah-ee	near
chizu	chee-zoo	map
gakkō	gahk-kohh	school
hakubutsukan	hah-koo-boo-tsoo-kahn	museum
jūsho	jooo-shoh	address
shiyakusho	shee-yah-koo-shoh	city hall
tōi	tohh-ee	far
yūbinkyoku	yooo-been-kyoh-koo	post office

Answering "Where" Questions

The easiest way to answer "where" questions is to use your index finger and point while saying **Asoko desu** (ah-soh-koh deh-soo; It's over there).

Other location words you can use in conjunction with pointing your index finger are **koko** (koh-koh) and **soko** (soh-koh). They all end in **oko.** Here's a breakdown for these three words that will make them easy to remember:

Japanese	Pronunciation	English	Location
koko	koh-koh	here	near the speaker
soko	soh-koh	there; near you	near the listener, but far from the speaker
asoko	a-soh-koh	over there	far from both the speaker and the listener

If the short location words listed above and your index finger don't work, describe the location with some of the position phrases in Table 12-1.

Table 12-1	Position Phrases	
Position Phrase	*Pronunciation*	*Translation*
chikaku	chee-kah-koo	near
hantai (gawa)	hahn-tah-ee (gah-wah)	opposite (side)
hidari (gawa)	hee-dah-ree (gah-wa)	left (side)
mae	mah-eh	front
migi (gawa)	mee-gee (gah-wah)	right (side)
mukai (gawa)	moo-kah-ee (gah-wah)	across the street from
soba	soh-bah	right near
ushiro	oo-shee-roh	behind
aida	ah-ee-dah	between

I want to warn you about one thing. You can't use one of the phases in the preceding table all by itself to describe the location of something. If you say *My house is on the left,* no one will understand you. You have to say *on the left of what.* The "of what" part is the important reference point. Use the particle **no** to create a modifier phrase that gives the reference point, and place it right before one of the position phrases in Table 12-1. For example, **hakubutsukan no hidari** means *the museum's left,* or *to the left of the museum.* Now, other people will understand where your house is. You need two reference points for the position **aida** (between). Connect the two points with the particle **to**.

Use **tonari** (toh-nah-ree; next to) only if you are dealing with two similar things like two buildings, two people, or two seats. But if you want to say that the hot dog vendor is next to the museum, for example, use **yoko** (yoh-koh) to express *next to.*

The following phrases put some of these modifiers in context:

- ✔ **Gakkō no ushiro desu.** (gahk-kohh noh oo-shee-roh deh-soo; It's behind the school.)

- ✔ **Gakkō wa byōin no mae desu.** (gah-kohh wah byohh-een noh mah-eh deh-soo; The school is in front of the hospital.)

- ✔ **Ginkō wa gasorin sutando no tonari desu.** (geen-kohh wah gah-soh-reen soo-tahn-doh noh toh-nah-ree deh-soo; The bank is next to the gas station.)

- ✔ **Yūbinkyoku wa toshokan to shiyakusho no aida desu.** (yooo-been-kyoh-koo wah toh-shoh-kahn toh shee-yah-koo-shoh noh ah-ee-dah deh-soo; The post office is between the library and the city hall.)

Specifying *how far* or *how near* you are to a location is often very helpful information. The word for *far* is **tōi** (tohh-ee), and the word for *near* is **chikai** (chee-kah-ee). I give you a few examples of how to use them in the following list.

- ✔ **Chotto tōi desu yo.** (choht-toh tohh-ee deh-soo yoh; It's a bit far.)

- ✔ **Sugu soko desu.** (soo-goo soh-koh deh-soo; It's right there.)

- ✔ **Totemo chikai desu.** (toh-teh-moh chee-kah-ee deh-soo; It's very close.)

By now, you must have noticed that **desu** is used a lot for expressing locations. **Desu** follows nouns and adjectives, and expresses the identity, property, characteristics, or the state of people and things.

- ✔ **Watashi wa gakusē desu.** (wah-tah-shee wah gah-koo-sehh deh-soo; I'm a student.)

- ✔ **Sushi wa oishii desu.** (soo-shee wah oh-ee-sheee deh-soo; Sushi is delicious.)

Check out Chapter 2 for information on how to conjugate **desu**.

CULTURAL WISDOM

Kōban (police box)

Japan is a very safe country. Many women feel very comfortable walking around the city at night. This level of safety has a lot to do with **koban** (kohh-bahn; police boxes). A **koban** is a tiny building or a small part of a big building. One or two police officers are in each **koban** 24 hours a day. They're located every few blocks in major towns.

Officers at a **koban** use bicycles to patrol the neighborhood several times a day. If you get lost, stop at the nearest **koban** and ask for directions. The officers know the neighborhood very well, and they have detailed maps.

Talkin' the Talk

Ben is looking for a subway station. He asks a woman where it is.

Ben: **Sumimasen. Chikatetsu no eki wa doko desu ka.**
soo-mee-mah-sehn. chee-kah-teh-tsoo noh
eh-kee wah doh-koh deh-soo kah.
Excuse me. Where is the subway station?

The woman points across the street.

Woman: **Chikatetsu no eki wa asoko desu.**
chee-kah-teh-tsoo noh eh-kee wah ah-soh-koh
deh-soo.
The subway station is over there.

Ben: **Ano yūbinkyoku no tonari desu ka.**
ah-noh yooo-been-kyoh-koo noh toh-nah-ree
deh-soo kah.
The one next to the post office?

Woman: **Hai.**
hah-ee.
Right.

Ben: **Arigatō gozaimashita.**
ah-ree-gah-tohh goh-zah-ee-mah-shee-tah.
Thank you very much.

Woman: **Īe.**
eee-eh.
Sure.

Words to Know

hidari	hee-dah-ree	left
mae	mah-eh	front
migi	mee-gee	right
tonari	toh-nah-ree	next to
ushiro	oo-shee-roh	behind

Giving Precise Directions with Cardinal Points and Ordinal Numbers

Being able to tell someone that the bank is over there is all well and good, but to be really helpful, you have to be able to give someone your street address or tell some young man to go west.

The following sections address the specifics of giving directions. And these expressions work just as well in reverse for those certainly very rare occasions when you need to ask for help to find your way.

Specifying cardinal points

Migi (mee-gee; right) and **hidari** (hee-dah-ree; left) are great. But after you turn 180 degrees or make a couple of lefts and rights, you may get confused. To avoid any confusion, specify *cardinal points* like north and east.

- ✔ **higashi** (hee-gah-shee; east)
- ✔ **kita** (kee-tah; north)
- ✔ **minami** (mee-nah-mee; south)
- ✔ **nishi** (nee-shee; west)

If you need to specify the direction more accurately, the following phrases are for you.

- ✔ **hokusē** (hoh-koo-sehh; northwest)
- ✔ **hokutō** (hoh-koo-tohh; northeast)

✔ **nansē** (nahn-sehh; southwest)

✔ **nantō** (nahn-tohh; southeast)

✔ **nannansē** (nahn-nahn-sehh; south-southwest)

Talkin' the Talk

 Masako is looking for the post office. She asks a man on the street to help her.

Masako:	**Sumimasen.** soo-mee-mah-sehn. Excuse me.
Man:	**Hai.** hah-ee. Yes.
Masako:	**Yūbinkyoku wa doko desu ka.** yooo-been-kyoh-koo wah doh-koh deh-soo kah. Where is the post office?
Man:	**Go-ban-dōri ni arimasu.** goh-bahn-dohh-ree nee ah-ree-mah-soo. It's on Fifth Street.
Masaki:	**Higashi gawa desu ka.** hee-gah-shee gah-wah deh-soo kah. Is it on the east side?
Man:	**Īe. Nishi gawa desu.** eee-eh. nee-shee gah-wah deh-soo. No, on the west side.
Masako:	**Ā, dōmo.** ahh, dohh-moh. Oh, thanks.
Man:	**Īe.** eee-eh. No problem.

Specifying ordinal numbers

Ordinal-number phrases like *the first* and *the second* are essential for pin-pointing houses, buildings, intersections, and streets. Remember that quantity phrases like **go-hon** (goh-hohn) and **mit-tsu** (meet-tso) express how many things there are, and depending on the type of the item, you need a different counter. (Chapter 2 has more on counters.) For example, you need the counter **-hon** if you're counting long, cylindrical-shaped items like straws or items that are just long like ribbons and streets. And you use the counter **-tsu** for inanimate objects that don't have a counter all to themselves — the counter to use when you're not sure what counter to use.

You can convert these quantity phrases into ordinal-number phrases just by adding **-me** after them. So, if you're talking about streets, **go-hon** (goh-hohn) means *five streets,* but **go-hon-me** (goh-hohn-meh) means *the fifth street.* If you're talking about intersections, **mit-tsu** (meet-tsoo) means *three intersections,* but **mit-tsu-me** (meet-tsoo-meh) means *the third intersection.* You see? Quantity phrases tell you how many, but ordinal-number phrases tells you which one in a sequence of items.

Now you're ready to specify at which intersection you should make a turn. Is it at the **hito-tsu-me** (hee-toh-tsoo-meh; first one), the **futa-tsu-me** (foo-tah-tsoo-meh; second one), or the **mit-tsu-me** (meet-tsoo-meh; third one). And you can also specify which building on the street has a public bathroom. Very important stuff in case of an emergency!

- **futa-tsu-me no kōsaten** (foo-tah-tsoo-meh noh kohh-sah-tehn; the second intersection)

- **hito-tsu-me no tatemono** (hee-toh-tsoo-meh noh tah-teh-moh-noh; the first building)

- **migi gawa no mit-tsu-me no ie** (mee-gee gah-wah noh meet-tsoo-meh noh ee-eh; the third house on the right-hand side)

- **yon-hon-me no michi** (yohn-hohn-meh noh mee-chee; the fourth street)

Table 12-2 lists a selection of ordinal numbers.

Table 12-2	Ordinal Numbers		
English	*Tsu-me (Various Items)*	*Hon-me (Long Items)*	*Mai-me (Flat Items)*
1st	hito-tsu-me (hee-toh-tsoo-meh)	ip-pon-me (eep-pohn-meh)	ichi-mai-me (ee-chee-mah-ee-meh)
2nd	futa-tsu-me (foo-tah-tsoo-meh)	ni-hon-me (nee-hohn-meh)	ni-mai-me (nee-mah-ee-meh)

English	Tsu-me (Various Items)	Hon-me (Long Items)	Mai-me (Flat Items)
3rd	mit-tsu-me (meet-tsoo-meh)	san-bon-me (sahn-bohn-meh)	san-mai-me (sahn-mah-ee-meh)
4th	yot-tsu-me (yoht-tsoo-meh)	yon-hon-me (yohn-hohn-meh)	yon-mai-me (yohn-mah-ee-meh)
5th	itsu-tsu-me (ee-tsoo-tsoo-meh)	go-hon-me (goh-hohn-meh)	go-mai-me (goh-mah-ee-meh)
6th	mut-tsu-me (moot-tsoo-meh)	rop-pon-me (rohp-pohn-meh)	roku-mai-me (roh-koo-mah-ee-meh)
7th	nana-tsu-me (nah-nah-tsoo-meh)	nana-hon-me (nah-nah-hohn-meh)	nana-mai-me (nah-nah-mah-ee-meh)
8th	yat-tsu-me (yaht-tsoo-meh)	hap-pon-me (hahp-pohn-meh)	hachi-mai-me (hah-chee-mah-ee-meh)
9th	kokono-tsu-me (koh-koh-noh-tsoo-meh)	kyū-hon-me (kyooo-hohn-meh)	kyū-mai-me (kyooo-mah-ee-meh)

Specifying how far

You can express distance by specifying the time it takes to get somewhere. Use the counter **-fun** (foon) for *minutes.* **-Fun** expresses both a point of time and a period of time as the following examples show. **-Fun** changes to **-pun** depending on the preceding sound — Chapter 7 has a table that shows you when this happens.

- ✔ **Ima gozen jū-ji jūgo-fun desu.** (ee-mah goh-zehn jooo-jee jooo-goh-foon deh-soo; It's 10:15 a.m. now.)

- ✔ **Uchi kara gakkō made 10-pun desu.** (oo-chee kah-rah gahk-kohh mah-deh joop-poon deh-soo; My school is ten minutes away from my house.)

Use **-jikan** (jee-kahn) for specifying *hours.* Just add **kan** after the counter **-ji** (jee; o'clock). That's how you get **-jikan.** To check out pronunciation guidelines for the counter **-ji** paired with numerals, see Chapter 7; for some practical examples, see the following list:

- ✔ **Aruite 30-pun desu.** (ah-roo-ee-teh sahn-joop-poon deh-soo; Thirty minutes on foot.)

- ✔ **Kūkō made basu de ni-jikan desu.** (kooo-kohh mah-deh bah-soo deh nee-jee-kahn deh-soo; It is two hours to the airport by bus.)

- ✔ **Koko kara kuruma de go-fun gurai desu.** (koh-koh kah-rah koo-roo-mah deh goh-foon goo-rah-ee deh-soo; It's about five minutes from here by car.)

You can also specify the actual distance.

- ✔ **Eki made ni-kiro desu.** (eh-kee mah-deh nee-kee-roh deh-soo; It's two kilometers to the railway station.)
- ✔ **Koko kara ichi-mairu gurai desu.** (koh-koh kah-rah ee-chee mah-ee-roo goo-rah-ee deh-soo; It's about one mile from here.)

Asking "How do I get to" Questions

"Where" questions are great, but sometimes you have to ask "how do I get to" questions to be able to reach your destination. Ask these questions at a **ryokō annaijo** (ryoh-kohh ahn-nah-ee-jo; tourist bureau), **eki no kippu uriba** (eh-kee noh keep-poo oo-ree-bah; railway-station ticket counter), **gasorin sutando** (gah-soh-reen soo-tahn-doh; gas station), or **hoteru no furonto** (hoh-teh-roo noh foo-rohn-toh; hotel front desk). People that work in these places are very knowledgeable and helpful.

You can also ask a fellow traveler at the bus stop or in the train or subway station for directions. Chances are you'll find someone who is heading in the same direction as you. If so, your journey will become easier and more fun. Just follow your new best friend.

To ask "how do I get to" questions, use the question word **dōyatte** (dohh-yaht-teh; how). Place it right after the destination phrase and the particle **wa** (wah) in the question. You can see it in the following examples:

- ✔ **Amerika taishikan wa dōyatte iku-n-desu ka.** (ah-meh-ree-kah tah-ee-shee-kahn wah dohh-yaht-teh ee-koon-deh-soo kah; How can I get to the American embassy?)
- ✔ **Shiyakusho wa dōyatte iku-n-desu ka.** (shee-yah-koo-shoh wah dohh-yaht-teh ee-koon-deh-soo kah; How can I get to city hall?)

It's a good idea to find out whether you need transportation to get to your destination. Ask whether your destination is within walking distance. Use the verb in the "can" form in this case. (Check out Chapter 8 for a discussion of "can.")

- ✔ **Koko kara Akihabara made arukemasu ka.** (koh-koh kah-rah ah-kee-hah-bah-rah mah-deh ah-roo-keh-mah-soo kah; Can I walk to Akihabara from here?)
- ✔ **Shiyakusho wa aruite ikemasu ka.** (shee-yah-koo-shoh wah ah-roo-ee-teh ee-keh-mah-soo kah; Can I get to city hall on foot?)

If your destination isn't within walking distance, ask which transportation method to use. Chapter 14 shows how to ask "which" questions and has an extensive inventory of transportation terms.

Conjugate the verb **aruku** (ah-roo-koo; to walk). It's a u-verb. Pay attention to the **k** syllables.

Form	Pronunciation
aruku	ah-roo-koo
arukanai	ah-roo-kah-nah-ee
aruki	ah-roo-kee
aruite	ah-roo-ee-teh

Talkin' the Talk

John wants to go to Takeya, a department store. He is wondering whether he should take a subway. He asks a construction worker on the street.

John: **Sumimasen. Takeya wa dōyatte iku-n-desu ka.**
soo-mee-mah-sehn. tah-keh-yah wah dohh-yaht-teh ee-koon-deh-soo kah.
Excuse me. How can I get to Takeya?

Worker: **Takeya desu ka.**
tah-keh-yah deh-soo kah.
Takeya. Let's see.

John: **Koko kara aruite ikemasu ka.**
koh-koh kah-rah ah-roo-ee-teh ee-keh-mah-soo kah.
Can I get there on foot from here?

Worker: **Chotto tōi yo.**
choht-toh tohh-ee yoh.
It's a bit far.

John: **Jā, chikatetsu desu ka.**
jahh, chee-kah-teh-tsoo deh-soo kah.
Then, should I take a subway?

Worker: **Chikatetsu no eki mo tōi yo.**
chee-kah-teh-tsoo noh eh-kee moh tohh-ee yoh.
The subway station is also far from here.

Answering "How to Go" Questions

If someone asks you for directions, can you help him or her? Do you focus on landmarks like a hill or a shopping mall when you give directions? If so, you are a very visual person and may be a great artist. Or, do you focus on the number of streets and intersections? If so, you're a very logical person, and you may be a great scientist or a mathematician. See, our personalities affect our daily lives, and we can't get away from it! In any case, don't forget to clarify the starting point when you give directions.

Referring to locations on the street

When giving directions, include several landmarks that the person has to pass to get to his or her destination. Pick any landmarks that are visible and semi-permanent. It can be a bridge, a stop sign, or a traffic light. But don't pick anything like a broken-down car that has been parked in the same spot for as long as you can remember. Who knows — the owner may surprise you and move that eyesore one day. Your directions will be more complete if you incorporate the terms in Table 12-3.

Table 12-3	Landmarks	
Landmark	*Pronunciation*	*Translation*
fumikiri	foo-mee-kee-ree	railway crossing
hashi	hah-shee	bridge
ichiji tēshi	ee-chee-jee tehh-shee	stop
kado	kah-doh	corner
kōsaten	kohh-sah-tehn	intersection
michi	mee-chee	road
shingō	sheen-gohh	traffic light
tōri	tohh-ree	street
tsukiatari	tsoo-kee-ah-tah-ree	dead end

As in English, there is a subtle difference between **michi** (mee-chee; road) and **tōri** (tohh-ree; street). They both have two functions — to connect locations and to accommodate stores and houses. And, while they each perform both functions, the emphasis of **michi** is on the connection and the emphasis of **tōri** is on the accommodation of shops or homes.

You can combine landmarks with the numbers introduced in the "Specifying ordinal numbers" section earlier in this chapter to give pretty specific directions, such as **mit-tsu-me no shingō** (meet-tsoo-meh noh sheen-gohh; the third traffic light) or **itsu-tsu-me no kado** (ee-tsoo-tsoo-meh noh kah-doh; the fifth corner).

Providing actions with directions

You can't give directions without telling someone how to move — walk, cross, pass, turn, and so on. You have to master these action words in Japanese. Check out Table 12-4 for some convenient actions to include in your directions. Memorize the words in the table and move around your room as you say them, just to practice. Use your kitchen, living room, and stairs if necessary. This is the part of the book where you get more dynamic and active. Absorb the Japanese language through your body. Good luck!

Table 12-4	Moving Verbs	
Verb (Dictionary, Negative, Stem, and Te-forms)	*Pronunciation*	*Translation*
aruku [u]	ah-roo-koo	to walk
arukanai	ah-roo-kah-nah-ee	
aruki	ah-roo-kee	
aruite	ah-roo-ee-teh	
kudaru [u]	koo-dah-roo	to go down
kudaranai	koo-dah-rah-nah-ee	
kudari	koo-dah-ree	
kudatte	koo-daht-teh	
magaru [u]	mah-gah-roo	to make a turn
magaranai	mah-gah-rah-nah-ee	
magari	mah-gah-ree	
magatte	mah-gaht-teh	

(continued)

Table 12-4 (continued)

Verb (Dictionary, Negative, Stem, and Te-forms)	Pronunciation	Translation
noboru [u]	noh-boh-roo	to go up
noboranai	noh-boh-rah-nah-ee	
nobori	noh-boh-ree	
nobotte	noh-boht-teh	
sugiru [ru]	soo-gee-roo	to pass
suginai	soo-gee-nah-ee	
sugi	soo-gee	
sugite	soo-gee-teh	
wataru [u]	wah-tah-roo	to cross
wataranai	wah-tah-rah-nah-ee	
watari	wah-tah-ree	
watatte	wah-taht-teh	

You need to specify where you move. Where do you make a turn? What do you cross? Which street do you take? Specify these locations by marking them with the particle **o**, directly following the word for the location or landmark. A smart person like you may wonder why you need the direct object particle **o** here, but that's just the way it is. Japanese is a human language, and as with English, the reason for a rule is not always obvious.

- ✔ **kōsaten o magaru** (kohh-sah-tehn oh mah-gah-roo; make a turn at the intersection)
- ✔ **hashi o wataru** (hah-shee oh wah-tah-roo; cross the bridge)
- ✔ **kono michi o aruku** (koh-noh mee-chee oh ah-roo-koo; walk along this road)

And specify the direction of your movement by marking it with the particle **ni.**

- ✔ **migi ni magaru** (mee-gee nee mah-gah-roo; make a right turn)
- ✔ **higashi ni iku** (hee-gah-shee nee ee-koo; go east)

Now you're ready to put everything together — where to make a move, which direction to move in, and how far to go. Give complete directions:

- ✔ **san-ban-dōri o minami ni iku** (sahn-bahn-dohh-ree oh mee-nah-mee nee ee-koo; go south on Third Street)

- ✔ **go-fun gurai aruku** (goh-foon goo-rah-ee ah-roo-koo; walk about five minutes)

- ✔ **futatsu-me no kado o migi ni magaru** (foo-tah-tsoo-meh noh kah-doh oh mee-gee nee mah-gah-roo; make a right at the second corner)

- ✔ **ginkō o sugiru** (geen-kohh oh soo-gee-roo; pass the bank)

- ✔ **kaidan o noboru** (kah-ee-dahn oh noh-boh-roo; go up the stairs)

- ✔ **kono michi o massugu iku** (koh-noh mee-chee oh mahs-soo-goo ee-koo; go straight on this street)

- ✔ **kōsaten o hidari ni magaru** (kohh-sah-tehn oh hee-dah-ree nee mah-gah-roo; make a left at the intersection)

Making directions flow

How do you usually give directions to others? Most people use an imperative like _Go straight on this street for five minutes or so_ or a request sentence such as _Please make a turn at the second intersection._ When you give directions in Japanese, use a _request sentence_ that consists of a verb in the te-form and **kudasai** (koo-dah-sah-ee). **Kudasai** literally means _Give it to me please,_ but when used right after a verb in the te-form, it doesn't mean _give it to me;_ it creates a polite request sentence. Conjugating verbs to the te-form is the first step of making a request sentence. You can look at Chapter 2 to find out how to get the te-form, but for your convenience, I list the dictionary forms and the te-forms of the verbs that you need for giving directions in Table 12-5.

Table 12-5	Verbs For Giving Directions	
English	_Dictionary Form_	_Te-form_
to go	iku (ee-koo)	itte (eet-teh)
to make a turn	magaru (mah-gah-roo)	magatte (mah-gaht-teh)
to cross	wataru (wah-tah-roo)	watatte (wah-taht-teh)
to pass	sugiru (soo-gee-roo)	sugite (soo-gee-teh)
to walk	aruku (ah-roo-koo)	aruite (ah-roo-ee-teh)
to go up	noboru (noh-boh-roo)	nobotte (noh-boht-teh)
to go down/to get off	oriru (oh-ree-roo)	orite (oh-ree-teh)
to get on	noru (noh-roo)	notte (noht-teh)

Now you're ready to give directions in Japanese.

- **San-ban-dōri o minami ni itte kudasai.** (sahn-bahn-dohh-ree oh mee-nah-mee nee eet-teh koo-dah-sah-ee; Go south on Third Street, please.)

- **Ano kado o migi ni magatte kudasai.** (ah-noh kah-doh oh mee-gee nee mah-gaht-teh koo-dah-sah-ee; Please make a right at that corner.)

- **Eki made aruite kudasai.** (eh-kee mah-deh ah-roo-ee-teh koo-dah-sah-ee; Walk to the railway station, please.)

- **Ginza kara densha ni notte kudasai.** (geen-zah kah-rah dehn-shah nee noht-teh koo-dah-sah-ee; Take a train from Ginza, please.)

To make your directions flow, connect your directions with the word **sorekara** (soh-reh-kah-rah; and then), as in these examples:

- **Kono michi o massugu itte kudasai. Sorekara, mit-tsu-me no kado o migi ni magatte kudasai.** (koh-noh mee-chee oh mahs-soo-goo eet-teh koo-dah-sah-ee. soh-reh-kah-rah, meet-tsoo-meh noh kah-doh oh mee-gee-nee mah-gaht-teh koo-dah-sah-ee; Go straight on this street. And then, make a right at the third corner.)

- **Hashi o watatte kudasai. Sorekara, kōban o sugite kudasai.** (hah-shee oh wah-taht-teh koo-dah-sah-ee. soh-reh-kah-rah, kohh-bahn oh soo-gee-teh koo-dah-sah-ee; Cross the bridge. And then, pass the police box.)

Talkin' the Talk

Daisuke is looking for Taketani shoten (tah-keh-tah-nee shoh-tehn; Taketani bookstore) in Shinjuku, Tokyo. He asks a stranger on the street for directions.

Daisuke: **Sumimasen. Taketani shoten wa doko desu ka.**
soo-mee-mah-sehn. tah-keh-tah-nee shoh-tehn
wah doh-koh deh-soo kah.
Excuse me. Where is Taketani bookstore?

Woman: **Tsugi no kōsaten o hidari ni magatte kudasai.**
tsoo-gee noh kohh-sah-tehn oh hee-dah-ree nee
mah-gaht-teh koo-dah-sah-ee.
Make a left turn at the next intersection.

Daisuke: **Ano shingō no kōsaten desu ne.**
ah-noh sheen-gohh noh kohh-sah-tehn deh-soo neh.
The one with the traffic light over there, right?

Woman: **Hai. Sorekara, fumikiri o watatte kudasai. Taketani shoten wa hidari gawa ni arimasu. Resutoran no tonari desu.**
hah-ee. sohh-reh-kah-rah, foo-mee-kee-ree oh wah-taht-teh koo-dah-sah-ee. tah-keh-tah-nee shoh-tehn wah hee-dah-ree gah-wah nee ah-ree-mah-soo. reh-soo-toh-rahn noh toh-nah-ree deh-soo.
Yes. Then, cross the railway crossing. Taketani book-store is on your left. It's next to the restaurant.

Daisuke: **Ā, sō desu ka. Dōmo.**
ahh, sohh deh-soo kah. dohh-moh.
Oh, I see. Thank you.

Woman: **Īe.**
eee-eh.
You're welcome.

Words to Know

kōsaten	kohh-sah-tehn	intersection
michi	mee-chee	street
shingō	sheen-gohh	traffic light
sorekara	soh-reh-kah-rah	and then
tsugi	tsoo-gee	next

Fun & Games

Match the pictures to the descriptions. Check the answers in Appendix C.

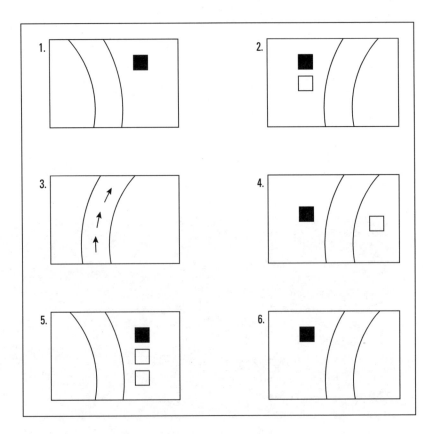

A. **Mukai gawa ni arimasu.**

B. **Michi no migi gawa desu.**

C. **Michi no migi gawa no mit-tsu-me desu.**

D. **Kono michi o massugu ikimasu.**

E. **Michi no hidari gawa desu.**

F. **Tonari ni arimasu.**

Chapter 13

Staying at a Hotel

. . . .

In This Chapter

▶ Finding accommodations

▶ Reserving the room

▶ Arriving at the hotel

▶ Paying the bill after your stay

. . . .

Choosing the right **hoteru** (hoh-teh-roo; hotel) can make any trip you take more enjoyable. Each day of your adventure starts and ends at the hotel.

In the morning, a good hotel offers you a refreshing breakfast, and at night, it offers you a comfortable bed. Hopefully, the clerks at the **furonto** (foo-rohn-toh; front desk) are kind and helpful. Having a great experience at a **hoteru** can help make your trip a success.

This chapter goes through the entire process of your hotel stay — choosing the right one, making a reservation, checking into the hotel, and checking out. Enjoy your visit!

Getting the Accommodations of Your Choice

Choose the right **shukuhaku shisetsu** (shoo-koo-hah-koo shee-seh-tsoo; accommodations) according to your needs and budget. Are you planning a family trip to a resort area near the coast? Get a nice **hoteru** (hoh-teh-roo; hotel) that features easy access to the beach. If you don't need any surprises, you may want to stay at a property owned by a well-known **hoteru chēn** (hoh-teh-roo chehhn; hotel chain). Are you going to celebrate your spouse's birthday? If so, save your money and book a **pentohausu** (pehn-toh-hah-oo-soo; penthouse).

Bathing Japanese style

A Japanese public bath is very different from a Western-style bath. A Japanese bathtub is very deep, and the water is very hot. The bath is only for soaking and relaxing — washing your body, face, or hair is taboo. You wash yourself outside the tub, in a space with faucets, showers, and mirrors on the wall. You can sit on a low stool as you wash. It's considered polite to wash your body first, before you get into the tub.

Public baths are everywhere in Japan. Do you enjoy bathing with others in public? Of course, you have to get completely naked. It may be a bit embarrassing, but you don't know any of the other people. What the heck? Go for it! The tub in a public bath is huge. It's a giant hot tub, but it's not a heated swimming pool. So, don't plan on taking a few laps. You can sing a song in the tub, though. You'll get a nice echo effect. Occasionally, check out the people around you just to make sure that your singing doesn't annoy them. And come out of the tub every 15 minutes or so; otherwise, you'll become a dizzy octopus.

If you're staying in a sleepy little town for a few weeks doing research for that thesis, try a **bī ando bī** (beee ahn-doh beee; bed-and-breakfast). Driving from coast to coast in the United States can take some time. If that kind of trip is in your future, why don't you save some money and stay in a **mōteru** (mohh-teh-roo; motel) or **in** (een; inn)? Or, I guess you could save even more money by sleeping in your car in a parking lot. Choose a parking lot close to a public bathroom and a bunch of vending machines. And don't forget to carry lots of coins and a blanket!

A **hoteru** (hoh-teh-roo; hotel) is a Western-style hotel. You can speak English in most major **hoteru** in Japan. You can also eat a Western-style **chōshoku** (chohh-shoh-koo; breakfast), sleep on a **beddo** (behd-doh; bed) instead of a futon, and use a Western-style **o-furo** (oh-foo-roh; bath). These amenities may be familiar to you and put you at ease, but then again, they don't set off any bells or alarms on the new-culture meter.

If you want to try authentic Japanese-style accommodations, go to a **ryokan** (ryoh-kahn; Japanese-style inn). At the entrance to the inn, a **nakai-san** (nah-kah-ee-sahn; maid) in kimono welcomes you. Enjoy a big **o-furo** with other guests, and have a Japanese-style breakfast. (See Chapter 5 for examples of Japanese-style breakfast dishes.) When you get back to your room for the evening, the **futon** (foo-tohn; thin, quilted mattress) is already spread out on the **tatami** (tah-tah-mee; straw mat) floor in your bedroom (see Chapter 10 for more about **futon**), and dinner is brought right to the living/dining area of your room. Wear a special kimono-like cotton robe, a **yukata** (yoo-kah-tah) while you enjoy a special dinner.

A **minshuku** (meen-shoo-koo) is a private home that offers lodging and meals to tourists. All the **minshuku** guests eat their meals together in a big dining room with a **tatami** floor. Guests have to spread out their own **futon** when they sleep and fold it up again in the morning. It's like visiting your uncle or aunt's big house in the countryside. A **minshuku** is similar to a bed-and-breakfast in Western countries, but a **minshuku** often provides dinner as well as breakfast.

If you're young and your budget is very tight (or does that go without saying?), you can stay in a **yūsu hosuteru** (yooo-soo-hoh-soo-teh-roo; youth hostel). You have to share a room and/or a bathroom with other travelers and follow the hostel's strict rules, but you can save your money for another part of your trip.

Words to Know

bī ando bī	beee ahn-doh beee	bed-and-breakfast
hoteru	hoh-teh-roo	hotel
in	een	inn
mōteru	mohh-teh-roo	motel
o-furo	oh-foo-roh	bath
ryokan	ryo-kahn	Japanese-style inn
yūsu hosuteru	yooo-soo hoh-soo-teh-roo	youth hostel

Making a Room Reservation

Before calling a hotel to **yoyaku suru** (yoh-yah-koo soo-roo; make a reservation), get a clear idea about how many people are staying, how many rooms you need, how long you're staying, and how much you can spend. Then, have your **kurejitto kādo** (koo-reh-jeet-toh kahh-doh; credit card) ready and dial the number. If you're already traveling, just walk into the hotel and ask them whether they have a room for you.

This section gives you important words to express room size, number of people, length of stay, and cost. In addition, I provide information about how to express ownership — you don't want your stuff getting mixed-up with other hotel guests' stuff. Be ready to say *That's mine*.

Japanese doesn't have simple verbs that mean *to plan* or *to make a reservation*. To say *to plan* and *to make a reservation,* you combine the verb **suru** (soo-roo; to do) with a noun — **kēkaku** (kehh-kah-koo; plan) and **yoyaku** (yoh-yah-koo; reservation). So, **kēkaku suru** means *to plan,* and **yoyaku suru** means *to make a reservation*. But how do you conjugate these verbs? You simply conjugate the **suru** part of the verb. **Suru** is an irregular verb, and I conjugate **suru** in a verb table in Chapter 8.

Checking out room size

Ask the folks at the front desk about the types of **heya** (heh-yah; rooms) they have. Suppose you're traveling with your mother, spouse, and two teenage children. Would it be better to get a big room that everyone can stay in together, or do you want a separate room for your kids and mom? Think about that. I know what my answer would be. Is anyone in your family a heavy snorer? Think about that too because you need a good night's sleep to have some energy for your trip.

- ✔ **shinguru** (sheen-goo-roo; single)
- ✔ **tsuin** (tsoo-een; twin)
- ✔ **semi-daburu** (seh-mee-dah-boo-roo; semi-double/a room with a full-size bed)
- ✔ **daburu** (dah-boo-roo; double)

Compare room sizes and prices. Which one would you like, a twin room or a double room? When asking a choice question involving two items, use **dochira** (doh-chee-rah; which one). (For more info on using **dochira** and making other comparisons, see Chapter 6.)

- ✔ **Daburu to tsuin to, dochira ga yoroshii desu ka.** (dah-boo-roo toh tsoo-een toh, doh-chee-rah gah yoh-roh-sheee deh-soo kah; We have double and twin rooms. Which one would you like?)
- ✔ **Dochira no heya ga hiroi desu ka. Tsuin no heya ga hiroi desu.** (doh-chee-rah noh heh-yah gah hee-roh-ee deh-soo kah. tsoo-een noh heh-yah gah hee-roh-ee deh-soo; Which room is bigger? A twin room is bigger.)
- ✔ **Dochira ga takai desu ka.** (doh-chee-rah gah tah-kah-ee deh-soo kah; Which one is more expensive?)

Counting the number of people staying

How many people are in your group? Room costs are always different in Japan, and often in other places too, depending on the number of people sharing the room. Express the number of people in your party by using the counter **-nin.** Watch out for the irregular *one person* and *two people.*

- ✔ **hitori** (hee-toh-ree; one person)
- ✔ **futari** (foo-tah-ree; two people)
- ✔ **san-nin** (sahn-neen; three people)
- ✔ **yo-nin** (yoh-neen; four people)
- ✔ **go-nin** (goh-neen; five people)

Suppose that there are five people in your family, and you reserved a big hotel room with two full-size beds. Only two people can sleep in each bed. What are you going to do with the fifth member of your family? And no, leaving him or her at home is not an option. Ask the front desk for an extra bed. Use the convenient word **mō hitotsu** (mohh hee-toh-tsoo; one more) and request a bed by saying **Beddo o mō hitotsu onegaishimasu** (behd-doh oh mohh hee-toh-tsoo oh-neh-gah-ee shee-mah-soo; One more bed please.).

Words to Know

daburu	dah-boo-roo	double
dochira	doh-chee-rah	which one (of two)
heya	heh-yah	room
nagame	nah-gah-meh	view
-nin	neen	counter for people
shinguru	sheen-goo-roo	single
tsuin	tsoo-een	twin
yoyaku	yoh-yah-koo	reservation

Indicating the length of your stay

Specify how long you want to **tomaru** (toh-mah-roo; stay). The longer the better, but nobody can stay forever in an expensive hotel. To start with, why don't you conjugate the verb **tomaru?** It's a u-verb.

Form	*Pronunciation*
tomaru	toh-mah-roo
tomaranai	toh-mah-rah-nah-ee
tomari	toh-mah-ree
tomatte	toh-maht-teh

Use the particles **kara** (kah-rah; from) and **made** (mah-deh; until) to talk about the duration of your visit. **Kara** and **made** look like English prepositions, but they have to follow, not precede, the relevant phrases. For example, *from the 15th* in English is *the 15th from* in Japanese. And *until the 23rd* in English is *the 23rd until* in Japanese. That's a mirror image. I didn't know that there was a mirror barrier between Japan and the English-speaking world, but we're still friends. So, you now know **15-nichi kara** (jooo-goh-nee-chee kah-rah) means *from the 15th,* and **23-nichi made** (nee-jooo-sahn-nee-chee mah-deh) means *until the 23rd.* Take a look at a few examples:

- ✔ **Raishū no getsuyōbi kara mokuyōbi made onegaishimasu.** (rah-ee-shooo noh geh-tsoo-yohh-bee kah-rah moh-koo-yohh-bee mah-deh oh-neh-gah-ee-shee-mah-soo; From Monday to Thursday of next week, please.)

- ✔ **San-gatsu 15-nichi kara 23-nichi made desu.** (sahn-gah-tsoo jooo-goh-nee-chee kah-rah nee-jooo-sahn-nee-chee mah-deh deh-soo; I want to stay from March 15th to the 23rd.)

- ✔ **Kyō kara asatte made tomarimasu.** (kyohh kah-rah ah-saht-teh mah-deh toh-mah-ree-mah-soo; I'll stay from today until the day after tomorrow.)

Use the counter **-haku** (hah-koo) to specify the number of nights that you're staying. **-Haku** is the counter for nights that one stays outside of his or her home. And remember to watch out for the **-haku/-paku** alternation. You may not like it, but you just have to memorize it.

- ✔ **ip-paku** (eep-pah-koo; one night)
- ✔ **ni-haku** (nee-hah-koo; two nights)
- ✔ **san-paku** (sahn-pah-koo; three nights)
- ✔ **yon-haku** (yohn-hah-koo; four nights)
- ✔ **go-haku** (goh-hah-koo; five nights)
- ✔ **rop-paku** (rohp-pah-koo; six nights)

Talkin' the Talk

 Toshi is going to Tokyo next month with his wife. He calls up Hotel Tokyo to make a reservation.

Clerk: **Hoteru Tōkyō de gozaimasu.**
hoh-teh-roo tohh-kyohh deh goh-zah-ee-mah-soo.
This is Hotel Tokyo.

Toshi: **Anō, ku-gatsu 12-nichi kara 16-nichi made yoyaku shitai-n-desu ga.**
ah-nohh, koo-gah-tsoo jooo-nee-nee-chee kah-rah jooo-roh-koo-nee-chee mah-deh yoh-yah-koo shee-tah-een-deh-soo gah.
I'd like to make a reservation for September 12th to the 16th.

Clerk: **Arigatō gozaimasu. O-hitori-sama desu ka.**
ah-ree-gah-tohh goh-zah-ee-mah-soo.
oh-hee-toh-ree-sah-mah deh-soo kah.
Thank you very much. Is it for one person?

Toshi: **Īe, futari desu.**
eee-eh, foo-tah-ree deh-soo.
No, it's for two.

Clerk: **Daburu to tsuin to, dochira ga yoroshii desu ka.**
dah-boo-roo toh tsoo-een toh, doh-chee-rah gah yoh-roh-sheee deh-soo kah.
Which would you prefer, a double or twin?

Toshi: **O-nedan wa.**
oh-neh-dahn wah.
What are the prices?

Clerk: **Daburu no o-heya wa ip-paku o-futari de 12,000-en de gozaimasu.**
dah-boo-roo noh oh-heh-yah wah eep-pah-koo oh-foo-tah-ree deh ee-chee-mahn-nee-sehn-ehn deh goh-zah-ee-mah-soo.
For a double room, for one night, for a two-person occupancy, 12,000 yen.

Tsuin no o-heya wa o-futari de 13,000-en de gozaimasu.
tsoo-een noh oh-heh-yah wah oh-foo-tah-ree deh ee-chee-mahn-sahn-zehn-ehn deh goh-zah-ee-mah-soo.
For a twin room, 13,000 yen for a two-person occupancy.

Toshi: **Dochira no heya ga hiroi desu ka.**
doh-chee-rah noh heh-yah gah hee-roh-ee deh-soo kah.
Which room is bigger?

Clerk: **Tsuin no o-heya ga sukoshi hiroi desu.**
tsoo-een noh oh-heh-yah gah soo-koh-shee hee-roh-ee deh-soo.
Twin rooms are a bit bigger.

Nagame mo, tsuin no o-heya ga yoroshii desu yo.
nah-gah-meh moh, tsoo-een noh oh-heh-yah gah yoh-roh-sheee deh-soo yoh.
And they have a nicer view too.

Toshi: **Jā, tsuin no heya o onegaishimasu.**
jahh, tsoo-een noh heh-yah oh oh-neh-gah-ee-shee-mah-soo.
Then, a twin room please.

Clerk: **Hai, kashikomarimashita.**
hah-ee, kah-shee-koh-mah-ree-mah-shee-tah.
Certainly.

Talking with insiders and outsiders: Using "uchi" and "soto"

The distinction between *inside* and *outside* is very important for communicating in Japanese. Your choice between using a formal speech style or an informal one heavily depends on whether the person you're talking to is your insider or outsider.

The two important words **uchi** (oo-chee; inside) and **soto** (soh-toh; outside) mean not only physical locations, such as inside the house or outside the house, but also social groupings: *our group* versus *their group*. So, the word

uchi can mean both one's household and one's group. For example, if a hotel clerk says **Uchi wa yasui desu yo** (oo-chee wah yah-soo-ee deh-soo yoh), it doesn't mean *My house doesn't charge much;* the phrase means *Our hotel doesn't charge much.*

Comparing costs

Cost is a major criterion when you choose a hotel. Suppose one hotel charges you $150, and another hotel charges you $200. The difference is $50, but if you're staying for 10 days, the difference becomes $500. That's quite a bit of money. But if you share a room with a friend, you can save money *and* take the $200 room. Figuring out the total cost is not always simple, but if you keep reading, you'll be able to do it in Japanese. Do all the research and **kēkaku suru** (kehh-kah-koo soo-roo; plan) carefully. In this section, I show you how to compare prices, how to express "times," like *twice* and *three times,* and how to express percentages.

It's very easy to make comparisons in Japanese. All you need is the particle **yori** (yoh-ree; than). For example, **Yūsu hosuteru wa yasui desu** (yooo-soo-hoh-soo-teh-roo wah yah-soo-ee deh-soo) means *Youth hostels are cheap.* If you want to say *Youth hostels are cheaper than hotels,* just stick in **hoteru yori** (hoh-teh-roo yoh-ree; than hotels) right before the adjective **yasui desu.** So, **Yūsu hosuteru wa hoteru yori yasui desu** means *Youth hostels are cheaper than hotels.* See Chapter 6 for additional examples of comparison sentences with **yori.**

To make a comparison by saying that something is a number of times more (or less) than something else, use the counter **-bai** (bah-ee). **Ni-bai** (nee-bah-ee) means *twice,* and **san-bai** means *three times.*

And here's one more convenient phrase that you can use when you compare prices. To express percentages, use the counter **-pāsento** (pahh-sehn-toh; percent). You can also use the same percentage symbol (%) in Japanese as you do in English. *Fifteen percent* is **15-pāsento** (jooo-goh-pahh-sehn-toh), and **20-pāsento** (nee-joop-pahh-sehn-toh) means *20 percent.*

- ✔ **Kanada no hoteru wa Amerika no hoteru yori 25-pāsento yasui desu.** (kah-nah-dah noh hoh-teh-roo wah ah-meh-ree-kah noh hoh-teh-roo yoh-ree nee-jooo-goh-pahh-sehn-toh yah-soo-ee deh-soo; Canadian hotels are 25 percent cheaper than American hotels.)

- ✔ **Ryokan wa yūsu hosuteru yori san-bai takai desu.** (ryoh-kahn wah yooo-soo hoh-soo-teh-roo yoh-ree sahn-bah-ee tah-kah-ee deh-soo; Japanese-style inns are three times more expensive than youth hostels.)

Talkin' the Talk

David has been traveling around Japan. It's 9 p.m. He's just decided to stay in Nagoya tonight, and he walks in to a youth hostel.

David: **Sumimasen. Kyō tomaritai-n-desu ga, heya wa aite arimasu ka.**
soo-mee-mah-sehn. kyohh toh-mah-ree-tah-een-deh-soo gah, heh-yah wah ah-ree-mah-soo kah.
Excuse me. I would like to stay here tonight, but do you have a vacancy?

Clerk: **Kyō wa manshitsu desu.**
kyohh wah mahn-shee-tsoo deh-soo.
No vacancy tonight.

David: **Ā, sō desu ka. Komatta nā.**
ahh, sohh deh-soo kah. koh-maht-tah nahh.
Oh really. That's a problem.

Clerk: **Mōshiwake gozaimasen.**
mohh-shee-wah-keh goh-zah-ee-mah-sehn.
I'm terribly sorry.

David: **Hoka no hoteru o oshiete kudasai masen ka.**
hoh-kah noh hoh-teh-roo oh oh-shee-eh-teh koo-dah-sah-ee mah-sehn kah.
Could you let me know of any other hotels?

Clerk: **Tonari no Hoteru Purinsu wa ikaga desu ka.**
toh-nah-ree noh hoh-teh-roo poo-reen-soo wah ee-kah-gah deh-soo kah.
How about next door, the Hotel Prince?

David: **Soko wa takai desu ka.**
soh-koh wah tah-kah-ee deh-soo kah.
Is it expensive there?

Clerk: **Uchi no san-bai gurai desu.**
oo-chee noh sahn-bah-ee goo-rah-ee deh-soo.
About three times more expensive than us.

Words to Know

-bai	bah-ee	times (more or less) [counter]
hoka no	hoh-kah noh	other
manshitsu	mahn-shee-tsoo	all occupied/ no vacancy
Mōshiwake gozaimasen.	mohh-shee-wah-keh goh-zah-ee-mah-sehn	I'm terribly sorry.
tomaru [u]	toh-mah-roo	to stay (overnight)
uchi	oo-chee	my house/ our institution

Keeping track of what's yours with possessive pronouns

Lots of mix-ups can happen when you're staying in a big hotel with 300 other guests. Keep track of your **sūtsukēsu** (sooo-tsoo-kehh-soo; suitcases), **saifu** (sah-ee-foo; wallet), and **kagi** (kah-gee; keys). If a guy reaches for your **kagi** on a table in the hotel lobby, tell him that the keys are yours right away.

How do you say *yours* and *mine* in Japanese? Actually, it's easy to create possessive pronouns. To say *yours* and *mine*, take the words that mean *you* and *I* and add the particle **no** after them. **Anata** (ah-nah-tah) is *you*, and **anata no** (ah-nah-tah noh) is *yours*. How about *mine?* **Watashi** (wah-tah-shee) is *I*, so **watashi no** (wah-tah-shee-noh) is *mine*. Piece of cake, right? Now you can say **Watashi no desu** (wah-tah-shee-noh deh-soo; That's mine!) to the guy reaching for your keys. But don't say **Watashi no desu** every time a guest touches stuff in your house. You'll sound like a five-year-old child who doesn't know how to share your toys with other kids.

And luckily, if you know *yours* and *mine* in Japanese, you already know *your* and *my* in Japanese. They're exactly the same — almost like a buy-one-get-one-free coupon at the supermarket. **Watashi no desu** (wah-tah-shee-noh deh-soo) means *That's mine,* and **Watashi no kagi desu** (wah-tah-shee noh kah-gee deh-soo) means *That's my key.* **Watashi no** means both *mine* and *my*. If it's followed by a noun like **kagi,** it means *my,* and if it's not followed by a noun, it means *mine*. Take a look at Table 13-1. It contains all the basic personal pronouns and their ownership counterparts.

Table 13-1		Personal and Possessive Pronouns	
Personal Pronouns	*Translation*	*Ownership Words*	*Translation*
watashi (wah-tah-shee)	I/me	watashi no (wah-tah-shee noh)	my/mine
watashi tachi (wah-tah-shee tah-chee)	we/us	watashi tachi no (wah-tah-shee tah-chee noh)	our/ours
anata (ah-nah-tah)	you	anata no (ah-nah-tah noh)	your/yours
anata tachi (ah-nah-tah tah-chee)	you *plural*	anata tachi no (ah-nah-tah tah-chee noh)	your/yours *plural*
kare (kah-reh)	he/him	kare no (kah-reh noh)	his
kanojo (kah-noh-joh)	she/her	kanojo no (kah-noh-joh noh)	her/hers
karera (kah-reh-rah)	they/them	karera no (kah-reh-rah noh)	their/theirs

Checking into a Hotel

As soon as you **tsuku** (tsoo-koo; arrive) at a hotel, a **bōi-san** (bohh-ee-sahn; bell hop) helps you with your baggage. (If you're in Japan, there's no need to tip him. Isn't that amazing?)

Conjugate the verb **tsuku** (tsoo-koo; to arrive). It's a u-verb.

Form	*Pronunciation*
tsuku	tsoo-koo
tsukanai	tsoo-kah-nah-ee
tsuki	tsoo-kee
tsuite	tsoo-ee-teh

Go to the **furonto** (foo-rohn-toh; front desk). If you don't have a reservation, ask them whether they have an **akibeya** (ah-kee-beh-yah; vacancy). You can say **Akibeya wa arimasu ka** (ah-kee-beh-yah wah ah-ree-mah-soo kah; Any vacancies?).

If you have a reservation or they have a vacancy, **chekku-in suru** (chehk-koo-een soo-roo; check in). Hotel clerks are trained to speak very politely. If you're in Japan, a hotel clerk will address you with your name and **-sama** (sah-mah; Mr./Ms.), which is the super-polite, business-like version of **-san** (sahn).

The clerk will probably give you a **yōshi** (yohh-shee; form). Write your **namae** (nah-mah-eh; name), **jūsho** (jooo-shoh; address), and **denwa-bangō** (dehn-wah-bahn-gohh; telephone number) on it. If the clerk asks, show him or her your **pasupōto** (pah-soo-pohh-toh; passport). Finally, get a **kagi** (kah-gee; key) for your **heya** (heh-yah; room).

Which floor is your room on? Is it on the **nana-kai** (nah-nah-kah-ee; seventh floor) or on the **37-kai** (sahn-jooo-nah-nah-kah-ee; 37th floor)? Specify your floor using a numeral plus the counter **-kai.**

Which room is yours? Refer to your room using a numeral plus the counter **-gōshitsu** (gohh-shee-tsoo). Is it **502-gōshitsu** (goh-hyah-koo-nee-gohh-shee-tsoo; room #502) or **2502-gōshitsu** (nee-sehn-goh-hyah-koo-nee-gohh-shee-tsoo; room #2502)?

As you check in, you may want to ask where the parking garage is, whether the hotel has room service, and how to get a wake-up call. You may want to request **kurīningu sābisu** (koo-reee-neen-goo sahh-bee-soo; laundry service) or use the hotel **kinko** (keen-koh; safe) to store your valuables. Ask all of your questions when you check in so that you can **neru** (neh-roo; sleep) well. Some or all of the following phrases may come in handy:

- **Chekku-auto wa nan-ji desu ka.** (chehk-koo-ah-oo-toh wah nahn-jee deh-soo kah; When is checkout time?)

- **Chōshoku wa tsuite imasu ka.** (chohh-shoh-koo wah tsoo-ee-teh ee-mah-soo kah; Is breakfast included?)

- **Chūshajō wa doko desu ka.** (chooo-shah-johh wah doh-koh deh-soo kah; Where is the parking garage?)

- **Watashi ni dengon wa arimasen ka.** (wah-tah-shee nee dehn-gohn wah ah-ree-mah-sehn kah; Are there any messages for me?)

- **Rūmu sābisu wa arimasu ka.** (rooo-moo sahh-bee-soo wah ah-ree-mah-soo kah; Do you offer room service?)

- **Ashita no roku-ji ni mōningu kōru o onegaishimasu.** (ah-shee-tah noh roh-koo-jee nee mohh-neen-goo kohh-roo oh oh-neh-gah-ee-shee-mah-soo; Give me a morning wake-up call at six o'clock tomorrow, please.)

Conjugate the verb **neru** (neh-roo; to sleep). It's a ru-verb.

Form	Pronunciation
neru	neh-roo
nenai	neh-nah-ee
ne	neh
nete	neh-teh

Talkin' the Talk

 Yoshi Kitayama has just arrived at Hotel New York and is checking in.

Yoshi: **Sumimasen. Kyō kara yon-haku yoyaku shita-n-desu ga.**
soo-mee-mah-sehn. kyohh kah-rah yohn-hah-koo yoh-yah-koo shee-tahn-deh-soo gah.
Excuse me. I made a reservation for a four-night stay starting today.

Clerk: **O-namae wa.**
oh-nah-mah-eh wah.
Your name sir?

Yoshi: **Kitayama Yoshi desu.**
kee-tah-yah-mah yoh-shee deh-soo.
Yoshi Kitayama.

Clerk: **Kitayama Yoshi-sama de gozaimasu ne.**
kee-tah-yah-mah yoh-shee-sah-mah deh goh-zah-ee-mah-soo neh.
Mr. Yoshi Kitayama, correct?

Yoshi: **Hai.**
hah-ee.
Yes.

The clerk checks the computer.

Clerk: **Kyō kara yon-haku, o-hitori-sama, shinguru no o-heya de gozaimasu ne.**
kyohh kah-rah yohn-hah-koo, oh-hee-toh-ree-sah-mah, sheen-goo-roo noh oh-heh-yah deh goh-zah-ee-mah-soo neh.
Starting today — four nights, one person, a single room, right?

Yoshi: **Hai.**
hah-ee.
Yes.

Clerk: **703-goshitsu de gozaimasu. Kochira ga kagi de gozaimasu.**
nah-nah-hyah-koo-sahn-gohh-shee-tsoo deh goh-zah-ee-mah-soo. koh-chee-rah gah kah-gee deh goh-zah-ee-mah-soo.
It's room 703. Here's your key.

Yoshi: **Ā, dōmo.**
            ahh, dohh-moh.
            Thank you.

Words to Know

chekku-in	chehk-koo-een	check-in
-gōshitsu	gohh-shee-tsoo	room number [counter]
kagi	kah-gee	key
mōningu kōru	mohh-neen-goo kohh-roo	wake-up call
neru [ru]	neh-roo	to sleep
rūmu sābisu	rooo-moo sahh-bee-soo	room service
tsuku [u]	tsoo-koo	to arrive

Checking out of a Hotel

It's **chekku-auto** (chehk-koo-ah-oo-toh; checkout) time! Pack up your stuff and don't **wasureru** (wah-soo-reh-roo; forget) anything in your room. Go to the **furonto** (foo-rohn-toh; front desk) to **chekku-auto** and pay your bill. You may see some additional charges on your bill:

- **denwaryō** (dehn-wah-ryohh; telephone usage charge)
- **inshokuryō** (een-shoh-koo-ryohh; food and drink charge)
- **kurīningudai** (koo-reee-neen-goo-dah-ee; laundry charge)
- **zēkin** (zehh-keen; tax)

If you need further assistance from the hotel staff after checking out, just ask them.

- **Go-ji made nimotsu o azukatte kudasai.** (goh-jee mah-deh nee-moh-tsoo oh ah-zoo-kaht-teh koo-dah-sah-ee; Please keep my baggage here until five o'clock.)
- **Ryōshūsho o kudasai.** (ryohh-shooo-shoh oh koo-dah-sah-ee; Please give me the receipt.)

✔ **Takushī o yonde kudasai.** (tah-koo-sheee oh yohn-deh koo-dah-sah-ee; Please call a taxi.)

If the clerks can accommodate your request, they'll say **kekkō desu** (kehk-kohh deh-soo; it's good). **Kekkō desu** is the polite version of **ii desu** (eee deh-soo; it's good).

Just be careful. Both **kekkō desu** and **ii desu** can mean either *that's fine* or *no thank you,* depending on the situation. If a clerk says **kekkō desu** as a reply to one of your requests, it means *that's fine.* But if someone says **kekkō desu** right after you offer him or her a drink, it means *no thank you.*

By adding **masen ka** (mah-sehn kah) at the end of a request like **tabete kudasai** (tah-beh-teh koo-dah-sah-ee; eat please), you can make the request sound a bit softer and more polite. For example, **tabete kudasai masen ka** sounds much more polite than **tabete kudasai. Masen** is just a polite suffix in the negative form and **ka** is the question particle. It means something like *Wouldn't you?* or *Would you mind?* Use **masenka** when you ask a favor of a hotel clerk, as Mayuko does in the following Talkin' the Talk dialogue.

Talkin' the Talk

Mayuko is about to check out of the hotel.

Mayuko: **Sumimasen. Chekku-auto o shitai-n-desu ga.**
soo-mee-mah-sehn. chehk-koo-ah-oo-toh oh
shee-tah-een-deh-soo gah.
Excuse me. I'd like to check out.

Clerk: **Hai, kashikomarimashita.**
hah-ee, kah-shee-koh-mah-ree-mah-shee-tah.
Yes, certainly.

The clerk prepares the bill.

Clerk: **Kochira ga sēkyūsho desu.**
koh-chee-rah gah sehh-kyooo-shoh deh-soo.
Here's your bill.

The clerk shows the bill to Mayuko.

Clerk: **Shukuhakuryō ga go-man-en to denwaryō ga 1,500
en, gōkē 51,500-en desu.**
shoo-koo-hah-koo-ryohh gah goh-mahn-ehn toh
dehn-wah-ryohh gah sehn-goh-hyah-koo-ehn, gohh-
kehh goh-mahn-sehn-goh-hyah-koo-ehn deh-soo.
Fifty thousand yen for the room charge and 1,500 yen
for the telephone usage, and it comes to a total of
51,500 yen.

Mayuko: **Hai. Jā, Biza de onegaishimasu.**
            hah-ee. jahh, bee-zah deh
            oh-neh-gah-ee-shee-mah-soo.
            Okay. Then, could you charge it to my Visa?

Clerk: **Hai, kashikomarimashita.**
            hah-ee, kah-shee-koh-mah-ree-mah-shee-tah.
            Certainly.

The clerk processes the charge.

Mayuko: **Go-ji made sūtsukēsu-o azukatte kudasai masen ka.**
            goh-jee mah-deh sooo-tsoo-kehh-soo-oh ah-zoo-
            kaht-teh koo-dah-sah-ee mah-sehn kah.
            Could you keep my suitcase here until five o'clock?

Clerk: **Hai, kekkō desu yo.**
            hah-ee, kehk-kohh deh-soo yoh.
            Sure. That's fine.

Words to Know

chekku-auto	chehk-koo-ah-oo-toh	checkout
denwaryō	dehn-wah-ryohh	telephone usage charge
harau [u]	hah-rah-oo	to pay
inshokuryō	een-shoh-koo-ryohh	food and drink charge
kurīningudai	koo-reee-neen-goo-dah-ee	laundry charge
nimotsu	nee-moh-tsoo	luggage/baggage
ryōshūsho	ryohh-shooo-shoh	receipt
sēkyūsho	sehh-kyooo-shoh	bill

Fun & Games

Fill in the blanks using the following words:

mōningu kōru, rūmu sābisu, chekku–auto, dengon, akibeya

The answers are in Appendix C.

1. _____ **wa nan–ji desu ka.**

    When is checkout time?

2. **Watashi ni _____ wa arimasu ka.**

    Are there any messages for me?

3. _____ **wa arimasu ka.**

    Do you offer room service?

4. _____ **wa arimasu ka.**

    Any vacancies?

5. **Ashita 6–ji ni _____ o onegaishimasu.**

    Give me a wake-up call at 6 a.m.

Chapter 14

Transportation

. . . .

In This Chapter

▶ Flying through the airport with the greatest of ease

▶ Deciding on the best mode of transportation

▶ Traveling by bus, train, and taxi

▶ Traveling by subway, car, and boat

. . . .

Kōtsū kikan (kohh-tsooo kee-kahn; transportation) is an indispensable part of life. Choose the **kōtsū kikan** that best meets your needs. Which one costs less, driving a car or taking a train? Which one is less hectic, taking a subway or taking a cab? Which one do you think is safer, flying or driving? Are you traveling or commuting? This chapter provides you with the essential phrases that you need to get around town using various **kōtsū kikan**.

Japan is a **shimaguni** (shee-mah-goo-nee; island country). If you go to Japan, your first stop will probably be the airport, unless you take a **fune** (foo-neh; ship). So, I start from the airport in this chapter, and then take you into town going through bus terminals, train stations, taxi stands, rental car shops, and harbors.

Getting Around at the Airport

In a big country like the United States, a **hikōki** (hee-kohh-kee; airplane) is often necessary for vacation travel and business trips, even if you're afraid of heights. If you take a **kokusaibin** (koh-koo-sah-ee-been; international flight), don't forget to bring your **pasupōto** (pah-soo-pohh-toh; passport). You also may need a **biza** (bee-zah; visa) depending on where you're coming from, where you're going, the purpose of your visit, and the duration of your trip.

Getting on board

Arrive at the **kūkō** (kooo-kohh; airport) early to get a good **seki** (seh-kee; seat) on your **bin** (been; flight). Do you prefer a **mado gawa no seki** (mah-doh gah-wah noh seh-kee; window seat) or a **tsūro gawa no seki** (tsooo-roh gah-wah noh seh-kee; aisle seat)?

If you finish your **tōjō tetsuzuki** (tohh-johh teh-tsoo-zoo-kee; check-in) quickly, you may have some time to enjoy shopping at the **menzēten** (mehn-zehh-tehn; duty-free shops). If you want to bring a duty-free gift to your friend in the foreign country you're visiting, don't miss this opportunity. Or, just wait near your **gēto** (gehh-toh; gate) until you **noru** (noh-roo; get on) the plane. In some countries, including Japan, you need to go through **shukkoku tetsuzuki** (shook-koh-koo teh-tsoo-zoo-kee; departure immigration) before leaving.

After you get on the plane, just relax. Ask the **suchuwādo** (soo-choo-wahh-doh; steward) or **suchuwādesu** (soo-choo-wahh-deh-soo; stewardess) any questions you may have.

- ✔ **Ēga wa nan-ji kara desu ka.** (ehh-gah wah nahn-jee kah-rah deh-soo kah; What time does the movie start?)

- ✔ **Nan-ban gēto ni tsukimasu ka.** (nahn-bahn gehh-toh nee tsoo-kee-mah-soo kah; Which gate are we arriving at?)

- ✔ **Nan-ji ni tsukimasu ka.** (nahn-jee nee tsoo-kee-mah-soo kah; What time will we arrive?)

The verb **noru** (noh-roo; to ride) is a u-verb. Pay close attention to the **r** syllables as you conjugate it. **Noru** is used for all forms of transportation including bicycles, buses, trains, ships, and airplanes. So, its translation can be *to ride, get on,* or *get in* any form of transportation, depending on the context. Remember to mark the form of transportation that you are taking with the particle **ni** (nee), as in the following examples:

- ✔ **hikōki ni noru** (hee-kohh-kee nee noh-roo; to get on an airplane)

- ✔ **jitensha ni noru** (jee-tehn-shah nee noh-roo; to ride a bike)

- ✔ **densha ni noru** (dehn-shah nee noh-roo; to get on a train)

- ✔ **takushī ni noru** (tah-koo-sheee nee noh-roo; to get in a taxi)

Form	Pronunciation
noru	noh-roo
noranai	noh-rah-nah-ee
nori	noh-ree
notte	noht-teh

If you know the verb **noru,** you have to know the verb **oriru** (oh-ree-roo; to get off), unless you want to live on an airplane. Like **noru,** you can use

oriru for any form of transportation. Here are a few examples in an airport context:

- **Hikōki kara orimashita.** (hee-kohh-kee kah-rah oh-ree-mah-shee-tah; I got off the airplane.)

- **Ushiro no deguchi kara orite kudasai.** (oo-shee-roh noh deh-goo-chee kah-rah oh-ree-teh koo-dah-sah-ee; Please get off via the rear exit.)

The verb **oriru** (oh-ree-roo; to get off) is a ru-verb.

Form	*Pronunciation*
oriru	oh-ree-roo
orinai	oh-ree-nah-ee
ori	oh-ree
orite	oh-ree-teh

Words to Know

bin	been	flight
biza	bee-zah	visa
gēto	gehh-toh	gate
hikōki	hee-kohh-kee	airplane
kōtsū kikan	kohh-tsooo kee-kahn	transportation
kūkō	kooo-kohh	airport
noru [u]	noh-roo	to ride/to get on
oriru [ru]	oh-ree-roo	to get off

Going through immigration

Before entering a foreign country, you have to meet the very serious folks in the **nyūkoku shinsa** (nyooo-koh-koo sheen-sah; immigration) and **zēkan** (zehh-kahn; customs) sections. If you're arriving in Japan, go to the **gaikokujin** (gah-ee-koh-koo-jeen; foreigner) booth. Be ready for some of these questions and requests:

- ✔ **Biza wa.** (bee-zah wah; How about your visa?)

- ✔ **Doko ni tomarimasu ka.** (doh-koh nee toh-mah-ree-mah-soo kah; Where are you staying?)

- ✔ **Jūsho wa.** (jooo-shoh wah; Your address?)

- ✔ **O-namae wa.** (oh-nah-mah-eh wah; Your name?)

- ✔ **Shigoto desu ka.** (shee-goh-toh deh-soo kah; Are you here for business?)

To specify what form of transportation you're using to go somewhere, use the particle **de** (deh). Place **de** at the end of the word for the mode of transportation, and place both of them before the verb. For example, **Hikōki de ikimasu.** (hee-kohh-kee deh ee-kee-mah-soo; I'll go by airplane.)

The general function of **de** is to specify how you perform a given action. Specifying the form of transportation is just one instance in which you use **de.** For other examples, see Chapter 2.

And if you need to specify a flight with its flight number, add **-bin** (been; flight), right after the number. For example, **18-bin** (jooo-hah-chee-been) means *Flight 18.* **Bin** is a word that means *flight,* and it also functions as a counter that specifies which flight.

Talkin' the Talk

Emily has just arrived at Narita Airport in Japan, and she's at the immigration booth.

Officer:	**Tsugi no kata. Dōzo.**
	tsoo-gee noh kah-tah. dohh-zoh.
	Next person please.

Emily:	**Hai.**
	hah-ee.
	Yes.

Officer:	**Pasupōto o misete kudasai.**
	pah-soo-pohh-toh oh mee-seh-teh koo-dah-sah-ee.
	Show me your passport please.

Emily:	**Dōzo.**
	dohh-zoh.
	Here you are.

Officer:	**Sēnengappi wa.**
	sehh-nehn-gahp-pee wah.
	Date of birth?

Emily: **1981-nen go-gatsu 25-nichi desu.**
sehn-kyooo-hyah-koo-hah-chee-jooo-ee-chee-nehn
goh-gah-tsoo nee-jooo-goh-nee-chee deh-soo.
May 25, 1981.

Officer: **Kankō desu ka.**
kahn-kohh deh-soo kah.
Are you here for sightseeing?

Emily: **Hai.**
hah-ee.
Yes.

Officer: **Dono bin de kimashita ka.**
doh-noh been deh kee-mah-shee-tah kah.
Which flight did you take to come here?

Emily: **Īsuto uesuto no 900-bin desu.**
eee-soo-toh oo-eh-soo-toh noh kyooo-hyah-koo-been
deh-soo.
Eastwest, Flight 900.

Officer: **Doko ni tomarimasu ka.**
doh-koh nee toh-mah-ree-mah-soo kah.
Where are you staying?

Emily: **Hoteru Tōkyō desu.**
hoh-teh-roo tohh-kyohh deh-soo.
Hotel Tokyo.

Officer: **Hai. Jā dōzo. Tsugi no kata.**
hah-ee. jahh dohh-zoh. tsoo-gee noh kah-tah.
Okay. You may go. Next person.

Words to Know

nyūkoku shinsa	nyooo-koh-koo sheen-sah	immigration
pasupōto	pah-soo-pohh-toh	passport
tsugi no kata	tsoo-gee noh kah-tah	next person
zēkan	zehh-kahn	customs

Going through customs

After you get through immigration, go to the **tenimotsu hikiwatashijō** (teh-nee-moh-tsoo hee-kee-wah-tah-shee-johh; baggage claim) and pick up your suitcases, bags, boxes, or whatever. Put them on a cart, proceed to **zēkan** (zehh-kahn; customs), and pay the **zēkin** (zehh-keen; tax), if necessary. Certain items are **menzē** (mehn-zehh; duty-free) only if you bring less than a certain amount or quantity of the item with you. Be familiar with the following questions and phrases:

- **Asoko de zēkin o haratte kudasai.** (ah-soh-koh deh zehh-keen oh hah-raht-teh koo-dah-sah-ee; Pay the tax over there please.)

- **Minomawari no mono desu.** (mee-noh-mah-wah-ree noh moh-noh deh-soo; They are my personal belongings.)

- **Shinkoku suru mono wa arimasen ka.** (sheen-koh-koo soo-roo moh-noh wah ah-ree-mah-sehn kah; Is there anything you want to declare?).

- **Sūtsukēsu o akete kudasai.** (sooo-tsoo-kehh-soo oh ah-keh-teh koo-dah-sah-ee; Open your suitcase please.)

Conjugate the verb **akeru** (ah-keh-roo; to open). It's a ru-verb.

Form	Pronunciation
akeru	ah-keh-roo
akenai	ah-keh-nah-ee
ake	ah-keh
akete	ah-keh-teh

Talkin' the Talk

Terry is about to go through customs at the airport.

Officer: **Tsugi no kata. Dōzo.**
tsoo-gee noh kah-tah. dohh-zoh.
Next person please.

Terry: **Hai.**
hah-ee.
Yes.

Officer: **Shinkoku suru mono wa arimasu ka.**
sheen-koh-koo soo-roo moh-noh wah
ah-ree-mah-soo kah.
Is there anything that you want to declare?

Terry: **Īe, arimasen.**
            eee-eh ah-ree-mah-sehn.
            No, I don't.

The officer points at Terry's suitcase.

Officer: **Kono kaban no naka wa.**
            koh-noh kah-bahn noh nah-kah wah.
            What's inside this bag?

Terry: **Zenbu minomawari no mono desu.**
            zehn-boo mee-noh-mah-wah-ree noh moh-noh
            deh-soo.
            Everything is my personal belongings.

Officer: **Chotto akete kudasai.**
            choht-toh ah-keh-teh koo-dah-sah-ee.
            Open it please.

Leaving the airport

When you're done at **zēkan,** grab your cart, pass through the **deguchi** (deh-goo-chee; exit), and go to the **tōchaku robī** (tohh-chah-koo roh-beee; arrival gate). You may see hundreds of faces looking at you, which can make you feel like you're either a movie star or a terrible criminal. Most of these people are just looking for their friends and relatives, not you, so don't get too excited. If no one is meeting you, you can find ground transportation on your own.

Ask for assistance at the **chiketto kauntā** (chee-keht-toh kah-oon-tahh; ticket counter) or **annaijo** (ahn-nah-ee-joh; information counter) in your quest to find ground transportation. You can use the following questions to arrange your transportation from the airport or any other location.

- ✔ **Monorēru wa doko de noremasu ka.** (moh-noh-rehh-roo wah doh-koh deh noh-reh-mah-soo kah; Where can I catch the monorail?)

- ✔ **Shinagawa yuki no rimujin basu wa arimasu ka.** (shee-nah-gah-wah yoo-kee noh ree-moo-jeen bah-soo wah ah-ree-mah-soo kah; Do you have a limousine to Shinagawa?)

- ✔ **Tsugi no Tōkyō eki yuki no rimujin basu wa nan-ji desu ka.** (tsoo-gee noh tohh-kyohh eh-kee yoo-kee noh ree-moo-jeen bah-soo wah nahn-jee deh-soo kah; What time is the next limousine bound for Tokyo Station?)

Words to Know

deguchi	deh-goo-chee	exit
monorēru	moh-noh-rehh-roo	monorail
rimujin basu	ree-moo-jeen bah-soo	limousine
tōchaku robī	tohh-chah-koo roh-beee	arrival gate

Getting Around In and Out of Town

Which is your favorite form of **kōtsū kikan** (kohh-tsooo kee-kahn; transportation)? Sure, it depends on where you are, and where you want to go. If you're going into town from the airport, a **shatoru basu** (shah-toh-roo bah-soo; shuttle bus) may be the most economical choice, but you can certainly take a **takushī** (tah-koo-sheee; taxi).

If you're just traveling around town, you have many choices. Which one would you pick? A young man in a leather jacket may pick a **baiku** (bah-ee-koo; motorcycle). Yes, it's cool. **Baiku** means only *motorcycle* in Japanese, not *bicycle.* **Jitensha** (jee-tehn-shah) is the word for *bicycle,* and it would probably be a health-conscious person's choice of transportation. A father with a family of five may prefer a **kuruma** (koo-roo-mah; car) to a **densha** (dehn-shah; train). And someone who likes the sun may not like the **chikatetsu** (chee-kah-teh-tsoo; subway). Table 14-1 lists several forms of transportation.

Table 14-1	**Forms of Transportation**	
Form of Transportation	***Pronunciation***	***Translation***
basu	bah-soo	bus
chikatetsu	chee-kah-teh-tsoo	subway
densha	dehn-shah	train
fune	foo-neh	ship
jitensha	jee-tehn-shah	bicycle

Form of Transportation	*Pronunciation*	*Translation*
kuruma	koo-roo-mah	car
rentakā	rehn-tah-kahh	rental car
takushī	tah-koo-sheee	taxi

Asking about the best

To ask questions like *Which transportation method is most economical?* or *Can you tell me the best way to get there?* use the question words **dono** (doh-noh; which) or **dore** (doh-reh; which one). If you're asking about *which* of a particular thing, use **dono** and add the thing you're asking about right after it, as in the following examples:

- ✔ **Dono basu ni norimasu ka.** (doh-noh bah-soo nee noh-ree-mah-soo kah; Which bus are you getting on?)
- ✔ **Dono densha de ikimasu ka.** (doh-noh dehn-shah deh ee-kee-mah-soo kah; By which train are you going there?)

If the name of the thing that you're asking about is understood in the context, or is stated separately, you don't have to repeat that word. Just use **dore** (which one) instead of **dono** (which).

- ✔ **Dore ni norimasu ka.** (doh-reh nee noh-ree-mah-soo kah; Which one are you getting on?)
- ✔ **Dore de ikimasu ka.** (doh-reh deh ee-kee-mah-soo kah; By which one are you going there?)

You already know how to form a question phrase (if you need a refresher, turn to Chapter 2). So, the next step is to make a question sentence using the **dono** or **dore** question phrase as the subject and to insert the key ingredient for a "most/-est" question — the adverb **ichi-ban** (ee-chee-bahn; the most/-est). If you recognize the word **ichi-ban** as the Japanese word for *first,* you're right. It literally means *number one.* Check out the following examples:

- ✔ **Dono basu ga ichi-ban hayai desu ka.** (doh-noh bah-soo gah ee-chee-bahn hah-yah-ee deh-soo kah; Which bus is the fastest?)
- ✔ **Dono densha ga ichi-ban benri desu ka.** (doh-noh dehn-shah gah ee-chee-bahn behn-ree deh-soo kah; Which train is the most convenient?)
- ✔ **Dore ga ichi-ban yasui desu ka.** (doh-reh gah ee-chee-bahn yah-soo-ee deh-soo kah; Which one is the cheapest?)

If you want to make a comparison and alert listeners that they must choose from the list that you provide, you can list the items at the beginning of a question. The only thing you have to do is to place the particle **to** (toh) at the end of each item, as in

- ✔ **Takushī to, densha to, basu to, dore ga ichi-ban hayai desu ka.** (tah-koo-sheee toh, dehn-shah toh, bah-soo toh, doh-reh gah ee-chee-bahn hah-yah-ee deh-soo kah; Which is the fastest, taxis, trains, or buses?)

- ✔ **Hikōki to, kuruma to, densha to, basu to, dore ga ichi-ban anzen desu ka.** (hee-kohh-kee toh, koo-roo-mah toh, dehn-shah toh, bah-soo toh, doh-reh gah ee-chee-bahn ahn-zehn deh-soo kah; Which is the safest, airplanes, cars, trains, or buses?)

The particle **to** lets you neatly list items one-by-one. It's almost like all the commas when you list things like A, B, C, and D in English.

If you're comparing people, use **dare** (dah-reh; who) instead of **dore**. And if you're comparing locations, use **doko** (doh-koh; where) instead of **dore**. To ask a question that compares just two items, use the question word **dochira** (doh-chee-rah; which one out of the two), regardless of what the two items are. See Chapter 6 for more information about **dochira** and a complete discussion of comparisons.

Getting on a bus

Basu (bah-soo; buses) are inexpensive and convenient, and they can take you across town or across the country. Taking a long-distance bus instead of a plane or train can save you a lot of money.

Go to a **basu tāminaru** (bah-soo tahh-mee-nah-roo; bus terminal) or **basutē** (bah-soo-tehh; bus stop) and find out which **basu** you should take. The **unchin** (oon-cheen; fare) may be a flat rate, or it may vary depending on how far you go. **Ireru** (ee-reh-roo; put) the **unchin** in the designated box. Don't forget to ask the driver for a transfer if you need to change buses.

Conjugate the verb **ireru** (ee-reh-roo; to put). It's a ru-verb.

Form	Pronunciation
ireru	ee-reh-roo
irenai	ee-reh-nah-ee
ire	ee-reh
irete	ee-reh-teh

Talkin' the Talk

Mrs. Tani is going to visit her friend in a different town for the first time. She's at the bus stop, and the bus has just arrived. Mrs. Tani asks the driver some questions.

Mrs. Tani: **Sumimasen. Kono basu wa Takada-chō ni ikimasu ne.**
soo-mee-mah-sehn. koh-noh bah-soo wah tah-kah-dah-chohh nee ee-kee-mah-soo neh.
Excuse me. This bus goes to Takada Town, right?

Driver: **Hai.**
hah-ee.
Yes.

Mrs. Tani: **Norikae wa arimasen ne.**
noh-ree-kah-eh wah ah-ree-mah-sehn neh.
No transfer needed, right?

Driver: **Hai, arimasen.**
hah-ee, ah-ree-mah-sehn.
Right, no transfer needed.

Mrs. Tani: **Ikura desu ka.**
ee-koo-rah deh-soo kah.
How much does it cost?

Driver: **250-en desu. Koko ni irete kudasai.**
nee-hyah-koo goh-jooo-ehn deh-soo. koh-koh nee ee-reh-teh koo-dah-sah-ee.
It's 250 yen. Please put it here.

Mrs. Tani: **Hai.**
hah-ee.
Sure.

Hai (hah-ee) in Japanese expresses agreement — *right or correct* — but it doesn't always express the affirmative *yes.* So, the driver's answer **hai, arimasen** in the above Talkin' the Talk means *Right, no transfer needed,* rather than *Yes, no transfer needed,* which is weird and confusing.

Words to Know

basu	bah-soo	bus
basu tāminaru	bah-soo tahh-mee-nah-roo	bus terminal
basutē	bah-soo-tehh	bus stop
ireru [ru]	ee-reh-roo	to put
norikae	noh-ree-kah-eh	transfer
unchin	oon-cheen	fare

Hopping a train

Return to the **eki** (eh-kee; train station) in your hometown if you haven't been there in a while. The smells and sounds and the platforms, stairs, and ticket gates always make me feel **natsukashii** (nah-tsoo-kah-sheee; nostalgic)! Traveling by **densha** (dehn-shah; train) is special because you go through many **eki,** each of which represents the people who live or work that town. In some **eki,** you see many businessmen and businesswomen, but in others you see children and their moms.

Check the direction of your train:

- ✔ **kudari densha** (koo-dah-ree dehn-shah; down train)
- ✔ **nobori densha** (noh-boh-ree dehn-shah; up train)
- ✔ **Ōsaka yuki** (ohh-sah-kah yoo-kee; bound for Osaka)
- ✔ **Tōkyō hatsu Nagoya yuki** (tohh-kyohh hah-tsoo nah-goh-yah yoo-kee; departing from Tokyo and bound for Nagoya)

You may be asking yourself, "What in the world are **nobori densha** (up trains) and **kudari densha** (down trains)?" You're in luck — I have the answer. **Nobori densha** refers to any train in Japan traveling toward Tokyo, and **kudari densha** refers to any train traveling away from Tokyo. Tokyo really is the center of Japan, as a glance at a map of Japan shows you. These strange terms may give the impression that Tokyo is the highest point in Japan, so the farthest location from Tokyo must be below sea level. But the allusion to altitude is only figurative, even if somewhat elitist on the part of Tokyo. The point of using these two terms is just to distinguish the directions of each railroad line, not the altitude.

CULTURAL WISDOM

Eating a box lunch from the train station

Ekiben (eh-kee-behn) is a box lunch sold at **eki** (eh-kee; train stations) or on the **densha** (dehn-shah; train). Different **eki** sell different **ekiben** with unique names. The name of my favorite **ekiben** is **Tōge no kamameshi** (tohh-geh noh kah-mah-meh-shee; Mountain Pass Chicken-Vegetable Rice in a Pot) from **Nagano-ken** (nah-gah-noh-kehn; Nagano Prefecture).

Some **ekiben** are famous, and people visit the **eki** or get on the **densha** just to buy one of these lunches. If you travel in Japan by train, buy an **ekiben** and a bottle of hot **o-cha** (oh-chah; green tea) at the platform. What a fun experience!

When you take a train, make sure you know what time it **deru** (deh-roo; leaves) and **tsuku** (tsoo-koo; arrives). Conjugate the verb **deru** (deh-roo; to leave). It's a ru-verb. The verb for *to arrive,* **tsuku** (tsoo-koo), is conjugated in Chapter 13.

Form	*Pronunciation*
deru	deh-roo
denai	deh-nah-ee
de	deh
dete	deh-teh

REMEMBER

Remember to check the **jikokuhyō** (jee-koh-koo-hyohh; time table) at the station. Be ready for the 24-hour system if you're traveling in Japan. **Jū-ji** (jooo-goh-jee; fifteen o'clock) means **gogo 3-ji** (goh-goh sahn-jee; 3 p.m.). Watch out for two important keywords on the timetable: **hatsu** (hah-tsoo; departure) and **chaku** (chah-koo; arrival). They're short forms of **hassha suru** (hahs-shah soo-roo; to depart) and **tōchaku suru** (tohh-chah-koo soo-roo; to arrive). Take a look at a few examples (and for a complete recap on telling time, check out Chapter 7):

- ✔ **16-ji 15-fun hatsu** (jooo-roh-koo-jee jooo-goh-foon hah-tsoo; 16:15 *or* 4:15 p.m. departure)

- ✔ **20-ji 57-fun chaku** (nee-jooo-jee goh-jooo-nah-nah-foon chah-koo; 20:57 *or* 8:57 p.m. arrival)

- ✔ **7-ji 5-fun Tōkyō hatsu 10-ji 7-fun Ōsaka chaku** (shee-chee-jee goh-foon tohh-kyohh hah-tsoo jooo-jee nah-nah-foon ohh-sah-kah chah-koo; 7:05 a.m. Tokyo departure, 10:07 a.m. Osaka arrival)

Depending on how much of a hurry you're in, choose from one of these types of trains, listed in descending order of speed and distance:

- **shinkansen** (sheen-kahn-sehn; bullet train)
- **tokkyū** (tohk-kyooo; super-express)
- **kaisoku** (kah-ee-soh-koo; rapid)
- **kyūkō** (kyooo-kohh; express)
- **futsū** (foo-tsooo; local)

Shinkansen got its English name, *bullet train,* from the bullet shape of the lead car. These trains run on special tracks at top speeds of 300 kilometers per hour (186 miles per hour) and connect all the major cities of **Honshū** (hohn-shooo), the main island of Japan.

For all trains, the **unchin** (oon-cheen; fare) is different for **otona** (oh-toh-nah; adults) and **kodomo** (koh-doh-moh; children). Be sure to specify the number of **otona** and the number of **kodomo** when buying your **kippu** (keep-poo; tickets). And ask whether they have any discounts or special assistance for **otoshiyori** (oh-toh-shee-yoh-ree; seniors) and other people, like **shintaishōgaisha** (sheen-tah-ee shohh-gah-ee-shah; handicapped people).

Use the counter **-mai** to express the number of tickets you want to purchase. (See Chapter 2 for information on counters.) Also specify whether you need an **ōfuku** (ohh-foo-koo; round-trip) or **katamichi** (kah-tah-mee-chee; one-way) ticket. If you're taking the **shinkansen** or another **tokkyū densha** (tohk-kyooo dehn-shah; super-express train) in Japan, you'll need to buy two tickets: a **tokkyūken** (tohk-kyooo-kehn; super-express ticket) plus the regular **jōshaken** (johh-shah-kehn; passenger ticket). You may make a request like:

- **Nagoya made otona san-mai ōfuku onegaishimasu.** (nah-goh-yah mah-deh oh-toh-nah sahn-mah-ee ohh-foo-koo oh-neh-gah-ee-shee-mah-soo; To Nagoya, three round-trip tickets for adults, please.)
- **Ōsaka made otona ichi-mai to kodomo ni-mai onegaishimasu.** (ohh-sah-kah mah-deh oh-toh-nah ee-chee-mah-ee toh koh-doh-moh nee-mah-ee oh-neh-gah-ee-shee-mah-soo; To Osaka, one ticket for an adult, and two tickets for children, please.)
- **Tōkyō made katamichi ichi-mai.** (tohh-kyohh mah-deh kah-tah-mee-chee ee-chee-mah-ee; To Tokyo, one one-way ticket, please.)
- **Tōkyō made no jōshaken to tokkyūken o kudasai.** (tohh-kyohh mah-deh noh johh-shah-kehn toh tohk-kyooo-kehn oh koo-dah-sah-ee; A passenger ticket and a super-express ticket to Tokyo, please.)

Find out which **hōmu** (hohh-moo; platform) you're leaving from and say the number with the counter **-ban-sen** (bahn-sehn), such as **ichi-ban-sen** (ee-chee-bahn-sehn; track one), **ni-ban-sen** (nee-bahn-sehn; track two), and **san-ban-sen** (sahn-bahn-sehn; track three).

Talkin' the Talk

Mr. Oda is about to visit his client in Kuwana City. He's at the train station.

Mr. Oda:	**Sumimasen. Kuwana made ichi-mai.** soo-mee-mah-sehn. koo-wah-nah mah-deh ee-chee-mah-ee. Excuse me. To Kuwana, one ticket.
Clerk:	**Jōshaken dake.** johh-shah-kehn dah-keh. Just the passenger ticket?
Mr. Oda:	**Tokkyūken mo.** tohk-kyooo-kehn moh. A super-express ticket too.
Clerk:	**Jā, jōshaken ga 550-en, tokkyūken ga 400-en de 950-en.** jahh, johh-shah-kehn gah goh-hyah-koo-goh-jooo-ehn, tohk-kyooo-kehn gah yohn-hyah-koo-ehn deh kyooo-hyah-koo-goh-jooo-ehn. Then, 550 yen for the passenger ticket, 400 yen for the super-express ticket, and the total is 950 yen.
Mr. Oda:	**Hai. Nan-ban-sen desu ka.** hah-ee. nahn-bahn-sehn deh-soo kah. Okay. Which track?
Clerk:	**Go-ban-sen desu.** goh-bahn-sehn deh-soo. Track Five.
Mr. Oda:	**Dōmo.** dohh-moh. Thanks.

Words to Know

chaku	chah-koo	arriving at
densha	dehn-shah	train
futsū densha	foo-tsooo dehn-shah	local train
hatsu	hah-tsoo	departing from
hōmu	hohh-moo	platform
kaisoku densha	kah-ee-soh-koo dehn-shah	rapid train
katamichi	kah-tah-mee-chee	one-way
kippu	keep-poo	ticket
kudari densha	koo-dah-ree dehn-shah	down train
kyūkō densha	kyooo-kohh dehn-shah	express train
nobori densha	noh-boh-ree dehn-shah	up train
ōfuku	ohh-foo-koo	round-trip
tokkyū densha	tohk-kyooo dehn-shah	super express train

Hailing a taxi

Takushī (tah-koo-sheee; taxis) are very convenient — they come to where you are, so there's no need to walk anywhere. Unlike trains, there's no need to figure out which one you should take. And unlike buses, there's no need to wait for them. Just call a taxi to pick you up wherever you are. If you have three or four people in your group, taking a **takushī** may be cheaper than taking a train or a bus.

Taxis in Japan

Takushī (tah-koo-sheee; taxies) in Japan are clean, neat, and comfortable. When a taxi stops for you, don't try to open the door — it opens automatically! The interiors are always clean, and the seats have white covers. I'd like to see taxis in some other countries try to get away with white interiors!

The drivers wear handsome uniforms, white gloves, and white caps. They're usually polite, friendly, and helpful, and they know the neighborhoods very well. If a driver doesn't know the directions to your destination, the main office guides him or her over the radio.

After you pay the fare, the door automatically opens again to let you out. Maybe the door won't open if you don't pay, so don't try to stiff the driver! One more thing that you should know: In Japan, tipping taxi drivers is totally optional. It's enough just to tip them when you ask for a special service.

These are some phrases you may say or hear in a taxi:

- ✔ **Kūkō made ikura gurai kakarimasu ka.** (kooo-kohh mah-deh ee-koo-rah goo-rah-ee kah-kah-ree-mah-soo kah; How much does it cost to the airport?)

- ✔ **Bijutsukan made onegai shimasu.** (bee-joo-tsoo-kahn mah-deh oh-neh-gah-ee shee-mah-soo; Please go to the art museum.)

- ✔ **Dochira made.** (doh-chee-rah mah-deh; To where?)

- ✔ **Otsuri wa kekkō desu.** (oh-tsoo-ree wah kehk-kohh deh-soo; Please keep the change.)

- ✔ **Tsukimashita yo.** (tsoo-kee-mah-shee-tah yoh; We're here.)

Kekkō desu (kehk-kohh deh-soo) means *good* or *fine* in some contexts, but it means *no thank you* in other contexts. It may sound like a contradiction, but in English you sometimes say *I'm fine* after being asked *Would you like some coffee?* when what you mean is *no thank you,* right? That's the spirit of **kekkō desu** as *no thank you.* When the driver is about to give you the **otsuri** (oh-tsoo-ree; change), you can refuse it by saying **kekkō desu.** Letting the driver keep the change is cool, but totally optional in Japan. Of course, estimate your change before you say **kekkō desu.**

Talkin' the Talk

Kent is trying to hail a taxi. A taxi finally stops in front of him, and the door opens.

Kent: **Akagi Ēgo Gakkō made onegaishimasu.**
ah-kah-gee ehh-goh gahk-kohh mah-deh oh-neh-gah-ee-shee-mah-soo.
To Akagi English School please.

Driver: **Yokohama Eki no mae desu ne.**
yoh-koh-hah-mah eh-kee noh mah-eh deh-soo neh.
That's in front of Yokohama Station, right?

Kent: **Hai.**
hah-ee.
Yes.

Driver: **O-kyaku-san wa ēgo no sensē desu ka.**
oh-kyah-koo-sahn wah ehh-goh noh sehn-sehh deh-soo kah.
Are you an English teacher?

Kent: **Hai.**
hah-ee.
Yes.

The taxi arrives in front of Akagi English School.

Driver: **Hai, tsukimashita yo.**
hah-ee, tsoo-kee-mah-shee-tah yoh.
Okay, we're here.

Kent: **Ikura desu ka.**
ee-koo-rah deh-soo kah.
How much?

Driver: **750-en desu.**
nah-nah-hyah-koo-goh-jooo-en deh-soo.
750 yen.

Kent: **Jā, dōzo. Otsuri wa kekkō desu.**
jahh, dohh-zoh. oh-tsoo-ree wah kehk-kohh deh-soo.
Here you are. Keep the change.

Driver: **Ā, arigatō gozaimasu.**
ahh, ah-ree-gah-tohh goh-zah-ee-mah-soo.
Oh, thank you very much.

Taking the subway

Subways are convenient and inexpensive. Which one would you take, a **takushī** (tah-koo-sheee; taxi) or the **chikatetsu** (chee-kah-teh-tsoo; subway)? A **takushī** usually costs a whole lot more than the **chikatetsu**. How about a **densha** (dehn-shah; train)? It may be fast, but the train may not go near your destination. Should you take a **basu** (bah-soo; bus)? It may bring you to your destination, but it may take forever. Considering all these factors, the **chikatetsu** may offer you the most convenience for your dollar.

When you make up your mind, say **ni suru** (nee soo-roo; to decide on). The verb **suru** is an irregular verb, and its polite counterpart is **shimasu**. Now you can understand the following decisions:

- ✔ **Chikatetsu ni shimasu.** (chee-kah-teh-tsoo nee shee-mah-soo; I'll decide on the subway.)
- ✔ **Takushī ni shimasu.** (tah-koo-sheee nee shee-mah-soo; I'll take a taxi.)

When you take a subway, be careful not to miss your station. At which station should you get off? **Hito-tsu-me** (hee-toh-tsoo-meh; the first one) or **futa-tsu-me** (foo-tah-tsoo-meh; the second one)? See Chapter 12 to find out how to express ordinal numbers using the ordinal counter -**me**.

Talkin' the Talk

Richard is asking for directions to Kabukiza Theater in Tokyo at the front desk of his hotel.

Richard: **Sumimasen. Kabukiza ni ikitai-n-desu ga, koko kara takushī de nan-pun gurai desu ka.**
soo-mee-mah-sehn. kah-boo-kee-zah nee ee-kee-tah-een-deh-soo gah, koh-koh kah-rah tah-koo-sheee deh nahn-poon goo-rah-ee deh-soo kah.
Excuse me. I want to go to Kabukiza. How long does it take from here by taxi?

Clerk: **15-fun gurai desu.**
jooo-goh-foon goo-rah-ee deh-soo.
About 15 minutes.

Richard: **Chikatetsu wa benri desu ka.**
chee-kah-teh-tsoo wah behn-ree deh-soo kah.
Is the subway convenient?

Clerk: **Hai. Benri desu yo.**
hah-ee. behn-ree deh-soo yoh.
Yes. It's convenient.

Richard:	**Jā, chikatetsu ni shimasu.**
	jahh, chee-kah-teh-tsoo nee shee-mah-soo.
	Then, I'll take the subway.

Clerk:	**Soko no eki kara notte, itsu-tsu-me no eki no Higashi Ginza de orite kudasai.**
	soh-koh noh eh-kee kah-rah noht-teh, ee-tsoo-tsoo-meh noh eh-kee noh hee-gah-shee geen-zah deh oh-ree-teh koo-dah-sah-ee.
	Take the subway from that station over there, and get off at the fifth station, Higashi Ginza.

Richard:	**Ā, wakarimashita. Arigatō gozaimashita.**
	ahh, wah-kah-ree-mah-shee-tah. ah-ree-gah-tohh goh-zah-ee-mah-shee-tah.
	Okay. I got it. Thank you very much.

Clerk:	**Īe.**
	eee-eh.
	My pleasure.

Renting a car

If you live in a big city, you may not want to own a **kuruma** (koo-roo-mah; car). Subways and buses are everywhere. Taxis are always on the street. Parking space is limited and very costly. And insurance is more expensive in the city than in the suburbs. Many city dwellers choose not to own a car. When it's time to take that weekend trip outside of the city, they often **kariru** (kah-ree-roo; rent) a car. It's not very expensive, you can get a nice car in good condition, usually, and the rental process isn't that difficult.

Even if you own a car, you may want to rent a big minivan to go to a ski resort with seven of your friends. A minivan can make the drive more fun. Take turns driving, and share the **kosuto** (koh-soo-toh; cost). You may also need to rent a car if you go to another city on business, after you fly there. A rental car gives you the freedom to travel around town.

If you go to Japan, you may think about renting a car. But it's a bit tricky to drive a car in Japan. You have to drive on the **hidari gawa** (hee-dah-ree gah-wah; left side), and your **handoru** (hahn-doh-roo; steering wheel) is on the **migi gawa** (mee-gee gah-wah; right side). The **dōro** (dohh-roh; roads) are clean and nice but very **semai** (seh-mah-ee; narrow). **Jitensha** (jee-tehn-shah; bicycles) and **hokōsha** (hoh-kohh-shah; pedestrians) always have the right of way in the neighborhood streets. And the **kōsoku dōro** (kohh-soh-koo dohh-roh; highways) are great, but the tolls are outrageous.

If you still decide to **unten suru** (oon-tehn soo-roo; to drive) in Japan after thinking about all of these factors, go to a **rentakā gaisha** (rehn-tah-kahh gah-ee-shah; rental-car company). Their **ryōkin** (ryohh-keen; charges) differ depending on the type of vehicle that you choose:

- **yon daburu dī** (yohn dah-boo-ruu deee; four-wheel drive)

- **hai gurēdo sarūn** (hah-ee goo-rehh-doh sah-rooon; luxury car)

- **konpakuto sedan** (kohn-pah-koo-toh seh-dahn; compact sedan)

- **supōtsu taipu** (soo-pohh-tsoo tah-ee-poo; sports car)

- **wagonsha** (wah-gohn-shah; station wagon)

Conjugate the verb **unten suru** (oon-tehn soo-roo; to drive). If you know how to conjugate the irregular verb **suru** (soo-roo; to do), it's a piece of cake.

Form	Pronunciation
unten suru	oon-tehn soo-roo
unten shinai	oon-tehn shee-nah-ee
unten shi	oon-tehn shee
unten shite	oon-tehn shee-teh

And ask about the rental car's features:

- **eakon** (eh-ah-kohn; air conditioning)

- **manyuaru** (mah-nyoo-ah-roo; stick shift)

- **ōtomachikku** (ohh-toh-mah-cheek-koo; automatic transmission)

- **sutereo** (soo-teh-reh-oh; stereo)

Show your **unten menkyoshō** (oon-tehn-mehn-kyoh-shohh; driver's license) to the clerk at the car-rental agency. You'll need a **kokusai menkyoshō** (koh-koo-sah-ee mehn-kyoh-shohh; international license) when you drive in Japan, unless you have a Japanese license. Some common phrases that you can use when renting a car are:

- **Hoken o kakemasu.** (hoh-kehn oh kah-keh-mah-soo; I'll take the insurance policy.)

- **Kogata no kuruma o karitai-n-desu ga.** (koh-gah-tah noh koo-roo-mah oh kah-ree-tah-een-deh-soo gah; I'd like to rent a small-size car, but do you have one?)

- **Kyō kara kinyōbi made tsukai-tai-n-desu.** (kyooo kah-rah keen-yohh-bee mah-deh tsoo-kah-ee-tah-een-deh-soo; I want it today through Friday.)

- **Mokuyōbi ni kaeshimasu.** (moh-koo-yohh-bee nee kah-eh-shee-mah-soo; I'll return it on Thursday.)

My ultimate piece of advice: Stop at a **gasorin sutando** (gah-soh-reen soo-tahn-doh; gas station) before you run out of **gasorin** (gah-soh-reen; gas).

Conjugate the verbs **kariru** (kah-ree-roo; to rent) and **kaesu** (kah-eh-soo; to return) — two essential words for visiting a rental-car agency. **Kariru** is a ru-verb, and **kaesu** is a u-verb. The conjugation table for **kariru** is in Chapter 11. The one for **kaesu** is provided below:

Form	Pronunciation
kaesu	kah-eh-soo
kaesanai	kah-eh-sah-nah-ee
kaeshi	kah-eh-shee
kaeshite	kah-eh-shee-teh

Words to Know

gasorin sutando	gah-soh-reen soo-tahn-doh	gas station
hoken	hoh-kehn	insurance
kaesu [u]	kah-eh-soo	to return
rentakā	rehn-tah-kahh	rental car

Boarding a boat

You may have a lot of chances to go to nearby islands or to towns across the lake, bay, or cove near your home. Some people even commute to work by ferry. What a romantic way to commute! Use some of the following terms to travel by water or just to have fun:

- **bōto** (bohh-toh; boat)
- **ferī** (feh-reee; ferry)
- **fune** (foo-neh; ship)
- **yotto** (yoht-toh; yacht)

If you don't know how to swim, find the life jackets right after you board. I'm just kidding. Relax and enjoy the nice breeze. If you spend some time on the water, you'll come ashore feeling refreshed!

Fun & Games

How do you say the following types of transportation in Japanese?

The answers are in Appendix C.

1. _____

2. _____

3. _____

4. _____

5. _____

Chapter 15

Planning a Trip

*J*insē (jeen-sehh; life) is like a **tabi** (tah-bee; journey), but it's also nice to go on an actual **ryokō** (ryoh-kohh; trip) to escape from the pressures of daily life. Everyone needs a little rest and relaxation, but careful planning is the key to a successful **ryokō**. With a little advance work, you can save lots of **jikan** (jee-kahn; time) and **o-kane** (oh-kah-neh; money). And you can avoid the stress and frustration that comes with doing anything at the last minute.

If you're a worrier, bring everything — bandages, a flashlight, emergency food and water, and so on. If you're more of a free spirit, just bring your money, your passport, and yourself.

Picking the Time for Your Trip

When's a good time for your two-week vacation? What do you want to do? No one wants to go snorkeling in freezing-cold water. (Trust me; I did it once and *no one* should attempt this mind — and body — numbing feat for a vacation.) And no one wants to climb a mountain in the rainy season, either. Pick the **kisetsu** (kee-seh-tsoo; season) for your trip wisely. For words that express each **kisetsu,** see Chapter 8.

Start looking at the **karendā** (kah-rehn-dahh; calendar) now. Pick the **tsuki** (tsoo-kee; months) in which you can do everything that you've planned and pick the least busy **shū** (shooo; week) and **hi** (hee; days).

Japan's climate

Japan has **shiki** (shee-kee; four seasons) plus a brief **tsuyu** (tsoo-yoo; rainy season), but the climate varies tremendously, depending on the location, because Japan is a long, narrow country. The north end of Japan is at the same latitude as Montreal, and its southern tip is at the same latitude as the Florida Keys.

Naming the months and counting them up

The Japanese word for *moon* is **tsuki** (tsoo-kee), which also means *month*. This doesn't cause as much confusion as you may think. Japanese doesn't have a separate word for each month — it uses a number paired with the counter **-gatsu** (gah-tsoo). So, *January* is **ichi-gatsu** (eeh-chee-gah-tsoo) and *December* is **jū-ni-gatsu** (jooo-nee-gah-tsoo).

Using a number to name a month may seem a bit strange at first glance, but in English, you use numbers to express months too — April 20 is 4/20. So, you shouldn't have any problem getting this concept down. Just add the counter **-gatsu** after the number that you normally use to refer to a month — but in Japanese of course. Table 15-1 lists all twelve **tsuki** of the year. Which **tsuki** were you born in?

Table 15-1	The Months	
English	**Japanese**	**Pronunciation**
January	ichi-gatsu	ee-chee-gah-tsoo
February	ni-gatsu	nee-gah-tsoo
March	san-gatsu	sahn-gah-tsoo
April	shi-gatsu	shee-gah-tsoo
May	go-gatsu	goh-gah-tsoo
June	roku-gatsu	roh-koo-gah-tsoo
July	shichi-gatsu	shee-chee-gah-tsoo

English	Japanese	Pronunciation
August	hachi-gatsu	hah-chee-gah-tsoo
September	ku-gatsu	koo-gah-tsoo
October	jū-gatsu	jooo-gah-tsoo
November	jū-ichi-gatsu	jooo-ee-chee-gah-tsoo
December	jū-ni-gatsu	jooo-nee-gah-tsoo

The number *four* is usually pronounced as **yon** (yohn), rather than **shi** (shee), because **shi** sounds the same as the word for death, **shi** (shee). Japanese usually avoid saying **shi** for the number four. Now that you know this fact, are you surprised by the pronunciation of **shi-gatsu** (shee-gah-tsoo; April)? **Shi-gatsu** is very exceptional.

To express a number of months, like *one month* and *two months,* use the counter **-kagetsu** (kah-geh-tsoo) or **-kagetsukan** (kah-geh-tsoo-kahn). In conversation, **-kagetsu** is more common than **-kagetsukan,** so you can just use **-kagetsu,** but it's good to know both of them because you may hear either one. Table 15-2 shows how **kagetsu** is pronounced when combined with numbers. Watch out for irregular sound changes!

April in Japan

Just because the words for *April,* **shi-gatsu** (shee-gah-tsoo), and *death,* **shi** (shee), sound alike doesn't mean that April is the death month. In Japan, April is the most lovely, beautiful, and admired month, even though it starts on **ēpuriru fūru** (ehh-poo-ree-roo fooo-roo; April Fool's Day). Oh, there's a spider on your head!!! April Fool! April Fool's Day isn't a Japanese custom, but Japanese kids enjoy this Western tradition.

Sakura no hana (sah-koo-rah noh hah-nah; cherry blossoms) are a symbolic image of April in Japan. You can experience a little taste of April in Japan by visiting Washington, D.C., when the cherry blossoms come out. In 1912, Japan sent about 3,000 cherry trees to the American capital as a sign of friendship between the United States and Japan. When the hundreds of trees around the tidal basin flower, politicians and plain folks make it a point to walk among the trees.

Another image of Japan in April is **nyūgakushiki** (nyooo-gah-koo-shee-kee; ceremonies for entering schools). A new academic year starts in **shi-gatsu** for all schools in Japan, including kindergartens and colleges. **Shi-gatsu** is surely the most beautiful month of the year, not the death month, as it's name may seem to imply.

Table 15-2	The Number of Months	
English	*Japanese*	*Pronunciation*
one month	ik-kagetsu	eek-kah-geh-tsoo
two months	ni-kagetsu	nee-kah-geh-tsoo
three months	san-kagetsu	sahn-kah-geh-tsoo
four months	yon-kagetsu	yohn-kah-geh-tsoo
five months	go-kagetsu	goh-kah-geh-tsoo
six months	rok-kagetsu	rohk-kah-geh-tsoo
seven months	nana-kagetsu	nah-nah-kah-geh-tsoo
eight months	hachi-kagetsu	hah-chee-kah-geh-tsoo
nine months	kyū-kagetsu	kyooo-kah-geh-tsoo
ten months	juk-kagetsu	jook-kah-geh-tsoo

Counting the days

When you specify dates in English, you use number words like *the first* and *the second.* In English, these words are used for specifying dates, and they're also used for specifying other items in a sequence, as in *the first building on the street, the second bottle of wine,* and *the third slice of pizza.* But in Japanese, you can't use the same number words for different type of items. *The first* for dates and *the first* for buildings are different: They're **tsuitachi** (tsoo-ee-tah-chee) and **hito-tsu-me** (hee-toh-tsoo-meh), respectively. *The first* for bottles and *the first* for slices are **ip-pon-me** (eep-pohn-meh) and **ichi-mai-me** (ee-chee-mah-ee-meh), respectively. Yes, it is cumbersome. In this section, I show you how you say *the first, the second,* and so on, for dates. To find out how you say these types of words in relation to other items like buildings, bottles, pizza slices, streets, and intersections, see Chapter 12.

The way that dates are pronounced in Japanese is not very systematic — it's full of irregularities. I know, it's not very encouraging. Sorry. Your best bet is to memorize Table 15-3.

Table 15-3	What's Today's Date?	
Date	*Japanese*	*Pronunciation*
1st	tsuitachi	tsoo-ee-tah-chee
2nd	futsuka	foo-tsoo-kah

Date	Japanese	Pronunciation
3rd	mikka	meek-kah
4th	yokka	yohk-kah
5th	itsuka	ee-tsoo-kah
6th	muika	moo-ee-kah
7th	nanoka	nah-noh-kah
8th	yōka	yohh-kah
9th	kokonoka	koh-koh-noh-kah
10th	tōka	tohh-kah
11th	11-nichi	jooo-ee-chee-nee-chee
12th	12-nichi	jooo-nee-nee-chee
13th	13-nichi	jooo-sahn-nee-chee
14th	jūyokka	jooo-yohk-kah
15th	15-nichi	jooo-goh-nee-chee
16th	16-nichi	jooo-roh-koo-nee-chee
17th	17-nichi	jooo-shee-chee-nee-chee
18th	18-nichi	jooo-hah-chee-nee-chee
19th	19-nichi	jooo-koo-nee-chee
20th	hatsuka	hah-tsoo-kah
21st	21-nichi	nee-jooo-ee-chee-nee-chee
22nd	22-nichi	nee-jooo-nee-nee-chee
23rd	23-nichi	nee-jooo-sahn-nee-chee
24th	nijūyokka	nee-jooo-yohk-kah
25th	25-nichi	nee-jooo-goh-nee-chee
26th	26-nichi	nee-jooo-roh-koo-nee-chee
27th	27-nichi	nee-jooo-shee-chee-nee-chee
28th	28-nichi	nee-jooo-hah-chee-nee-chee
29th	29-nichi	nee-jooo-koo-nee-chee
30th	30-nichi	sahn-jooo-nee-chee
31st	31-nichi	sahn-jooo-ee-chee-nee-chee

The dates shown in the Table 15-3 also can be interpreted as the *number of days*. For example, **futsuka** can mean either *the second* or *two days,* and **11-nichi** can mean either *the 11th* or *11 days*. So, if you remember this one form, you can use it for two purposes: to specify the date and to express the number of days. To make it crystal clear that you're talking about the *number of days,* just add **-kan** (kahn) to this form — **futsukakan** (foo-tsoo-kah-kahn; two days) and **11-nichikan** (jooo-ee-chee-nee-chee-kahn; 11 days). Then there's no more ambiguity. The only exception to these rules for dates and the number of days is **tsuitachi. Tsuitachi** means only *the first* and not *one day.* To say *one day,* use **ichi-nichi** (ee-chee-nee-chee) or **ichi-nichikan** (ee-chee-nee-chee-kahn), which are much more fun to say than **tsuitachi** anyway.

Counting the weeks

One week has seven days: **getsuyōbi** (geh-tsoo-yohh-bee; Monday), **kayōbi** (kah-yohh-bee; Tuesday), **suiyōbi** (soo-ee-yohh-bee; Wednesday), **mokuyōbi** (moh-koo-yohh-bee; Thursday), **kinyōbi** (keen-yohh-bee; Friday), **doyōbi** (doh-yohh-bee; Saturday), and **nichiyōbi** (nee-chee-yohh-bee; Sunday). And each month has four or five weeks.

You can specify the weeks in a month, or the weeks in any cycle, by saying **dai** (dah-ee), the number, and then **-shū** (shooo):

- **dai is-shū** (dah-ee ees-shooo; the first week)
- **dai ni-shū** (dah-ee nee-shooo; the second week)
- **dai san-shū** (dah-ee sahn-shooo; the third week)
- **dai yon-shū** (dah-ee yohn-shoo; the fourth week)

To count weeks, use the counter **-shūkan,** as in **is-shūkan** (ees-shooo-kahn; one week), **ni-shūkan** (nee-shooo-kahn; two weeks), **san-shūkan** (sahn-shooo-kahn; three weeks), **yon-shūkan** (yohn-shooo-kahn; four weeks), and **go-shūkan** (goh-shooo-kahn; five weeks).

Reeling off the years

To specify the **toshi** (toh-shee; year), just add the counter **-nen** after the number that expresses the year — **1998-nen** (sehn-kyooo-hyah-koo-kyooo-jooo-hah-chee-nehn; 1998) and **2002-nen** (nee-sehn-nee-nehn; 2002), for example.

Follow this advice, and you'll be understood perfectly in Japan. But, be ready to hear a year referred to with a unique **nengō** (nehn-gohh; era name), as in **Hēsē 14-nen** (hehh-sehh jooo-yoh-nehn), which is equivalent to 2002. Check out the "Era names in Japan" sidebar in this section.

CULTURAL WISDOM

Era names in Japan

Years can be expressed in two ways in Japan:

- Using the Western system with the counter **-nen** (nehn), as in **2002-nen** (nee-sehn-nee-nehn; 2002)

- Using the Japanese system with the **nengō** (nehn-gohh; era name) and the counter **-nen**, as in **Hēsē 14-nen** (hehh-sehh jooo-yoh-nehn; 2002)

A new **nengō** is created every time a new emperor ascends the throne in Japan and continues to be used until a different emperor takes his place. The first year of any era is called **gan-nen** (gahn-nehn).

For example, the year Emperor **Hēsē** (hehh-sehh) ascended the throne (1989) was called **Hēsē gan-nen** (hehh-sehh gahn-nehn) in the Japanese system. And the following year (1990) was called **Hēsē 2-nen** (hehh-sehh nee-nehn). Previous Japanese **nengō** include **Shōwa** (shohh-wah) (1926–1989), **Taishō** (tah-ee-shohh) (1912–1926), and **Mēji** (mehh-jee) (1868–1912).

Government officials tend to use only the Japanese system, but many companies and institutions use the Western systems.

If you want to count years, use either **-nenkan** or **-nen** as counters. So, *one year* is **ichi-nen** (ee-chee-nehn) or **ichi-nenkan** (ee-chee-nehn-kahn), and *two years* is **ni-nen** (nee-nehn) or **ni-nenkan** (nee-nehn-kahn). In conversation, the shorter version, **-nen,** is used more frequently than **-nenkan,** but again, it's good to be aware of both forms.

Specifying dates and times

When specifying a date the Japanese way, start from the largest unit of time in a date, the **toshi** (toh-shee; year), and then move to successively smaller units, the **tsuki** (tsoo-kee; month), the **hi** (hee; day of the month), and the **yōbi** (yohh-bee; day of the week) in that order, as in **2002-nen 8-gatsu 29-nichi mokuyōbi** (nee-sehn nee-nehn hah-chee-gah-tsoo nee-jooo-koo-nee-chee moh-koo-yohh-bee; August 29th, 2002, Thursday).

To specify *when* something happens or happened, insert a time phrase into the sentence. You can place the time phrase anywhere in a sentence, as long as it's before the verb. If you're dealing with a *specific time* — a specific day, month, year, hour, and so on — like **getsuyōbi** (geh-tsoo-yohh-bee; Monday), **shi-gatsu** (shee-gah-tsoo; April), or **7-ji** (shee-chee-jee; 7:00), place the particle **ni** (nee) after the time phrase.

You may have noticed that **ni** is a frequently-used particle in Japanese. It marks the destination as well as the time of the action. So, you may have two occurrences of **ni** in the same sentence, but that's perfectly fine. If you're dealing with relative time expressions like **kyonen** (kyoh-nehn; last year), **kyō** (kyohh; today), or **raishū** (rah-ee-shooo; next week), you don't need to use the particle **ni**. For more information on and examples of relative time phrases, check out Chapter 7; meanwhile, check out the following examples:

- ✔ **12-gatsu 28-nichi ni ikimasu.** (jooo-nee-gah-tsoo nee-jooo-hah-chee-nee-chee nee ee-kee-mah-soo; I'll go there on December 28th.)

- ✔ **1989-nen ni Hawai ni ikimashita.** (sehn-kyooo-hyah-koo-hah-chee-jooo-kyooo-nehn nee hah-wah-ee nee ee-kee-mah-shee-tah; I went to Hawaii in 1989.)

- ✔ **Nan-gatsu ni umaremashita ka.** (nahn-gah-tsoo nee oo-mah-reh-mah-shee-tah kah; Which month were you born in?)

- ✔ **Kyō ēga o mimasu.** (kyohh ehh-gah oh mee-mah-soo; I'll see a movie today.)

- ✔ **Senshū o-kane o haraimashita.** (sehn-shooo oh-kah-neh oh hah-rah-ee-mah-shee-tah; I paid last week.)

To list a number of activities in the same sentence, put all the verbs, except the last one, into the te-form. You don't need to use any particle that would correspond to *and* in English — converting all the verbs, except the last one, into the te-form handles the *and* concept. The last verb expresses the tense of all the activities.

- ✔ **Kinō wa ku-ji ni ginkō ni itte, jū-ji ni depāto ni itte, go-ji ni kaerimashita.** (kee-nohh wah koo-jee nee geen-kohh nee eet-teh, jooo-jee nee deh-pahh-toh nee eet-teh, goh-jee nee kah-eh-ree-mah-shee-tah; Yesterday, I went to the bank at nine o'clock, went to the department store at ten o'clock, and went home at five o'clock.)

- ✔ **15-nichi ni itte, 18-nichi ni kaerimasu.** (jooo-goh-nee-chee nee eet-teh, jooo-hah-chee-nee-chee nee kah-eh-ree-mah-soo; I'll go there on the 15th, and I'll be back on the 18th.)

- ✔ **Raigetsu Furansu ni itte, Supein ni itte, Itaria ni ikimasu.** (rah-ee-geh-tsoo foo-rahn-soo nee eet-teh, soo-peh-een nee eet-teh, ee-tah-ree-ah nee ee-kee-mah-soo; Next month, I'll go to France, Spain, and Italy.)

In the following Talkin' the Talk section, Eleanor talks about her vacation plans for Hawaii. Notice that her first sentence ends with **-n-desu** (n-deh-soo).

Remember that **-n-desu** doesn't add any literal meaning to the sentence, but it invites a response from the listener. Eleanor also talks about when she will leave and when she will return from her trip. The Japanese verb *to return* is **kaeru** (kah-eh-roo). Before going over the Talkin' the Talk section, practice conjugating the verb **kaeru** (kah-eh-roo; to return, go back). It's a u-verb.

Form	*Pronunciation*
kaeru	kah-eh-roo
kaeranai	kah-eh-rah-nah-ee
kaeri	kah-eh-ree
kaette	kah-eht-teh

Talkin' the Talk

Eleanor is planning to go to Hawaii next month. She talks about it with Kevin.

Eleanor: **Raigetsu Hawai ni iku-n-desu.**
rah-ee-geh-tsoo hah-wah-ee nee ee-koon-deh-soo.
I'm going to Hawaii next month.

Kevin: **Hontō. Nan-nichikan.**
hohn-tohh. nahn-nee-chee-kahn.
Really? For how many days?

Eleanor: **Mikkakan.**
meek-kah-kahn.
Three days.

Kevin: **Mijikai desu ne.**
mee-jee-kah-ee deh-soo neh.
That's short, isn't it?

Eleanor: **Ē, 15-nichi ni itte, 18-nichi ni kaeru-n-desu.**
ehh, jooo-goh-nee-chee nee eet-teh, jooo-hah-chee-nee-chee nee kah-eh-roon-deh-soo.
Uh-huh. I'll go there on the 15th, and I'll be back on the 18th.

Words to Know

ē	ehh	yeah/right/uh-huh
hi	hee	day
kaeru [u]	kah-eh-roo	to return
karendā	kah-rehn-dahh	calendar
kisetsu	kee-seh-tsoo	seasons
mijikai	mee-jee-kah-ee	short
ryokō	ryoh-kohh	trip/travel
shū	shooo	week
tabi	tah-bee	journey
toshi	toh-shee	year
tsuki	tsoo-kee	month
yōbi	yohh-bee	day of the week

Picking the Place for Your Trip

After you secure the cash and the time for your **ryokō** (ryoh-kohh; trip), pick the location. Do you want to visit a **gaikoku** (gah-ee-koh-koo; foreign country)? Or, do you prefer **kokunai** (koh-koo-nah-ee; domestic) travel. **Erabu** (eh-rah-boo; choose) the location carefully after considering all of your options.

Are you into **rekishi** (reh-kee-shee; history)? If so, visit a **kuni** (koo-nee; country) in **Yōroppa** (yohh-rohp-pah; Europe) or **Ajia** (ah-jee-ah; Asia) and look for these structures:

- **jinja** (jeen-jah; Shinto shrines)
- **kyōkai** (kyohh-kah-ee; churches)
- **o-shiro** (oh-shee-roh; castles)
- **o-tera** (oh-teh-rah; temples)

Do you want to spend a little time connecting with **shizen** (shee-zehn; nature)? How about **Ierōsutōn Kokuritsu Kōen** (ee-eh-rohh-soo-tohhn koh-koo-ree-tsoo kohh-ehn; Yellowstone National Park)? If you like **yama** (yah-mah; mountains) or **umi** (oo-mee; oceans), see Chapter 8 for more words and phrases related to nature.

Do you want to go to somewhere to play your favorite **supōtsu** (soo-pohh-tsoo; sport)? You can always go skiing in the **Arupusu** (ah-roo-poo-soo; Alps). (See Chapter 8 for more words related to sports.) Or, is shopping your idea of a contact sport? If so, go to **Honkon** (hohn-kohn; Hong Kong). I'll take this option every time.

In the following Talkin' the Talk section, two girls are trying to decide where to go for their year-end vacation. They speak casually, using the female ending **wa** (wah) a lot. Don't get it confused with the topic particle **wa.** I'm talking about the particle **wa** at the end of the statement. It makes a woman sound feminine. If men use it, they sound like women. Be careful. The sentence-ending particle **yo** (yoh) is for emphasis. Depending on the intonation and the context, you may sound very pushy, very helpful, or very enthusiastic when you use **yo.** So, you better not use **yo** when you talk to your teacher or boss until you understand exactly when and how to use it. Often, the feminine ending **wa** occurs right before the emphasis particle **yo.**

Keep in mind that **aru** (ah-roo; to exist) is slightly irregular — its negative form is **nai,** which Junko uses in the following Talkin' the Talk section. When you talk about whether you have something or you don't have something, say **aru** and **nai,** respectively.

Talkin' the Talk

Junko and Hiroko are co-workers at a company that is going to be closed for one week at the end of the year. They decided to go on a trip together, and they're debating where to go.

Junko: **Yōroppa wa.**
yohh-rohp-pah wah.
How about Europe?

Hiroko: **Amerika ga ii wa yo.**
ah-meh-ree-kah gah eee wah yoh.
America is better.

Junko: **Demo, Amerika wa furui tatemono ga nai wa yo.**
deh-moh, ah-meh-ree-kah wah foo-roo-ee tah-teh-moh-noh gah nah-ee wah yoh.
But there are no old buildings in America.

Hiroko: **Demo, Amerika wa omoshiroi wa yo.**
deh-moh, ah-meh-ree-kah wah oh-moh-shee-roh-ee
wah yoh.
But America is fun.

Words to Know

gaikoku	gah-ee-koh-koo	foreign country
jinja	jeen-jah	Shinto shrine
kokuritsu kōen	koh-koo-ree-tsoo kohh-ehn	national park
kuni	koo-nee	country
kyōkai	kyohh-kah-ee	church
o-shiro	oh-shee-roh	castle
o-tera	oh-teh-rah	temple

Packing for Your Trip

Do you like a big **sūtsukēsu** (sooo-tsoo-kehh-soo; suitcase) or a soft leather **ryokō kaban** (ryoh-kohh kah-bahn; travel bag)? Or, do you only want to carry a **deibaggu** (deh-ee-bahg-goo; backpack) on your trip? Choose one of them and start packing. What do you want to **ireru** (ee-reh-roo; put) into your bag? Table 15-4 lists some items you may need for a vacation at the beach. (The shopping chapter — Chapter 6 — also has clothing items.)

Table 15-4	Clothing	
Japanese	*Pronunciation*	*Translation*
beruto	beh-roo-toh	belt
bōshi	bohh-shee	hat/cap
han-zubon	hahn-zoo-bohn	shorts/short pants
puruōbā	poo-roo-ohh-bahh	pullover
sandaru	sahn-dah-roo	sandals

Japanese	Pronunciation	Translation
sangurasu	sahn-goo-rah-soo	sunglasses
sunīkā	soo-neee-kahh	sneakers
T-shatsu	teee-shah-tsoo	T-shirt

And remember to pack your toiletries and makeup:

- ✔ **haburashi** (hah-boo-rah-shee; toothbrush)
- ✔ **keshōhin** (keh-shohh-heen; cosmetics)
- ✔ **kushi** (koo-shee; comb)
- ✔ **sekken** (sehk-kehn; soap)
- ✔ **taoru** (tah-oh-roo; towel)

Other items that may be useful include a **chizu** (chee-zoo; map) to help you get there and a **kaichūdentō** (kah-ee-chooo-dehn-tohh; flashlight) to help you see the map in the dark. If you're going to the beach, you need some **hiyakedome** (hee-yah-keh-doh-meh; sunscreen). And, wherever you go, don't forget your **kamera** (kah-meh-rah; camera) and a **kasa** (kah-sah; umbrella), just in case.

Using Mood and Attitude Suffixes

When you say something, you may want to indicate how sure you are about your statement. Suppose that you're a notoriously bad cook, but to save money, you decide to cook for 30 guests instead of hiring a caterer. Now, your family is asking, *Will the guests eat your food?* You think they will, but you have a bunch of phrases to choose from that express how confident you are. You can say *They will definitely eat, They will probably eat, They will eat, I think,* or *They may eat.* Don't be that pessimistic — your food can't be that bad.

In this section, I show you the most convenient way to express your mood and attitude in Japanese — with mood and attitude suffixes that you can add to the end of sentences.

Verbs have two versions: plain/informal and polite/neutral (see Chapter 2 or the Cheat Sheet for more on verb forms). For example, *to eat* can be said using both **taberu** (tah-beh-roo), the plain/informal form, and **tabemasu** (tah-beh-mah-soo), the polite/neutral form. Mood/attitude suffixes also have these two forms. When you want to say *They may eat,* you can add either **kamoshirenai** (kah-moh-shee-reh-nah-ee) or **kamoshiremasen** (kah-moh-she-reh-mah-sehn) at the end of the verb *to eat.* Suppose you're talking informally to your wife. You can say **taberu kamoshirenai** (tah-beh-roo kah-moh-shee-reh-nah-ee; They may eat.). Got it? Now, suppose you're talking politely to your neighbor. In this situation, the correct form isn't **tabemasu kamoshire-masen;** it's **taberu kamoshiremasen.** At first glance, this phrase may look like it's only 50 percent polite. However, these suffixes must be used after a verb in the plain/informal form.

Regardless of whether you want to be polite or not, a verb before a mood/attitude suffix must be in the plain/informal form, although the suffix itself can be either plain/informal or polite/neutral. Listen, I'm not the one who invented Japanese, I'm just trying to share the rules. Table 15-5 provides a ton of examples for mood/attitude suffixes.

Table 15-5	Mood/Attitude Suffixes		
Suffix	*Pronunciation*	*Meaning*	*Example*
deshō (polite/neutral)	deh-shohh	It's probably so./ I guess so.	Ano hoteru wa takai deshō. (That hotel is probably expensive.)
darō (plain/informal)	dah-rohh		Ame ga furu darō. (It'll rain, I guess.)
deshō ka (polite/neutral)	deh-shohh kah	I'm wondering.	Kore de ii deshō ka. (Is this one okay, I'm wondering.)
ka na (plain/informal)	kah nah		Ame wa furu ka na. (I wonder whether it'll rain.)
kamoshiremasen (polite/neutral) (See Chapter 10 for more information)	kah-moh-shee-reh-mah-sehn	It's possible./ Maybe	Beddo ga warui kamoshiremasen yo. (Your bed may be bad.)
kamoshirenai (plain/informal) (See Chapter 10 for more information.)	kah-moh-shee-reh-nah-ee		Hiyakedome ga iru kamoshirenai. (We may need sun-screen lotion.)

Suffix	Pronunciation	Meaning	Example
n-desu (polite/neutral) (See Chapter 5 for more information.)	n-deh-soo	I'll tell you./ What do you think?	Yoyaku o shitai-n-desu. (I'd like to make a reservation, if I could.)
n-da (plain/informal)	n-dah	You know.	Mekishiko ni iku-n-da. (I'm going to Mexico, you know.)
to omoimasu (polite/neutral)	toh oh-moh-ee-mah-soo	I think so.	Kono kuruma wa yoku ureru to omoimasu. (I think this car can sell very easily.)
to omou (plain/informal)	toh oh-moh-oo		Mō dame da to omou. (I think there's no hope anymore.)
wake ga arimasen (polite/neutral)	wah-keh gah ah-ree-mah-sehn	It's impossible!/ No way!	Wakaru wake ga arimasen. (There's no way that I can understand it!)
wake ga nai (plain/informal)	wah-keh gah nah-ee		Biza ga iru wake ga nai. (No way that we need a visa.)

Practice conjugating the verb **omou** (oh-moh-oo; to think). It's a u-verb. Don't forget the **w** sound in the negative form.

Form	Pronunciation
omou	oh-moh-oo
omowanai	oh-moh-wah-nah-ee
omoi	oh-moh-ee
omotte	oh-moht-teh

Both **omou** and **kangaeru** (kahn-gah-eh-roo) mean *to think*, but they're not interchangeable. Sorry. **Omou** is *to think* in the sense of having an opinion, and **kangaeru** expresses more of a sense of pondering.

✔ **Kore wa ii to omou.** (koh-reh wah eee toh oh-moh-oo; I think this is good.)

✔ **Sore o yoku kangaete kudasai.** (soh-reh oh yoh-koo kahn-gah-eh-teh koo-dah-sah-ee; Please think carefully about that.)

In the following Talkin' the Talk section, a husband and wife are talking informally. While you read it, try to catch the mood/attitude enhancing suffixes from Table 15-5. But before you do that, conjugate the verb **iru** (ee-roo; to need) because it shows up a few times in the conversation. Here's the only criterion to follow when you pack for your trip: Do you *need* the item or do you *not need* the item? **Iru** (ee-roo; to need) is a u-verb. Don't get it confused with the verb **iru** (ee-roo; to exist), which is a ru-verb.

Form	Pronunciation
iru	ee-roo
iranai	ee-rah-nah-ee
iri	ee-ree
itte	eet-teh

The verb **ireru** (ee-reh-roo; to put) also shows up in the following Talkin' the Talk section. You *put* a lot of stuff in your suitcase when you go somewhere, right? Check out Chapter 14 for the verb table for **ireru**.

Talkin' the Talk

It's 9 p.m. Mari and her husband, Shin, have finished their dinner, and they're relaxing in the living room. They're going to the ballpark tomorrow morning to see a professional baseball game. Shin is very excited about it, and Mari has started putting some things in a bag for the trip.

Mari: **Kasa wa iru ka na.**
kah-sah wah ee-roo kah nah.
I wonder whether we need an umbrella.

Shin: **Iranai darō.**
ee-rah-nah-ee dah-rohh.
We probably won't need it.

Mari: **Jā, hiyakedome wa.**
jahh, hee-yah-keh-doh-meh wah.
Then, how about sunscreen?

Shin: **Iru kamoshirenai ne.**
ee-roo kah-moh-shee-reh-nah-ee neh.
We might need that.

Mari: **Jā, ireru wa. Mizu wa iru.**
jahh, ee-reh-roo wah. mee-zoo wah ee-roo.
Okay, I'll put it in. Do we need bottled water?

Shin:	**Iru to omou.**
	ee-roo toh oh-moh-oo.
	We need it, I think.

Mari:	**Ōkē. Jā, pasupōto wa.**
	ohh-kehh. jahh, pah-soo-pohh-toh wah.
	All right. Then, how about our passports?

Shin:	**Iru wake nai yo. Nani o kangaete iru no.**
	ee-roo wah-keh nah-ee yoh. nah-nee oh kahn-gah-eh-teh ee-roo noh.
	We won't need them for goodness sake. What are you thinking about?

Mari:	**Raigetsu no Mekishiko ryokō yo.**
	rah-ee-geh-tsoo noh meh-kee-shee-koh ryoh-kohh yoh.
	Our trip to Mexico next month.

Shin:	**Ā.**
	ahh.
	Oh.

Words to Know

hiyakedome	hee-yah-keh-doh-meh	sunscreen
iru [u]	ee-roo	to need
kangaeru [ru]	kahn-gah-eh-roo	to think
kasa	kah-sah	umbrella
mizu	mee-zoo	water
omou [u]	oh-moh-oo	to think

Getting Help from a Travel Agency

If arranging the **kōtsū kikan** (kohh-tsooo-kee-kahn; transportation) and **shukuhaku shisetsu** (shoo-koo-hah-koo shee-seh-tsoo; accommodations) is too much for you, get help from a **ryokō gaisha** (ryoh-kohh gah-ee-shah; travel agency) and choose the plan that satisfies your needs.

You can join their **tsuā** (tsoo-ahh; tour) and benefit from the presence of a knowledgeable **tenjōin** (tehn-johh-een; tour guide). Check what **pakkēji** (pahk-kehh-jee; packages) they offer. Also, check how much they charge for the **mōshikomiryō** (mohh-shee-koh-mee-ryohh; application fee), **ryokō daikin** (ryoh-kohh dah-ee-keen; travel fares), and **torikeshiryō** (toh-ree-keh-shee-ryohh; cancellation fee).

Tell the agency where you want to go and how many days and nights you want to spend there. In Japanese, say the number of nights first, and then say the number of days. To specify the number of nights, use the counter -**haku**, which is explained in Chapter 13. For specifying the number of days, see the "Counting the days" section earlier in this chapter. Here's the general pattern:

- ✔ **ip-paku futsuka** (eep-pah-koo foo-tsoo-kah; one night, two days)

- ✔ **ni-haku mikka** (nee-hah-koo meek-kah; two nights, three days)

- ✔ **nana-haku yōka** (nah-nah-hah-koo yohh-kah; seven nights, eight days)

And check what the travel agency's packages include:

- ✔ **Chōshoku to yūshoku ga tsukimasu.** (chohh-shoh-koo toh yooo-shoh-koo gah tsoo-kee-mah-soo; Breakfast and dinner are included.)

- ✔ **Hikōki to hoteru tsuki desu.** (hee-kohh-kee toh hoh-teh-roo tsoo-kee deh-soo; The fees for the hotel and airfare are included.)

- ✔ **Tenjōin ga dōkō shimasu.** (tehn-johh-een gah dohh-kohh shee-mah-soo; A tour guide will accompany you.)

- ✔ **Hariuddo ichi-nichi kankō desu.** (hah-ree-ood-doh ee-chee-nee-chee kahn-kohh deh-soo; It's a one-day sightseeing trip to Hollywood.)

Tsukimasu (tsoo-kee-mah-soo) means *to be included.* Its dictionary form is **tsuku** (tsoo-koo). The following Talkin' the Talk section discusses what's included in Toshi's trip to Hokkaido. Before going through it, conjugate the verb **tsuku** (tsoo-koo; to be included), a u-verb.

Form	*Pronunciation*
tsuku	tsoo-koo
tsukanai	tsoo-kah-nah-ee
tsuki	tsoo-kee
tsuite	tsoo-ee-teh

Talkin' the Talk

Toshi is planning to go on a trip to Hokkaido with his friend. He visits a travel agency near his company and asks a few questions.

Toshi: **Tomodachi to Hokkaidō ni ikitai-n-desu.**
toh-moh-dah-chee toh hohk-kah-ee-dohh
nee ee-kee-tah-een-deh-soo.
I want to go to Hokkaido with my friend.

Agent: **Yasui pakkēji ga arimasu yo.**
yah-soo-ee pahk-kehh-jee gah ah-ree-mah-soo yoh.
We offer an inexpensive package.

Toshi: **Nani ga tsukimasu ka.**
nah-nee gah tsoo-kee-mah-soo kah.
What's included?

Agent: **Hikōki to hoteru ga tsukimasu.**
hee-kohh-kee toh hoh-teh-roo gah tsoo-kee-mah-soo.
The fees for the hotel and airfare are included.

Toshi: **Shokuji wa tsukimasu ka.**
shoh-koo-jee wah tsoo-kee-mah-soo kah.
Are meals included?

Agent: **Īe, tsukimasen.**
eee-eh, tsoo-kee-mah-sehn.
No, they aren't included.

Words to Know

mōshikomiryō	mohh-shee-koh-mee-ryohh	application fee
pakkēji	pahk-kehh-jee	package
ryokō daikin	ryoh-kohh dah-ee-keen	travel fares
ryokō gaisha	ryoh-kohh gah-ee-shah	travel agency
tenjōin	tehn-johh-een	tour guide
torikeshiryō	toh-ree-keh-shee-ryohh	cancellation fee
tsuā	tsoo-ahh	tour
tsuku [u]	tsoo-koo	to be included

Fun & Games

Name the marked items in Japanese.

The answers are in Appendix C.

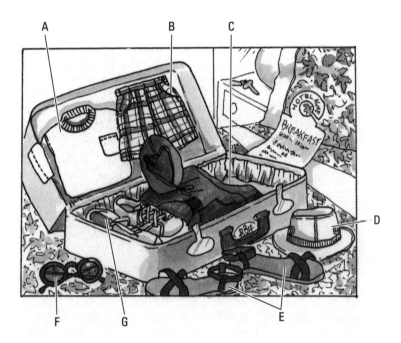

A. _____

B. _____

C. _____

D. _____

E. _____

F. _____

G. _____

Chapter 16

Handling an Emergency

- -

In This Chapter

▶ Finding help when you need it

▶ Talking to the police

▶ Visiting a doctor's office

▶ Diagnosing and treating illness

- -

*I*t's great to think about all the good things in life like eating, shopping, having fun, and making friends, but it's also important to think about what to do in case an illness, injury, or emergency pops up. Handling these situations isn't a big deal when you know the ABCs of emergencies and sickness. This chapter provides you with the confidence and the Japanese to act wisely when faced with an emergency.

Shouting Out for Help

When you're really in a panic, it may be difficult to make even the slightest of sounds, but don't give in. Use your stomach power and shout it out! But what should you shout? Just the vowel **a** (ah)? Its longer counterpart **ā** (aah)? Or maybe its super-long counterpart **āāāāā** (aaaaaaaaah)? Even a crow can do that. To be more sophisticated than a crow, use the following phrases and scream

- ✔ **Dareka.** (dah-reh-kah; Someone help!)
- ✔ **Tasukete.** (tah-soo-keh-teh; Help me!)
- ✔ **Dorobō.** (doh-roh-bohh; A thief!)
- ✔ **Kaji.** (kah-jee; Fire!)
- ✔ **Kēsatsu.** (kehh-sah-tsoo; Police!)

Tasukete, in the list above, is the te-form of the verb **tasukeru** (tah-soo-keh-roo; to help). It's in the te-form because it's the product of omitting **kudasai** (koo-dah-sah-ee) from the complete request sentence **Tasukete kudasai** (tah-soo-keh-teh koo-dah-sah-ee; Please help me.). Remember that a request is expressed by a verb in the te-form plus **kudasai. Kudasai** is a sort of helping verb for expressing a request. In an informal context or in emergency, you can omit it. See Chapter 12 to find out more about **kudasai.**

Conjugate the verb **tasukeru** (tah-soo-keh-roo; to help). It's a ru-verb. Use its te-form **(tasukete)** to call for help.

Form	Pronunciation
tasukeru	tah-soo-keh-roo
tasukenai	tah-soo-keh-nah-ee
tasuke	tah-soo-keh
tasukete	tah-soo-keh-teh

If you see someone who appears to be having a problem, don't scream. Just ask

- ✔ **Daijōbu desu ka.** (dah-ee-johh-boo deh-soo kah; Are you all right?)

- ✔ **Dōshita-n-desu ka.** (dohh-shee-tahn-deh-soo kah; What happened?)

To call for help, it helps to know the verb *to call,* **yobu** (yoh-boo). It means *to call* in a general sense, not necessarily by telephone. Practice conjugating the verb **yobu.** It's a u-verb. The **b** syllables are fun to say, but make sure you end the te-form with **nde.**

Form	Pronunciation
yobu	yoh-boo
yobanai	yoh-bah-nah-ee
yobi	yoh-bee
yonde	yohn-deh

Be a good person and offer help to those in need. The best way to express your helpful intentions is to ask a question that ends in **-mashō ka** (mah-shohh kah; shall I). **-Mashō ka** follows a verb in the stem form. The stem form of **yobu** (yoh-boo; to call) is **yobi** (yoh-bee); therefore, **Kēsatsu o yobimashō ka** (kehh-sah-tsoo oh yoh-bee-mah-shohh kah) means *Shall I call the police?*

- ✔ **Go-kazoku ni denwa shimashō ka.** (goh-kah-zoh-koo nee dehn-wah shee-mah-shohh kah; Shall I telephone your family?)

✔ **Kyūkyūsha o yobimashō ka.** (kyooo-kyooo-shah oh yoh-bee-mah-shohh kah; Shall I call an ambulance?)

✔ **Unten shimashō ka.** (oon-tehn shee-mah-shohh kah; Shall I drive?)

If you think you can't handle a situation alone, ask the people around you to help out too. To express your request, use a verb in the te-form and add **kudasai** (koo-dah-sah-ee), as discussed earlier in this section. You can also check out Chapter 12 for more info on **kudasai.** For now, here are a few examples:

✔ **Kēsatsu ni denwa shite kudasai.** (kehh-sah-tsoo nee dehn-wah shee-teh koo-dah-sah-ee; Phone the police please.)

✔ **Kyūkyūsha o yonde kudasai.** (kyooo-kyooo-shah oh yohn-deh koo-dah-sah-ee; Call an ambulance please.)

✔ **Shōbōsho ni denwa shite kudasai.** (shohh-bohh-shoh nee dehn-wah shee-teh koo-dah-sah-ee; Please phone the fire department.)

Talkin' the Talk

Hiroshi sees a woman slumped down next to her car in the parking lot.

Hiroshi:	**Daijōbu desu ka.** dah-ee-johh-boo deh-soo kah. Are you all right?
Woman:	**Ē.** ehh. Kind of.
Hiroshi:	**Kyūkyūsha o yobimashō ka.** kyooo-kyooo-shah oh yoh-bee-mah-shohh kah. Shall I call an ambulance?
Woman:	**Daijōbu desu. Sugu naorimasu.** dah-ee-johh-boo deh-soo. soo-goo nah-oh-ree-mah-soo. I'm all right. I'll be better soon.
Hiroshi:	**Sō desu ka.** sohh deh-soo kah. Are you sure?

Words to Know

Daijōbu desu ka.	dah-ee-johh-boo deh-soo kah	Are you all right?
dorobō	doh-roh-bohh	thief
kaji	kah-jee	fire
kēsatsu	kehh-sah-tsoo	police
kyūkyūsha	kyooo-kyooo-shah	ambulance
shōbōsho	shohh-bohh-shoh	fire department
tasukeru [ru]	tah-soo-keh-roo	to help
tasukete	tah-soo-keh-teh	help me
yobu [u]	yoh-boo	to call for

Calling the Police

The police emergency number in Japan is 110. Japanese call it **110-ban** (hyah-koo-tohh-bahn). Yes, they usually say **hyakutō-ban** (hyah-koo-tohh-bahn) rather than **hyakujū-ban** (hyah-koo-jooo-bahn) — just one of those things. The number for an accident or fire is different: **119-ban** (hyah-koo-jooo-kyooo-bahn). Don't confuse these numbers with your own emergency number — 911 in the United States, for example. When you call emergency numbers, calm down and first tell the dispatcher where you are. Then explain what happened.

Reporting an accident to the police

If you see a **jiko** (jee-koh; accident), report it to the **kēsatsu** (kehh-sah-tsoo; police). The verb you need to report a **jiko** is **aru** (ah-roo; to exist). When you call the police, use the past tense in reporting the problem — *There was an accident.* And remember to use the polite/neutral style when you talk to a police officer. So, you need to conjugate **aru** into the polite past tense form, **arimashita** (ah-ree-mah-shee-tah).

- **Jiko ga arimashita.** (jee-koh gah ah-ree-mah-shee-tah; There was an accident.)

- **Takada-chō de jiko ga arimashita.** (tah-kah-dah-chohh deh jee-koh gah ah-ree-mah-shee-tah; There was an accident in Takada Town.)

I hope you don't **okosu** (oh-koh-soo; cause) a **jiko** (accident), and I don't want you to **au** (ah-oo; be involved in) a **jiko,** either. When you use the verb **au,** make sure to mark **jiko** with the particle **ni,** as in **jiko ni au** (jee-koh nee ah-oo; to be involved in an accident). The polite past tense forms of **okosu** and **au** are **okoshimashita** and **aimashita.** Here are a couple examples:

- **Hidoi jiko ni aimashita.** (hee-doh-ee jee-koo nee ah-ee-mah-shee-tah; I was involved in a terrible accident.)

- **Kinō otōto ga jiko o okoshimashita.** (kee-nohh oh-tohh-toh gah jee-koh oh oh-koh-shee-mah-shee-tah; My brother caused an accident yesterday.)

Conjugate the verb **au** (ah-oo; to encounter). It's a u-verb. Watch out for the **w** sound in the negative form.

Form	Pronunciation
au	ah-oo
awanai	ah-wah-nah-ee
ai	a-ee
atte	aht-teh

Conjugate the verb **okosu** (o-koh-soo; to cause). It's also a u-verb. Create **s/sh**-syllables.

Form	Pronunciation
okosu	o-koh-soo
okosanai	oh-koh-sah-nah-ee
okoshi	oh-koh-shee
okoshite	oh-koh-shee-teh

It's often necessary to specify the nature of an accident so that the people responding know what to expect. The following list gives you an idea of some of the types of **jiko** you may encounter:

- **gasumore jiko** (gah-soo-moh-reh jee-koh; gas leak accident)

- **jidōsha jiko** (jee-dohh-shah jee-koh; auto accident)

- **baiku no jiko** (bah-ee-koo noh jee-koh; motorcycle accident)

  ✔ **kaji** (kah-jee; fire)

  ✔ **kega** (keh-gah; injury)

  ✔ **kōtsū jiko** (kohh-tsoo jee-koh; traffic accident)

Unfortunately, **kōtsū jiko** (kohh-tsoo jee-koh; traffic accidents) are everyday events in most cities. If you're involved in an accident and no one gets hurt, consider yourself lucky in an unlucky situation, even if it's your fault.

To avoid future legal complications over responsibilities, call the **kēsatsu** (kehh-sah-tsoo; police). Tell them where you are and **matsu** (mah-tsoo; wait for) the **kēsatsukan** (kehh-sah-tsoo-kahn; police officer) to arrive. To tell the police how to find you, use the location and direction words listed in Chapter 12.

Conjugate the verb **matsu** (mah-tsoo; to wait). It's a u-verb.

Form	Pronunciation
matsu	mah-tsoo
matanai	mah-tah-nah-ee
machi	mah-chee
matte	maht-teh

Talkin' the Talk

Takeshi was just involved in a collision. He calls the police using his cellular phone.

Takeshi: **Moshimoshi. Ima kuruma no jiko ni atta-n-desu.**
moh-shee-moh-shee. ee-mah koo-roo-mah noh jee-koh nee aht-tahn-deh-soo.
Hello. I was just in a car accident.

Police: **Dareka kega o shimashita ka.**
dah-reh-kah keh-gah oh shee-mah-shee-tah kah.
Did anyone get injured?

Takeshi: **Īe.**
eee-eh.
No.

Police: **Ima doko desu ka.**
ee-mah doh-koh deh-soo kah.
Where are you now?

Takeshi:	**Takada-chō no yūbinkyoku no mae no kōsaten desu.**
	tah-kah-dah-chohh noh yooo-been-kyoh-koo noh mah-eh noh kohh-sah-tehn deh-soo.
	I'm at the intersection in front of the post office in Takada Town.
Police:	**Kōsaten no kita desu ka. Minami desu ka.**
	kohh-sah-tehn noh kee-tah deh-soo kah. mee-nah-mee deh-soo kah.
	On the north of the intersection? Or, the south side?
Takeshi:	**Kita desu.**
	kee-tah deh-soo.
	The north side.
Police:	**Sugu kēsatsukan ga ikimasu. Go-fun gurai matte kudasai.**
	soo-goo kehh-sah-tsoo-kahn gah ee-kee-mah-soo. goh-foon goo-rah-ee maht-teh koo-dah-sah-ee.
	An officer will be there soon. Please wait for about five minutes.

Words to Know

au [u]	ah-oo	to encounter
jidosha jiko	jee-dohh-shah jee-koh	auto accident
jiko	jee-koh	accident
kēsatsukan	kehh-sah-tsoo-kahn	police officer
matsu [u]	mah-tsoo	to wait
okosu [u]	oh-koh-soo	to cause

Finding the lost and found

Hotels, airlines, and taxi companies are always dealing with lost items. Their lost and found departments contain tons of umbrellas, wallets, cameras, watches, jackets, socks, and a little bit of everything else. When you travel, don't lose the important stuff like your wallet, purse, or money. Socks are okay — you can always buy a new pair. Have you ever lost something important, such as your **handobaggu** (hahn-doh-bahg-goo; handbag), **saifu** (sah-ee-foo; wallet), or **sūtsukēsu** (sooo-tsoo-kehh-soo; suitcase)?

If you lose a bag or a wallet, tell the authorities where you lost it and what it looks like. (Use the words from Chapter 6 that describe colors and sizes.) And think about what was in it.

- ✔ **genkin** (gehn-keen; cash)
- ✔ **kagi** (kah-gee; keys)
- ✔ **kurejitto kādo** (koo-reh-jeeht-toh kahh-doh; credit cards)
- ✔ **shashin** (shah-sheen; photos)
- ✔ **unten menkyoshō** (oon-tehn mehn-kyoh-shohh; driver's license)

To describe the contents of your bag or wallet, use the phrase **haitte iru** (hah-eet-teh ee-roo; to be in it). **Haitte** is the te-form of the verb **hairu** (hah-ee-roo; to be placed in somewhere).

Conjugate the verb **hairu** (hah-ee-roo; to be placed in somewhere). It also means *to enter* in some contexts. It's a u-verb.

Form	Pronunciation
hairu	hah-ee-roo
hairanai	hah-ee-rah-nah-ee
hairi	hah-ee-ree
haitte	hah-eet-teh

If you add the verb **iru** (ee-roo; to exist) after another verb in the te-form, you're talking about a state. For example, **haitte iru** is the state after something entered. It's hard to understand that something would be in the state of having entered somewhere, but it just means *Something is in it.* That's it. **Haitte iru** (hah-eet-teh ee-roo) means *It's in it.* **Genkin ga haitte iru** (gehn-keehn gah hah-eet-teh ee-roo) means *Some cash is in it.* In a polite/neutral context, say **Genkin ga haitte imasu** (gehn-keen gah hah-eet-teh ee-mah-soo). And if you have more than one item in your bag, list everything using the particle **to** (toh). Simply place the particle **to** after each item except the last one.

- ✔ **Shashin ga haitte imasu.** (shah-sheen gah hah-eet-teh ee-mah-soo; A photo is in it.)
- ✔ **Saifu to pasupōto ga haitte imasu.** (sah-ee-foo toh pah-soo-pohh-toh gah hah-eet-teh ee-mah-soo; My wallet and my passport are in it.)
- ✔ **Genkin to kurejitto kādo to shashin ga haitte imasu.** (gehn-keen toh koo-reh-jeet-toh kahh-doh toh shah-sheen gah hah-eet-teh ee-mah-soo; Some cash, a credit card, and a photograph are in it.)

I've been so lucky so far. I've later found most of the things that I thought I had lost. Thank you **kami-sama** (kah-mee-sah-mah; God)! But, I said *most*. I didn't say *all*.

Conjugate the two important verbs in this section — **nakusu** (nah-koo-soo; to lose) and **mitsukaru** (mee-tsoo-kah-roo; to be found). They're both u-verbs.

Form	*Pronunciation*
nakusu	nah-koo-soo
nakusanai	nah-koo-sah-nah-ee
nakushi	nah-koo-shee
nakushite	nah-koo-shee-teh

Form	*Pronunciation*
mitsukaru	mee-tsoo-kah-roo
mitsukaranai	mee-tsoo-kah-rah-nah-ee
mitsukari	mee-tsoo-kah-ree
mitsukatte	mee-tsoo-kaht-teh

If you lose something in a store, airport, or train station, listen for an announcement. If you're paged over the public address system, it's a good sign. An announcement states your name and **o-koshi kudasai** (oh-koh-shee koo-dah-sah-ee). This is a super-polite, business-like phrase that means *please come* and uses the stem form — **koshi** — of the verb **kosu** (koh-soo). **Kosu** means *to pass, to move,* or *to come,* depending on the context. In this case, it obviously means *to come.* If you're curious about what the **o** and **kudasai** are doing, take a look at Chapter 11. In the following Talkin' the Talk section, Naomi is paged at an airport. Pay attention to where she's asked to come to. The location is marked by the particle **made** (mah-deh) and placed before **o-koshi kudasai.**

Talkin' the Talk

Naomi is at an airport waiting for her plane. Trying to buy a cup of coffee, she realizes that she doesn't have her handbag with her. She talks to a security guard standing nearby.

Naomi: **Anō, handobaggu o nakushimashita.**
ah-nohh, hahn-doh-bahg-goo oh nah-koo-shee-mah-shee-tah.
Excuse me, I lost my handbag.

Guard: **Donna handobaggu desu ka.**
dohn-nah hahn-doh-bahg-goo deh-soo kah.
What kind of handbag is it?

Naomi: **Chīsai pinku no handobaggu desu.**
cheee-sah-ee peen-koo noh hahn-doh-bahg-goo deh-soo.
It's a small pink handbag.

Saifu to pasupōto ga haitte imasu.
sah-ee-foo toh pah-soo-pohh-toh gah hah-eet-teh ee-mah-soo.
My wallet and my passport are in it.

All of a sudden, they hear an announcement.

Voice: **Katō Naomi-sama. Katō Naomi-sama. Uesuto Eā kauntā made o-koshi kudasai.**
kah-tohh nah-oh-mee-sah-mah. kah-tohh nah-oh-mee-sah-mah. oo-eh-soo-toh eh-ahh kah-oon-tahh mah-deh oh-koh-shee koo-dah-sah-ee.
Ms. Naomi Kato. Ms. Naomi Kato. Please come to the West Air counter.

Naomi: **Ā. Watashi desu. Chotto shitsurēshimasu.**
ahh. wah-tah-shee deh-soo. choht-toh shee-tsoo-rehh-shee-mah-soo.
Oh! That's me. Excuse me.

Naomi runs to the West Air counter where she receives her bag. She goes back to find the security guard she was talking to earlier.

Naomi: **Dōmo arigatō gozaimashita. Handobaggu ga mitsukarimashita.**
dohh-moh ah-ree-gah-tohh goh-zah-ee-mah-shee-tah. hahn-doh-bahg-goo gah mee-tsoo-kah-ree-mah-shee-tah.
Thank you very much. My handbag was found!

Guard: **Yokatta desu ne.**
yoh-kaht-tah deh-soo neh.
Gee, that's great.

Words to Know

hairu [u]	hah-ee-roo	to enter
handobaggu	hahn-doh-bahg-goo	handbag
kagi	kah-gee	keys
mitsukaru [u]	mee-tsoo-kah-roo	to be found
nakusu [u]	nah-koo-soo	to lose
saifu	sah-ee-foo	wallet

Getting Legal Help

Japan is not a very litigious society, and Japanese don't settle disputes through the courts as often as Americans seem to, but if you find that you need legal assistance in Japan, you can always **hanasu** (hah-nah-soo; talk) to a **bengoshi** (behn-goh-shee; lawyer). (The u-verb **hanasu** is conjugated below.) It's also a good idea to **renraku suru** (rehn-rah-koo soo-roo; contact) your country's consulate if you run into trouble.

Form	Pronunciation
hanasu	hah-nah-soo
hanasanai	hah-nah-sah-nah-ee
hanashi	hah-nah-shee
hanashite	hah-nah-shee-teh

You may find these sentences helpful.

- ✔ **Amerika ryōjikan ni renraku shite kudasai.** (ah-meh-ree-kah ryohh-jee-kahn nee rehn-rah-koo shee-teh koo-dah-sah-ee; Please contact the American consulate.)

- ✔ **Bengoshi o yonde kudasai.** (behn-goh-shee oh yohn-deh koo-dah-sah-ee; Please call a lawyer.)

- ✔ **Watashi no bengoshi ni hanashite kudasai.** (wah-tah-shee noh behn-goh-shee nee hah-nah-shee-teh koo-dah-sah-ee; Please talk to my lawyer.)

Words to Know

bengoshi	behn-goh-shee	lawyer
hanasu [u]	hah-nah-soo	to talk
ryōjikan	ryohh-jee-kahn	consulate

Getting Medical Help

Sometimes it's hard enough to understand doctor-talk in your own language, let alone in a foreign one. If you happen to get sick in Japan, you may want to prepare for your visit to the **o-isha-san** (oh-ee-shah-sahn; doctor) by going over the keywords for your **shōjō** (shohh-johh; symptoms) and for the **kensa** (kehn-sah; tests), **shindan** (sheen-dahn; diagnoses), **kusuri** (koo-soo-ree; medications), and **chiryō** (chee-ryohh; treatments) that you may receive.

Looking for a doctor

If you have a medical emergency, go to the **kyūkyū byōin** (kyooo-kyooo byohh-een; emergency hospital) and don't forget to bring your identification and insurance cards. If it's not an emergency, choose a **byōin** (byohh-een; hospital/doctor's office) and see a **senmon-i** (sehn-mohn-ee; medical specialist):

- **ganka-i** (gahn-kah-ee; ophthalmologist)
- **haisha** (hah-ee-shah; dentist)
- **hifuka-i** (hee-foo-kah-ee; dermatologist)
- **naika-i** (nah-ee-kah-ee; internist)
- **sanfujinka-i** (sahn-foo-jeen-kah-ee; obstetrician and gynecologist)
- **sēkē geka-i** (sehh-kehh geh-kah-ee; orthopedist)
- **shōnika-i** (shohh-nee-kah-ee; pediatrician)

O-isha-san ni iku (oh-ee-shah-sahn nee ee-koo) literally means *to go to a doctor,* but it actually means *to go to see a doctor.* So, use the verb **iku** (ee-koo; to go) when you go to see any kind of doctor.

Giving advice

If you want to recommend that your friend do something, place **hō ga ii** (hohh gah eee; it's better to) after a verb in the past tense. Isn't it strange? Even though such a recommendation refers to the future, you use the past tense of the verb. If you think someone should eat, say **tabeta hō ga ii** (tah-beh-tah hohh gah eee), which, if you were to insist on a literal translation, would translate as *the ate-alternative is good.* And that, my friend, is why we don't do literal translations.

The past tense of the verb **taberu** (tah-beh-roo) is **tabeta** (tah-beh-tah). It's very easy to form the past tense of a verb if you know the te-form. Replace the final **e** in the te-form with an **a,** and you instantly get the past tense. And if you want to speak politely, add **desu** to the end of **hō ga ii.** Check out these examples:

- ✔ **Haisha ni itta hō ga ii desu.** (hah-ee-shah nee eet-tah hohh gah eee deh-soo; You'd better see a dentist.)
- ✔ **Yasunda hō ga ii yo.** (yah-soon-dah hohh gah eee yoh; You'd better rest.)

In the following Talkin' the Talk section, Hiroshi is complaining about his headache. To introduce personal matters into a conversation, it's nice to end the sentence with **-n-desu** to sound polite and invite a response. (For more on **-n-desu,** see Chapter 5.)

Talkin' the Talk

Hiroshi has been suffering from a minor headache for two weeks. He talks about it to his co-worker, Yukiko.

Hiroshi:	**Saikin atama ga itai-n-desu. Itsumo hidari no mimi no ue ga itai-n-desu.** sah-ee-keen ah-tah-mah gah ee-tah-een-deh-soo. ee-tsoo-moh hee-dah-ree noh mee-mee noh oo-eh gah ee-tah-een-deh-soo. Lately, I've been suffering from a headache. It's always the spot right above my left ear that hurts.
Yukiko:	**Hen ne. Byōin ni itta hō ga ii desu yo.** hehn neh. byohh-een nee eet-tah hohh gah eee deh-soo yoh. That's strange. You'd better go to a hospital.

Hiroshi: **Naika.**
nah-ee-kah.
Internal medicine?

Yukiko: **Haisha ni itta hō ga ii desu yo.**
hah-ee-sha nee eet-tah hohh gah eee deh-soo yoh.
It's better to go to see a dentist.

Words to Know

byōin	byohh-een	hospital
haisha	hah-ee-shah	dentist
hen desu ne	hehn deh-soo neh	that's strange
naika	nah-ee-kah	internal medicine
naika-i	nah-ee-kah-ee	internist
o-isha-san	oh-ee-shah-sahn	medical doctors (in general)
saikin	sah-ee-keen	lately
senmon-i	sehn-mohn-ee	medical specialist

Pointing at your body parts

To explain your **shōjō** (shohh-johh; symptoms) to the doctor, specify *where* it hurts. It may be just one location, or it may be several locations. If you have arthritis, all your joints may hurt on cold, rainy days, but they may get better on warm, sunny days.

Now you need Japanese words for body parts. Go over the terms in Table 16-1. Touch your body parts as you say the words. The first one is **ashi** (ah-shee), which means both *foot* and *leg*. And even though there's a perfectly good word for *arm* — **ude** (oo-deh) — the word **te** (teh) means both *hand* and *arm*. How do you know which is which? Context is everything.

Table 16-1	Parts of the Body	
Body Part	*Pronunciation*	*Translation*
ashi	ah-shee	foot/leg
atama	ah-tah-mah	head
hiza	hee-zah	knee
kata	kah-tah	shoulder
koshi	koh-shee	hip
kubi	koo-bee	neck
kuchi	koo-chee	mouth
me	meh	eyes
mimi	mee-mee	ears
mune	moo-neh	chest
nodo	noh-doh	throat
onaka	oh-nah-kah	belly
senaka	seh-nah-kah	back
te	teh	hand/arm
ude	oo-deh	arm

If some part of your body hurts, say the body part that hurts, plus **ga** (gah), plus **itai** (ee-tah-ee) or **itai-n-desu** (ee-tah-een-deh-soo). By adding **-n-desu** you sound polite and receptive to your partner's response. (See Chapter 5 to find out about the basic function of **-n-desu**.) **Itai** (ee-tah-ee) is an adjective meaning painful, although in English, you often say *it hurts*. **Itai** is also what Japanese say for *ouch*. So, **atama ga itai** basically means *head is ouch* — in other words, *I have a headache*. If more than one part hurts, list all the parts using the particle **to** (toh) as a type of verbal comma and a stand-in for *and*. Place **to** after each body part, except the last one, as seen in the following examples:

- ✔ **Kata to kubi ga totemo itai-n-desu.** (kah-tah toh koo-bee gah toh-teh-moh ee-tah-een-deh-soo; My shoulder and neck hurt a lot.)

- ✔ **Kata to koshi to kubi ga itai-n-desu.** (kah-tah toh koh-shee toh koo-bee gah ee-tah-een-deh-soo; My shoulder, back, and neck hurt.)

Complaining about your discomfort

Expressing exactly how you're feeling with specific symptoms is crucial for receiving the right diagnosis. A few symptoms may occur together. For example, bad stomach viruses cause nausea, which is usually followed by diarrhea. Upper respiratory infections can give you a runny nose, a cough, and a very stuffy and congested night's sleep or cause a lack of sleep. All this talk of symptoms reminds me of a quick question that I have for all doctors out there: Why do flu shots never seem to work for me? I took the shot, but I'm suffering again this year. Check out the symptoms that you have in Table 16-2 before you go to the doctor.

Table 16-2	Suffering from Symptoms	
Symptom	*Pronunciation*	*Translation*
geri o shite iru	geh-ree oh shee-teh ee-roo	to have diarrhea
hakike ga suru	hah-kee-keh gah soo-roo	to have nausea
hana ga tsumatte iru	hah-nah gah tsoo-maht-teh ee-roo	to have a stuffy nose
hanamizu ga deru	hah-nah-mee-zoo gah deh-roo	to have a runny nose
kushami ga deru	koo-shah-mee gah deh-roo	to sneeze
me ga kayui	meh gah kah-yoo-ee	to have itchy eyes
netsu ga aru	neh-tsoo gah ah-roo	to have a fever
nodo ga itai	noh-doh gah ee-tah-ee	to have a sore throat
seki ga deru	seh-kee gah deh-roo	to cough
zutsū ga suru	zoo-tsoo gah soo-roo	to have a headache
zē zē suru	zehh zehh soo-roo	to wheeze

To describe how it hurts, you can use funny image-sound words like the ones in the following bulleted list. No translations here, just descriptions. Sorry.

- **chiku-chiku** (chee-koo-chee-koo): Sharp, needle-like pain, like you might have with stomach complaints

- **gan-gan** (gahn-gahn): Hammering or banging pain, as with a pounding headache

- **gohon-gohon** (goh-hohn-goh-hohn): Deep coughing sounds

- **hiri-hiri** (hee-ree-hee-ree): Smarting pain, as with a bad sunburn

✔ **zuki-zuki** (zoo-kee-zoo-kee): Nailing or screwing pain in the head

✔ **zē-zē** (zehh zehh): Wheezing sound in the chest

Conjugate the verb **deru** (deh-roo; to come out). You need it to describe all the annoying mucus that comes out when you cough, sneeze, and blow your nose when you have a code. **Gohon-gohon-gohon.** Sorry, I mean cold. It's a ru-verb.

Form	Pronunciation
deru	deh-roo
denai	deh-nah-ee
de	deh
dete	deh-teh

Talkin' the Talk

Miki is not feeling well, and she visits her doctor.

Doctor:	**Dōshimashita ka.** dohh-shee-mah-shee-tah kah. What happened?
Miki:	**Netsu ga aru-n-desu.** neh-tsoo gah ah-roon-deh-soo. I've been running a fever.
Doctor:	**Sorekara.** soh-reh-kah-rah. And.
Miki:	**Kushami ga demasu. Hanamizu mo hidoi-n-desu.** koo-shah-mee gah deh-mah-soo. hah-nah-mee-zoo moh hee-doh-een-deh-soo. I sneeze. I also have a terrible runny nose.
Doctor:	**Atama wa itai desu ka.** ah-tah-mah wah ee-tah-ee deh-soo kah. Do you have a headache?
Miki:	**Īe.** eee-eh. No.

Words to Know

deru [ru]	deh-roo	to come out
geri	geh-ree	diarreah
hanamizu	hah-nah-mee-zoo	runny nose
hidoi	hee-doh-ee	terrible
itai	ee-tah-ee	painful/ouch!
kushami	koo-shah-mee	sneeze
netsu	neh-tsoo	fever
seki	seh-kee	cough

Getting a diagnosis

A doctor can usually diagnose a minor cold or the flu just by talking with you, but sometimes you have to have tests done. No one wants to have a painful or time-consuming test, but if the doctor tells you that you need it, you'd better take it.

The test I hate the most is the blood test that requires the patient to fast for 12 hours beforehand. The feeling of not being able to eat or drink for 12 hours makes me nuts. My neighbor's sister is afraid of taking an MRI. She suffers from claustrophobia, the fear of confined spaces. The bad part of this story is that she didn't know that she was claustrophobic until she had an MRI!

A few tests and procedures that a doctor may recommend are:

- **chōonpa** (chohh-ohn-pah; sonogram)
- **ketsueki kensa** (keh-tsoo-eh-kee kehn-sah; blood test)
- **nyō kensa** (nyohh kehn-sah; urine test)
- **rentogen** (rehn-toh-gehn; X-ray)

After you explain your symptoms to the doctor, have an exam, and give some bodily fluid, it's judgment time. I hope the diagnosis is not serious. Possible diagnoses include

- ✔ **haien** (hah-ee-ehn; pneumonia)
- ✔ **infuruenza** (een-foo-roo-ehn-zah; influenza/flu)
- ✔ **kafunshō** (kah-foon-shohh; hay fever)
- ✔ **kansetsuen** (kahn-seh-tsoo-ehn; arthritis)
- ✔ **kaze** (kah-zeh; cold)
- ✔ **kossetsu** (kohs-seh-tsoo; broken bone)
- ✔ **nenza** (nehn-zah; sprain)
- ✔ **shokuchūdoku** (shoh-koo-chooo-doh-koo; food poisoning)
- ✔ **zensoku** (zehn-soh-koo; asthma)

In the following Talkin' the Talk section, Kazuo starts discussing yesterday's car accident at the doctor's office. **Jiko ni au** means *be involved in an accident,* and Kazuo says **jiko ni atta** because the accident is a past event. Be aware that **atta** (aht-tah) is the past tense of the verb **au** (ah-oo; to be involved).

Talkin' the Talk

Kazuo's car was hit by another car yesterday, and he had a stiff neck this morning. He talks about it with his doctor.

Kazuo: **Kinō kuruma no jiko ni atta-n-desu.**
kee-nohh koo-roo-mah noh jee-koh nee aht-tahn-deh-soo.
I had an auto accident yesterday.

Doctor: **Sorede. . .**
soh-reh-deh.
And. . .

Kazuo: **Kubi ga itai-n-desu.**
koo-bee gah ee-tah-een-deh-soo.
I've been having a pain in my neck.

Doctor: **Ue o muite kudasai.**
oo-eh oh moo-ee-teh koo-dah-sah-ee.
Turn your head up.

Kazuo slowly lifts his head and looks up.

Doctor: **Jā, shita o muite kudasai.**
jahh, shee-tah oh moo-ee-teh koo-dah-sah-ee.
Then, turn your head down a little.

Kazuo slowly lowers his head and looks down.

Doctor: **Daijōbu desu.**
dah-ee-johh-boo deh-soo.
You are fine.

Kazuo: **Rentogen wa.**
rehn-toh-gehn wah.
How about an X-ray?

Doctor: **Hitsuyō arimasen.**
hee-tsoo-yohh ah-ree-mah-sehn.
It's not necessary.

Words to Know

hitsuyō	hee-tsoo-yohh	necessity
infuruenza	een-foo-roo-ehn-zah	influenza/flu
kaze	kah-zeh	cold
kensa	kehn-sah	test
muku [u]	moo-koo	to turn one's head (toward)
rentogen	rehn-toh-gehn	X-ray

Getting treatment

There's no cure for a **kaze** (kah-zeh; cold), unless it's a bacterial infection, which then requires **kōsē busshitsu** (kohh-sehh boos-shee-tsoo; antibiotics). All you can do is try to treat your symptoms and make your life a little less miserable. Ask your grandma for her natural home remedy. One Japanese traditional cold remedy is **tamago zake** (tah-mah-goh zah-keh; egg sake) — heated sake with beaten egg. What's your secret remedy? Ginger tea? Chicken soup? Honey? Orange juice?

Your doctor may give you some **kusuri** (koo-soo-ree; medication) that makes you a bit more comfortable:

- **asupirin** (ah-soo-poo-reen; asprin)
- **itamidome** (ee-tah-mee-doh-meh; pain reliever)
- **genetsuzai** (geh-neh-tsoo-zah-ee; fever reducer)
- **sekidome** (seh-kee-doh-meh; cough suppressant)

If you have an injury, you may come home with one of these:

- **gipusu** (gee-poo-soo; cast)
- **hōtai** (hohh-tah-ee; bandage)
- **matsubazue** (mah-tsoo-bah-zoo-eh; crutches)
- **shippu** (sheep-poo; hot or cold compress)

Fun & Games

How do you say the following body parts in Japanese?

Check the answers in Appendix C.

1. _____   7. _____

2. _____   8. _____

3. _____   9. _____

4. _____   10. _____

5. _____   11. _____

6. _____

Part IV
The Part of Tens

The 5th Wave   By Rich Tennant

"So, you're learning conversational Japanese from a former Sumo wrestler. Besides, 'Ouch, I give up', 'Stop pushing', and 'Hey, let go of my belt', what else can you say?"

In this part . . .

This part is short but sweet. It contains a bunch of good, practical tips that you can keep in mind as you immerse yourself in the Japanese language. I give you ten ways to pick up Japanese quickly. And believe me; they can make a huge difference in your progress. Next, I introduce you to ten Japanese expressions and phrases that are guaranteed to make you sound Japanese. Enjoy using them. Finally, I include ten things that you shouldn't do in front of Japanese. You may thank me one day if you avoid one of these potentially embarrassing situations.

Chapter 17

Ten Ways to Pick Up Japanese Quickly

In This Chapter

▶ Cooking up language skills

▶ Reading comic books

▶ Watching movies

▶ Staying curious

Y ou have a hope; you have a dream. There's no time like the present to make it happen. Be creative. Create your own path to success. Picking up Japanese, or any new language, takes some work, but with these ten tips, you'll be rattling off Japanese phrases and sentences in no time. After you're through with these tips, invent some clever shortcuts of your own.

Use Japanese Language Tapes, CDs, and CD-ROMs

Think of this as the *good student approach* to picking up Japanese. Go to a bookstore and buy audiovisual materials. Bookstores have all sorts of language aids — audio tapes, videotapes, CDs, CD-ROMs, and the materials that often accompany Japanese language books. Listen to or watch your new collection and imitate the pronunciations, intonations, and rhythms of a native Japanese speaker's speech. And don't forget to listen to the audio CD included with this book.

Cook or Eat Japanese Foods

I call this tip the *gourmet way*. Find a Japanese cookbook at your local bookstore or order one on the Internet. Pick a dish that really makes your mouth water and whip up a Japanese meal next weekend! As you read over the recipe for your fabulous feast, be sure to have your trusty Japanese-English dictionary close by. After you understand the entire recipe, memorize keywords for ingredients and actions. Now, it's time to start cookin', good lookin'. Each time you wash, cut, grate, mix, bake, or grill, say what you're doing in Japanese. And call out the ingredients as you add them.

If you don't want to cook, go to a Japanese restaurant. Talk to a Japanese waiter, waitress, or sushi chef. Make it a goal to master the names of at least five Japanese dishes before you leave the restaurant.

Make Japanese Friends

Look around you. Okay, now stop looking around and read the rest of this paragraph. Are there any Japanese in your school, company, neighborhood, or church? If you find a few Japanese folks, become friends with them. Exchange telephone numbers and get together sometime. You could spend a nice afternoon together drinking tea. Ask them about Japanese culture, society, and daily life.

You may be communicating with them in English, but they'll surely let you know some Japanese words that are important for what you're talking about. Make a mental note of them.

Hang Out with Someone Who Understands Only Japanese

I call this an *immersion experience*. Do some fun activities like shopping or cooking with a Japanese person who only understands Japanese. Maybe it's your Japanese friend's grandma. As you speak nothing but Japanese, your tongue and lips will definitely get a workout.

Remember — language doesn't come from your head. It comes from your heart, and your head just provides a little help. Feeling that you have to speak Japanese to do something is a great driving force to increase your speaking ability. If you don't know a word in Japanese, use hand gestures or drawings to express it. And listen carefully to what the Japanese person says.

If you do this for a few hours each day for a week, by the end of the week, you'll be using fewer and fewer hand gestures and drawings, and more and more Japanese words. Think of it as an exchange program without ever leaving your home.

Read Japanese Comic Books

Japanese comic books are very popular among both young and old. The good part: Thousands of pictures that show detailed background scenes, actions, and facial expressions of characters accompany the written speech in balloons. Some comic books have English translations, too. Look for them in Japanese bookstores, comic book shops, and larger bookstores in your town or city.

Surf the Net

A tremendous amount of information is available right there in your computer. When you have time, surf the Net. Use your favorite search engine and simply punch in Japanese cultural keywords like *kimono* and *sushi,* Japanese artists' names, or Japanese place names like *Tokyo, Asakusa,* and *Akihabara.* You'll be amazed at the tons of useful information these searches return.

Watch Japanese Animation and Movies

Check out your local public library. They probably have videotapes, DVDs, or CD-ROMs of Japanese movies and animation with English subtitles. Pick one that looks interesting. Try one of Akira Kurosawa's movies, such as *Seven Samurai* and *Ran,* or other Japanese films that have received good reviews, such as *Tampopo* and *Shall We Dance?.* You may also want to check out Hayao Miyazaki's animation films — *Kiki's Delivery Service, My Neighbor Totoro,* and *Princess Mononoke,* to name a few.

When you watch the video for the first time, just watch the whole thing for enjoyment. Then, watch it a second time and try to catch some Japanese words and phrases. You'll learn the meaning of words, and you'll also figure out what context they're used in. Knowing when, where, and how words and phrases are used is very important for speaking Japanese naturally.

Do Karaoke

Get a Japanese karaoke set and sing as you read the lyrics that appear on the screen. If you like the song, memorize it by heart. Imitate the real singer's pronunciation very closely. After you master it perfectly, sing it in front of your friends and family. They'll be impressed by your use of Japanese, even if your singing ability leaves something to be desired!

Exchange Language Lessons

Did you know that helping others helps you a lot? Find a Japanese who wants to learn English, and teach him or her English. In exchange, ask him or her to teach you Japanese.

Local colleges and universities may have some Japanese international students who need English help. Contact them. You can also contact local Japanese associations. Find them in your local phone book. I'm sure you can find at least one Japanese person who needs some help perfecting his or her English in your area.

Be Positive, Curious, and Creative

Don't worry about making mistakes. Relax your mind when you talk. It's not a job interview. It won't be recorded. And, it won't be aired on TV. Be positive and praise yourself when you communicate in Japanese.

Don't wait until someone talks to you in Japanese. Initiate conversations yourself. Ask questions in Japanese. Regain the curious and worry-free spirit of your childhood.

Be creative and make opportunities to use Japanese in your daily life. Write down your weekly schedule in Japanese. Say the time and date in Japanese. Memorize your home phone number in Japanese. Address your family in Japanese. Greet your friends in Japanese. Don't wait until someone helps you; help yourself. Be creative, be curious, stay positive, and enjoy talking.

Chapter 18

Ten Things Never to Do in Japan

Social customs are culturally created rules that differ from the country to country. Different sets of values and ideas of what constitutes common sense are often tied to the histories of nations and peoples. Pasts rooted in democracy, feudalism, totalitarianism, a pioneer spirit, liberal values, or conservative values, to name a few, can be expected to give rise to different customs. So, what is polite for Americans, for example, may be rude for Japanese at times. This chapter alerts you to ten things that you shouldn't do when you're with Japanese people.

Don't Blow Your Nose in Public

Slurping noodles in front of other people is acceptable in Japanese culture, but blowing your nose isn't. People don't like the sound. A slurping sound is okay, but a blowing sound isn't.

When you need to blow your nose, leave the room. Do it in a hallway, a bathroom, or any other semi-private area. And when you blow your nose, use tissues, not your handkerchief. Don't wrap your germs and bacteria in a handkerchief and carry them around with you in your pocket. That's an unsanitary crime for Japanese.

Don't Walk in the House with Your Shoes On

Walking in a house with your shoes on is not just taboo; it's outrageously rude to Japanese. If you're visiting your Japanese friend's house, take off your shoes right away, or at least ask him or her whether you should take them off. In any case, remember to wear clean socks before visiting your Japanese friend. You probably want to avoid socks with holes in them too.

Don't Say That Your Mom Is Pretty

Don't tell other people that your mom is pretty. It sounds childish and immodest to Japanese. If someone tells you that your mom is pretty, deny it. Say that your mom is not pretty at all. You may think that my saying that is terrible, but that's the way the Japanese do it. Japanese moms never get upset when their children say this to others. Similarly, if someone tells you that your sweater is beautiful, don't say *Thank you*. Say *It's not beautiful; it was cheap* or *It's very old and worn out*. The basic rule: Deny every compliment you receive.

Don't Wash Yourself in the Bathtub

If you stay at your Japanese friend's house and use their bath, check whether you can use soap in the tub. The typical Japanese bath has a deep bathtub and a separate space outside the tub for actually washing your body. The tub is for soaking and relaxing, and other people in the house may use the same water. You need to keep the water in the tub as clean as possible.

Don't Say "San" After Your Own Name

When you talk with Japanese people, they'll say your name and say **-san** (sahn) after your name all the time. But don't copy them by placing **-san** after your own name when you refer to yourself. For example, don't say **Watashi wa Sumisu-san desu** (wah-tah-shee wah soo-mee-soo-sahn deh-soo; I'm Mr. Smith.). You'll sound like a kid. Instead, say **Watashi wa Sumisu desu** (wah-tah-shee wah soo-mee-soo deh-soo; I'm Smith.). The function of **-san** is to show respect to others; therefore, use it after other people's names but not after your own name.

Don't Kiss on the Lips in Public

Japanese don't kiss or hug their family or friends in public. They occasionally shake hands, but that's it as far as publicly touching bodies is concerned. Don't take this custom to mean that they're not affectionate. They simply aren't used to hugging and kissing people in public — it's not a cultural tradition as it is for people in some parts of the world. Japanese try to understand and accept a hug and a kiss on the cheek from westerners, but don't ever kiss them on their lips.

Don't Rip the Wrapping Paper Off of Presents

To Japanese, a present is more than just what's inside the package. The presentation itself is part of the present, and the gift-wrapping is part of the presentation. Even if you receive a store-wrapped present, don't haphazardly tear off the wrapping paper in front of the person who gave you the gift — it will break his or her heart. Remove the tape carefully, unwrap the present, and save the wrapping paper, even if you end up recycling it later.

Don't Use First Names or "Anata" with Your Boss or Teacher

Don't ever call your Japanese teacher or your Japanese boss by their first name. Call them by their last name with the appropriate title, like **sensē** (sehn-sehh; professor) or **shachō** (shah-chohh; company president), or use the suffix **-san** following their last name.

Don't use the pronoun **anata** (ah-nah-tah; you) with them either. Whenever you feel like saying *you,* use their last name plus their title again and again (and again). The pronoun **anata** is almost forbidden in Japanese conversations. For some reason, it sounds snobby or arrogant.

Don't Take the First "No, Thank You" Literally

Japanese say *No, thank you* at least once when someone offers food or beverages, even if they're very hungry or thirsty. So, don't take their first *No, thank you* literally. Even if they say *No, thank you,* make the offer again. If they want whatever it is you're offering, Japanese usually accept the offer after the second or the third time. If you understand how to play this game, you can become a great host or hostess for a Japanese guest.

Don't Start Eating Without Saying "Itadakimasu"

Don't ever start eating without saying **Itadakimasu** (ee-tah-dah-kee-mah-soo). **Itadakimasu** is the polite form of the humble verb **itadaku** (ee-tah-dah-koo; to receive), but it's also a set phrase used when you start eating, as if to say *I humbly receive this food.* Starting to eat without saying it is very rude. And if you're eating with a bunch of people, don't start eating until the host or the hostess tells you to start. When you finish eating, say **Gochisōsama** (goh-chee-sohh-sah-mah). It literally means *It was a great feast.* It's the set phrase used when you finish eating. Leaving the table without saying this phrase is also very rude.

Chapter 19

Ten Favorite Japanese Expressions

Life is full of **ki-do-ai-raku** (kee-doh-ah-ee-rah-koo; delight-anger-sorrow-fun), and some phrases slip out of our mouths repeatedly in response to different daily situations. Master these common Japanese expressions and use them casually.

Yatta

(yaht-tah; I did it!)

Say **yatta** when you accomplish something big, receive a great opportunity, or feel victorious. Passing a difficult test, getting the job you wanted, or winning the lottery — these all qualify as **yatta** material. I hope you get the opportunity to use this expression every day.

Hontō

(hohn-tohh; Really?)

Say **hontō** to confirm what you've just heard. Suppose your colleague tells you that she's getting married to your boss. Respond to the news by saying **hontō.**

What if your friend says that he'll give his car to you for free? Say **hontō** before saying thank you. You can say **hontō** in a lot of situations in your daily life because so many unbelievable things happen every day.

Ā, sō desu ka

(ahh, sohh deh-soo kah; Oh, I see.)

Say **Ā, sō desu ka** every time your conversational partner provides a new piece of information. You need to acknowledge each new bit of info by saying, *Oh, I see*. Be sure to nod as you say this expression. If you talk casually with a Japanese person, you may use this phrase 200 times in one hour.

Mochiron

(moh-chee-rohn; Of course!)

This is the favorite adverb of confident people. Use it when you're 100 percent confident in your opinion. If you were a married man, how would you answer this question, posed to you by your wife: *Would you marry me if you had a chance to do it all over again?* A word of advice: Don't think about it; just say **mochiron** to her because you only live once, and you'll never actually be faced with the decision.

Ā, yokatta

(ahh, yoh-kaht-tah; Oh, good.)

Say **Ā, yokatta** every time you feel like saying *What a relief* or *Oh, good*. If you're Mr. or Ms. Worrier, you may say **Ā, yokatta** ten times a day:

> Did I turn off the stove?
>
> Yes, you did.
>
> **Ā, yokatta.**
>
> My daughter was kidnapped!
>
> No, she's right there behind you.
>
> **Ā, yokatta.**

Zenzen

(zehn-zehn; Not at all.)

Zenzen is the phrase of denial. Suppose that someone asks you, "Am I disturbing you?" when they're not bothering you at all. Say **zenzen** and shake your head. Suppose that your spouse or friend asks whether you understand why he or she is so mad. If you don't have any idea, say **zenzen,** if you have the courage.

Nani

(nah-nee; What?)

Nani is a question word. It's handy when you talk with a Japanese person. Say **nani** when you don't hear or understand what the other person said.

You can also say **nani** when you can't believe or don't like what you hear. For example, your fiancée suddenly announces, "I'm getting married to Tom." If your name is Frank, you can surely say **nani.** That's assuming you have the ability to form words at that point.

Dōshiyō

(dohh-shee-yohh; What shall I do?)

Say **dōshiyō** when you're in a panic and have no idea what to do. You can repeat it over and over while you try to think of what to do: **Dōshiyō, dōshiyō, dōshiyō.** Now, you sound like you're in big trouble. What happened? Oh, you've locked your car door with your keys and your coat inside?!

Ā, bikkurishita

(ahh, beek-koo-ree-shee-tah; What a surprise!)

Say **Ā, bikkurishita** when you're very surprised. Is your family known for throwing surprise parties? If so, say **Ā, bikkurishita** after they shout out *Surprise* on your birthday.

Yappari

(yahp-pah-ree; I knew it would happen.)

Sometimes you have a vague suspicion that something will happen, and then it actually happens. At times like that, say **yappari.** Suppose that you haven't received a newspaper for the last month, but the newspaper delivery person says that he has dropped it off in front of your door every day. One day, you wake up earlier than usual, and you see your neighbor picking up your newspaper. If you had a suspicion that your neighbor was up to something, say **yappari.**

Chapter 20

Ten Phrases That Make You Sound Japanese

In This Chapter

▶ Greeting guests
▶ Giving it your best shot
▶ Expressing sympathy

*A*ll languages have some obscure or unique expressions that provide an authentic flavor of the culture. The literal translations are often not transparent, and your command of these expressions depends upon a deep understanding of the culture and values behind the language. In this chapter, I give you ten phrases that can make you sound Japanese. Master these expressions and use them in the right context and feel the Japanese mentality and spirit.

Enryo shinaide

(ehn-ryoh shee-nah-ee-deh; Don't be shy.)

Japanese guests often appear to be very shy. They usually refuse offers of food or drink at least once, no matter what. If you're the host or the hostess, say **Enryo shinaide** right after your guest says *No, thank you.*

Mottainai

(moht-tah-ee-nah-ee; What a waste./It's too good.)

Even though Japanese have become spoiled by disposable goods, such as plastic diapers, paper cups, and paper towels, they still hate to waste things, and they constantly express their objections to waste by saying **mottainai.** *What? Are you going to throw away that sweater? Ā, **mottainai.** Give it to me.*

This phrase is like a two-for-one special. It doesn't just express your objection to throwing away things; you can also say **Ā, mottainai** if someone lacks a true appreciation for something of value. You would use this phrase when your children don't appreciate good food. *What? You gave steak to the dog?* **Ā, mottainai.**

Osakini

(oh-sah-kee-nee; Pardon me, but I'm leaving now.)

The literal meaning of **osakini** is *earlier.* When you have to leave someplace earlier than a friend who is staying behind, or even a stranger that you've struck up a conversation with, tell them **osakini. Osakini** displays your thoughtfulness for the people who can't leave the place yet. It's commonly used to say goodbye politely in all sorts of contexts and locations — a waiting room, restaurant, library, party, and so on.

Sasuga

(sah-soo-gah; I'm impressed by you, as usual.)

The literal meaning of **sasuga** is *as might have been expected,* but the expression is commonly used as a compliment when someone has done an impressive job. Suppose your friend John is a good athlete, and he has just won the gold medal in a skiing competition. You can tell him **sasuga,** meaning *I knew that you could win the prize! You were cool, as usual.* If your company president has just created a new day-care center and a recreation facility for the employees, you can say **sasuga shachō** (sah-soo-gah shah-chohh) to her. It means *I admire your usual thoughtfulness, president.*

Gambatte

(gahm-baht-teh; Try your best!)

Japanese often believe that the effort is more important than the result. Trying one's best is the only way to go. When your friend is going to take an important exam, say **gambatte** to him or her. And, if you are seriously studying Japanese, I want to tell you **gambatte.**

Shōganai

(shohh-gah-nah-ee; There's no choice.)

When you're in a difficult situation, look at all the possible solutions. If none of them will work well, accept the fact or choose a solution that you know isn't part of the best-case scenario and say **Shōganai. Shōganai** conveys your disappointment and your attitude that you have given up and resigned yourself to the situation. Suppose that you miss your plane home and no other flights are departing until tomorrow morning. You have to give up the idea of going home today. In such a context, say **Shōganai** and start looking for a hotel. Suppose that you can't find a hotel. Then, you have to give up the idea of sleeping on a bed. Say **Shōganai** again and sleep on a bench at the airport. It somehow smoothes out inevitably bad situations. Life goes on.

Okage-sama de

(oh-kah-geh-sah-mah de; Luckily.)

If someone asks you **Ogenki desu ka** (oh-gehn-kee deh-soo kah; How are you?), answer it with **Okage-sama de,** instead of **Genki desu** (gehn-kee deh-soo; I'm fine). You'll sound modest, thankful, and sophisticated. The original meaning is that your good being and health are due to God and other people, including the person you're talking to. It's a very modest expression.

Gokurō-sama

(goh-koo-rohh-sah-mah; Thank you for your trouble.)

This is a phrase of appreciation from a boss to his or her subordinates. If you're the boss at work, say **Gokurō-sama** to each of your workers and assistants when they say goodbye to you at the end of the workday. So everyday around 5:00, you may have to say **Gokurō-sama** about fifty times or more an hour.

Yoroshiku

(yoh-roh-shee-koo; I'm pleased to meet you./I appreciate your helping me.)

The literal meaning of **yoroshiku** is *appropriately* or *as needed,* but you can say **yoroshiku** when you meet someone for the very first time. In this case, it means *I'm pleased to meet you.* The concept behind this use is *Please treat me appropriately.* You can also say **yoroshiku** right after asking a favor of someone. Then, it means *I appreciate your helping me.* The underlying idea is *Thank you for helping me, and I hope you handle it for me appropriately.* In both cases, **yoroshiku** shows your polite and modest attitude.

Taihen desu ne

(tah-ee-hen deh-soo neh; That's tough.)

This is a phrase of sympathy. Use it when your friends tell you about their hardships related to sickness, financial problems, relationship troubles, or any other kind of difficult situation. Suppose that your friend tells you that he has to pay for five kids to go to college. You can tell him **Taihen desu ne.**

Part V
Appendixes

The 5th Wave · By Rich Tennant

"I think you meant to ask for more 'wasabi', not, 'Kemosabe'."

In this part . . .

The appendixes in this part give you verb tables so that you can conjugate most regular verbs and many irregular ones. I also provide a mini-dictionary with some of the words you'll use most often. Next comes the answers to the Fun and Games exercises at the end of most chapters. Finally, I list the tracks of the audio CD included with this book so that you can read along as you listen.

Appendix A
Verb Tables

Regular Japanese Verbs

Regular ru-verbs Ending with -eru
For example: taberu (to eat)

	Present	Negative	Past
Plain/Informal	taberu	tabenai	tabeta
Polite/Neutral	tabemasu	tabemasen	tabemashita

Stem: tabe

Te-form: tabete

Regular ru-verbs Ending with -iru
For example: miru (to watch)

	Present	Negative	Past
Plain/Informal	miru	minai	mita
Polite/Neutral	mimasu	mimasen	mimashita

Stem: mi

Te-form: mite

Regular u-verbs Ending with -ku
For example: kaku (to write)

	Present	Negative	Past
Plain/Informal	kaku	kakanai	kaita
Polite/Neutral	kakimasu	kakimasen	kakimashita

Stem: kaki

Te-form: kaite

Regular u-verbs Ending with -gu
For example: oyogu (to swim)

	Present	Negative	Past
Plain/Informal	oyogu	oyoganai	oyoida
Polite/Neutral	oyogimasu	oyogimasen	oyogimashita

Stem: oyogi

Te-form: oyoide

Regular u-verbs Ending with -su
For example: hanasu (to speak)

	Present	Negative	Past
Plain/Informal	hanasu	hanasanai	hanashita
Polite/Neutral	hanashimasu	hanashimasen	hanashimashita

Stem: hanashi

Te-form: hanashite

Regular u-verbs Ending with -bu
For example: asobu (to play)

	Present	Negative	Past
Plain/Informal	asobu	asobanai	asonda
Polite/Neutral	asobimasu	asobimasen	asobimashita

Stem: asobi

Te-form: asonde

Regular u-verbs Ending with -mu
For example: nomu (to drink)

	Present	Negative	Past
Plain/Informal	nomu	nomanai	nonda
Polite/Neutral	nomimasu	nomimasen	nomimashita

Stem: nomi

Te-form: nonde

Regular u-verbs Ending with -nu
For example: shinu (to die)

	Present	Negative	Past
Plain/Informal	shinu	shinanai	shinda
Polite/Neutral	shinimasu	shinimasen	shinimashita

Stem: shini
Te-form: shinde

Regular u-verbs Ending with -u
For example: kau (to buy)

	Present	Negative	Past
Plain/Informal	kau	kawanai	katta
Polite/Neutral	kaimasu	kaimasen	kaimashita

Stem: kai
Te-form: katte

Regular u-verbs Ending with -ru
For example: kaeru (to go home)

	Present	Negative	Past
Plain/Informal	kaeru	kaeranai	kaetta
Polite/Neutral	kaerimasu	kaerimasen	kaerimashita

Stem: kaeri
Te-form: kaette

Regular u-verbs Ending with -tsu
For example: matsu (to wait)

	Present	Negative	Past
Plain/Informal	matsu	matanai	matta
Polite/Neutral	machimasu	machimasen	machimashita

Stem: machi
Te-form: matte

Irregular Japanese Verbs

suru
to do

	Present	Negative	Past
Plain/Informal	suru	shinai	shita
Polite/Neutral	shimasu	shimasen	shimashita

Stem: shi
Te-form: shite

kuru
to come

	Present	Negative	Past
Plain/Informal	kuru	konai	kita
Polite/Neutral	kimasu	kimasen	kimashita

Stem: ki
Te-form: kite

aru
to exist

	Present	Negative	Past
Plain/Informal	aru	nai	atta
Polite/Neutral	arimasu	arimasen	arimashita

Stem: ari
Te-form: atte

iku
to go

	Present	Negative	Past
Plain/Informal	iku	ikanai	itta
Polite/Neutral	ikimasu	ikimasen	ikimashita

Stem: iki
Te-form: itte

irassharu
to exist (honorific)

	Present	Negative	Past
Plain/Informal	irassharu	irassharanai	irasshatta
Polite/Neutral	irasshaimasu	irasshaimasen	irasshaimashita

Stem: irasshai
Te-form: irasshatte

Japanese-English Mini-Dictionary

A

aida (ah-ee-dah): between

aisu kurīmu (ah-ee-soo koo-reee-moo): ice cream

aka (ah-kah): red

akeru (ah-keh-roo): to open

ame (ah-meh): rain

Amerika (ah-meh-ree-kah): America

Amerikajin (ah-meh-ree-kah-jeen): American person

anata (ah-nah-tah): you

ao (ah-oh): blue

apāto (ah-pahh-toh): apartment

are (ah-reh): that one over there

arigatō (ah-ree-gah-tohh): thanks

aruku (ah-roo-koo): to walk

asa (ah-sah): morning

ashi (ah-shee): foot

ashita (ah-shee-tah): tomorrow

asoko (ah-soh-koh): over there

atama (ah-tah-mah): head

atarashii (ah-tah-rah-sheee): new

B

basu (bah-soo): bus

beddo (behd-doh): bed

bengoshi (behn-goh-shee): lawyer

benkyō suru (behn-kyohh soo-roo): to study

bifuteki (bee-foo-teh-kee): beef steak

bīru (beee-roo): beer

bōshi (bohh-shee): hat

burausu (boo-rah-oo-soo): blouse

butaniku (boo-tah-nee-koo): pork

byōin (byohh-een): hospital

byōki (byohh-kee): illness

C

chairo (chah-ee-roh): brown

chikaku (chee-kah-koo): near

chikatetsu (chee-kah-teh-tsoo): subway

chiketto (chee-keht-toh): ticket

chippu (cheep-poo): tip

chīsai (cheee-sah-ee): small

chizu (chee-zoo): map

chōshoku (chohh-shoh-koo): breakfast

Chūgoku (chooo-goh-koo): China

chūshoku (chooo-shoh-koo): lunch

chūshajō (chooo-shah-johh): parking lot

D

daidokoro (dah-ee-doh-koh-roh): kitchen

daigaku (dah-ee-gah-koo): university

dare (dah-reh): who

dareka (dah-reh-kah): somebody

deguchi (deh-goo-chee): exit

demo (deh-moh): but

densha (dehn-shah): train

denwa (dehn-wah): telephone

denwa-bangō (dehn-wah-bahn-gohh): telephone number

depāto (deh-pahh-toh): department store

dezāto (deh-zahh-toh): dessert

dō (dohh): how

Doitsu (doh-ee-tsoo): Germany

doko (doh-koh): where

dōmo (dohh-moh): thanks

dore (doh-reh): which one

dōryō (dohh-ryohh): co-worker

doyōbi (doh-yohh-bee): Saturday

E

ēga (ehh-gah): movie

ēgo (ehh-goh): English

F

Furansu (foo-rahn-soo): France

furui (foo-roo-ee): old

G

gakkō (gahk-kohh): school

gekijō (geh-kee-johh): theater

genkin (gehn-keen): cash

getsuyōbi (geh-tsoo-yohh-bee): Monday

ginkō (geen-kohh): bank

gitā (gee-tahh): guitar

go (goh): five

go-gatsu (goh-gah-tsoo): May

gohan (goh-hahn): cooked rice

gorufu (goh-roo-foo): golf

gyūniku (gyooo-nee-koo): beef

gyūnyū (gyooo-nyooo): milk

H

hachi (hah-chee): eight

hachi-gatsu (hah-chee-gah-tsoo): August

hairu (hah-ee-roo): to enter

haisha (hah-ee-shah): dentist

hakubutsukan (hah-koo-boo-tsoo-kahn): museum

hana (1) (hah-nah): flower

hana (2) (hah-nah): nose

hanasu (hah-nah-soo): to speak

harau (hah-rah-oo): to pay

hataraku (hah-tah-rah-koo): to work

hayaku (hah-yah-koo): quickly

hen (hehn): weird

heya (heh-yah): room

hi (hee): day

hidari (hee-dah-ree): left

higashi (hee-gah-shee): east

hikōki (hee-kohh-kee): airplane

hiroi (hee-roh-ee): wide

hisho (hee-shoh): secretary

hiza (hee-zah): knee

hon (hohn): book

hoshii (hoh-sheee): to want

hoteru (hoh-teh-roo): hotel

hyaku (hyah-koo): hundred

I

ichi (ee-chee): one

ichi-gatsu (ee-chee-gah-tsoo): January

ie (ee-eh): house

Igirisu (ee-gee-ree-soo): England

ii (eee): good

iku (ee-koo): to go

ikura (ee-koo-rah): how much

ima (ee-mah): now

imōto (ee-mohh-toh): younger sister

inaka (ee-nah-kah): countryside

inu (ee-noo): dog

iriguchi (ee-ree-goo-chee): entrance

iro (ee-roh): color

isha (ee-shah): physician

Itaria (ee-tah-ree-ah): Italy

itoko (ee-toh-koh): cousin

itsu (ee-tsoo): when

itsumo (ee-tsoo-moh): always

J

jaketto (jah-keht-toh): jacket

jiko (jee-koh): accident

jīnzu (jeeen-zoo): jeans

jitensha (jee-tehn-shah): bicycle

jū (jooo): ten

jū-gatsu (jooo-gah-tsoo): October

jūgo (jooo-goh): fifteen

jūgyōin (jooo-gyohh-een): employee

jūhachi (jooo-hah-chee): eighteen

jūichi-gatsu (jooo-ee-chee-gah-tsoo): November

jūkyū (jooo-kyooo): nineteen

jūnana (jooo-nah-nah): seventeen

jūni (jooo-nee): twelve

jūni-gatsu (jooo-nee-gah-tsoo): December

jūroku (jooo-roh-koo): sixteen

jūsan (jooo-sahn): thirteen

jūsho (jooo-shoh): address

jūsu (jooo-soo): juice

jūyon (jooo-yohn): fourteen

K

kaban (kah-bahn): bag

kaeru (kah-eh-roo): to return

kagi (kah-gee): key

kaisha (kah-ee-shah): company

kaishain (kah-ee-shah-een): company employee

kaku (kah-koo): to write

kami (1) (kah-mee): hair

kami (2) (kah-mee): paper

Kanada (kah-nah-dah): Canada

kangofu (kahn-goh-foo): nurse

Kankoku (kahn-koh-koo): Korea

kanojo (kah-noh-joh): she

kantan (kahn-tahn): easy

kao (kah-oh): face

kare (kah-reh): he

karendā (kah-rehn-dahh): calendar

kasa (kah-sah): umbrella

kata (kah-tah): shoulder

kau (kah-oo): buy

kawa (kah-wah): river

kayōbi (kah-yohh-bee): Tuesday

kēsatsu (kehh-sah-tsoo): police

ki (kee): tree

kinō (kee-nohh): yesterday

kinyōbi (keen-yohh-bee): Friday

kirē (kee-rehh): beautiful

kīro (keee-roh): yellow

kita (kee-tah): north

kitte (keet-teh): stamp

kodomo (koh-doh-moh): child

kōen (kohh-ehn): park

kōhī (kohh-heee): coffee

kōkō (kohh-kohh): high school

koko (koh-koh): here

kokuseki (koh-koo-seh-kee): nationality

konban (kohn-bahn): tonight

kongetsu (kohn-geh-tsoo): this month

konnichiwa (kohn-nee-chee-wah): hello/good afternoon

konshū (kohn-shooo): this week

kore (koh-reh): this one

kōsaten (kohh-sah-tehn): intersection

kotoshi (koh-toh-shee): this year

kubi (koo-bee): neck

kuchi (koo-chee): mouth

kudamono (koo-dah-moh-noh): fruit

ku-gatsu (koo-gah-tsoo): September

kūkō (kooo-kohh): airport

kuni (koo-nee): country

kurai (koo-rah-ee): dark

kurejitto kādo (koo-reh-jeet-toh kahh-doh): credit card

kuro (koo-roh): black

kuru (koo-roo): to come

kuruma (koo-roo-mah): car

kusuri (koo-soo-ree): medicine

kutsu (koo-tsoo): shoe

kyō (kyohh): today

kyōkai (kyohh-kah-ee): church

kyonen (kyoh-nehn): last year

kyū (kyooo): nine

kyūkyūsha (kyooo-kyooo-shah): ambulance

M

mado (mah-doh): window

mae (mah-eh): front

matsu (mah-tsoo): to wait

me (meh): eye

midori (mee-doh-ree): green

migi (mee-gee): right

mikan (mee-kahn): orange

mimi (mee-mee): ear

minami (mee-nah-mee): south

mise (mee-seh): store

mizu (mee-zoo): water

mizuumi (mee-zoo-oo-mee): lake

mokuyōbi (moh-koo-yohh-bee): Thursday

moshimoshi (moh-shee-moh-shee): hello (telephone)

mune (moo-neh): chest

mura (moo-rah): village

muzukashii (moo-zoo-kah-sheee): difficult

N

namae (nah-mah-eh): name

nana (nah-nah): seven

nani (nah-nee): what

nanika (nah-nee-kah): something

neko (neh-koh): cat

neru (neh-roo): to sleep

netsu (neh-tsoo): fever

ni (nee): two

nichiyōbi (nee-chee-yohh-bee): Sunday

ni-gatsu (nee-gah-tsoo): February

Nihon (nee-hohn): Japan

Nihongo (nee-hohn-goh): Japanese language

Nihonjin (nee-hohn-jeen): Japanese person

niku (nee-koo): meat

nimotsu (nee-moh-tsoo): luggage

nishi (nee-shee): west

nomu (noh-moo): to drink

O

oboeru (oh-boh-eh-roo): to remember

o-cha (oh-chah): tea

odoru (oh-doh-roo): to dance

ohayō (oh-hah-yohh): good morning

o-kane (oh-kah-neh): money

okāsan (oh-kahh-sahn): mother

ōkii (ohh-keee): big

o-kome (oh-koh-meh): uncooked rice

oku (oh-koo): to put

omoshiroi (oh-moh-shee-roh-ee): interesting

onaka (oh-nah-kah): abdomen

onēsan (oh-nehh-sahn): older sister

onĭsan (oh-neee-sahn): older brother

onna (ohn-nah): female

onna no hito (ohn-nah noh hee-toh): woman

osoi (oh-soh-ee): late

Ōsutoraria (ohh-soo-toh-rah-ree-ah): Australia

otoko (oh-toh-koh): male

otoko no hito (oh-toh-koh noh hee-toh): man

otōsan (oh-tohh-sahn): father

otōto (oh-tohh-toh): younger brother

owaru (oh-wah-roo): to end

oyasuminasai (oh-yah-soo-mee-nah-sah-ee): good night

P

pan (pahn): bread

pasupōto (pah-soo-pohh-toh): passport

piano (pee-ah-noh): piano

piza (pee-zah): pizza

R

raigetsu (rah-ee-geh-tsoo): next month

rainen (rah-ee-nehn): next year

raishū (rah-ee-shooo): next week

resutoran (reh-soo-toh-rahn): restaurant

ringo (reen-goh): apple

roku (roh-koo): six

roku-gatsu (roh-koo-gah-tsoo): June

ryōjikan (ryohh-jee-kahn): consulate

ryokō (ryoh-kohh): trip

ryōri (ryohh-ree): cooking

ryōshūsho (ryohh-shooo-shoh): receipt

S

saifu (sah-ee-foo): wallet

sakana (sah-kah-nah): fish

sakkā (sahk-kahh): soccer

san (sahn): three

san-gatsu (sahn-gah-tsoo): March

sarada (sah-rah-dah): salad

satō (sah-tohh): sugar

sayōnara (sah-yohh-nah-rah): goodbye

sengetsu (sehn-geh-tsoo): last month

sensē (sehn-sehh): teacher

senshū (sehn-shooo): last week

sētā (sehh-tahh): sweater

shachō (shah-chohh): company president

shashin (shah-sheen): photograph

shatsu (shah-tsoo): shirt

shichi-gatsu (shee-chee-gah-tsoo): July

shi-gatsu (shee-gah-tsoo): April

shinbun (sheen-boon): newspaper

shiro (shee-roh): white

shitsumon (shee-tsoo-mohn): question

shizen (shee-zehn): nature

shizuka (shee-zoo-kah): quiet

shokugyŏ (shoh-koo-gyohh): occupation

shokuji (shoh-koo-jee): meal

shomĕ (shoh-mehh): signature

shŭ (shooo): week

shumi (shoo-mee): hobby

shuppatsu (shoop-pah-tsoo): departure

soko (soh-koh): there near you

sore (soh-reh): that one near you

soto (soh-toh): outside

suiĕ (soo-ee-ehh): swimming

suiyŏbi (soo-ee-yohh-bee): Wednesday

sukăto (soo-kahh-toh): skirt

suki (soo-kee): to like

supagettĭ (soo-pah-geht-teee): spaghetti

sŭpămăketto (sooo-pahh-mahh-keht-toh): supermarket

Supein (soo-peh-een): Spain

suru (soo-roo): to do

sŭtsu (sooo-tsoo): suit

sŭtsukĕsu (sooo-tsoo-kehh-soo): suitcase

suwaru (soo-wah-roo): to sit down

T

taberu (tah-beh-roo): to eat

taishikan (tah-ee-shee-kahn): embassy

taiyŏ (tah-ee-yohh): sun

takai (tah-kah-ee): expensive

takushĭ (tah-koo-sheee): taxi

te (teh): hand

tegami (teh-gah-mee): letter

tenisu (teh-nee-soo): tennis

terebi (teh-reh-bee): TV

tŏi (tohh-ee): far

tomodachi (toh-moh-dah-chee): friend

tonari (toh-nah-ree): next door

toriniku (toh-ree-nee-koo): chicken

toru (toh-roo): to take

totemo (toh-teh-moh): very

tsukau (tsoo-kah-oo): to use

tsuku (tsoo-koo): to arrive

tsukuru (tsoo-koo-roo): to make

U

ude (oo-deh): arm

uma (oo-mah): horse

umi (oo-mee): ocean

unten suru (oon-tehn soo-roo): to drive

uru (oo-roo): to sell

urusai (oo-roo-sah-ee): noisy

ushiro (oo-shee-roh): behind

utau (oo-tah-oo): to sing

W

wain (wah-een): wine

warui (wah-roo-ee): bad

watashi (wah-tah-shee): I

Y

yakyŭ (yah-kyooo): baseball

yama (yah-mah): mountain

yasai (yah-sah-ee): vegetable

yasui (yah-soo-ee): cheap

yasumi (yah-soo-mee): vacation

yomu (yoh-moo): to read

yon (yohn): four

yoyaku (yoh-yah-koo): reservation

yubi (yoo-bee): finger

yūbin bangō (yooo-been bahn-gohh): zip code

yūbinkyoku (yooo-been-kyoh-koo): post office

yuki (yoo-kee): snow

yūshoku (yooo-shoh-koo): dinner

Z

zenzen (zehn-zehn): not at all

zubon (zoo-bohn): pants

English-Japanese Mini-Dictionary

A

abdomen: **onaka** (oh-nah-kah)

accident: **jiko** (jee-koh)

address: **jūsho** (jooo-shoh)

airplane: **hikōki** (hee-kohh-kee)

airport: **kūkō** (kooo-kohh)

always: **itsumo** (ee-tsoo-moh)

ambulance: **kyūkyūsha**
   (kyooo-kyooo-shah)

America: **Amerika** (ah-meh-ree-kah)

American person: **Amerikajin**
   (ah-meh-ree-kah-jeen)

apartment: **apāto** (ah-pahh-toh)

apple: **ringo** (reen-goh)

April: **shi-gatsu** (shee-gah-tsoo)

arm: **ude** (oo-deh)

arrive: **tsuku** (tsoo-koo)

August: **hachi-gatsu** (hah-chee-gah-tsoo)

Australia: **Ōsutoraria**
   (ohh-soo-toh-rah-ree-ah)

B

bad: **warui** (wah-roo-ee)

bag: **kaban** (kah-bahn)

bank: **ginkō** (geen-kohh)

baseball: **yakyū** (yah-kyooo)

beautiful: **kirē** (kee-rehh)

bed: **beddo** (behd-doh)

beef: **gyūniku** (gyooo-nee-koo)

beef steak: **bifuteki** (bee-foo-teh-kee)

beer: **bīru** (beee-roo)

behind: **ushiro** (oo-shee-roh)

between: **aida** (ah-ee-dah)

bicycle: **jitensha** (jee-tehn-shah)

big: **ōkii** (ohh-keee)

black: **kuro** (koo-roh)

blouse: **burausu** (boo-rah-oo-soo)

blue: **ao** (ah-oh)

book: **hon** (hohn)

bread: **pan** (pahn)

breakfast: **chōshoku** (chohh-shoh-koo)

brother, younger: **otōto** (oh-tohh-toh)

brother, older: **onīsan** (oh-neee-sahn)

brown: **chairo** (chah-ee-roh)

bus: **basu** (bah-soo)

but: **demo** (deh-moh)

buy: **kau** (kah-oo)

C

calendar: **karendā** (kah-rehn-dahh)

Canada: **Kanada** (kah-nah-dah)

car: **kuruma** (koo-roo-mah)

cash: **genkin** (gehn-keen)

cat: **neko** (neh-koh)

cheap: **yasui** (yah-soo-ee)

cheese: **chīzu** (cheee-zoo)

chest: **mune** (moo-neh)

chicken: **toriniku** (toh-ree-nee-koo)

child: **kodomo** (koh-doh-moh)

China: **Chūgoku** (chooo-goh-koo)

church: **kyōkai** (kyohh-kah-ee)

coffee: **kōhī** (kohh-heee)

color: **iro** (ee-roh)

come (v.): **kuru** (koo-roo)

company: **kaisha** (kah-ee-shah)

company employee: **kaishain**
   (kah-ee-shah-een)

company president: **shachō** (shah-chohh)

consulate: **ryōjikan** (ryohh-jee-kahn)

cooking: **ryōri** (ryohh-ree)

country: **kuni** (koo-nee)

countryside: **inaka** (ee-nah-kah)

cousin: **itoko** (ee-toh-koh)

co-worker: **dōryō** (dohh-ryohh)

credit card: **kurejitto kādo** (koo-reh-jeet-
   toh kahh-doh)

D

dance (v.): **odoru** (oh-doh-roo)

dark: **kurai** (koo-rah-ee)

day: **hi** (hee)

December: **jūni-gatsu** (jooo-nee-gah-tsoo)

dentist: **haisha** (hah-ee-shah)

department store: **depāto** (deh-pahh-toh)

departure: **shuppatsu** (shoop-pah-tsoo)

dessert: **dezāto** (deh-zahh-toh)

dinner: **yūshoku** (yooo-shoh-koo)

difficult: **muzukashii** (moo-zoo-kah-sheee)

do: **suru** (soo-roo)

dog: **inu** (ee-noo)

dress: **wanpīsu** (wahn-peee-soo)

drink (v.): **nomu** (noh-moo)

drive (v.): **unten suru** (oon-tehn soo-roo)

E

ear: **mimi** (mee-mee)

east: **higashi** (hee-gah-shee)

easy: **kantan** (kahn-tahn)

eat (v.): **taberu** (tah-beh-roo)

eight: **hachi** (hah-chee)

eighteen: **jūhachi** (jooo-hah-chee)

embassy: **taishikan** (tah-ee-shee-kahn)

employee: **jūgyōin** (jooo-gyohh-een)

end (v.): **owaru** (oh-wah-roo)

England: **Igirisu** (ee-gee-ree-soo)

English: **ēgo** (ehh-goh)

enter (v.): **hairu** (hah-ee-roo)

entrance: **iriguchi** (ee-ree-goo-chee)

exit: **deguchi** (deh-goo-chee)

expensive: **takai** (tah-kah-ee)

eye: **me** (meh)

F

face: **kao** (kah-oh)

far: **tōi** (tohh-ee)

father: **otōsan** (oh-tohh-sahn)

February: **ni-gatsu** (nee-gah-tsoo)

female: **onna** (ohn-nah)

fever: **netsu** (neh-tsoo)

fifteen: **jūgo** (jooo-goh)

finger: **yubi** (yoo-bee)

fish: **sakana** (sah-kah-nah)

five: **go** (goh)

(v. indicates a verb)

flower: **hana** (hah-nah)

foot: **ashi** (ah-shee)

four: **yon** (yohn)

fourteen: **jūyon** (jooo-yohn)

France: **Furansu** (foo-rahn-soo)

Friday: **kinyōbi** (keen-yohh-bee)

friend: **tomodachi** (toh-moh-dah-chee)

front: **mae** (mah-eh)

fruit: **kudamono** (koo-dah-moh-noh)

G

Germany: **Doitsu** (doh-ee-tsoo)

go (v.): **iku** (ee-koo)

golf: **gorufu** (goh-roo-foo)

good: **ii** (eee)

good afternoon: **konnichiwa**
    (kohn-nee-chee-wah)

goodbye: **sayōnara** (sah-yohh-nah-rah)

good morning: **ohayō** (oh-hah-yohh)

good night: **oyasuminasai**
    (oh-yah-soo-mee-nah-sah-ee)

green: **midori** (mee-doh-ree)

guitar: **gitā** (gee-tahh)

H

hair: **kami** (kah-mee)

hand: **te** (teh)

hat: **bōshi** (bohh-shee)

he: **kare** (kah-reh)

head: **atama** (ah-tah-mah)

hello: **konnichiwa** (kohn-nee-chee-wah)

hello (telephone): **moshimoshi**
    (moh-shee-moh-shee)

here: **koko** (koh-koh)

high school: **kōkō** (kohh-kohh)

hobby: **shumi** (shoo-mee)

horse: **uma** (oo-mah)

hospital: **byōin** (byohh-een)

hotel: **hoteru** (hoh-teh-roo)

house: **ie** (ee-eh)

how: **dō** (dohh)

how much: **ikura** (ee-koo-rah)

hundred: **hyaku** (hyah-koo)

I

I: **watashi** (wah-tah-shee)

ice cream: **aisu kurīmu**
    (ah-ee-soo koo-reee-moo)

illness: **byōki** (byohh-kee)

interesting: **omoshiroi**
    (oh-moh-shee-roh-ee)

intersection: **kōsaten** (kohh-sah-tehn)

Italy: **Itaria** (ee-tah-ree-ah)

J

jacket: **jaketto** (jah-keht-toh)

January: **ichi-gatsu** (ee-chee-gah-tsoo)

Japan: **Nihon** (nee-hohn)

Japanese language: **Nihongo**
    (nee-hohn-goh)

Japanese person: **Nihonjin**
    (nee-hohn-jeen)

jeans: **jīnzu** (jeeen-zoo)

juice: **jūsu** (jooo-soo)

July: **shichi-gatsu** (shee-chee-gah-tsoo)

June: **roku-gatsu** (roh-koo-gah-tsoo)

K

key: **kagi** (kah-gee)
kitchen: **daidokoro** (dah-ee-doh-koh-roh)
knee: **hiza** (hee-zah)
Korea: **Kankoku** (kahn-koh-koo)

L

lake: **mizuumi** (mee-zoo-oo-mee)
last month: **sengetsu** (sehn-geh-tsoo)
last week: **senshū** (sehn-shooo)
last year: **kyonen** (kyoh-nehn)
late: **osoi** (oh-soh-ee)
lawyer: **bengoshi** (behn-goh-shee)
left: **hidari** (hee-dah-ree)
letter: **tegami** (teh-gah-mee)
like: **suki** (soo-kee)
luggage: **nimotsu** (nee-moh-tsoo)
lunch: **chūshoku** (chooo-shoh-koo)

M

make (v.): **tsukuru** (tsoo-koo-roo)
male: **otoko** (oh-toh-koh)
man: **otoko no hito**
    (oh-toh-koh noh hee-toh)
March: **san-gatsu** (sahn-gah-tsoo)
May: **go-gatsu** (goh-gah-tsoo)
meal: **shokuji** (shoh-koo-jee)
meat: **niku** (nee-koo)
medicine: **kusuri** (koo-soo-ree)
milk: **gyūnyū** (gyooo-nyooo)
Monday: **getsuyōbi** (geh-tsoo-yohh-bee)
money: **o-kane** (oh-kah-neh)
morning: **asa** (ah-sah)

mother: **okāsan** (oh-kahh-sahn)
mountain: **yama** (yah-mah)
mouth: **kuchi** (koo-chee)
movie: **ēga** (ehh-gah)
museum: **hakubutsukan**
    (hah-koo-boo-tsoo-kahn)

N

name: **namae** (nah-mah-eh)
nationality: **kokuseki** (koh-koo-seh-kee)
nature: **shizen** (shee-zehn)
near: **chikaku** (chee-kah-koo)
neck: **kubi** (koo-bee)
new: **atarashii** (ah-tah-rah-sheee)
newspaper: **shinbun** (sheen-boon)
next door: **tonari** (toh-nah-ree)
next month: **raigetsu** (rah-ee-geh-tsoo)
next week: **raishū** (rah-ee-shooo)
next year: **rainen** (rah-ee-nehn)
nine: **kyū** (kyooo)
nineteen: **jūkyū** (jooo-kyooo)
noisy: **urusai** (oo-roo-sah-ee)
north: **kita** (kee-tah)
nose: **hana** (hah-nah)
not at all: **zenzen** (zehn-zehn)
November: **jūichi-gatsu**
    (jooo-ee-chee-gah-tsoo)
now: **ima** (ee-mah)
nurse: **kangofu** (kahn-goh-foo)

O

occupation: **shokugyō** (shoh-koo-gyohh)
ocean: **umi** (oo-mee)
October: **jū-gatsu** (jooo-gah-tsoo)
(v. indicates a verb)

old: **furui** (foo-roo-e)
one: **ichi** (ee-chee)
open (v.): **akeru** (ah-keh-roo)
orange: **mikan** (mee-kahn)
outside: **soto** (soh-toh)
over there: **asoko** (ah-soh-koh)

P

pants: **zubon** (zoo-bohn)
paper: **kami** (kah-mee)
park: **kōen** (kohh-ehn)
parking lot: **chūshajō** (chooo-shah-johh)
passport: **pasupōto** (pah-soo-pohh-toh)
pay (v.): **harau** (hah-rah-oo)
photograph: **shashin** (shah-sheen)
physician: **isha** (ee-shah)
piano: **piano** (pee-ah-noh)
pizza: **piza** (pee-zah)
police: **kēsatsu** (kehh-sah-tsoo)
pork: **butaniku** (boo-tah-nee-koo)
post office: **yūbinkyoku**
   (yooo-been-kyoh-koo)
put (v.): **oku** (oh-koo)

Q

question: **shitsumon** (shee-tsoo-mohn)
quickly: **hayaku** (hah-yah-koo)
quiet: **shizuka** (shee-zoo-kah)

R

rain: **ame** (ah-meh)
read (v.): **yomu** (yoh-moo)
receipt: **ryōshūsho** (ryohh-shooo-shoh)

red: **aka** (ah-kah)
remember (v.): **oboeru** (oh-boh-eh-roo)
reservation: **yoyaku** (yoh-yah-koo)
restaurant: **resutoran** (reh-soo-toh-rahn)
return: **kaeru** (kah-eh-roo)
rice, cooked: **gohan** (goh-hahn)
rice, uncooked: **o-kome** (oh-koh-meh)
right: **migi** (mee-gee)
river: **kawa** (kah-wah)
room: **heya** (heh-yah)

S

salad: **sarada** (sah-rah-dah)
Saturday: **doyōbi** (doh-yohh-bee)
school: **gakkō** (gahk-kohh)
secretary: **hisho** (hee-shoh)
sell (v.): **uru** (oo-roo)
September: **ku-gatsu** (koo-gah-tsoo)
seven: **nana** (nah-nah)
seventeen: **jūnana** (jooo-nah-nah)
she: **kanojo** (kah-noh-joh)
shirt: **shatsu** (shah-tsoo)
shoe: **kutsu** (koo-tsoo)
shoulder: **kata** (kah-tah)
signature: **shomē** (shoh-mehh)
sing (v.): **utau** (oo-tah-oo)
sister, older: **onēsan** (oh-nehh-sahn)
sister, younger sister: **imōto**
   (ee-mohh-toh)
sit down (v.): **suwaru** (soo-wah-roo)
six: **roku** (roh-koo)
sixteen: **jūroku** (jooo-roh-koo)
skirt: **sukāto** (soo-kahh-toh)
sleep: **neru** (neh-roo)
small: **chīsai** (cheee-sah-ee)

snow: **yuki** (yoo-kee)

soccer: **sakkā** (sahk-kahh)

somebody: **dareka** (dah-reh-kah)

something: **nanika** (nah-nee-kah)

south: **minami** (mee-nah-mee)

spaghetti: **supagettī** (soo-pah-geht-teee)

Spain: **Supein** (soo-peh-een)

speak (v.): **hanasu** (hah-nah-soo)

stamp: **kitte** (keet-teh)

store: **mise** (mee-seh)

study (v.): **benkyō suru**
(behn-kyohh soo-roo)

subway: **chikatetsu** (chee-kah-teh-tsoo)

sugar: **satō** (sah-tohh)

suit: **sūtsu** (sooo-tsoo)

suitcase: **sūtsukēsu** (sooo-tsoo-kehh-soo)

sun: **taiyō** (tah-ee-yohh)

Sunday: **nichiyōbi** (nee-chee-yohh-bee)

supermarket: **sūpāmāketto**
(sooo-pahh-mahh-keht-toh)

sweater: **sētā** (sehh-tahh)

swimming: **suiē** (soo-ee-ehh)

T

take (v.): **toru** (toh-roo)

taxi: **takushī** (tah-koo-sheee)

tea: **o-cha** (oh-chah)

teacher: **sensē** (sehn-sehh)

telephone: **denwa** (dehn-wah)

telephone number: **denwa-bangō**
(dehn-wah-bahn-gohh)

ten: **jū** (jooo)

tennis: **tenisu** (teh-nee-soo)

thanks: **arigatō** (ah-ree-gah-tohh) / **dōmo**
(dohh-moh)

that one near you: **sore** (soh-reh)

that one over there: **are** (ah-reh)

theater: **gekijō** (geh-kee-johh)

there near you: **soko** (soh-koh)

thirteen: **jūsan** (jooo-sahn)

this month: **kongetsu** (kohn-geh-tsoo)

this one: **kore** (koh-reh)

this week: **konshū** (kohn-shooo)

this year: **kotoshi** (koh-toh-shee)

three: **san** (sahn)

Thursday: **mokuyōbi**
(moh-koo-yohh-bee)

ticket: **chiketto** (chee-keht-toh)

tip: **chippu** (cheep-poo)

today: **kyō** (kyohh)

tomorrow: **ashita** (ah-shee-tah)

tonight: **konban** (kohn-bahn)

train: **densha** (dehn-shah)

tree: **ki** (kee)

trip: **ryokō** (ryoh-kohh)

Tuesday: **kayōbi** (kah-yohh-bee)

TV: **terebi** (teh-reh-bee)

twelve: **jūni** (jooo-nee)

two: **ni** (nee)

U

umbrella: **kasa** (kah-sah)

university: **daigaku** (dah-ee-gah-koo)

use (v.): **tsukau** (tsoo-kah-oo)

V

vacation: **yasumi** (yah-soo-mee)

vegetable: **yasai** (yah-sah-ee)

very: **totemo** (toh-teh-moh)

village: **mura** (moo-rah)

(v. indicates a verb)

W

wait (v.): **matsu** (mah-tsoo)

walk (v.): **aruku** (ah-roo-koo)

wallet: **saifu** (sah-ee-foo)

want (v.): **hoshii** (hoh-sheee)

water: **mizu** (mee-zoo)

Wednesday: **suiyōbi** (soo-ee-yohh-bee)

week: **shū** (shooo)

weird: **hen** (hehn)

west: **nishi** (nee-shee)

what: **nani** (nah-nee)

when: **itsu** (ee-tsoo)

where: **doko** (doh-koh)

which one: **dore** (doh-reh)

white: **shiro** (shee-roh)

who: **dare** (dah-reh)

wide: **hiroi** (hee-roh-ee)

window: **mado** (mah-doh)

wine: **wain** (wah-een)

woman: **onna no hito**
  (ohn-nah noh hee-toh)

work (v.): **hataraku** (hah-tah-rah-koo)

write (v.): **kaku** (kah-koo)

Y

yellow: **kīro** (keee-roh)

yesterday: **kinō** (kee-nohh)

you: **anata** (ah-nah-tah)

Z

zip code: **yūbin bangō**
  (yooo-been bahn-gohh)

(v. indicates a verb)

Appendix C

Answer Key

Chapter 1: You Already Know a Little Japanese

1. **obāsan** 2. **ojīsan** 3. **dōmo** 4. **karaoke** 5. **jūdō**

Chapter 2: The Nitty Gritty: Basic Japanese Grammar and Numbers

3. **san** 6. **roku** 8. **hachi** 9. **kyū** 14. **jū-yon**

Chapter 3: Introductions and Greetings

1. c 2. d 3. e 4. b 5. a

Chapter 4: Getting to Know You: Making Small Talk

1. d 2. a 3. b 4. c

Chapter 5: Eating and Drinking: Itadakimasu!

A. **ringo** (apples) B. **ichigo** (strawberries) C. **banana** (bananas) D. **mikan** (oranges) E. **retasu** (lettuce) F. **remon** (lemons) G. **masshurūmu** (mushrooms) H. **tamanegi** (onions)

Chapter 6: Shopping Around

1. **yunomi** 2. **kimono** 3. **geta** 4. **origami**

Chapter 7: Exploring the Town

ā	w	u	r	y	z	i	d	f	b	f	ō
g	e	k	i	j	ō	z	p	d	i	h	t
a	b	t	h	ī	e	a	a	k	j	p	r
r	h	o	k	o	s	k	z	k	u	r	h
ō	i	s	ī	ō	t	a	ā	h	t	k	e
ū	o	h	b	w	ā	y	ē	f	s	h	ō
k	ā	o	k	m	t	a	z	ē	u	t	u
h	a	k	u	b	u	t	s	u	k	a	n
ē	y	a	n	j	t	z	ā	u	a	u	ī
n	f	n	e	ē	g	a	k	a	n	o	ō

Chapter 8: Enjoying Yourself: Recreation

A. **fuyu** B. **natsu** C. **haru** D. **aki**

Chapter 9: Talking on the Telephone

1. e 2. b 3. a 4. c 5. d

Chapter 10: At the Office and Around the House

1. **o-furoba** 2. **shinshitsu** 3. **beddo** 4. **ima** 5. **sofā** 6. **konro** 7. **daidokoro** 8. **shokudō**

Chapter 11: Money, Money, Money

							¹d	¹o	r	u
								k		
					²g	a	i	k	a	
					i			a	n	
³y	o	k	i	n				e		
					k					
			⁴r	y	ō	g	a	e		

Chapter 12: Asking for Directions

1. B 2. F 3. D 4. A 5. C 6. E

Chapter 13: Staying at a Hotel

1. **chekku-auto** 2. **dengon** 3. **rūmu sābisu** 4. **akibeya** 5. **mōningu kōru**

Chapter 14: Transportation

1. **takushī** 2. **hikōki** 3. **densha** or **shinkansen** 4. **basu** 5. **fune**

Chapter 15: Planning a Trip

A. **shatsu** B. **han zubon** C. **puruōbā** D. **bōshi** E. **sandaru** F. **sangurasu** G. **sunīkā**

Chapter 16: Handling an Emergency

1. **atama** 2. **mimi** 3. **me** 4. **kuchi** 5. **kubi** 6. **kata** 7. **ude** 8. **mune** 9. **te** 10. **hiza** 11. **ashi**

Appendix D

On the CD

• •

*F*ollowing is the list of the tracks that appear on this book's audio CD, which you can find inside the back cover. Note that this is an audio-only CD — just pop it into your CD player (or whatever you use to listen to music CDs).

Track 1: Introduction and basic Japanese sounds (Chapter 1)

Track 2: Asking people where they're from (Chapter 3)

Track 3: Greeting people formally (Chapter 3)

Track 4: Apologizing to a stranger (Chapter 3)

Track 5: Asking the time (Chapter 4)

Track 6: Chatting with a stranger in a train (Chapter 4)

Track 7: Talking about family members (Chapter 4)

Track 8: Making a restaurant reservation (Chapter 5)

Track 9: Ordering at a restaurant (Chapter 5)

Track 10: Shopping at a fish market (Chapter 5)

Track 11: Shopping at a souvenir store (Chapter 6)

Track 12: Looking for the jewelry section in a department store (Chapter 6)

Track 13: Negotiating the price (Chapter 6)

Track 14: Buying a ticket at a theater (Chapter 7)

Track 15: Going to a bar (Chapter 7)

Index